FRC Financial Reporting Council

September 2015

FRS 102
The Financial Reporting Standard applicable in the UK and Republic of Ireland

GH00493886

1AC.23 *Where financial instruments or other assets have been measured at fair value through profit or loss there must be stated for each class of derivatives, the extent and nature of the instruments, including significant terms and conditions that may affect the amount, timing and certainty of future cash flows. (Schedule 1, paragraph 51(2)(c))*

1AC.24 *Where any amount is transferred to or from the fair value reserve during the reporting period, there must be stated in tabular form:*

    (a) *the amount of the reserve as at the beginning of the reporting period and as at the reporting date respectively; and*

    (b) *the amount transferred to or from the reserve during that year. (Schedule 1, paragraph 51(3))*

Paragraphs 6.3A, 12.29(c) and 12.29(d) address similar requirements.

1AC.25 *The treatment for taxation purposes of amounts credited or debited to the fair value reserve must be disclosed in a note to the financial statements. (Schedule 1, paragraph 41(2))*

Paragraph 29.27(a) addresses similar requirements.

Financial instruments measured at fair value

1AC.26 *Financial instruments which under international accounting standards may be included in accounts at fair value, may be so included, provided that the disclosures required by such accounting standards are made. (Schedule 1, paragraph 36(4))*

This only applies in certain circumstances; for example, it does not apply to derivatives. It applies where investments in subsidiaries, associates and joint ventures are measured at fair value through profit or loss. When it applies, the disclosures required by Section 11 that relate to financial assets and financial liabilities measured at fair value, including paragraph 11.48A, shall be given.

Indebtedness, guarantees and financial commitments

1AC.27 *For the aggregate of all items shown under 'creditors' in the small entity's statement of financial position there must be stated the aggregate of the following amounts:*

    (a) *the amount of any debts included under 'creditors' which are payable or repayable otherwise than by instalments and fall due for payment or repayment after the end of the period of five years beginning with the day next following the reporting date; and*

    (b) *in the case of any debts so included which are payable or repayable by instalments, the amount of any instalments which fall due for payment after the end of that period. (Schedule 1, paragraph 55(1))*

1AC.28 *In respect of each item shown under 'creditors' in the small entity's statement of financial position there must be stated the aggregate amount of any debts included under that item in respect of which any security has been given by the small entity with an indication of the nature and form of any such security. (Schedule 1, paragraph 55(2))*

Paragraphs 11.46, 13.22(e), 16.10(c), 17.32(a) and 18.28(c) address similar requirements.

1AC.29 *The total amount of any financial commitments, guarantees and contingencies that are not included in the balance sheet must be stated. (Schedule 1, paragraph 57(1))*

The total amount of any commitments concerning pensions must be separately disclosed. (Schedule 1, paragraph 57(3))

The total amount of any commitments which are undertaken on behalf of or for the benefit of:

(a)   any parent, fellow subsidiary or any subsidiary of the small entity; or

(b)   any undertaking in which the small entity has a participating interest,

must be separately stated and those within (a) must also be stated separately from those within (b). (Schedule 1, paragraph 57(4))

Such commitments can arise in a variety of situations, including in relation to group entities, investments, property, plant and equipment, leases and pension obligations. Paragraphs 15.19(d), 16.10(d), 17.32(b), 18.28(d), 20.16, 21.15, 28.40A(a), 28.40A(b), 28.41A(d), 33.9(b)(ii) and 34.62 address similar requirements.

1AC.30   *An indication of the nature and form of any valuable security given by the small entity in respect of commitments, guarantees and contingencies within paragraph 1AC.29 must be given. (Schedule 1, paragraph 57(2))*

Paragraphs 11.46, 13.22(e), 16.10(c), 17.32(a) and 18.28(c) address similar requirements.

1AC.31   *If in any reporting period a small entity is or has been party to arrangements that are not reflected in its statement of financial position and at the reporting date the risks or benefits arising from those arrangements are material the nature and business purpose of the arrangements must be given in the notes to the financial statements to the extent necessary for enabling the financial position of the small entity to be assessed. (Section 410A of the Act)*

Examples of off-balance sheet arrangements include risk and benefit-sharing arrangements or obligations arising from a contract such as debt factoring, combined sale and repurchase arrangements, consignment stock arrangements, take or pay arrangements, securitisation arranged through separate entities, pledged assets, operating lease arrangements, outsourcing and the like. In many cases the disclosures about financial commitments and contingencies required by paragraphs 1AC.29 and 1AC.30 will also address such arrangements.

Notes supporting the income statement

1AC.32   *The amount and nature of any individual items of income or expenses of exceptional size or incidence must be stated. (Schedule 1, paragraph 61(2))*

Paragraph 5.9A addresses a similar requirement in relation to material items.

1AC.33   *The notes to a small entity's financial statements must disclose the average number of persons employed by the small entity in the reporting period. (Section 411 of the Act)*

Related party disclosures

1AC.34   *Where the small entity is a subsidiary, the following information must be given in respect of the parent of the smallest group for which consolidated financial statements are drawn up of which the small entity is a member:*

(a)   the name of the parent which draws up the consolidated financial statements;

(b)   the address of the parent's registered office (whether in or outside the UK); or

(c)   if it is unincorporated, the address of its principal place of business. (Schedule 1, paragraph 65)

Paragraph 33.5 addresses a similar requirement to paragraph (a).

1AC.35   *Particulars must be given of material transactions the small entity has entered into that have not been concluded under normal market conditions with:*

(a)   *owners holding a participating interest in the small entity;*

(b)   *companies in which the small entity itself has a participating interest; and*

(c)   *the small entity's directors [or members of its governing body].*

Particulars must include:

(a)   *the amount of such transactions;*

(b)   *the nature of the related party relationship; and*

(c)   *other information about the transactions necessary for an understanding of the financial position of the small entity.*

Information about individual transactions may be aggregated according to their nature, except where separate information is necessary for an understanding of the effects of the related party transactions on the financial position of the small entity.

Particulars need not be given of transactions entered into between two or more members of a group, provided that any subsidiary which is a party to the transaction is wholly-owned by such a member. (Schedule 1, paragraph 66)

Although disclosure is only required of material transactions with the specified related parties that have not been concluded under normal market conditions, small entities disclosing all transactions with such related parties would still be compliant with company law.

Transactions with directors, or members of an entity's governing body, include directors' remuneration and dividends paid to directors.

Paragraphs 33.9 and 33.14 address similar requirements for all related parties.

1AC.36   *Details of advances and credits granted by the small entity to its directors and guarantees of any kind entered into by the small entity on behalf of its directors must be shown in the notes to the financial statements.*

The details required of an advance or credit are:

(a)   *its amount;*

(b)   *an indication of the interest rate;*

(c)   *its main conditions;*

(d)   *any amounts repaid;*

(e)   *any amounts written off; and*

(f)   *any amounts waived.*

There must also be stated in the notes to the financial statements the totals of amounts stated under (a), (d), (e) and (f).

The details required of a guarantee are:

(a)   its main terms;

(b)   the amount of the maximum liability that may be incurred by the small entity; and

(c)   any amount paid and any liability incurred by the small entity for the purpose of fulfilling the guarantee (including any loss incurred by reason of enforcement of the guarantee).

There must also be stated in the notes to the financial statements the totals of amounts stated under (b) and (c). (Section 413 of the Act)

Paragraph 33.9 addresses similar requirements for all related parties.

A small entity that is not a company shall provide this disclosure in relation to members of its governing body.

Other

1AC.37   *The financial statements must state:*

(a)   the part of the UK in which the small entity is registered;

(b)   the small entity's registered number;

(c)   whether the small entity is a public or a private company and whether the small entity is limited by shares or by guarantee;

(d)   the address of the small entity's registered office; and

(e)   where appropriate, the fact that the entity is being wound up. (Section 396 of the Act)

Paragraph 3.24(a) addresses similar requirements.

1AC.38   *Where items to which Arabic numbers are given in any of the formats have been combined, unless they are not material, the individual amounts of any items which have been combined must be disclosed in a note to the financial statements. (Schedule 1, paragraph 4(3))*

1AC.39   *The nature and financial effect of material events arising after the reporting date which are not reflected in the income statement or statement of financial position must be stated. (Schedule 1, paragraph 64)*

Paragraphs 32.10 and 32.11 address similar requirements.

Appendix D to Section 1A

Additional disclosures encouraged for small entities

This appendix is an integral part of the Standard.

1AD.1   Where relevant to its transactions, other events and conditions, a small entity is encouraged to provide the following disclosures:

(a)   a statement of compliance with this FRS as set out in paragraph 3.3, adapted to refer to Section 1A;

(b)   a statement that it is a public benefit entity as set out in paragraph PBE3.3A;

(c)   the disclosures relating to going concern set out in paragraph 3.9;

(d)   dividends declared and paid or payable during the period (for example, as set out in paragraph 6.5(b)); and

(e)   on first-time adoption of this FRS an explanation of how the transition has affected its financial position and financial performance as set out in paragraph 35.13.

Section 2
Concepts and Pervasive Principles

Scope of this section

2.1 This section describes the **objective of financial statements** of entities within the scope of this FRS and the qualities that make the information in the **financial statements** of entities within the scope of this FRS useful. It also sets out the concepts and basic principles underlying the financial statements of entities within the scope of this FRS.

2.1A Although this section sets out the concepts and pervasive principles underlying financial statements, in some circumstances there may be inconsistencies between the concepts and principles in this section of the FRS and the specific requirements of another section. In these circumstances the specific requirements of the other section within the FRS take precedence over this section.

Objective of financial statements

2.2 The objective of financial statements is to provide information about the **financial position**, **performance** and **cash flows** of an entity that is useful for economic decision-making by a broad range of users who are not in a position to demand reports tailored to meet their particular information needs.

2.3 Financial statements also show the results of the stewardship of management—the accountability of management for the resources entrusted to it.

Qualitative characteristics of information in financial statements

Understandability

2.4 The information provided in financial statements should be presented in a way that makes it comprehensible by users who have a reasonable knowledge of **business** and economic activities and accounting and a willingness to study the information with reasonable diligence. However, the need for **understandability** does not allow relevant information to be omitted on the grounds that it may be too difficult for some users to understand.

Relevance

2.5 The information provided in financial statements must be relevant to the decision-making needs of users. Information has the quality of **relevance** when it is capable of influencing the economic decisions of users by helping them evaluate past, present or future events or confirming, or correcting, their past evaluations.

Materiality

2.6 Information is **material**—and therefore has relevance—if its omission or misstatement, individually or collectively, could influence the economic decisions of users taken on the basis of the financial statements. Materiality depends on the size and nature of the omission or misstatement judged in the surrounding circumstances. The size or nature of the item, or a combination of both, could be the determining factor. However, it is inappropriate to make, or leave uncorrected, immaterial departures from this FRS to achieve a particular presentation of an entity's financial position, financial performance or cash flows.

Reliability

2.7   The information provided in financial statements must be reliable. Information is reliable when it is free from material **error** and bias and represents faithfully that which it either purports to represent or could reasonably be expected to represent. Financial statements are not free from bias (ie not neutral) if, by the selection or presentation of information, they are intended to influence the making of a decision or judgement in order to achieve a predetermined result or outcome.

Substance over form

2.8   Transactions and other events and conditions should be accounted for and presented in accordance with their substance and not merely their legal form. This enhances the **reliability** of financial statements.

Prudence

2.9   The uncertainties that inevitably surround many events and circumstances are acknowledged by the disclosure of their nature and extent and by the exercise of **prudence** in the preparation of the financial statements. Prudence is the inclusion of a degree of caution in the exercise of the judgements needed in making the estimates required under conditions of uncertainty, such that **assets** or **income** are not overstated and **liabilities** or **expenses** are not understated. However, the exercise of prudence does not allow the deliberate understatement of assets or income, or the deliberate overstatement of liabilities or expenses. In short, prudence does not permit bias.

Completeness

2.10   To be reliable, the information in financial statements must be complete within the bounds of materiality and cost. An omission can cause information to be false or misleading and thus unreliable and deficient in terms of its relevance.

Comparability

2.11   Users must be able to compare the financial statements of an entity through time to identify trends in its financial position and performance. Users must also be able to compare the financial statements of different entities to evaluate their relative financial position, performance and cash flows. Hence, the **measurement** and display of the financial effects of like transactions and other events and conditions must be carried out in a consistent way throughout an entity and over time for that entity, and in a consistent way across entities. In addition, users must be informed of the **accounting policies** employed in the preparation of the financial statements, and of any changes in those policies and the effects of such changes.

Timeliness

2.12   To be relevant, financial information must be able to influence the economic decisions of users. **Timeliness** involves providing the information within the decision time frame. If there is undue delay in the reporting of information it may lose its relevance. Management may need to balance the relative merits of timely reporting and the provision of reliable information. In achieving a balance between relevance and reliability, the overriding consideration is how best to satisfy the needs of users in making economic decisions.

Balance between benefit and cost

2.13   The benefits derived from information should exceed the cost of providing it. The evaluation of benefits and costs is substantially a judgemental process. Furthermore, the costs are not necessarily borne by those users who enjoy the benefits, and often the benefits of the information are enjoyed by a broad range of external users.

2.14   Financial reporting information helps capital providers make better decisions, which results in more efficient functioning of capital markets and a lower cost of capital for the economy as a whole. Individual entities also enjoy benefits, including improved access to capital markets, favourable effect on public relations, and perhaps lower costs of capital. The benefits may also include better management decisions because financial information used internally is often based at least partly on information prepared for general purpose financial reporting purposes.

Financial position

2.15   The financial position of an entity is the relationship of its assets, liabilities and **equity** as of a specific date as presented in the **statement of financial position**. These are defined as follows:

(a)   An asset is a resource controlled by the entity as a result of past events and from which future economic benefits are expected to flow to the entity.

(b)   A liability is a present obligation of the entity arising from past events, the settlement of which is expected to result in an outflow from the entity of resources embodying economic benefits.

(c)   Equity is the residual interest in the assets of the entity after deducting all its liabilities.

2.16   Some items that meet the definition of an asset or a liability may not be recognised as assets or liabilities in the statement of financial position because they do not satisfy the criteria for **recognition** in paragraphs 2.27 to 2.32. In particular, the expectation that future economic benefits will flow to or from an entity must be sufficiently certain to meet the probability criterion before an asset or liability is recognised.

Assets

2.17   The future economic benefit of an asset is its potential to contribute, directly or indirectly, to the flow of **cash** and **cash equivalents** to the entity. Those cash flows may come from using the asset or from disposing of it.

2.18   Many assets, for example **property, plant and equipment**, have a physical form. However, physical form is not essential to the existence of an asset. Some assets are intangible.

2.19   In determining the existence of an asset, the right of ownership is not essential. Thus, for example, property held on a **lease** is an asset if the entity controls the benefits that are expected to flow from the property.

Liabilities

2.20   An essential characteristic of a liability is that the entity has a present obligation to act or perform in a particular way. The obligation may be either a legal obligation or a **constructive obligation**. A legal obligation is legally enforceable as a consequence of a binding contract or statutory requirement. A constructive obligation is an obligation that derives from an entity's actions when:

(a)   by an established pattern of past practice, published policies or a sufficiently specific current statement, the entity has indicated to other parties that it will accept certain responsibilities; and

(b)   as a result, the entity has created a valid expectation on the part of those other parties that it will discharge those responsibilities.

2.21   The settlement of a present obligation usually involves the payment of cash, transfer of other assets, provision of services, the replacement of that obligation with another obligation, or conversion of the obligation to equity. An obligation may also be extinguished by other means, such as a creditor waiving or forfeiting its rights.

Equity

2.22   Equity is the residual interest in the assets of the entity after deducting all its liabilities. It may be sub-classified in the statement of financial position. For example, in a corporate entity, sub-classifications may include funds contributed by shareholders, retained earnings and **gains** or losses recognised in **other comprehensive income**.

Performance

2.23   Performance is the relationship of the income and expenses of an entity during a **reporting period**. This FRS permits entities to present performance in a single financial statement (a **statement of comprehensive income**) or in two financial statements (an **income statement** and a statement of comprehensive income). **Total comprehensive income** and **profit or loss** are frequently used as measures of performance or as the basis for other measures, such as return on investment or earnings per share. Income and expenses are defined as follows:

(a)   Income is increases in economic benefits during the reporting period in the form of inflows or enhancements of assets or decreases of liabilities that result in increases in equity, other than those relating to contributions from equity investors.

(b)   Expenses are decreases in economic benefits during the reporting period in the form of outflows or depletions of assets or incurrences of liabilities that result in decreases in equity, other than those relating to distributions to equity investors.

2.24   The recognition of income and expenses results directly from the recognition and measurement of assets and liabilities. Criteria for the recognition of income and expenses are discussed in paragraphs 2.27 to 2.32.

Income

2.25   The definition of income encompasses both **revenue** and gains.

(a)   Revenue is income that arises in the course of the ordinary activities of an entity and is referred to by a variety of names including sales, fees, interest, dividends, royalties and rent.

(b)   Gains are other items that meet the definition of income but are not revenue. When gains are recognised in the statement of comprehensive income, they are usually displayed separately because knowledge of them is useful for making economic decisions.

Expenses

2.26 The definition of expenses encompasses losses as well as those expenses that arise in the course of the ordinary activities of the entity.

(a) Expenses that arise in the course of the ordinary activities of the entity include, for example, cost of sales, wages and **depreciation**. They usually take the form of an outflow or depletion of assets such as cash and cash equivalents, **inventory**, or property, plant and equipment.

(b) Losses are other items that meet the definition of expenses and may arise in the course of the ordinary activities of the entity. When losses are recognised in the statement of comprehensive income, they are usually presented separately because knowledge of them is useful for making economic decisions.

Recognition of assets, liabilities, income and expenses

2.27 Recognition is the process of incorporating in the statement of financial position or statement of comprehensive income an item that meets the definition of an asset, liability, equity, income or expense and satisfies the following criteria:

(a) it is **probable** that any future economic benefit associated with the item will flow to or from the entity; and

(b) the item has a cost or value that can be measured reliably.

2.28 The failure to recognise an item that satisfies those criteria is not rectified by disclosure of the accounting policies used or by **notes** or explanatory material.

The probability of future economic benefit

2.29 The concept of probability is used in the first recognition criterion to refer to the degree of uncertainty that the future economic benefits associated with the item will flow to or from the entity. Assessments of the degree of uncertainty attaching to the flow of future economic benefits are made on the basis of the evidence relating to conditions at the end of the reporting period available when the financial statements are prepared. Those assessments are made individually for individually significant items, and for a group for a large population of individually insignificant items.

Reliability of measurement

2.30 The second criterion for the recognition of an item is that it possesses a cost or value that can be measured with reliability. In many cases, the cost or value of an item is known. In other cases it must be estimated. The use of reasonable estimates is an essential part of the preparation of financial statements and does not undermine their reliability. When a reasonable estimate cannot be made, the item is not recognised in the financial statements.

2.31 An item that fails to meet the recognition criteria may qualify for recognition at a later date as a result of subsequent circumstances or events.

2.32 An item that fails to meet the criteria for recognition may nonetheless warrant disclosure in the notes or explanatory material or in supplementary schedules. This is appropriate when knowledge of the item is relevant to the evaluation of the financial position, performance and changes in financial position of an entity by the users of financial statements.

Measurement of assets, liabilities, income and expenses

2.33   Measurement is the process of determining the monetary amounts at which an entity measures assets, liabilities, income and expenses in its financial statements. Measurement involves the selection of a basis of measurement. This FRS specifies which measurement basis an entity shall use for many types of assets, liabilities, income and expenses.

2.34   Two common measurement bases are historical cost and **fair value**:

     (a)   For assets, historical cost is the amount of cash or cash equivalents paid or the fair value of the consideration given to acquire the asset at the time of its acquisition. For liabilities, historical cost is the amount of proceeds of cash or cash equivalents received or the fair value of non-cash assets received in exchange for the obligation at the time the obligation is incurred, or in some circumstances (for example, **income tax**) the amounts of cash or cash equivalents expected to be paid to settle the liability in the normal course of business. Amortised historical cost is the historical cost of an asset or liability plus or minus that portion of its historical cost previously recognised as an expense or income.

     (b)   Fair value is the amount for which an asset could be exchanged, a liability settled, or an equity instrument granted could be exchanged, between knowledgeable, willing parties in an arm's length transaction. In the absence of any specific guidance provided in the relevant section of this FRS, where fair value measurement is permitted or required the guidance in paragraphs 11.27 to 11.32 shall be applied.

Pervasive recognition and measurement principles

2.35   The requirements for recognising and measuring assets, liabilities, income and expenses in this FRS are based on pervasive principles that are derived from the IASB *Framework for the Preparation and Presentation of Financial Statements*[7] and from **EU-adopted IFRS**. In the absence of a requirement in this FRS that applies specifically to a transaction or other event or condition, paragraph 10.4 provides guidance for making a judgement and paragraph 10.5 establishes a hierarchy for an entity to follow in deciding on the appropriate accounting policy in the circumstances. The second level of that hierarchy requires an entity to look to the definitions, recognition criteria and measurement concepts for assets, liabilities, income and expenses and the pervasive principles set out in this section.

Accrual basis

2.36   An entity shall prepare its financial statements, except for cash flow information, using the **accrual basis** of accounting. On the accrual basis, items are recognised as assets, liabilities, equity, income or expenses when they satisfy the definitions and recognition criteria for those items.

---

[7] In 2010 the IASB issued the *Conceptual Framework for Financial Reporting*, which superseded the *Framework for the Preparation and Presentation of Financial Statements*.

Recognition in financial statements

Assets

2.37   An entity shall recognise an asset in the statement of financial position when it is probable that the future economic benefits will flow to the entity and the asset has a cost or value that can be measured reliably. An asset is not recognised in the statement of financial position when expenditure has been incurred for which it is considered not probable that economic benefits will flow to the entity beyond the current reporting period. Instead such a transaction results in the recognition of an expense in the statement of comprehensive income (or in the income statement, if presented).

2.38   An entity shall not recognise a **contingent asset** as an asset. However, when the flow of future economic benefits to the entity is virtually certain, then the related asset is not a contingent asset, and its recognition is appropriate.

Liabilities

2.39   An entity shall recognise a liability in the statement of financial position when:

(a)   the entity has an obligation at the end of the reporting period as a result of a past event;

(b)   it is probable that the entity will be required to transfer resources embodying economic benefits in settlement; and

(c)   the settlement amount can be measured reliably.

2.40   A **contingent liability** is either a possible but uncertain obligation or a present obligation that is not recognised because it fails to meet one or both of the conditions (b) and (c) in paragraph 2.39. An entity shall not recognise a contingent liability as a liability, except for contingent liabilities of an acquiree in a **business combination** (see Section 19 *Business Combinations and Goodwill*).

Income

2.41   The recognition of income results directly from the recognition and measurement of assets and liabilities. An entity shall recognise income in the statement of comprehensive income (or in the income statement, if presented) when an increase in future economic benefits related to an increase in an asset or a decrease of a liability has arisen that can be measured reliably.

Expenses

2.42   The recognition of expenses results directly from the recognition and measurement of assets and liabilities. An entity shall recognise expenses in the statement of comprehensive income (or in the income statement, if presented) when a decrease in future economic benefits related to a decrease in an asset or an increase of a liability has arisen that can be measured reliably.

Total comprehensive income and profit or loss

2.43   Total comprehensive income is the arithmetical difference between income and expenses. It is not a separate element of financial statements, and a separate recognition principle is not needed for it.

2.44   Profit or loss is the arithmetical difference between income and expenses other than those items of income and expense that this FRS classifies as items of other comprehensive income. It is not a separate element of financial statements, and a separate recognition principle is not needed for it.

2.45 Generally this FRS does not allow the recognition of items in the statement of financial position that do not meet the definition of assets or of liabilities regardless of whether they result from applying the notion commonly referred to as the 'matching concept' for measuring profit or loss.

Measurement at initial recognition

2.46 At initial recognition, an entity shall measure assets and liabilities at historical cost unless this FRS requires initial measurement on another basis such as fair value.

Subsequent measurement

Financial assets and financial liabilities

2.47 An entity measures basic **financial assets** and basic **financial liabilities** at **amortised cost** less impairment except for:

(a) investments in non-convertible preference shares and non-puttable ordinary and preference shares that are **publicly traded** or whose fair value can otherwise be measured reliably, which are measured at fair value with changes in fair value recognised in profit or loss; and

(b) any financial instruments that upon their initial recognition were designated by the entity as at fair value through profit or loss.

2.48 An entity generally measures all other financial assets and financial liabilities at fair value, with changes in fair value recognised in profit or loss, unless this FRS requires or permits measurement on another basis such as cost or amortised cost.

Non-financial assets

2.49 Most non-financial assets that an entity initially recognised at historical cost are subsequently measured on other measurement bases. For example:

(a) An entity measures property, plant and equipment using either the cost model or the revaluation model.

(b) An entity measures inventories at the lower of cost and selling price less costs to complete and sell.

Measurement of assets at amounts lower than initial historical cost is intended to ensure that an asset is not measured at an amount greater than the entity expects to recover from the sale or use of that asset.

2.50 For certain types of non-financial assets, this FRS permits or requires measurement at fair value. For example:

(a) Investments in **associates** and **joint ventures** that an entity measures at fair value (see paragraphs 14.4(b) and 14.4B, and 15.9(b) and 15.9B respectively).

(b) **Investment property** that an entity measures at fair value (see paragraph 16.7).

(c) **Biological assets** that an entity measures at fair value less estimated costs to sell in accordance with the fair value model (see paragraph 34.3A(a)) and **agricultural produce** that an entity measures, at the point of harvest, at fair value less estimated costs to sell in accordance with either the fair value model (see paragraph 34.3A(a)) or cost model (see paragraph 34.9).

(d) Property, plant and equipment that an entity measures in accordance with the revaluation model (see paragraph 17.15B).

(e) **Intangible assets** that an entity measures in accordance with the revaluation model (see paragraph 18.18B).

Liabilities other than financial liabilities

2.51 Most liabilities other than financial liabilities are measured at the best estimate of the amount that would be required to settle the obligation at the **reporting date**.

Offsetting

2.52 An entity shall not offset assets and liabilities, or income and expenses, unless required or permitted by an FRS.

(a) Measuring assets net of valuation allowances (for example, allowances for inventory obsolescence and allowances for uncollectible receivables) is not offsetting.

(b) If an entity's normal **operating activities** do not include buying and selling **fixed assets**, including investments and operating assets, then the entity reports gains and losses on disposal of such assets by deducting from the proceeds on disposal the **carrying amount** of the asset and related selling expenses.

Section 3
Financial Statement Presentation

Scope of this section

3.1 This section explains that the **financial statements** of an entity shall give a true and fair view, what compliance with this FRS requires, and what is a complete set of financial statements.

3.1A A **small entity** applying Section 1A *Small Entities* is not required to comply with paragraphs 3.3, PBE3.3A, 3.9, 3.17, 3.18, 3.19 and 3.24(b).

True and fair view

3.2 The financial statements shall give a true and fair view of the **assets, liabilities, financial position**, financial **performance** and, when required to be presented, **cash flows** of an entity.

    (a) The application of this FRS, with additional disclosure when necessary, is presumed to result in financial statements that give a true and fair view of the financial position, financial performance and, when required to be presented, cash flows of entities within the scope of this FRS.

    (b) [Not used]

The additional disclosures referred to in (a) are necessary when compliance with the specific requirements in this FRS is insufficient to enable users to understand the effect of particular transactions, other events and conditions on the entity's financial position and financial performance.

Compliance with this FRS

3.3 An entity whose financial statements comply with this FRS shall make an explicit and unreserved statement of such compliance in the **notes**. Financial statements shall not be described as complying with this FRS unless they comply with all the requirements of this FRS.

PBE3.3A A **public benefit entity** that applies the 'PBE' prefixed paragraphs shall make an explicit and unreserved statement that it is a public benefit entity.

* 3.4 In special circumstances when management concludes that compliance with any requirement of this FRS or applicable legislation (only when it allows for a true and fair override) is inconsistent with the requirement to give a true and fair view, the entity shall depart from that requirement in the manner set out in paragraph 3.5.

* 3.5 When an entity departs from a requirement of this FRS in accordance with paragraph 3.4, or from a requirement of applicable legislation, it shall disclose the following:

    (a) that management has concluded that the financial statements give a true and fair view of the entity's financial position, financial performance and, when required to be presented, cash flows;

    (b) that it has complied with this FRS or applicable legislation, except that it has departed from a particular requirement of this FRS or applicable legislation to the extent necessary to give a true and fair view; and

(c)   the nature and effect of the departure, including the treatment that this FRS or applicable legislation would require, the reason why that treatment would be so misleading in the circumstances that it would conflict with the objective of financial statements set out in Section 2, and the treatment adopted.

3.6   When an entity has departed from a requirement of this FRS or applicable legislation in a prior period, and that departure affects the amounts recognised in the financial statements for the current period, it shall make the disclosures set out in paragraph 3.5(c).

3.7   [Not used]

Going concern

3.8   When preparing financial statements, the management of an entity using this FRS shall make an assessment of the entity's ability to continue as a **going concern**. An entity is a going concern unless management either intends to liquidate the entity or to cease trading, or has no realistic alternative but to do so. In assessing whether the going concern assumption is appropriate, management takes into account all available information about the future, which is at least, but is not limited to, twelve months from the date when the financial statements are authorised for issue.

3.9   When management is aware, in making its assessment, of **material** uncertainties related to events or conditions that cast significant doubt upon the entity's ability to continue as a going concern, the entity shall disclose those uncertainties. When an entity does not prepare financial statements on a going concern basis, it shall disclose that fact, together with the basis on which it prepared the financial statements and the reason why the entity is not regarded as a going concern.

Frequency of reporting

3.10   An entity shall present a complete set of financial statements (including comparative information as set out in paragraph 3.14) at least annually. When the end of an entity's **reporting period** changes and the annual financial statements are presented for a period longer or shorter than one year, the entity shall disclose the following:

(a)   that fact;

(b)   the reason for using a longer or shorter period; and

(c)   the fact that comparative amounts presented in the financial statements (including the related notes) are not entirely comparable.

Consistency of presentation

3.11   An entity shall retain the presentation and classification of items in the financial statements from one period to the next unless:

(a)   it is apparent, following a significant change in the nature of the entity's operations or a review of its financial statements, that another presentation or classification would be more appropriate having regard to the criteria for the selection and application of **accounting policies** in Section 10 *Accounting Policies, Estimates and Errors*; or

(b)   this FRS, or another applicable FRS or FRC Abstract, requires a change in presentation.

* 3.12 When the presentation or classification of items in the financial statements is changed, an entity shall reclassify comparative amounts unless the reclassification is **impracticable**. When comparative amounts are reclassified, an entity shall disclose the following:

(a) the nature of the reclassification;

(b) the amount of each item or class of items that is reclassified; and

(c) the reason for the reclassification.

* 3.13 If it is impracticable to reclassify comparative amounts, an entity shall disclose why reclassification was not practicable.

Comparative information

3.14 Except when this FRS permits or requires otherwise, an entity shall present comparative information in respect of the preceding period for all amounts presented in the current period's financial statements. An entity shall include comparative information for narrative and descriptive information when it is relevant to an understanding of the current period's financial statements.

Materiality and aggregation

3.15 An entity shall present separately each material class of similar items. An entity shall present separately items of a dissimilar nature or function unless they are immaterial.

3.16 Financial statements result from processing large numbers of transactions or other events that are aggregated into classes according to their nature or function. The final stage in the process of aggregation and classification is the presentation of condensed and classified data, which form line items in the financial statements. If a line item is not individually material, it is aggregated with other items either in those statements or in the notes. An item that may not warrant separate presentation in those statements may warrant separate presentation in the notes.

3.16A An entity need not provide a specific disclosure required by this FRS if the information is not material.

Complete set of financial statements

3.17 A complete set of financial statements of an entity shall include all of the following:

(a) a **statement of financial position** as at the **reporting date**;

(b) either:

(i) a single **statement of comprehensive income** for the reporting period displaying all items of income and expense recognised during the period including those items recognised in determining **profit or loss** (which is a subtotal in the statement of comprehensive income) and items of **other comprehensive income**; or

(ii) a separate **income statement** and a separate statement of comprehensive income. If an entity chooses to present both an income statement and a statement of comprehensive income, the statement of comprehensive income begins with profit or loss and then displays the items of other comprehensive income;

(c) a **statement of changes in equity** for the reporting period;

(d) a **statement of cash flows** for the reporting period; and

(e) notes, comprising a summary of significant accounting policies and other explanatory information.

3.18   If the only changes to **equity** during the periods for which financial statements are presented arise from profit or loss, payment of dividends, corrections of prior period **errors**, and changes in accounting policy, the entity may present a single **statement of income and retained earnings** in place of the statement of comprehensive income and statement of changes in equity (see paragraph 6.4).

3.19   If an entity has no items of other comprehensive income in any of the periods for which financial statements are presented, it may present only an income statement, or it may present a statement of comprehensive income in which the 'bottom line' is labelled 'profit or loss'.

3.20   Because paragraph 3.14 requires comparative amounts in respect of the previous period for all amounts presented in the financial statements, a complete set of financial statements means that an entity shall present, as a minimum, two of each of the required financial statements and related notes.

3.21   In a complete set of financial statements, an entity shall present each financial statement with equal prominence.

3.22   An entity may use titles for the financial statements other than those used in this FRS as long as they are not misleading.

Identification of the financial statements

3.23   An entity shall clearly identify each of the financial statements and the notes and distinguish them from other information in the same document. In addition, an entity shall display the following information prominently, and repeat it when necessary for an understanding of the information presented:

(a) the name of the reporting entity and any change in its name since the end of the preceding reporting period;

(b) whether the financial statements cover the individual entity or a group of entities;

(c) the date of the end of the reporting period and the period covered by the financial statements;

(d) the **presentation currency**, as defined in Section 30 *Foreign Currency Translation*; and

(e) the level of rounding, if any, used in presenting amounts in the financial statements.

3.24   An entity shall disclose the following in the notes:

* (a) the legal form of the entity, its country of incorporation and the address of its registered office (or principal place of business, if different from the registered office); and

(b) a description of the nature of the entity's operations and its principal activities, unless this is disclosed in the business review (or similar statement) accompanying the financial statements.

Presentation of information not required by this FRS

3.25   This FRS does not address presentation of **interim financial reports**. An entity that prepares such reports shall describe the basis for preparing and presenting the information. **FRS 104** sets out a basis for the preparation and presentation of interim financial reports that an entity may apply.

Section 4
Statement of Financial Position

Scope of this section

4.1 This section sets out the information that is to be presented in a **statement of financial position** and how to present it. The statement of financial position (which is referred to as the balance sheet in the **Act**) presents an entity's **assets, liabilities** and **equity** as of a specific date—the end of the **reporting period**. This section applies to all entities, whether or not they report under the Act. Entities that do not report under the Act should comply with the requirements of this section, and with the **Regulations** (or, where applicable, the **LLP Regulations**) where referred to in this section, except to the extent that these requirements are not permitted by any statutory framework under which such entities report.

4.1A A **small entity** applying Section 1A *Small Entities* is not required to comply with this section.

Information to be presented in the statement of financial position

4.2 An entity shall present a statement of financial position in accordance with one of the following requirements for a balance sheet:

(a) Part 1 *General Rules and Formats* of Schedule 1 to the Regulations.

(b) Part 1 *General Rules and Formats* of Schedule 2 to the Regulations.

(c) Part 1 *General Rules and Formats* of Schedule 3 to the Regulations.

(d) Part 1 *General Rules and Formats* of Schedule 1 to the LLP Regulations.

The consolidated statement of financial position of a **group** shall be presented in accordance with the requirements for a consolidated balance sheet in Schedule 6 to the Regulations or Schedule 3 to the LLP Regulations.

4.2A An entity choosing to apply paragraph 1A(1) of Schedule 1 to the Regulations and adapt one of the balance sheet formats shall, as a minimum, include in its statement of financial position line items that present the following, distinguishing between those items that are **current** and those that are **non-current**:

(a) **property, plant and equipment**;

(b) **investment property** carried at **fair value** through profit or loss;

(c) **intangible assets**;

(d) **financial assets** (excluding amounts shown under (e), (f), (j) and (k));

(e) investments in **associates**;

(f) investments in **jointly controlled entities**;

(g) **biological assets** carried at cost less accumulated **depreciation** and impairment;

(h) biological assets carried at fair value through profit or loss;

(i) **inventories**;

(j) trade and other receivables;

(k) **cash** and **cash equivalents**;

(l) trade and other payables;

(m) **provisions**;

(n) financial liabilities (excluding amounts shown under (l) and (m));

(o) liabilities and assets for **current tax**;

(p) **deferred tax liabilities** and **deferred tax assets** (classified as non-current);

(q) **non-controlling interest**, presented within equity separately from the equity attributable to the owners of the **parent**; and

(r) equity attributable to the owners of the parent.

4.2B An entity choosing to apply paragraph 1A(1) of Schedule 1 to the Regulations shall also disclose, either in the statement of financial position or in the **notes**, the following sub-classifications of the line items presented:

(a) property, plant and equipment in classifications appropriate to the entity;

(b) intangible assets and **goodwill** in classifications appropriate to the entity;

(c) investments, showing separately shares and loans;

(d) trade and other receivables showing separately amounts due from **related parties**, amounts due from other parties, prepayments and receivables arising from accrued income not yet billed;

(e) inventories, showing separately amounts of inventories:

(i) held for sale in the ordinary course of business;

(ii) in the process of production for such sale; and

(iii) in the form of materials or supplies to be consumed in the production process or in the rendering of services.

(f) trade and other payables, showing separately amounts payable to trade suppliers, payable to related parties, deferred income and accruals; and

(g) classes of equity, such as share capital, share premium, retained earnings, revaluation reserve, fair value reserve and other reserves.

4.2C The descriptions used in paragraphs 4.2A and 4.2B, and the ordering of items or aggregation of similar items, may be amended according to the nature of the entity and its transactions, to provide information that is relevant to an understanding of the entity's financial position, providing the information given is at least equivalent to that required by the balance sheet format had it not been adapted.

4.2D In order to comply with the requirement to distinguish between those items that are current and those that are non-current an entity shall present current and non-current assets, and current and non-current liabilities, as separate classifications in its statement of financial position.

4.3 An entity shall present additional line items, headings and subtotals in the statement of financial position when such presentation is relevant to an understanding of the entity's **financial position**.

Debtors due after more than one year

4.4 [Not used]

4.4A Unless an entity chooses to apply paragraph 1A(1) of Schedule 1 to the Regulations, in instances where the amount of debtors due after more than one year is so **material** in the context of the total net current assets that in the absence of disclosure of the debtors due after more than one year on the face of the statement of financial position readers may misinterpret the **financial statements**, the amount should be disclosed on the face of the statement of financial position within **current assets**. In most cases it will be satisfactory to disclose the amount due after more than one year in the **notes** to the financial statements.

4.5   [Not used]

4.6   [Not used]

Creditors: amounts falling due within one year

4.7   Unless an entity chooses to apply paragraph 1A(1) of Schedule 1 to the Regulations, an entity shall classify a creditor as due within one year when the entity does not have an unconditional right, at the end of the reporting period, to defer settlement of the creditor for at least 12 months after the **reporting date**. For example, this would be the case if the earliest date on which the lender, exercising all available options and rights, could require repayment or (as the case may be) payment was within 12 months after the reporting date.

4.8   [Not used]

Information to be presented either in the statement of financial position or in the notes

4.9   [Not used]

4.10   [Not used]

4.11   [Not used]

4.12   An entity with share capital shall disclose the following, either in the statement of financial position or in the notes:

(a)   For each class of share capital:

(i)   [Not used]

(ii)   The number of shares issued and fully paid, and issued but not fully paid.

(iii) Par value per share, or that the shares have no par value.

(iv) A reconciliation of the number of shares outstanding at the beginning and at the end of the period. This reconciliation need not be presented for prior periods.

(v)   The rights, preferences and restrictions attaching to that class including restrictions on the distribution of dividends and the repayment of capital.

(vi) Shares in the entity held by the entity or by its **subsidiaries**, **associates**, or **joint ventures**.

(vii) Shares reserved for issue under options and contracts for the sale of shares, including the terms and amounts.

(b)   A description of each reserve within equity.

4.13   An entity without share capital, such as a partnership or trust, shall disclose information equivalent to that required by paragraph 4.12(a), showing changes during the period in each category of equity, and the rights, preferences and restrictions attaching to each category of equity.

Information to be presented in the notes

4.14   If, at the reporting date, an entity has a binding sale agreement for a major disposal of assets, or a **disposal group**, the entity shall disclose the following information:

(a)   a description of the asset(s) or the disposal group;

(b)   a description of the facts and circumstances of the sale; and

(c)   the **carrying amount** of the assets or, for a disposal group, the carrying amounts of the underlying assets and liabilities.

Section 5
Statement of Comprehensive Income and Income Statement

Scope of this section

5.1   This section requires an entity to present its **total comprehensive income** for a period—ie its financial **performance** for the period—in one or two statements. It sets out the information that is to be presented in those statements and how to present it. This section applies to all entities, whether or not they report under the **Act**. Entities that do not report under the Act should comply with the requirements of this section, and with the **Regulations** (or, where applicable, the **LLP Regulations**) where referred to in this section, except to the extent that these requirements are not permitted by any statutory framework under which such entities report. If an entity meets specified conditions and chooses to do so, it may present a **statement of income and retained earnings** as set out in Section 6 *Statement of Change in Equity and Statement of Income and Retained Earnings*.

5.1A   A **small entity** applying Section 1A *Small Entities* is not required to comply with this section.

Presentation of total comprehensive income

5.2   An entity shall present its total comprehensive income for a period either:

(a)   in a single **statement of comprehensive income**, in which case the statement of comprehensive income presents all items of **income** and **expense** recognised in the period; or

(b)   in two statements—an **income statement** (which is referred to as the profit and loss account in the Act) and a statement of comprehensive income—in which case the income statement presents all items of income and expense recognised in the period except those that are recognised in total comprehensive income outside of **profit or loss** as permitted or required by this FRS.

5.3   A change from the single-statement approach to the two-statement approach, or vice versa, is a change in **accounting policy** to which Section 10 *Accounting Policies, Estimates and Errors* applies.

Single-statement approach

5.4   [Not used]

5.5   An entity shall present, in the statement of comprehensive income, the items to be included in a profit and loss account in accordance with one of the following requirements:

(a)   Part 1 *General Rules and Formats* of Schedule 1 to the Regulations;

(b)   Part 1 *General Rules and Formats* of Schedule 2 to the Regulations;

(c)   Part 1 *General Rules and Formats* of Schedule 3 to the Regulations; or

(d)   Part 1 *General Rules and Formats* of Schedule 1 to the LLP Regulations.

The consolidated statement of comprehensive income of a **group** shall be presented in accordance with the requirements for a consolidated profit and loss account of Schedule 6 to the Regulations or Schedule 3 to the LLP Regulations.

5.5A   In addition an entity shall include, in the statement of comprehensive income, line items that present the following amounts for the period:

(a)   Classified by nature (excluding amounts in (b)), the components of **other comprehensive income** recognised as part of total comprehensive income outside profit or loss as permitted or required by this FRS. An entity may present the components of other comprehensive income either:

(i)   net of related tax effects; or

(ii)   before the related tax effects with one amount shown for the aggregate amount of **income tax** relating to those components.

(b)   Its share of the other comprehensive income of **associates** and **jointly controlled entities** accounted for by the equity method.

(c)   Total comprehensive income.

5.5B   An entity choosing to apply paragraph 1A(2) of Schedule 1 to the Regulations and adapt one of the profit and loss account formats shall, as a minimum, include in its statement of comprehensive income line items that present the following amounts for the period:

(a)   **revenue**;

(b)   finance costs;

(c)   share of the profit or loss of investments in **associates** (see Section 14 *Investments in Associates*) and **jointly controlled entities** (see Section 15 *Investments in Joint Ventures*) accounted for using the equity method;

(d)   profit or loss before taxation;

(e)   **tax expense** excluding tax allocated to items (h) and (i) below or to **equity** (see paragraph 29.27);

(f)   as set out in paragraph 5.7E (including a column identified as **discontinued operations**) a single amount comprising the total of:

(i)   the post-tax profit or loss of a discontinued operation, and

(ii)   the post-tax gain or loss recognised on the remeasurement of the impairment or on the disposal of the **assets** or **disposal group(s)** constituting discontinued operations.

(g)   profit or loss;

(h)   each item of other comprehensive income classified by nature (excluding amounts in (i));

(i)   share of other comprehensive income of associates and jointly controlled entities accounted for by the equity method; and

(j)   total comprehensive income.

5.5C   An entity may include additional line items in the income statement and amend the descriptions used in paragraph 5.5B, and the ordering of items, when this is necessary to explain the elements of financial performance, providing the information given is at least equivalent to that required by the profit and loss account format had it not been adapted.

5.6   An entity shall present the following items as allocations of profit or loss and other comprehensive income in the statement of comprehensive income for the period:

(a)   Profit or loss for the period attributable to:

(i)   **non-controlling interest**; and

(ii) **owners** of the **parent**.

(b) Total comprehensive income for the period attributable to:

(i) non-controlling interest; and

(ii) owners of the parent.

Two-statement approach

5.7 Under the two-statement approach, an entity shall present in an income statement, the items to be included in a profit and loss account in accordance with one of the following requirements:

(a) Part 1 *General Rules and Formats* of Schedule 1 to the Regulations;

(b) Part 1 *General Rules and Formats* of Schedule 2 to the Regulations;

(c) Part 1 *General Rules and Formats* of Schedule 3 to the Regulations; or

(d) Part 1 *General Rules and Formats* of Schedule 1 to the LLP Regulations.

The consolidated income statement of a group shall be presented in accordance with the requirements for a consolidated profit and loss account of Schedule 6 to the Regulations or Schedule 3 to the LLP Regulations.

5.7A An entity choosing to apply paragraph 1A(2) of Schedule 1 to the Regulations and adapt one of the profit and loss account formats shall, as a minimum, include in its income statement line items that present the amounts in paragraphs 5.5B(a) to 5.5B(g), with profit or loss as the last line. The statement of comprehensive income shall begin with profit or loss as its first line and shall display, as a minimum, line items that present the amounts in paragraphs 5.5B(h) to 5.5B(j) and paragraph 5.6(b) for the period, with total comprehensive income as the last line.

5.7B If an entity presents profit or loss in an income statement, it shall present the information required in paragraph 5.6(a) in that statement.

5.7C The statement of comprehensive income shall begin with profit or loss as its first line and shall display, as a minimum, line items that present the amounts in paragraphs 5.5A and 5.6(b) for the period.

Requirements applicable to both approaches

5.7D In addition to the requirements of paragraphs 5.5 or 5.7, as a minimum, **turnover** must be presented on the face of the income statement (or statement of comprehensive income if presented).

5.7E An entity shall also disclose on the face of the income statement (or statement of comprehensive income if presented) an amount comprising the total of:

(a) the post-tax profit or loss of discontinued operations; and

(b) the post-tax gain or loss attributable to the impairment or on the disposal of the assets or disposal group(s) constituting discontinued operations.

A line-by-line analysis shall be presented in the income statement (or statement of comprehensive income if presented), in a column identified as relating to discontinued operations, ie separately from continuing operations; a total column shall also be presented.

5.7F   An entity shall re-present the disclosures in paragraph 5.7D for prior periods presented in the **financial statements** so that the disclosures relate to all operations that have been discontinued by the end of the **reporting period** for the latest period presented.

5.8   Under this FRS, the effects of corrections of **material errors** and changes in accounting policies are presented as retrospective adjustments of prior periods rather than as part of profit or loss in the period in which they arise (see Section 10).

5.9   An entity shall present additional line items, headings and subtotals in the statement of comprehensive income (and in the income statement, if presented), when such presentation is relevant to an understanding of the entity's financial performance.

* 5.9A When items included in total comprehensive income are material, an entity shall disclose their nature and amount separately, in the statement of comprehensive income (and in the income statement, if presented) or in the **notes**.

5.9B   This FRS does not require disclosure of 'operating profit'. However, if an entity elects to disclose the results of **operating activities** the entity should ensure that the amount disclosed is representative of activities that would normally be regarded as 'operating'. For example, it would be inappropriate to exclude items clearly related to operations (such as inventory write-downs and restructuring and relocation expenses) because they occur irregularly or infrequently or are unusual in amount. Similarly, it would be inappropriate to exclude items on the grounds that they do not involve **cash flows**, such as **depreciation** and **amortisation** expenses.

Ordinary activities and extraordinary items

5.10   An entity applying paragraph 5.5(a) or 5.7(a) shall not present or describe any items of income or expense as 'extraordinary items' in the statement of comprehensive income (or in the income statement, if presented) or in the notes.

        Paragraphs 5.10A and 5.10B apply to entities applying paragraphs 5.5(b), 5.5(c), 5.5(d), 5.7(b), 5.7(c) or 5.7(d).

5.10A   Ordinary activities are any activities which are undertaken by a reporting entity as part of its business and such related activities in which the reporting entity engages in furtherance of, incidental to, or arising from, these activities. Ordinary activities include any effects on the reporting entity of any event in the various environments in which it operates, including the political, regulatory, economic and geographical environments, irrespective of the frequency or unusual nature of the events.

5.10B   Extraordinary items are material items possessing a high degree of abnormality which arise from events or transactions that fall outside the ordinary activities of the reporting entity and which are not expected to recur. The additional line items required to be presented by paragraph 5.9 and material items required to be disclosed by paragraph 5.9A, are not extraordinary items when they arise from the ordinary activities of the entity. Extraordinary items do not include prior period items merely because they relate to a prior period.

Analysis of expenses

5.11   Unless otherwise required under the Regulations, an entity shall present an analysis of expenses using a classification based on either the nature of expenses or the function of expenses within the entity, whichever provides information that is reliable and more relevant.

Analysis by nature of expense

(a)   Under this method of classification, expenses are aggregated in the statement of comprehensive income (or in the income statement, under the two-statement approach) according to their nature (eg depreciation, raw materials and consumables and staff costs), and are not reallocated among various functions within the entity.

Analysis by function of expense

(b)   Under this method of classification, expenses are aggregated according to their function as part of cost of sales or, for example, the costs of distribution or administrative activities.

Appendix to Section 5

Example showing presentation of discontinued operations

This appendix accompanies, but is not part of, Section 5. It provides guidance on applying the requirements of Section 5 paragraph 5.7E for presenting discontinued operations. The example illustrates the presentation of comprehensive income in a single statement and the classification of expenses within profit by function. A columnar format is used in order to present a single line item as required by paragraph 5.7E, while still complying with the requirements of the Act to show totals for ordinary activities of items such as turnover, profit or loss before taxation and tax.

Statement of comprehensive income

for the year ended 31 December 20X1

	20X1			20X0		
	Continuing operations	Discontinued operations	Total	Continuing operations (as restated)	Discontinued operations (as restated)	Total
	CU	CU	CU	CU	CU	CU
Turnover	4,200	1,232	5,432	3,201	1,500	4,701
Cost of Sales	(2,591)	(1,104)	(3,695)	(2,281)	(1,430)	(3,711)
Gross profit	1,609	128	1,737	920	70	990
Administrative expenses	(452)	(110)	(562)	(418)	(120)	(538)
Other operating income	212	–	212	198	–	198
Profit on disposal of operations	–	301	301	–	–	–
Operating profit	1,369	319	1,688	700	(50)	650
Interest receivable and similar income	14	–	14	16	–	16
Interest payable and similar charges	(208)	–	(208)	(208)	–	(208)
Profit on ordinary activities before tax	1,175	319	1,494	508	(50)	458
Taxation	(390)	(4)	(394)	(261)	3	(258)
Profit on ordinary activities after taxation and profit for the financial year	785	315	1,100	247	(47)	200
Other comprehensive income						
Actuarial losses on defined benefit pension plans			(108)			(68)
Deferred tax movement relating to actuarial losses			28			18
Total comprehensive income for the year			1,020			150

Section 6
Statement of Changes in Equity and Statement of Income and Retained Earnings

Scope of this section

6.1   This section sets out requirements for presenting the changes in an entity's **equity** for a period, either in a statement of changes in equity or, if specified conditions are met and an entity chooses, in a **statement of income and retained earnings**.

6.1A   A **small entity** applying Section 1A *Small Entities* is not required to comply with this section. However, paragraph 1A.9 encourages a small entity to present a statement of changes in equity or a statement of income and retained earnings.

Statement of changes in equity

Purpose

6.2   The statement of changes in equity presents an entity's **profit or loss** for a **reporting period**, **other comprehensive income** for the period, the effects of changes in **accounting policies** and corrections of **material errors** recognised in the period, and the amounts of investments by, and dividends and other distributions to, equity investors during the period.

Information to be presented in the statement of changes in equity

6.3   An entity shall present a statement of changes in equity showing in the statement:

(a) **total comprehensive income** for the period, showing separately the total amounts attributable to **owners** of the **parent** and to **non-controlling interests**;

(b) for each component of equity, the effects of **retrospective application** or retrospective restatement recognised in accordance with Section 10 *Accounting Policies, Estimates and Errors*; and

(c) for each component of equity, a reconciliation between the **carrying amount** at the beginning and the end of the period, separately disclosing changes resulting from:

(i)   profit or loss;

(ii) other comprehensive income; and

(iii) the amounts of investments by, and dividends and other distributions to, owners, showing separately issues of shares, purchase of own share transactions, dividends and other distributions to owners, and changes in ownership interests in **subsidiaries** that do not result in a loss of **control**.

Information to be presented in the statement of changes in equity or in the notes

* 6.3A   For each component of equity, an entity shall present, either in the statement of changes in equity or in the **notes**, an analysis of other comprehensive income by item (see paragraph 6.3(c)(ii)).

Statement of income and retained earnings

Purpose

6.4   The statement of income and retained earnings presents an entity's profit or loss and changes in retained earnings for a reporting period. Paragraph 3.18 permits an entity to present a statement of income and retained earnings in place of a **statement of comprehensive income** and a statement of changes in equity if the only changes to its equity during the periods for which **financial statements** are presented arise from profit or loss, payment of dividends, corrections of prior period material errors, and changes in accounting policy.

Information to be presented in the statement of income and retained earnings

6.5   An entity shall present, in the statement of income and retained earnings, the following items in addition to the information required by Section 5 *Statement of Comprehensive Income and Income Statement*:

(a)   retained earnings at the beginning of the reporting period;

(b)   dividends declared and paid or payable during the period;

(c)   restatements of retained earnings for corrections of prior period material errors;

(d)   restatements of retained earnings for changes in accounting policy; and

(e)   retained earnings at the end of the reporting period.

Section 7
Statement of Cash Flows

Scope of this section

7.1   This section sets out the information that is to be presented in a **statement of cash flows** and how to present it. The statement of cash flows provides information about the changes in **cash** and **cash equivalents** of an entity for a **reporting period**, showing separately changes from **operating activities, investing activities** and **financing activities**.

7.1A   This section and paragraph 3.17(d) do not apply to:

     (a)   mutual life assurance companies;

     (b)   **retirement benefit plans**; or

     (c)   investment funds that meet all the following conditions:

         (i)   substantially all of the entity's investments are highly liquid;

         (ii)   substantially all of the entity's investments are carried at market value; and

         (iii)   the entity provides a statement of changes in net assets.

7.1B   A **small entity** is not required to comply with this section.

Cash equivalents

7.2   Cash equivalents are short-term, highly liquid investments that are readily convertible to known amounts of cash and that are subject to an insignificant risk of changes in value. Therefore, an investment normally qualifies as a cash equivalent only when it has a short maturity of, say, three months or less from the date of acquisition. Bank overdrafts are normally considered financing activities similar to borrowings. However, if they are repayable on demand and form an integral part of an entity's cash management, bank overdrafts are a component of cash and cash equivalents.

Information to be presented in the statement of cash flows

7.3   An entity shall present a statement of cash flows that presents **cash flows** for a reporting period classified by operating activities, investing activities and financing activities.

Operating activities

7.4   Operating activities are the principal revenue-producing activities of the entity. Therefore, cash flows from operating activities generally result from the transactions and other events and conditions that enter into the determination of **profit or loss**. Examples of cash flows from operating activities are:

     (a)   cash receipts from the sale of goods and the rendering of services;

     (b)   cash receipts from royalties, fees, commissions and other revenue;

     (c)   cash payments to suppliers for goods and services;

     (d)   cash payments to and on behalf of employees;

     (e)   cash payments or refunds of **income tax**, unless they can be specifically identified with financing and investing activities;

(f) cash receipts and payments from investments, loans and other contracts held for dealing or trading purposes, which are similar to **inventory** acquired specifically for resale; and

(g) cash advances and loans made to other parties by **financial institutions**.

Some transactions, such as the sale of an item of plant by a manufacturing entity, may give rise to a **gain** or loss that is included in profit or loss. However, the cash flows relating to such transactions are cash flows from investing activities.

Investing activities

7.5 Investing activities are the acquisition and disposal of long-term assets and other investments not included in cash equivalents. Examples of cash flows arising from investing activities are:

(a) cash payments to acquire **property, plant and equipment** (including self-constructed property, plant and equipment), **intangible assets** and other long-term assets. These payments include those relating to capitalised development costs and self-constructed property, plant and equipment;

(b) cash receipts from sales of property, plant and equipment, intangibles and other long-term assets;

(c) cash payments to acquire **equity** or debt instruments of other entities and interests in **joint ventures** (other than payments for those instruments classified as cash equivalents or held for dealing or trading);

(d) cash receipts from sales of equity or debt instruments of other entities and interests in joint ventures (other than receipts for those instruments classified as cash equivalents or held for dealing or trading);

(e) cash advances and loans made to other parties (except those made by financial institutions – see paragraph 7.4(g));

(f) cash receipts from the repayment of advances and loans made to other parties;

(g) cash payments for futures contracts, forward contracts, option contracts and swap contracts, except when the contracts are held for dealing or trading, or the payments are classified as financing activities; and

(h) cash receipts from futures contracts, forward contracts, option contracts and swap contracts, except when the contracts are held for dealing or trading, or the receipts are classified as financing activities.

When a contract is accounted for as a hedge (see Section 12 *Other Financial Instruments Issues*), an entity shall classify the cash flows of the contract in the same manner as the cash flows of the item being hedged.

Financing activities

7.6 Financing activities are activities that result in changes in the size and composition of the contributed equity and borrowings of an entity. Examples of cash flows arising from financing activities are:

(a) cash proceeds from issuing shares or other equity instruments;

(b) cash payments to **owners** to acquire or redeem the entity's shares;

(c) cash proceeds from issuing debentures, loans, notes, bonds, mortgages and other short-term or long-term borrowings;

(d) cash repayments of amounts borrowed; and

(e) cash payments by a lessee for the reduction of the outstanding **liability** relating to a **finance lease**.

Reporting cash flows from operating activities

7.7   An entity shall present cash flows from operating activities using either:

(a)   the indirect method, whereby profit or loss is adjusted for the effects of non-cash transactions, any deferrals or accruals of past or future operating cash receipts or payments, and items of **income** or **expense** associated with investing or financing cash flows; or

(b)   the direct method, whereby major classes of gross cash receipts and gross cash payments are disclosed.

Indirect method

7.8   Under the indirect method, the net cash flow from operating activities is determined by adjusting profit or loss for the effects of:

(a)   changes during the period in inventories and operating receivables and payables;

(b)   non-cash items such as **depreciation**, **provisions**, **deferred tax**, accrued income (expenses) not yet received (paid) in cash, unrealised foreign currency gains and losses, undistributed profits of **associates**, and **non-controlling interests**; and

(c)   all other items for which the cash effects relate to investing or financing.

Direct method

7.9   Under the direct method, net cash flow from operating activities is presented by disclosing information about major classes of gross cash receipts and gross cash payments. Such information may be obtained either:

(a)   from the accounting records of the entity; or

(b)   by adjusting sales, cost of sales and other items in the **statement of comprehensive income** (or the **income statement**, if presented) for:

(i)   changes during the period in inventories and operating receivables and payables;

(ii)   other non-cash items; and

(iii)   other items for which the cash effects are investing or financing cash flows.

Reporting cash flows from investing and financing activities

7.10   An entity shall present separately major classes of gross cash receipts and gross cash payments arising from investing and financing activities, except to the extent that net presentation is permitted by paragraphs 7.10A to 7.10E. The aggregate cash flows arising from acquisitions and from disposals of **subsidiaries** or other business units shall be presented separately and classified as investing activities.

Reporting cash flows on a net basis

7.10A   Cash flows arising from the following operating, investing or financing activities may be reported on a net basis:

(a)   cash receipts and payments on behalf of customers when the cash flows reflect the activities of the customer rather than those of the entity; and

(b)   cash receipts and payments for items in which the turnover is quick, the amounts are large, and the maturities are short.

7.10B   Examples of cash receipts and payments referred to in paragraph 7.10A(a) are:

   (a)   the acceptance and repayment of demand deposits of a bank;

   (b)   funds held for customers by an investment entity; and

   (c)   rents collected on behalf of, and paid over to, the owners of properties.

7.10C   Examples of cash receipts and payments referred to in paragraph 7.10A(b) are advances made for, and the repayment of:

   (a)   principal amounts relating to credit card customers;

   (b)   the purchase and sale of investments; and

   (c)   other short-term borrowings, for example, those which have a maturity period of three months or less.

7.10D   Financial institutions may report cash flows described in paragraph 34.33 on a net basis.

7.10E   A financial institution that undertakes the business of effecting or carrying out **insurance contracts**, other than mutual life assurance companies scoped out of this section in paragraph 7.1A(a), should include the cash flows of their long-term business only to the extent of cash transferred and available to meet the obligations of the company or group as a whole.

Foreign currency cash flows

7.11   An entity shall record cash flows arising from transactions in a foreign currency in the entity's **functional currency** by applying to the foreign currency amount the exchange rate between the functional currency and the foreign currency at the date of the cash flow or an exchange rate that approximates the actual rate (for example, a weighted average exchange rate for the period).

7.12   An entity shall translate cash flows of a foreign subsidiary at the exchange rate between the entity's functional currency and the foreign currency at the date of the cash flow or at an exchange rate that approximates the actual rate (for example, a weighted average exchange rate for the period).

7.13   Unrealised gains and losses arising from changes in foreign currency exchange rates are not cash flows. However, to reconcile cash and cash equivalents at the beginning and the end of the period, the effect of exchange rate changes on cash and cash equivalents held or due in a foreign currency must be presented in the statement of cash flows. Therefore, the entity shall remeasure cash and cash equivalents held during the reporting period (such as amounts of foreign currency held and foreign currency bank accounts) at period-end exchange rates. The entity shall present the resulting unrealised gain or loss separately from cash flows from operating, investing and financing activities.

Interest and dividends

7.14   An entity shall present separately cash flows from interest and dividends received and paid. The entity shall classify these cash flows consistently from period to period as operating, investing or financing activities.

7.15   An entity may classify interest paid and interest and dividends received as operating cash flows because they are included in profit or loss. Alternatively, the entity may classify interest paid and interest and dividends received as financing cash flows and investing cash flows respectively, because they are costs of obtaining financial resources or returns on investments.

7.16 An entity may classify dividends paid as a financing cash flow because they are a cost of obtaining financial resources. Alternatively, the entity may classify dividends paid as a component of cash flows from operating activities because they are paid out of operating cash flows.

Income tax

7.17 An entity shall present separately cash flows arising from income tax and shall classify them as cash flows from operating activities unless they can be specifically identified with financing and investing activities. When tax cash flows are allocated over more than one class of activity, the entity shall disclose the total amount of taxes paid.

Non-cash transactions

7.18 An entity shall exclude from the statement of cash flows investing and financing transactions that do not require the use of cash or cash equivalents. An entity shall disclose such transactions elsewhere in the **financial statements** in a way that provides all the relevant information about those investing and financing activities.

7.19 Many investing and financing activities do not have a direct impact on current cash flows even though they affect the capital and asset structure of an entity. The exclusion of non-cash transactions from the statement of cash flows is consistent with the objective of a statement of cash flows because these items do not involve cash flows in the current period. Examples of non-cash transactions are:

(a) the acquisition of assets either by assuming directly related liabilities or by means of a finance lease;

(b) the acquisition of an entity by means of an equity issue; and

(c) the conversion of debt to equity.

Components of cash and cash equivalents

7.20 An entity shall present the components of cash and cash equivalents and shall present a reconciliation of the amounts presented in the statement of cash flows to the equivalent items presented in the **statement of financial position**. However, an entity is not required to present this reconciliation if the amount of cash and cash equivalents presented in the statement of cash flows is identical to the amount similarly described in the statement of financial position.

7.20A Entities applying Part 1 *General Rules and Formats* of Schedule 2 to the **Regulations** should include as cash, only cash and balances at central banks and loans and advances to banks repayable on demand.

Other disclosures

7.21 An entity shall disclose, together with a commentary by management, the amount of significant cash and cash equivalent balances held by the entity that are not available for use by the entity. Cash and cash equivalents held by an entity may not be available for use by the entity because of, among other reasons, foreign exchange controls or legal restrictions.

Section 8
Notes to the Financial Statements

Scope of this section

8.1 This section sets out the principles underlying information that is to be presented in the **notes** to the **financial statements** and how to present it. Notes contain information in addition to that presented in the **statement of financial position**, **statement of comprehensive income** (if presented), **income statement** (if presented), combined **statement of income and retained earnings** (if presented), **statement of changes in equity** (if presented), and **statement of cash flows**. Notes provide narrative descriptions or disaggregations of items presented in those statements and information about items that do not qualify for **recognition** in those statements. In addition to the requirements of this section, nearly every other section of this FRS requires disclosures that are normally presented in the notes.

Structure of the notes

8.2 The notes shall:

(a) present information about the basis of preparation of the financial statements and the specific **accounting policies** used, in accordance with paragraphs 8.5 to 8.7;

(b) disclose the information required by this FRS that is not presented elsewhere in the financial statements; and

(c) provide information that is not presented elsewhere in the financial statements but is relevant to an understanding of any of them.

* 8.3 An entity shall, as far as practicable, present the notes in a systematic manner. An entity shall cross-reference each item in the financial statements to any related information in the notes.

* 8.4 An entity normally[8] presents the notes in the following order:

(a) a statement that the financial statements have been prepared in compliance with this FRS (see paragraph 3.3);

(b) a summary of significant accounting policies applied (see paragraph 8.5);

(c) supporting information for items presented in the financial statements, in the sequence in which each statement and each line item is presented; and

(d) any other disclosures.

Disclosure of accounting policies

* 8.5 An entity shall disclose the following in the summary of significant accounting policies:

(a) the measurement basis (or bases) used in preparing the financial statements; and

(b) the other accounting policies used that are relevant to an understanding of the financial statements.

---

[8] Company law requires the notes to be presented in the order in which, where relevant, the items to which they relate are presented in the statement of financial position and in the income statement.

Information about judgements

* 8.6   An entity shall disclose, in the summary of significant accounting policies or other notes, the judgements, apart from those involving estimations (see paragraph 8.7), that management has made in the process of applying the entity's accounting policies and that have the most significant effect on the amounts recognised in the financial statements.

Information about key sources of estimation uncertainty

8.7   An entity shall disclose in the notes information about the key assumptions concerning the future, and other key sources of estimation uncertainty at the reporting date, that have a significant risk of causing a **material** adjustment to the **carrying amounts** of **assets** and **liabilities** within the next financial year. In respect of those assets and liabilities, the notes shall include details of:

(a)   their nature; and

(b)   their carrying amount as at the end of the **reporting period**.

Section 9
Consolidated and Separate Financial Statements

Scope of this section

9.1   This section applies to all **parents** that present **consolidated financial statements** (which are referred to as group accounts in the **Act**) intended to give a true and fair view of the **financial position** and **profit or loss** (or **income and expenditure**) of their **group**, whether or not they report under the Act. Parents that do not report under the Act should comply with the requirements of this section, and of the Act where referred to in this section, except to the extent that these requirements are not permitted by any statutory framework under which such entities report. This section also includes guidance on **individual financial statements** and **separate financial statements.**

Requirement to present consolidated financial statements

9.2   Except as permitted or required by paragraph 9.3, a parent entity shall present consolidated financial statements in which it consolidates all its investments in **subsidiaries** in accordance with this FRS. A parent entity need only prepare consolidated accounts under the Act if it is a parent at the year end.

9.3   A parent is exempt from the requirement to prepare consolidated financial statements on any one of the following grounds:

When its immediate parent is established under the law of an EEA State (Section 400 of the Act):

(a)   The parent is a wholly-owned subsidiary. Exemption is conditional on compliance with certain further conditions set out in section 400(2) of the Act.

(b)   The immediate parent holds 90% or more of the allotted shares in the entity and the remaining shareholders have approved the exemption. Exemption is conditional on compliance with certain further conditions set out in section 400(2) of the Act.

(bA) The immediate parent holds more than 50% (but less than 90%) of the allotted shares in the entity, and notice requesting the preparation of consolidated financial statements has not been served on the entity by shareholders holding in aggregate at least 5% of the allotted shares in the entity. Exemption is conditional on compliance with certain further conditions set out in section 400(2) of the Act.

When its parent is not established under the law of an EEA State (Section 401 of the Act):

(c)   The parent is a wholly-owned subsidiary. Exemption is conditional on compliance with certain further conditions set out in section 401(2) of the Act.

(d)   The parent holds 90% or more of the allotted shares in the entity and the remaining shareholders have approved the exemption. Exemption is conditional on compliance with certain further conditions set out in section 401(2) of the Act.

(dA) The parent holds more than 50% (but less than 90%) of the allotted shares in the entity, and notice requesting the preparation of consolidated financial statements has not been served on the entity by shareholders holding in aggregate at least 5% of the allotted shares in the entity. Exemption is conditional on compliance with certain further conditions set out in section 401(2) of the Act.

Other situations

(e)   The parent, and the group headed by it, qualify as small as set out in section 383 of the Act and the parent and the group are considered eligible for the exemption as determined by reference to sections 384 and 399(2A) of the Act.

(f)   All of the parent's subsidiaries are required to be excluded from consolidation by paragraph 9.9 (Section 402 of the Act).

(g)   For a parent not reporting under the Act, if its statutory framework does not require the preparation of consolidated financial statements.

In sub-paragraphs (a) to (dA), the parent is not exempt if any of its transferable securities are admitted to trading on a regulated market of any EEA State within the meaning of Directive 2004/39/EC.

9.4   A subsidiary is an entity that is controlled by the parent. **Control** is the power to govern the financial and operating policies of an entity so as to obtain benefits from its activities.

9.5   Control is presumed to exist when the parent owns, directly or indirectly through subsidiaries, more than half of the voting power of an entity. That presumption may be overcome in exceptional circumstances if it can be clearly demonstrated that such ownership does not constitute control. Control also exists when the parent owns half or less of the voting power of an entity but it has:

(a)   power over more than half of the voting rights by virtue of an agreement with other investors;

(b)   power to govern the financial and operating policies of the entity under a statute or an agreement;

(c)   power to appoint or remove the majority of the members of the board of directors or equivalent governing body and control of the entity is by that board or body; or

(d)   power to cast the majority of votes at meetings of the board of directors or equivalent governing body and control of the entity is by that board or body.

9.6   Control can also be achieved by having options or convertible instruments that are currently exercisable or by having an agent with the ability to direct the activities for the benefit of the controlling entity.

9.6A   Control can also exist when the parent has the power to exercise, or actually exercises, dominant influence or control over the undertaking or it and the undertaking are managed on a unified basis.

9.7   [Not used]

9.8   A subsidiary is not excluded from consolidation because its business activities are dissimilar to those of the other entities within the consolidation. Relevant information is provided by consolidating such subsidiaries and disclosing additional information in the consolidated financial statements about the different business activities of subsidiaries.

9.8A   A subsidiary is not excluded from consolidation because the information necessary for the preparation of consolidated financial statements cannot be obtained without disproportionate **expense** or undue delay, unless its inclusion is not **material** (individually or collectively for more than one subsidiary) for the purposes of giving a true and fair view in the context of the group.

9.9   A subsidiary shall be excluded from consolidation where:

   (a) severe long-term restrictions substantially hinder the exercise of the rights of the parent over the **assets** or management of the subsidiary; or

   (b) the interest in the subsidiary is **held exclusively with a view to subsequent resale**; and the subsidiary has not previously been consolidated in the consolidated financial statements prepared in accordance with this FRS.

9.9A   A subsidiary excluded from consolidation on the grounds set out in paragraph 9.9(a) shall be measured using an accounting policy selected by the parent in accordance with paragraph 9.26, except where the parent still exercises a significant influence over the subsidiary. If this is the case, the parent should treat the subsidiary as an associate using the equity method set out in paragraph 14.8.

9.9B   A subsidiary excluded from consolidation on the grounds set out in paragraph 9.9(b) which is:

   (a) **held as part of an investment portfolio** shall be measured at **fair value** with changes in fair value recognised in profit or loss;[9] or

   (b) not held as part of an investment portfolio shall be measured using an **accounting policy** selected by the parent in accordance with paragraph 9.26.

Special purpose entities

9.10   An entity may be created to accomplish a narrow objective (eg to effect a **lease**, undertake **research** and **development** activities, securitise **financial assets** or facilitate employee shareholdings under remuneration schemes, such as Employee Share Ownership Plans (ESOPs)). Such a special purpose entity (SPE) may take the form of a corporation, trust, partnership or unincorporated entity. Often, SPEs are created with legal arrangements that impose strict requirements over the operations of the SPE.

9.11   Except as permitted or required by paragraph 9.3, a parent entity shall prepare consolidated financial statements that include the entity and any SPEs that are controlled by that entity. In addition to the circumstances described in paragraph 9.5, the following circumstances may indicate that an entity controls a SPE (this is not an exhaustive list):

   (a) the activities of the SPE are being conducted on behalf of the entity according to its specific business needs;

   (b) the entity has the ultimate decision-making powers over the activities of the SPE even if the day-to-day decisions have been delegated;

   (c) the entity has rights to obtain the majority of the benefits of the SPE and therefore may be exposed to risks incidental to the activities of the SPE; and

   (d) the entity retains the majority of the residual or ownership risks related to the SPE or its assets.

9.12   Paragraphs 9.10 and 9.11 do not apply to **post-employment benefit plans** or other long-term employee benefit plans to which Section 28 *Employee Benefits* applies. A special purpose entity that is an intermediate payment arrangement shall be accounted for in accordance with paragraphs 9.33 to 9.38.

---

[9] Additional disclosures may need to be provided in accordance with company law (see Appendix IV, paragraph A4.17).

Consolidation procedures

9.13 The consolidated financial statements present financial information about the group as a single economic entity. In preparing consolidated financial statements, an entity shall:

(a) combine the **financial statements** of the parent and its subsidiaries line by line by adding together like items of assets, **liabilities**, **equity**, **income** and expenses;

(b) eliminate the **carrying amount** of the parent's investment in each subsidiary and the parent's portion of equity of each subsidiary;

(c) measure and present **non-controlling interest** in the profit or loss of consolidated subsidiaries for the **reporting period** separately from the interest of the **owners** of the parent; and

(d) measure and present non-controlling interest in the net assets of consolidated subsidiaries separately from the parent shareholders' equity in them. Non-controlling interest in the net assets consists of:

(i) the amount of the non-controlling interest's share in the net amount of the identifiable assets, liabilities and contingent liabilities recognised and measured in accordance with Section 19 *Business Combinations and Goodwill* at the date of the original combination; and

(ii) the non-controlling interest's share of changes in equity since the date of the combination.

9.14 The proportions of profit or loss and changes in equity allocated to the owners of the parent and to the non-controlling interest are determined on the basis of existing ownership interests and do not reflect the possible exercise or conversion of options or convertible instruments.

Intragroup balances and transactions

9.15 Intragroup balances and transactions, including income, expenses and dividends, are eliminated in full. Profits and losses resulting from intragroup transactions that are recognised in assets, such as **inventory** and **property, plant and equipment**, are eliminated in full. Intragroup losses may indicate an impairment that requires **recognition** in the consolidated financial statements (see Section 27 *Impairment of Assets*). Section 29 *Income Tax* applies to **timing differences** that arise from the elimination of profits and losses resulting from intragroup transactions.

Uniform reporting date and reporting period

9.16 The financial statements of the parent and its subsidiaries used in the preparation of the consolidated financial statements shall be prepared as of the same **reporting date**, and for the same reporting period, unless it is **impracticable** to do so. Where the reporting date and reporting period of a subsidiary are not the same as the parent's reporting date and reporting period, the consolidated financial statements must be made up:

(a) from the financial statements of the subsidiary as of its last reporting date before the parent's reporting date, adjusted for the effects of significant transactions or events that occur between the date of those financial statements and the date of the consolidated financial statements, provided that reporting date is no more than three months before that of the parent; or

(b) from interim financial statements prepared by the subsidiary as at the parent's reporting date.

Uniform accounting policies

9.17 Consolidated financial statements shall be prepared using uniform accounting policies for like transactions and other events and conditions in similar circumstances. If a member of the group uses accounting policies other than those adopted in the consolidated financial statements for like transactions and events in similar circumstances, appropriate adjustments are made to its financial statements in preparing the consolidated financial statements.

Acquisition and disposal of subsidiaries

9.18 The income and expenses of a subsidiary are included in the consolidated financial statements from the **acquisition date**, except when a **business combination** is accounted for by using the merger accounting method under Section 19 or, for certain public benefit entity combinations, Section 34 *Specialised Activities*. The income and expenses of a subsidiary are included in the consolidated financial statements until the date on which the parent ceases to control the subsidiary. A parent may cease to control a subsidiary with or without a change in absolute or relative ownership levels. This could occur, for example, when a subsidiary becomes subject to the control of a government, court, administrator or regulator.

Disposal – where control is lost

9.18A Where a parent ceases to control a subsidiary, a **gain** or loss is recognised in the consolidated statement of comprehensive income (or in the **income statement**, if presented) calculated as the difference between:

(a) the proceeds from the disposal (or the event that resulted in the loss of control); and

(b) the proportion of the carrying amount of the subsidiary's net assets, including any related **goodwill**, disposed of (or lost) as at the date of disposal (or date control is lost).

The cumulative amount of any exchange differences that relate to a foreign subsidiary recognised in equity in accordance with Section 30 *Foreign Currency Translation* is not recognised in profit or loss as part of the gain or loss on disposal of the subsidiary and shall be transferred directly to retained earnings.

9.18B The gain or loss arising on the disposal shall also include those amounts that have been recognised in **other comprehensive income** in relation to that subsidiary, where those amounts are required to be reclassified to profit or loss upon disposal in accordance with other sections of this FRS. Amounts that are not required to be reclassified to profit or loss upon disposal of the related assets or liabilities in accordance with other sections of this FRS shall be transferred directly to retained earnings.

9.19 If an entity ceases to be a subsidiary but the investor (former parent) continues to hold:

(a) an investment that is not an **associate** (see paragraph 9.19(b)) or a **jointly controlled entity** (see paragraph 9.19(c)), that investment shall be accounted for as a financial asset in accordance with Section 11 *Basic Financial Instruments* or Section 12 *Other Financial Instruments Issues* from the date the entity ceases to be a subsidiary;

(b) an associate, that associate shall be accounted for in accordance with Section 14 *Investments in Associates*; or

(c)   a jointly controlled entity, that jointly controlled entity shall be accounted for in accordance with Section 15 *Investments in Joint Ventures*.

The carrying amount of the net assets (and goodwill) attributable to the investment at the date that the entity ceases to be a subsidiary shall be regarded as the cost on initial **measurement** of the financial asset, investment in associate or jointly controlled entity, as appropriate. In applying the equity method to investments in associate or jointly controlled entities as required in sub-paragraphs (b) and (c) above, paragraph 14.8(c) shall not be applied.

Disposal – where control is retained

9.19A   Where a parent reduces its holding in a subsidiary and control is retained, it shall be accounted for as a transaction between equity holders and the resulting change in non-controlling interest shall be accounted for in accordance with paragraph 22.19. No gain or loss shall be recognised at the date of disposal.

Acquisition – Control achieved in stages

9.19B   Where a parent acquires control of a subsidiary in stages, the transaction shall be accounted for in accordance with paragraphs 19.11A and 19.14 applied at the date control is achieved.

Acquisition – Increasing a controlling interest in a subsidiary

9.19C   Where a parent increases its controlling interest in a subsidiary, the identifiable assets and liabilities and a **provision** for **contingent liabilities** of the subsidiary shall not be revalued to fair value and no additional goodwill shall be recognised at the date the controlling interest is increased.

9.19D   The transaction shall be accounted for as a transaction between equity holders and the resulting change in non-controlling interest shall be accounted for in accordance with paragraph 22.19.

Non-controlling interest in subsidiaries

9.20   An entity shall present non-controlling interest in the consolidated statement of financial position within equity, separately from the equity of the owners of the parent.

9.21   An entity shall disclose non-controlling interest in the profit or loss of the group separately in the **statement of comprehensive income** (or income statement, if presented).

9.22   Profit or loss and each component of other comprehensive income shall be attributed to the owners of the parent and to non-controlling interest. **Total comprehensive income** shall be attributed to the owners of the parent and to non-controlling interest even if this results in non-controlling interest having a deficit balance.

Disclosures in consolidated financial statements

9.23   The following disclosures shall be made in consolidated financial statements:

(a)   the fact that the statements are consolidated financial statements;

(b)   the basis for concluding that control exists when the parent does not own, directly or indirectly through subsidiaries, more than half of the voting power;

(c) any difference in the reporting date of the financial statements of the parent and its subsidiaries used in the preparation of the consolidated financial statements;

(d) the nature and extent of any significant restrictions (eg resulting from borrowing arrangements or regulatory requirements) on the ability of subsidiaries to transfer funds to the parent in the form of cash dividends or to repay loans; and

(e) the name of any subsidiary excluded from consolidation and the reason for exclusion.

Individual and separate financial statements

Preparation of individual and separate financial statements

9.23A The requirements for the preparation of individual financial statements are set out in the Act or other statutory framework.

9.24 Separate financial statements are those prepared by a parent in which the investments in subsidiaries, associates or jointly controlled entities are accounted for either at cost or fair value rather than on the basis of the reported results and net assets of the investees. Separate financial statements are included within the meaning of individual financial statements.

9.25 An entity that is not a parent shall account for any investments in associates and any interests in jointly controlled entities in accordance with paragraph 14.4 or 15.9, as appropriate in its individual financial statements.

Accounting policy election in separate financial statements

9.26 When an entity that is a parent prepares separate financial statements and describes them as conforming to this FRS, those financial statements shall comply with all of the requirements of this FRS. The parent shall select and adopt a policy of accounting for its investments in subsidiaries, associates and jointly controlled entities either:

(a) at cost less impairment;

(b) at fair value with changes in fair value recognised in other comprehensive income in accordance with paragraphs 17.15E and 17.15F; or

(c) at fair value with changes in fair value recognised in profit or loss (paragraphs 11.27 to 11.32 provide guidance on fair value).

The entity shall apply the same accounting policy for all investments in a single class (subsidiaries, associates or jointly controlled entities), but it can elect different policies for different classes.

9.26A A parent that is exempt in accordance with paragraph 9.3 from the requirement to present consolidated financial statements, and presents separate financial statements as its only financial statements, shall account for its investments in subsidiaries, associates and jointly controlled entities in accordance with paragraph 9.26.

Disclosures in separate financial statements

9.27 When a parent prepares separate financial statements, those separate financial statements shall disclose:

(a) that the statements are separate financial statements; and

* (b) a description of the methods used to account for the investments in subsidiaries, jointly controlled entities and associates.

9.27A A parent that uses one of the exemptions from presenting consolidated financial statements (described in paragraph 9.3) shall disclose the grounds on which the parent is exempt.

9.27B When a parent adopts a policy of accounting for its investments in subsidiaries, associates or jointly controlled entities at fair value with changes in fair value recognised in profit or loss, it must comply with the requirements of paragraph 36(4) of Schedule 1 to the **Regulations** by applying the disclosure requirements of Section 11 *Basic Financial Instruments* to those investments.

9.28 [Not used]

9.29 [Not used]

9.30 [Not used]

Exchanges of businesses or other non-monetary assets for an interest in a subsidiary, jointly controlled entity or associate

9.31 Where a reporting entity exchanges a **business**, or other non-monetary assets, for an interest in another entity, and that other entity thereby becomes a subsidiary, jointly controlled entity or associate of the reporting entity, the following accounting treatment shall apply in the consolidated financial statements of the reporting entity:

(a) To the extent that the reporting entity retains an ownership interest in the business, or other non-monetary assets, exchanged, even if that interest is then held through the other entity, that retained interest, including any related goodwill, is treated as having been owned by the reporting entity throughout the transaction and should be included at its pre-transaction carrying amount.

(b) Goodwill should be recognised as the difference between:

(i) the fair value of the consideration given; and

(ii) the fair value of the reporting entity's share of the pre-transaction identifiable net assets of the other entity.

The consideration given for the interest acquired in the other entity will include that part of the business, or other non-monetary assets, exchanged and no longer owned by the reporting entity. The consideration may also include **cash** or monetary assets to achieve equalisation of values. Where it is difficult to value the consideration given, the best estimate of its value may be given by valuing what is acquired.

(c) To the extent that the fair value of the consideration received by the reporting entity exceeds the carrying value of the part of the business, or other non-monetary assets exchanged and no longer owned by the reporting entity, and any related goodwill together with any cash given up, the reporting entity should recognise a gain. Any unrealised gain arising on the exchange shall be recognised in other comprehensive income.

(d) To the extent that the fair value of the consideration received by the reporting entity is less than the carrying value of the part of the business, or other non-monetary assets no longer owned by the reporting entity, and any related goodwill, together with any cash given up, the reporting entity should recognise a loss. This loss should be recognised either as an impairment in accordance with Section 27 *Impairment of Assets* or, for any loss remaining after an impairment review of the relevant assets, in profit or loss.

9.32   No gain or loss should be recognised in those rare cases where the artificiality or lack of substance of the transaction is such that a gain or loss on the exchange could not be justified. Where a gain or loss on the exchange is not taken into account because the transaction is artificial or has no substance, the circumstances should be explained.

Intermediate payment arrangements

9.33   Intermediate payment arrangements may take a variety of forms:

(a)   The intermediary is usually established by a sponsoring entity and constituted as a trust, although other arrangements are possible.

(b)   The relationship between the sponsoring entity and the intermediary may take different forms. For example, when the intermediary is constituted as a trust, the sponsoring entity will not have a right to direct the intermediary's activities. However, in these and other cases the sponsoring entity may give advice to the intermediary or may be relied on by the intermediary to provide the information it needs to carry out its activities. Sometimes, the way the intermediary has been set up gives it little discretion in the broad nature of its activities.

(c)   The arrangements are most commonly used to pay employees, although they are sometimes used to compensate suppliers of goods and services other than employee services. Sometimes the sponsoring entity's employees and other suppliers are not the only beneficiaries of the arrangement. Other beneficiaries may include past employees and their dependants, and the intermediary may be entitled to make charitable donations.

(d)   The precise identity of the persons or entities that will receive payments from the intermediary, and the amounts that they will receive, are not usually agreed at the outset.

(e)   The sponsoring entity often has the right to appoint or veto the appointment of the intermediary's trustees (or its directors or the equivalent).

(f)   The payments made to the intermediary and the payments made by the intermediary are often cash payments but may involve other transfers of value.

Examples of intermediate payment arrangements are employee share ownership plans (ESOPs) and employee benefit trusts that are used to facilitate employee shareholdings under remuneration schemes. In a typical employee benefit trust arrangement for share-based payments, an entity makes payments to a trust or guarantees borrowing by the trust, and the trust uses its funds to accumulate assets to pay the entity's employees for services the employees have rendered to the entity.

Although the trustees of an intermediary must act at all times in accordance with the interests of the beneficiaries of the intermediary, most intermediaries (particularly those established as a means of remunerating employees) are specifically designed so as to serve the purposes of the sponsoring entity, and to ensure that there will be minimal risk of any conflict arising between the duties of the trustees of the intermediary and the interest of the sponsoring entity, such that there is nothing to encumber implementation of the wishes of the sponsoring entity in practice. Where this is the case, the sponsoring entity has de facto control.

Accounting for intermediate payment arrangements

9.34   When a sponsoring entity makes payments (or transfers assets) to an intermediary, there is a rebuttable presumption that the entity has exchanged one asset for another and that the payment itself does not represent an immediate expense. To rebut this presumption at the time the payment is made to the intermediary, the entity must demonstrate:

(a)   it will not obtain future economic benefit from the amounts transferred; or

(b)   it does not have control of the right or other access to the future economic benefit it is expected to receive.

9.35   Where a payment to an intermediary is an exchange by the sponsoring entity of one asset for another, any assets that the intermediary acquires in a subsequent exchange transaction will also be under the control of the entity. Accordingly, assets and liabilities of the intermediary shall be accounted for by the sponsoring entity as an extension of its own business and recognised in its own individual financial statements. An asset will cease to be recognised as an asset of the sponsoring entity when, for example, the asset of the intermediary vests unconditionally with identified beneficiaries.

9.36   A sponsoring entity may distribute its own equity instruments, or other equity instruments, to an intermediary in order to facilitate employee shareholdings under a remuneration scheme. Where this is the case and the sponsoring entity has control, or de facto control, of the assets and liabilities of the intermediary, the commercial effect is that the sponsoring entity is, for all practical purposes, in the same position as if it had purchased the shares directly.

9.37   Where an intermediary holds the sponsoring entity's equity instruments, the sponsoring entity shall account for the equity instruments as if it had purchased them directly. The sponsoring entity shall account for the assets and liabilities of the intermediary in its individual financial statements as follows:

(a)   The consideration paid for the equity instruments of the sponsoring entity shall be deducted from equity until such time that the equity instruments **vest** unconditionally with employees.

(b)   Consideration paid or received for the purchase or sale of the sponsoring entity's own equity instruments shall be shown as separate amounts in the **statement of changes in equity**.

(c)   Other assets and liabilities of the intermediary shall be recognised as assets and liabilities of the sponsoring entity.

(d)   No gain or loss shall be recognised in profit or loss or other comprehensive income on the purchase, sale, issue or cancellation of the entity's own equity instruments.

(e)   Finance costs and any administration expenses shall be recognised on an accruals basis rather than as funding payments are made to the intermediary.

(f)   Any dividend income arising on the sponsoring entity's own equity instruments shall be excluded from profit or loss and deducted from the aggregate of dividends paid.

Disclosures in individual and separate financial statements

9.38   When a sponsoring entity recognises the assets and liabilities held by an intermediary, it should disclose sufficient information in the **notes** to its financial statements to enable users to understand the significance of the intermediary and the arrangement in the context of the sponsoring entity's financial statements. This should include:

(a)   a description of the main features of the intermediary including the arrangements for making payments and for distributing equity instruments;

(b)   any restrictions relating to the assets and liabilities of the intermediary;

(c)   the amount and nature of the assets and liabilities held by the intermediary, which have not yet vested unconditionally with the beneficiaries of the arrangement;

(d)   the amount that has been deducted from equity and the number of equity instruments held by the intermediary, which have not yet vested unconditionally with the beneficiaries of the arrangement;

(e)   for entities that have their equity instruments listed or **publicly traded** on a stock exchange or market, the market value of the equity instruments held by the intermediary which have not yet vested unconditionally with employees;

(f)   the extent to which the equity instruments are under option to employees, or have been conditionally gifted to them; and

(g)   the amount that has been deducted from the aggregate dividends paid by the sponsoring entity.

Section 10
Accounting Policies, Estimates and Errors

Scope of this section

10.1   This section provides guidance for selecting and applying the **accounting policies** used in preparing **financial statements**. It also covers **changes in accounting estimates** and corrections of **errors** in prior period financial statements.

Selection and application of accounting policies

10.2   Accounting policies are the specific principles, bases, conventions, rules and practices applied by an entity in preparing and presenting financial statements.

10.3   If an FRS or FRC Abstract specifically addresses a transaction, other event or condition, an entity shall apply that FRS or FRC Abstract. However, the entity need not follow a requirement in an FRS or FRC Abstract if the effect of doing so would not be **material**.

10.4   If an FRS or FRC Abstract does not specifically address a transaction, other event or condition, an entity's management shall use its judgement in developing and applying an accounting policy that results in information that is:

(a)   relevant to the economic decision-making needs of users; and

(b)   reliable, in that the financial statements:

   (i)   represent faithfully the **financial position**, financial **performance** and **cash flows** of the entity;

   (ii)   reflect the economic substance of transactions, other events and conditions, and not merely the legal form;

   (iii)   are neutral, ie free from bias;

   (iv)   are prudent; and

   (v)   are complete in all material respects.

10.5   In making the judgement described in paragraph 10.4, management shall refer to and consider the applicability of the following sources in descending order:

(a)   the requirements and guidance in an FRS or FRC Abstract dealing with similar and related issues;

(b)   where an entity's financial statements are within the scope of a **Statement of Recommended Practice (SORP)** the requirements and guidance in that SORP dealing with similar and related issues; and

(c)   the definitions, **recognition** criteria and measurement concepts for **assets**, **liabilities**, **income** and **expenses** and the pervasive principles in Section 2 *Concepts and Pervasive Principles*.

10.6   In making the judgement described in paragraph 10.4, management may also consider the requirements and guidance in **EU-adopted IFRS** dealing with similar and related issues. Paragraphs 1.4 to 1.7 require certain entities to apply IAS 33 *Earnings per Share* (as adopted in the EU) , IFRS 8 *Operating Segments* (as adopted in the EU) or IFRS 6 *Exploration for and Evaluation of Mineral Resources*.

Consistency of accounting policies

10.7   An entity shall select and apply its accounting policies consistently for similar transactions, other events and conditions, unless an FRS or FRC Abstract specifically requires or permits categorisation of items for which different policies may be appropriate. If an FRS or FRC Abstract requires or permits such categorisation, an appropriate accounting policy shall be selected and applied consistently to each category.

Changes in accounting policies

10.8   An entity shall change an accounting policy only if the change:

(a)   is required by an FRS or FRC Abstract; or

(b)   results in the financial statements providing reliable and more relevant information about the effects of transactions, other events or conditions on the entity's financial position, financial performance or cash flows.

10.9   The following are not changes in accounting policies:

(a)   the application of an accounting policy for transactions, other events or conditions that differ in substance from those previously occurring;

(b)   the application of a new accounting policy for transactions, other events or conditions that did not occur previously or were not material; and

(c)   a change to the cost model when a reliable measure of **fair value** is no longer available (or vice versa) for an asset that an FRS or FRC Abstract would otherwise require or permit to be measured at fair value.

10.10   If an FRS or FRC Abstract allows a choice of accounting treatment (including the measurement basis) for a specified transaction or other event or condition and an entity changes its previous choice, that is a change in accounting policy.

10.10A The initial application of a policy to revalue assets in accordance with Section 17 *Property, Plant and Equipment* or Section 18 *Intangible Assets other than Goodwill* is a change in accounting policy to be dealt with as a revaluation in accordance with those sections, rather than in accordance with paragraphs 10.11 and 10.12.

Applying changes in accounting policies

10.11   An entity shall account for changes in accounting policy as follows:

(a)   an entity shall account for a change in accounting policy resulting from a change in the requirements of an FRS or FRC Abstract in accordance with the transitional provisions, if any, specified in that amendment;

(b)   when an entity has elected to follow IAS 39 *Financial Instruments: Recognition and Measurement* and/or IFRS 9 *Financial Instruments* instead of following Section 11 *Basic Financial Instruments* and Section 12 *Other Financial Instruments Issues* as permitted by paragraph 11.2, and the requirements of IAS 39 and/or IFRS 9 change, the entity shall account for that change in accounting policy in accordance with the transitional provisions, if any, specified in the revised IAS 39 and/or IFRS 9; and

(c)   when an entity is required or has elected to follow IAS 33, IFRS 8 or IFRS 6 and the requirements of those standards change, the entity shall account for that change in accounting policy in accordance with the transitional provisions, if any, specified in those standards as amended; and

(d) an entity shall account for all other changes in accounting policy retrospectively (see paragraph 10.12).

Retrospective application

10.12 When a change in accounting policy is applied retrospectively in accordance with paragraph 10.11, the entity shall apply the new accounting policy to comparative information for prior periods to the earliest date for which it is practicable, as if the new accounting policy had always been applied. When it is **impracticable** to determine the individual-period effects of a change in accounting policy on comparative information for one or more prior periods presented, the entity shall apply the new accounting policy to the **carrying amounts** of assets and liabilities as at the beginning of the earliest period for which **retrospective application** is practicable, which may be the current period, and shall make a corresponding adjustment to the opening balance of each affected component of **equity** for that period.

Disclosure of a change in accounting policy

* 10.13 When an amendment to an FRS or FRC Abstract has an effect on the current period or any prior period, or might have an effect on future periods, an entity shall disclose the following:

(a) the nature of the change in accounting policy;

(b) for the current period and each prior period presented, to the extent practicable, the amount of the adjustment for each financial statement line item affected;

(c) the amount of the adjustment relating to periods before those presented, to the extent practicable; and

(d) an explanation if it is impracticable to determine the amounts to be disclosed in (b) or (c) above.

Financial statements of subsequent periods need not repeat these disclosures.

* 10.14 When a voluntary change in accounting policy has an effect on the current period or any prior period, an entity shall disclose the following:

(a) the nature of the change in accounting policy;

(b) the reasons why applying the new accounting policy provides reliable and more relevant information;

(c) to the extent practicable, the amount of the adjustment for each financial statement line item affected, shown separately:

(i) for the current period;

(ii) for each prior period presented; and

(iii) in the aggregate for periods before those presented; and

(d) an explanation if it is impracticable to determine the amounts to be disclosed in (c) above.

Financial statements of subsequent periods need not repeat these disclosures.

Changes in accounting estimates

10.15 A **change in accounting estimate** is an adjustment of the carrying amount of an asset or a liability, or the amount of the periodic consumption of an asset, that results from the assessment of the present status of, and expected future benefits and obligations associated with, assets and liabilities. Changes in accounting estimates result from new information or new developments and, accordingly, are not corrections of errors. When it is difficult to distinguish a change in an accounting policy from a change in an accounting estimate, the change is treated as a change in an accounting estimate.

10.16   An entity shall recognise the effect of a change in an accounting estimate, other than a change to which paragraph 10.17 applies, **prospectively** by including it in **profit or loss** in:

(a)   the period of the change, if the change affects that period only; or

(b)   the period of the change and future periods, if the change affects both.

10.17   To the extent that a change in an accounting estimate gives rise to changes in assets and liabilities, or relates to an item of equity, the entity shall recognise it by adjusting the carrying amount of the related asset, liability or equity item in the period of the change.

Disclosure of a change in estimate

10.18   An entity shall disclose the nature of any change in an accounting estimate and the effect of the change on assets, liabilities, income and expense for the current period. If it is practicable for the entity to estimate the effect of the change in one or more future periods, the entity shall disclose those estimates.

Corrections of prior period errors

10.19   Prior period errors are omissions from, and misstatements in, an entity's financial statements for one or more prior periods arising from a failure to use, or misuse of, reliable information that:

(a)   was available when financial statements for those periods were authorised for issue; and

(b)   could reasonably be expected to have been obtained and taken into account in the preparation and presentation of those financial statements.

10.20   Such errors include the effects of mathematical mistakes, mistakes in applying accounting policies, oversights or misinterpretations of facts, and fraud.

10.21   To the extent practicable, an entity shall correct a material prior period error retrospectively in the first financial statements authorised for issue after its discovery by:

(a)   restating the comparative amounts for the prior period(s) presented in which the error occurred; or

(b)   if the error occurred before the earliest prior period presented, restating the opening balances of assets, liabilities and equity for the earliest prior period presented.

10.22   When it is impracticable to determine the period-specific effects of a material error on comparative information for one or more prior periods presented, the entity shall restate the opening balances of assets, liabilities and equity for the earliest period for which retrospective restatement is practicable (which may be the current period).

Disclosure of prior period errors

* 10.23   An entity shall disclose the following about material prior period errors:

(a)   the nature of the prior period error;

(b) for each prior period presented, to the extent practicable, the amount of the correction for each financial statement line item affected;

(c) to the extent practicable, the amount of the correction at the beginning of the earliest prior period presented; and

(d) an explanation if it is not practicable to determine the amounts to be disclosed in (b) or (c) above.

Financial statements of subsequent periods need not repeat these disclosures.

Section 11
Basic Financial Instruments

Scope of Sections 11 and 12

11.1   Section 11 *Basic Financial Instruments* and Section 12 *Other Financial Instruments Issues* together deal with recognising, derecognising, measuring and disclosing **financial instruments** (**financial assets** and **financial liabilities**). Section 11 applies to basic financial instruments and is relevant to all entities. Section 12 applies to other, more complex financial instruments and transactions. If an entity enters into only basic financial instrument transactions then Section 12 is not applicable. However, even entities with only basic financial instruments shall consider the scope of Section 12 to ensure they are exempt.

PBE11.1A   **Public benefit entities** and other members of a **public benefit entity group** that make or receive **public benefit entity concessionary loans** shall refer to the relevant paragraphs of Section 34 *Specialised Activities* for the accounting requirements for such loans.

Accounting policy choice

11.2   An entity shall choose to apply either:

(a)   the provisions of both Section 11 and Section 12 in full; or

(b)   the **recognition** and **measurement** provisions of IAS 39 *Financial Instruments: Recognition and Measurement* (as adopted for use in the EU), the disclosure requirements of Sections 11 and 12 and the presentation requirements of paragraphs 11.38A or 12.25B; or

(c)   the recognition and measurement provisions of IFRS 9 *Financial Instruments* and/or IAS 39 (as amended following the publication of IFRS 9) subject to the restriction in paragraph 11.2A, the disclosure requirements of Sections 11 and 12 and the presentation requirements of paragraphs 11.38A or 12.25B;

to account for all of its financial instruments. Where an entity chooses (b) or (c) it applies the scope of the relevant standard to its financial instruments. An entity's choice of (a), (b) or (c) is an **accounting policy** choice. Paragraphs 10.8 to 10.14 contain requirements for determining when a change in accounting policy is appropriate, how such a change should be accounted for and what information should be disclosed about the change.

11.2A   An entity, including an entity that is not a company, that has made the accounting policy choice in paragraph 11.2(c) to apply the recognition and measurement provisions of IFRS 9 shall depart from the provisions of IFRS 9 as follows:

A financial asset that is not permitted by the **Small Companies Regulations**, the **Regulations, the Small LLP Regulations** or the **LLP Regulations** to be measured at **fair value** through **profit or loss** shall be measured at **amortised cost** in accordance with paragraphs 5.4.1 to 5.4.4 of IFRS 9.

Introduction to Section 11

11.3   A financial instrument is a contract that gives rise to a financial asset of one entity and a financial liability or equity instrument of another entity.

11.4   [Not used]

11.5   Basic financial instruments within the scope of Section 11 are those that satisfy the conditions in paragraph 11.8. Examples of financial instruments that normally satisfy those conditions include:

(a)   **cash**;

(b)   demand and fixed-term deposits when the entity is the depositor, eg bank accounts;

(c)   commercial paper and commercial bills held;

(d)   accounts, notes and loans receivable and payable;

(e)   bonds and similar debt instruments;

(f)   investments in non-convertible preference shares and non-puttable ordinary and preference shares; and

(g)   commitments to receive a loan and commitments to make a loan to another entity that meet the conditions of paragraph 11.8(c).

11.6   Examples of financial instruments that do not normally satisfy the conditions in paragraph 11.8, and are therefore within the scope of Section 12, include:

(a)   asset-backed securities, such as collateralised mortgage obligations, repurchase agreements and securitised packages of receivables;

(b)   options, rights, warrants, futures contracts, forward contracts and interest rate swaps that can be settled in cash or by exchanging another financial instrument;

(c)   financial instruments that qualify and are designated as hedging instruments in accordance with the requirements in Section 12; and

(d)   commitments to make a loan to another entity and commitments to receive a loan, if the commitment can be settled net in cash.

(e)   [not used]

Scope of Section 11

11.7   Section 11 applies to all financial instruments meeting the conditions of paragraph 11.8 except for the following:

(a)   Investments in **subsidiaries, associates** and **joint ventures** that are accounted for in accordance with Section 9 *Consolidated and Separate Financial Statements*, Section 14 *Investments in Associates* or Section 15 *Investments in Joint Ventures*.

(b)   Financial instruments that meet the definition of an entity's own equity and the equity component of **compound financial instruments** issued by the reporting entity that contain both a **liability** and an equity component (see Section 22 *Liabilities and Equity*).

(c)   **Leases**, to which Section 20 *Leases* applies. However, the **derecognition** requirements in paragraphs 11.33 to 11.35 and impairment accounting requirements in paragraphs 11.21 to 11.26 apply to derecognition and impairment of receivables recognised by a lessor and the derecognition requirements in paragraphs 11.36 to 11.38 apply to payables recognised by a lessee arising under a **finance lease**. Section 12 applies to leases with characteristics specified in paragraph 12.3(f).

(d) Employers' rights and obligations under employee benefit plans, to which Section 28 *Employee Benefits* applies, although paragraphs 11.27 to 11.32 do apply in determining the fair value of **plan assets**.

(e) Financial instruments, contracts and obligations to which Section 26 *Share-based Payment* applies, and contracts within the scope of paragraph 12.5.

(f) **Insurance contracts** (including **reinsurance contracts**) that the entity issues and reinsurance contracts that the entity holds (see FRS 103 *Insurance Contracts*).

(g) Financial instruments issued by an entity with a **discretionary participation feature** (see FRS 103 *Insurance Contracts*).

(h) Reimbursement assets accounted for in accordance with Section 21 *Provisions and Contingencies*.

(i) **Financial guarantee contracts** (see Section 21).

A reporting entity that issues the financial instruments set out in (f) or (g) or holds the financial instruments in (f) is required by paragraph 1.6 of this FRS to apply FRS 103 to those financial instruments.

Basic financial instruments

11.8 An entity shall account for the following financial instruments as basic financial instruments in accordance with Section 11:

(a) cash;

(b) a debt instrument (such as an account, note, or loan receivable or payable) that meets the conditions in paragraph 11.9 and is not a financial instrument described in paragraph 11.6(b);

(c) commitments to receive or make a loan to another entity that:

　　(i) cannot be settled net in cash; and

　　(ii) when the commitment is executed, are expected to meet the conditions in paragraph 11.9; and

(d) an investment in non-convertible preference shares and non-puttable **ordinary shares** or preference shares.

11.9 The conditions a debt instrument shall satisfy in accordance with paragraph 11.8(b) are:

(a) The contractual return to the holder (the lender), assessed in the currency in which the debt instrument is denominated, is:

　　(i) a fixed amount;

　　(ii) a positive fixed rate or a positive variable rate[10]; or

　　(iii) [not used]

　　(iv) a combination of a positive or a negative fixed rate and a positive variable rate (eg LIBOR plus 200 basis points or LIBOR less 50 basis points, but not 500 basis points less LIBOR).

---

[10] A variable rate for this purpose is a rate which varies over time and is linked to a single observable interest rate or to a single relevant observable index of general price inflation of the currency in which the instrument is denominated, provided such links are not leveraged.

(aA) The contract may provide for repayments of the principal or the return to the holder (but not both) to be linked to a single relevant observable index of general price inflation of the currency in which the debt instrument is denominated, provided such links are not leveraged.

(aB) The contract may provide for a determinable variation of the return to the holder during the life of the instrument, provided that:

> (i) the new rate satisfies condition (a) and the variation is not contingent on future events other than:
>
> > (1) a change of a contractual variable rate;
> >
> > (2) to protect the holder against credit deterioration of the issuer;
> >
> > (3) changes in levies applied by a central bank or arising from changes in relevant taxation or law; or
>
> (ii) the new rate is a market rate of interest and satisfies condition (a).

Contractual terms that give the lender the unilateral option to change the terms of the contract are not determinable for this purpose.

(b) There is no contractual provision that could, by its terms, result in the holder losing the principal amount or any interest attributable to the current period or prior periods. The fact that a debt instrument is subordinated to other debt instruments is not an example of such a contractual provision.

(c) Contractual provisions that permit the issuer (the borrower) to prepay a debt instrument or permit the holder (the lender) to put it back to the issuer before maturity are not contingent on future events other than to protect:

> (i) the holder against the credit deterioration of the issuer (eg defaults, credit downgrades or loan covenant violations), or a change in control of the issuer; or
>
> (ii) the holder or issuer against changes in levies applied by a central bank or arising from changes in relevant taxation or law.

The inclusion of contractual terms that, as a result of the early termination, require the issuer to compensate the holder for the early termination does not, in itself, constitute a breach of this condition.

(d) [Not used]

(e) Contractual provisions may permit the extension of the term of the debt instrument, provided that the return to the holder and any other contractual provisions applicable during the extended term satisfy the conditions of paragraphs (a) to (c).

Examples – Debt instruments

1 **A zero-coupon loan**

For a zero-coupon loan, the holder's return is the difference between the nominal value of the loan and the issue price. The holder (lender) receives a fixed amount when the loan matures and the issuer (borrower) repays the loan. The return to the holder meets the condition of paragraph 11.9(a)(i).

2 **A fixed interest rate loan with an initial tie-in period which reverts to the bank's standard variable interest rate after the tie-in period**

The initial fixed rate is a return permitted by paragraph 11.9(a)(ii). A bank's standard variable interest rate is an observable interest rate and, in accordance with the definition of a variable rate, is a permissible link. In

---

accordance with paragraph 11.9(a)(ii) the variable rate should be a positive rate.

The variation of the interest rate after the tie-in period is non-contingent and since the new rate (ie the bank's standard variable rate) meets the condition of paragraph 11.9(a), paragraph 11.9(aB)(i) is met.

3   **A loan with interest payable at the bank's standard variable rate plus 1 per cent throughout the life of the loan**

As discussed under Example 2 above, a bank's standard variable rate is a permitted variable rate in accordance with the definition of variable rate. The combination of a positive fixed rate (ie plus 1 per cent) and a positive variable rate is a permitted return under paragraph 11.9(a)(iv). The combination of a bank's standard variable rate plus a fixed interest rate of 1 per cent therefore meets the condition in paragraph 11.9(a)(iv).

4   **A loan with interest payable at the bank's standard variable rate less 1 per cent throughout the life of the loan, with the condition that the interest rate can never fall below 2 per cent**

Paragraph 11.9(aB)(i)(1) permits variation of a return to a holder (lender) that is contingent on a change of a contractual variable rate. In this example the contractual variable rate is the bank's standard variable rate. The variation of the return to the holder is between the bank's standard variable rate less 1 and 2 per cent, depending on the bank's standard variable rate. For example, if the bank's standard variable rate is less than 3 per cent, the return to the holder is fixed at 2 per cent; if the bank's standard variable rate is higher than 3 per cent, the return to the holder is the bank's standard variable rate less 1 per cent. The contractual variation meets the condition of paragraph 11.9(aB)(i)(1).

The holder is protected against the risk of losing the principal amount of the loan via the interest rate floor of 2 per cent. The requirement of paragraph 11.9(b) is therefore also met.

5   **Interest on a loan is referenced to 2 times the bank's standard variable rate**

In accordance with the definition of a variable rate, the contractual interest rate payable can be linked to a single observable interest rate. A bank's standard variable rate is an observable rate and meets the definition of a variable rate, but the rate in this example is 2 times the bank's standard variable rate and the link to the observable interest rate is leveraged. Therefore, the rate in this example is not a variable rate as described in paragraph 11.9(a). The instrument is measured at fair value in accordance with Section 12.

6   **Interest on a loan is charged at 10 per cent less 6-month LIBOR over the life of the loan**

The effect of combining a negative variable rate with a positive fixed rate is that the interest on the loan increases as and when the variable rate decreases and vice versa (so called inverse floating interest).

Under paragraph 11.9(a)(iv) the combination of positive or negative fixed rate and positive variable rate is a permitted return. The variable rate (6-month LIBOR) meets the definition of a variable rate, as the rate is a quoted interest rate. However, since the variable rate is negative (minus 6-month LIBOR), the rate is in breach of paragraph 11.9(a)(iv). The instrument is measured at fair value in accordance with Section 12.

7 **Interest on a GBP denominated mortgage is linked to the UK Land Registry House Price Index (HPI) plus 3 per cent**

In accordance with paragraph 11.9(aA) the holder's return may be linked to an index of general price inflation of the currency of the debt instrument. The mortgage is denominated in GBP and a permitted inflation index would be an index that measures general price inflation of goods and services denominated in GBP.

The HPI measures inflation for residential properties in the UK and is not a measure of general price inflation. The return to the holder therefore fails to meet the condition in paragraph 11.9(aA). The instrument is measured at fair value in accordance with Section 12.

11.10   Examples of financial instruments that would normally satisfy the conditions in paragraph 11.9 are:

(a)   trade accounts and notes receivable and payable, and loans from banks or other third parties;

(b)   accounts payable in a foreign currency. However, any change in the account payable because of a change in the exchange rate is recognised in profit or loss as required by paragraph 30.10;

(c)   loans to or from subsidiaries or associates that are due on demand; and

(d)   a debt instrument that would become immediately receivable if the issuer defaults on an interest or principal payment (such a provision does not violate the conditions in paragraph 11.9).

11.11   Examples of financial instruments that do not satisfy the conditions in paragraph 11.9 (and are therefore within the scope of Section 12) include:

(a)   an investment in another entity's equity instruments other than non-convertible preference shares and non-puttable ordinary and preference shares (see paragraph 11.8(d)); and

(b)   [not used]

(c)   [not used]

(d)   investments in convertible debt, because the return to the holder can vary with the price of the issuer's equity shares rather than just with market interest rates.

(e)   [not used]

Initial recognition of financial assets and liabilities

11.12   An entity shall recognise a financial asset or a financial liability only when the entity becomes a party to the contractual provisions of the instrument.

Initial measurement

11.13   When a financial asset or financial liability is recognised initially, an entity shall measure it at the transaction price (including **transaction costs** except in the initial measurement of financial assets and liabilities that are measured at fair value through profit or loss) unless the arrangement constitutes, in effect, a financing transaction. A financing transaction may take place in connection with the sale of goods or services, for example, if payment is deferred beyond normal business terms or is financed at a rate of interest that is not a market rate. If the arrangement constitutes a financing transaction, the entity shall measure the financial asset or financial liability at the **present value** of the future payments discounted at a market rate of interest for a similar debt instrument.

Examples – financial assets

1   For a long-term loan at a market rate of interest made to another entity, a receivable is recognised at the amount of the cash advanced to that entity plus transaction costs incurred by the entity (see the example following paragraph 11.20).

2   For goods sold to a customer on short-term credit, a receivable is recognised at the undiscounted amount of cash receivable from that entity, which is normally the invoice price.

3   For an item sold to a customer on two-years interest-free credit, a receivable is recognised at the current cash sale price for that item (in financing transactions conducted on an arm's length basis the cash sales price would normally approximate to the present value). If the current cash sale price is not known, it may be estimated as the present value of the cash receivable discounted using the **prevailing market rate(s)** of interest for a similar receivable.

4   For a cash purchase of another entity's ordinary shares, the investment is recognised at the amount of cash paid to acquire the shares.

Examples – financial liabilities

1   For a loan received from a bank at a market rate of interest, a payable is recognised initially at the amount of the cash received from the bank less separately incurred transaction costs.

2   For goods purchased from a supplier on short-term credit, a payable is recognised at the undiscounted amount owed to the supplier, which is normally the invoice price.

Subsequent measurement

11.14   At the end of each **reporting period**, an entity shall measure financial instruments as follows, without any deduction for transaction costs the entity may incur on sale or other disposal:

(a)   Debt instruments that meet the conditions in paragraph 11.8(b) shall be measured at amortised cost using the **effective interest method**. Paragraphs 11.15 to 11.20 provide guidance on determining amortised cost using the effective interest method. Debt instruments that are payable or receivable within one year shall be measured at the undiscounted amount of the cash or other consideration expected to be paid or received (ie net of impairment—see paragraphs 11.21 to 11.26) unless the arrangement constitutes, in effect, a financing transaction (see paragraph 11.13). If the arrangement constitutes a financing transaction, the entity shall measure the debt instrument at the present value of the future payments discounted at a market rate of interest for a similar debt instrument.

(b) Debt instruments that meet the conditions in paragraph 11.8(b) and commitments to receive a loan and to make a loan to another entity that meet the conditions in paragraph 11.8(c) may upon their initial recognition be designated by the entity as at fair value through profit or loss (paragraphs 11.27 to 11.32 provide guidance on fair value) provided doing so results in more relevant information, because either:

   (i) it eliminates or significantly reduces a measurement or recognition inconsistency (sometimes referred to as 'an accounting mismatch') that would otherwise arise from measuring assets or debt instruments or recognising the **gains** and losses on them on different bases; or

   (ii) a group of debt instruments or financial assets and debt instruments is managed and its performance is evaluated on a fair value basis, in accordance with a documented risk management or investment strategy, and information about the group is provided internally on that basis to the entity's **key management personnel** (as defined in Section 33 *Related Party Disclosures*, paragraph 33.6), for example members of the entity's board of directors and its chief executive officer.

(c) Commitments to receive a loan and to make a loan to another entity that meet the conditions in paragraph 11.8(c) shall be measured at cost (which sometimes is nil) less impairment.

(d) Investments in non-convertible preference shares and non-puttable ordinary shares or preference shares shall be measured as follows (paragraphs 11.27 to 11.32 provide guidance on fair value):

   (i) if the shares are **publicly traded** or their fair value can otherwise be measured reliably, the investment shall be measured at fair value with changes in fair value recognised in profit or loss; and

   (ii) all other such investments shall be measured at cost less impairment.

Impairment or uncollectability must be assessed for financial assets in (a), (c) and (d)(ii) above. Paragraphs 11.21 to 11.26 provide guidance.

Amortised cost and effective interest method

11.15 The amortised cost of a financial asset or financial liability at each **reporting date** is the net of the following amounts:

(a) the amount at which the financial asset or financial liability is measured at initial recognition;

(b) minus any repayments of the principal;

(c) plus or minus the cumulative amortisation using the effective interest method of any difference between the amount at initial recognition and the maturity amount;

(d) minus, in the case of a financial asset, any reduction (directly or through the use of an allowance account) for impairment or uncollectability.

Financial assets and financial liabilities that have no stated interest rate (and do not constitute a financing transaction) and are classified as payable or receivable within one year are initially measured at an undiscounted amount in accordance with paragraph 11.14(a). Therefore, (c) above does not apply to them.

11.16 The effective interest method is a method of calculating the amortised cost of a financial asset or a financial liability (or a group of financial assets or financial liabilities) and of allocating the interest income or interest expense over the relevant period. The **effective interest rate** is the rate that exactly discounts estimated future cash payments or receipts through the expected life of the financial instrument or, when appropriate, a shorter period, to the **carrying amount** of the financial asset or financial liability. The effective interest rate is determined on the basis of the carrying amount of the financial asset or liability at initial recognition. Under the effective interest method:

(a) the amortised cost of a financial asset (liability) is the present value of future cash receipts (payments) discounted at the effective interest rate; and

(b) the interest expense (income) in a period equals the carrying amount of the financial liability (asset) at the beginning of a period multiplied by the effective interest rate for the period.

11.17   When calculating the effective interest rate, an entity shall estimate cash flows considering all contractual terms of the financial instrument (eg prepayment, call and similar options) and known credit losses that have been incurred, but it shall not consider possible future credit losses not yet incurred.

11.18   When calculating the effective interest rate, an entity shall amortise any related fees, finance charges paid or received (such as 'points'), transaction costs and other premiums or discounts over the expected life of the instrument, except as follows. The entity shall use a shorter period if that is the period to which the fees, finance charges paid or received, transaction costs, premiums or discounts relate. This will be the case when the variable to which the fees, finance charges paid or received, transaction costs, premiums or discounts relate is repriced to market rates before the expected maturity of the instrument. In such a case, the appropriate amortisation period is the period to the next such repricing date.

11.19   For variable rate financial assets and variable rate financial liabilities, periodic re-estimation of cash flows to reflect changes in market rates of interest alters the effective interest rate. If a variable rate financial asset or variable rate financial liability is recognised initially at an amount equal to the principal receivable or payable at maturity, re-estimating the future interest payments normally has no significant effect on the carrying amount of the asset or liability.

11.20   If an entity revises its estimates of payments or receipts, the entity shall adjust the carrying amount of the financial asset or financial liability (or group of financial instruments) to reflect actual and revised estimated cash flows. The entity shall recalculate the carrying amount by computing the present value of estimated future cash flows at the financial instrument's original effective interest rate. The entity shall recognise the adjustment as **income** or **expense** in profit or loss at the date of the revision.

Impairment of financial instruments measured at cost or amortised cost

Recognition

11.21 At the end of each reporting period, an entity shall assess whether there is objective evidence of impairment of any financial assets that are measured at cost or amortised cost. If there is objective evidence of impairment, the entity shall recognise an **impairment loss** in profit or loss immediately.

11.22 Objective evidence that a financial asset or group of assets is impaired includes observable data that come to the attention of the holder of the asset about the following loss events:

(a) significant financial difficulty of the issuer or obligor;

(b) a breach of contract, such as a default or delinquency in interest or principal payments;

(c) the creditor, for economic or legal reasons relating to the debtor's financial difficulty, granting to the debtor a concession that the creditor would not otherwise consider;

(d) it has become **probable** that the debtor will enter bankruptcy or other financial reorganisation; and

(e) observable data indicating that there has been a measurable decrease in the estimated future cash flows from a group of financial assets since the initial recognition of those assets, even though the decrease cannot yet be identified with the individual financial assets in the group, such as adverse national or local economic conditions or adverse changes in industry conditions.

11.23   Other factors may also be evidence of impairment, including significant changes with an adverse effect that have taken place in the technological, market, economic or legal environment in which the issuer operates.

11.24   An entity shall assess the following financial assets individually for impairment:

(a)   all equity instruments regardless of significance; and

(b)   other financial assets that are individually significant.

An entity shall assess other financial assets for impairment either individually or grouped on the basis of similar **credit risk** characteristics.

Measurement

11.25   An entity shall measure an impairment loss on the following instruments measured at cost or amortised cost as follows:

(a)   For an instrument measured at amortised cost in accordance with paragraph 11.14(a), the impairment loss is the difference between the asset's carrying amount and the present value of estimated cash flows discounted at the asset's original effective interest rate. If such a financial instrument has a variable interest rate, the discount rate for measuring any impairment loss is the current effective interest rate determined under the contract.

(b)   For an instrument measured at cost less impairment in accordance with paragraph 11.14(c) and (d)(ii) the impairment loss is the difference between the asset's carrying amount and the best estimate (which will necessarily be an approximation) of the amount (which might be zero) that the entity would receive for the asset if it were to be sold at the reporting date.

Reversal

11.26   If, in a subsequent period, the amount of an impairment loss decreases and the decrease can be related objectively to an event occurring after the impairment was recognised (such as an improvement in the debtor's credit rating), the entity shall reverse the previously recognised impairment loss either directly or by adjusting an allowance account. The reversal shall not result in a carrying amount of the financial asset (net of any allowance account) that exceeds what the carrying amount would have been had the impairment not previously been recognised. The entity shall recognise the amount of the reversal in profit or loss immediately.

Fair value

11.27   Paragraph 11.14(b) and other sections of this FRS make reference to the fair value guidance in paragraphs 11.27 to 11.32, including Section 9 *Consolidated and Separate Financial Statements*, Section 12 *Other Financial Instruments Issues*, Section 13 *Inventories*, Section 14 *Investments in Associates*, Section 15 *Investments in Joint Ventures*, Section 16 *Investment Property*, Section 17 *Property, Plant and Equipment*, Section 18 *Intangible Assets other than Goodwill*, Section 27 *Impairment of Assets,* Section 28 *Employee Benefits* (in relation to plan assets) and Section 34 *Specialised Activities*. In applying the fair value guidance to assets or liabilities accounted for in accordance with those sections, the reference to ordinary shares or preference shares in these paragraphs should be read to include the types of assets and liabilities addressed in those sections.

Paragraph 11.14(d)(i) requires an investment in non-convertible preference shares and non-puttable ordinary shares or preference shares to be measured at fair value if the shares are publicly traded or if their fair value can otherwise be measured reliably. An entity shall use the following hierarchy to estimate the fair value of the shares:

(a) The best evidence of fair value is a quoted price for an identical asset in an **active market**. Quoted in an active market in this context means quoted prices are readily and regularly available and those prices represent actual and regularly occurring market transactions on an arm's length basis. The quoted price is usually the current bid price.

(b) When quoted prices are unavailable, the price of a recent transaction for an identical asset provides evidence of fair value as long as there has not been a significant change in economic circumstances or a significant lapse of time since the transaction took place. If the entity can demonstrate that the last transaction price is not a good estimate of fair value (eg because it reflects the amount that an entity would receive or pay in a forced transaction, involuntary liquidation or distress sale), that price is adjusted.

(c) If the market for the asset is not active and recent transactions of an identical asset on their own are not a good estimate of fair value, an entity estimates the fair value by using a valuation technique. The objective of using a valuation technique is to estimate what the transaction price would have been on the measurement date in an arm's length exchange motivated by normal business considerations.

Valuation technique

11.28 Valuation techniques include using recent arm's length market transactions for an identical asset between knowledgeable, willing parties, if available, reference to the current fair value of another asset that is substantially the same as the asset being measured, discounted cash flow analysis and option pricing models. If there is a valuation technique commonly used by market participants to price the asset and that technique has been demonstrated to provide reliable estimates of prices obtained in actual market transactions, the entity uses that technique.

11.29 The objective of using a valuation technique is to establish what the transaction price would have been on the measurement date in an arm's length exchange motivated by normal business considerations. Fair value is estimated on the basis of the results of a valuation technique that makes maximum use of market inputs, and relies as little as possible on entity-determined inputs. A valuation technique would be expected to arrive at a reliable estimate of the fair value if:

(a) it reasonably reflects how the market could be expected to price the asset; and

(b) the inputs to the valuation technique reasonably represent market expectations and measures of the risk return factors inherent in the asset.

No active market

11.30 The fair value of ordinary shares or preference shares that do not have a quoted market price in an active market is reliably measurable if:

(a) the variability in the range of reasonable fair value estimates is not significant for that asset; or

(b) the probabilities of the various estimates within the range can be reasonably assessed and used in estimating fair value.

11.31 There are many situations in which the variability in the range of reasonable fair value estimates of assets that do not have a quoted market price is likely not to be significant. Normally it is possible to estimate the fair value of ordinary shares or preference shares that an entity has acquired from an outside party. However, if the range of reasonable fair value estimates is significant and the probabilities of the various estimates cannot be reasonably assessed, an entity is precluded from measuring the ordinary shares or preference shares at fair value.

11.32   If a reliable measure of fair value is no longer available for an asset measured at fair value (eg ordinary shares or preference shares measured at fair value through profit or loss), its carrying amount at the last date the asset was reliably measurable becomes its new cost. The entity shall measure the ordinary shares or preference shares at this cost amount less impairment until a reliable measure of fair value becomes available.

Derecognition of a financial asset

11.33   An entity shall derecognise a financial asset only when:

(a)   the contractual rights to the cash flows from the financial asset expire or are settled; or

(b)   the entity transfers to another party substantially all of the risks and rewards of ownership of the financial asset; or

(c)   the entity, despite having retained some significant risks and rewards of ownership, has transferred control of the asset to another party and the other party has the practical ability to sell the asset in its entirety to an unrelated third party and is able to exercise that ability unilaterally and without needing to impose additional restrictions on the transfer. In this case, the entity shall:

(i)   derecognise the asset; and

(ii)   recognise separately any rights and obligations retained or created in the transfer.

The carrying amount of the transferred asset shall be allocated between the rights or obligations retained and those transferred on the basis of their relative fair values at the transfer date. Newly created rights and obligations shall be measured at their fair values at that date. Any difference between the consideration received and the amounts recognised and derecognised in accordance with this paragraph shall be recognised in profit or loss in the period of the transfer.

11.34   If a transfer does not result in derecognition because the entity has retained significant risks and rewards of ownership of the transferred asset, the entity shall continue to recognise the transferred asset in its entirety and shall recognise a financial liability for the consideration received. The asset and liability shall not be offset. In subsequent periods, the entity shall recognise any income on the transferred asset and any expense incurred on the financial liability.

11.35   If a transferor provides non-cash collateral (such as debt or equity instruments) to the transferee, the accounting for the collateral by the transferor and the transferee depends on whether the transferee has the right to sell or repledge the collateral and on whether the transferor has defaulted. The transferor and transferee shall account for the collateral as follows:

(a)   If the transferee has the right by contract or custom to sell or repledge the collateral, the transferor shall reclassify that asset in its **statement of financial position** (eg as a loaned asset, pledged equity instruments or repurchase receivable) separately from other assets.

(b)   If the transferee sells collateral pledged to it, it shall recognise the proceeds from the sale and a liability measured at fair value for its obligation to return the collateral.

(c) If the transferor defaults under the terms of the contract and is no longer entitled to redeem the collateral, it shall derecognise the collateral, and the transferee shall recognise the collateral as its asset initially measured at fair value or, if it has already sold the collateral, derecognise its obligation to return the collateral.

(d) Except as provided in (c), the transferor shall continue to carry the collateral as its asset, and the transferee shall not recognise the collateral as an asset.

Example: Transfer that qualifies for derecognition

An entity sells a group of its accounts receivable to a bank at less than their face amount. The entity continues to handle collections from the debtors on behalf of the bank, including sending monthly statements, and the bank pays the entity a market-rate fee for servicing the receivables. The entity is obliged to remit promptly to the bank any and all amounts collected, but it has no obligation to the bank for slow payment or non-payment by the debtors. In this case, the entity has transferred to the bank substantially all of the risks and rewards of ownership of the receivables. Accordingly, it removes the receivables from its statement of financial position (ie derecognises them), and it shows no liability in respect of the proceeds received from the bank. The entity recognises a loss calculated as the difference between the carrying amount of the receivables at the time of sale and the proceeds received from the bank. The entity recognises a liability to the extent that it has collected funds from the debtors but has not yet remitted them to the bank.

Example: Transfer that does not qualify for derecognition

The facts are the same as the preceding example except that the entity has agreed to buy back from the bank any receivables for which the debtor is in arrears as to principal or interest for more than 120 days.

In this case, the entity has retained the risk of slow payment or non-payment by the debtors—a significant risk with respect to receivables. Accordingly, the entity does not treat the receivables as having been sold to the bank, and it does not derecognise them. Instead, it treats the proceeds from the bank as a loan secured by the receivables. The entity continues to recognise the receivables as an asset until they are collected or written off as uncollectible.

Derecognition of a financial liability

11.36   An entity shall derecognise a financial liability (or a part of a financial liability) only when it is extinguished—ie when the obligation specified in the contract is discharged, is cancelled or expires.

11.37   If an existing borrower and lender exchange financial instruments with substantially different terms, the entities shall account for the transaction as an extinguishment of the original financial liability and the recognition of a new financial liability. Similarly, an entity shall account for a substantial modification of the terms of an existing financial liability or a part of it (whether or not attributable to the financial difficulty of the debtor) as an extinguishment of the original financial liability and the recognition of a new financial liability.

11.38   The entity shall recognise in profit or loss any difference between the carrying amount of the financial liability (or part of a financial liability) extinguished or transferred to another party and the consideration paid, including any non-cash assets transferred or liabilities assumed.

Presentation

11.38A A financial asset and a financial liability shall be offset and the net amount presented in the statement of financial position when, and only when, an entity:

(a) currently has a legally enforceable right to set off the recognised amounts; and

(b) intends either to settle on a net basis, or to realise the asset and settle the liability simultaneously.

Disclosures

11.39 The disclosures below make reference to disclosures for certain financial instruments measured at fair value through profit or loss. Entities that have only basic financial instruments (and therefore do not apply Section 12), and have not chosen to designate financial instruments as at fair value through profit or loss (in accordance with paragraph 11.14(b)) will not have any financial instruments measured at fair value through profit or loss and hence will not need to provide such disclosures.

Disclosure of accounting policies for financial instruments

11.40 In accordance with paragraph 8.5, an entity shall disclose, in the summary of significant accounting policies, the measurement basis (or bases) used for financial instruments and the other accounting policies used for financial instruments that are relevant to an understanding of the **financial statements**.

Statement of financial position – categories of financial assets and financial liabilities

11.41 An entity shall disclose the carrying amounts of each of the following categories of financial assets and financial liabilities at the reporting date, in total, either in the statement of financial position or in the **notes**:

* (a) financial assets measured at fair value through profit or loss (paragraphs 11.14(b), 11.14(d)(i), 12.8 and 12.9);

(b) financial assets that are debt instruments measured at amortised cost (paragraph 11.14(a));

(c) financial assets that are equity instruments measured at cost less impairment (paragraphs 11.14(d)(ii), 12.8 and 12.9);

* (d) financial liabilities measured at fair value through profit or loss (paragraphs 11.14(b), 12.8 and 12.9). Financial liabilities that are not held as part of a trading portfolio and are not **derivatives** shall be shown separately;

(e) financial liabilities measured at amortised cost (paragraph 11.14(a)); and

(f) loan commitments measured at cost less impairment (paragraph 11.14(c)).

11.42 An entity shall disclose information that enables users of its financial statements to evaluate the significance of financial instruments for its **financial position** and **performance**. For example, for long-term debt such information would normally include the terms and conditions of the debt instrument (such as interest rate, maturity, repayment schedule, and restrictions that the debt instrument imposes on the entity).

* 11.43 For all financial assets and financial liabilities measured at fair value, the entity shall disclose the basis for determining fair value, eg quoted market price in an active market or a valuation technique. When a valuation technique is used, the entity shall disclose the assumptions applied in determining fair value for each class of financial assets or financial liabilities. For example, if applicable, an entity discloses information about the assumptions relating to prepayment rates, rates of estimated credit losses, and interest rates or discount rates.

11.44 If a reliable measure of fair value is no longer available for ordinary or preference shares measured at fair value through profit or loss, the entity shall disclose that fact.

Derecognition

11.45 If an entity has transferred financial assets to another party in a transaction that does not qualify for derecognition (see paragraphs 11.33 to 11.35), the entity shall disclose the following for each class of such financial assets:

(a) the nature of the assets;

(b) the nature of the risks and rewards of ownership to which the entity remains exposed; and

(c) the carrying amounts of the assets and of any associated liabilities that the entity continues to recognise.

Collateral

* 11.46 When an entity has pledged financial assets as collateral for liabilities or **contingent liabilities**, it shall disclose the following:

(a) the carrying amount of the financial assets pledged as collateral; and

(b) the terms and conditions relating to its pledge.

Defaults and breaches on loans payable

11.47 For **loans payable** recognised at the reporting date for which there is a breach of terms or default of principal, interest, sinking fund, or redemption terms that has not been remedied by the reporting date, an entity shall disclose the following:

(a) details of that breach or default;

(b) the carrying amount of the related loans payable at the reporting date; and

(c) whether the breach or default was remedied, or the terms of the loans payable were renegotiated, before the financial statements were authorised for issue.

Items of income, expense, gains or losses

11.48 An entity shall disclose the following items of income, expense, gains or losses:

(a) income, expense, net gains or net losses, including changes in fair value, recognised on:

* (i) financial assets measured at fair value through profit or loss;

* (ii) financial liabilities measured at fair value through profit or loss (with separate disclosure of movements on those which are not held as part of a trading portfolio and are not derivatives);

(iii) financial assets measured at amortised cost; and

(iv) financial liabilities measured at amortised cost;

(b)   total interest income and total interest expense (calculated using the effective interest method) for financial assets or financial liabilities that are not measured at fair value through profit or loss; and

(c)   the amount of any impairment loss for each class of financial asset. A class of financial asset is a grouping that is appropriate to the nature of the information disclosed and that takes into account the characteristics of the financial assets.

Financial instruments at fair value through profit or loss

* 11.48A   An entity, including an entity that is not a company, shall provide the following disclosures only for financial instruments measured at fair value through profit or loss in accordance with paragraph 36(4) of Schedule 1 to the Regulations[11]. This does not include financial liabilities held as part of a trading portfolio nor derivatives. The required disclosures are:

(a)   The amount of change, during the period and cumulatively, in the fair value of the financial instrument that is attributable to changes in the credit risk of that instrument, determined either:

(i)   as the amount of change in its fair value that is not attributable to changes in market conditions that give rise to **market risk**; or

(ii)   using an alternative method the entity believes more faithfully represents the amount of change in its fair value that is attributable to changes in the credit risk of the instrument.

(b)   The method used to establish the amount of change attributable to changes in own credit risk, or, if the change cannot be measured reliably or is not **material**, that fact.

(c)   For a financial liability, the difference between the financial liability's carrying amount and the amount the entity would be contractually required to pay at maturity to the holder of the obligation.

(d)   If an instrument contains both a liability and an equity feature, and the instrument has multiple features that substantially modify the cash flows and the values of those features are interdependent (such as a callable convertible debt instrument), the existence of those features.

(e)   If there is a difference between the fair value of a financial instrument at initial recognition and the amount determined at that date using a valuation technique, the aggregate difference yet to be recognised in profit or loss at the beginning and end of the period and a reconciliation of the changes in the balance of this difference.

(f)   Information that enables users of the entity's financial statements to evaluate the nature and extent of relevant risks arising from financial instruments to which the entity is exposed at the end of the reporting period. These risks typically include, but are not limited to, credit risk, **liquidity risk** and market risk. The disclosure should include both the entity's exposure to each type of risk and how it manages those risks.

Financial institutions

11.48B   A **financial institution** (other than a **retirement benefit plan**) shall, in addition, apply the requirements of paragraph 34.17.

11.48C   A retirement benefit plan shall, in addition, apply the requirements of paragraphs 34.39 to 34.48.

---

[11] And the equivalent requirements of the Small Companies Regulations, the Small LLP Regulations and the LLP Regulations.

Section 12
Other Financial Instruments Issues

Scope of Sections 11 and 12

12.1   Section 11 *Basic Financial Instruments* and Section 12 *Other Financial Instruments Issues* together deal with recognising, derecognising, measuring, and disclosing **financial instruments** (**financial assets** and **financial liabilities**). Section 11 applies to basic financial instruments and is relevant to all entities. Section 12 applies to other, more complex financial instruments and transactions. If an entity enters into only basic financial instrument transactions then Section 12 is not applicable. However, even entities with only basic financial instruments shall consider the scope of Section 12 to ensure they are exempt.

PBE12.1A   **Public benefit entities** or other members of a **public benefit entity group** that make or receive **public benefit entity concessionary loans** shall refer to the relevant paragraphs of Section 34 *Specialised Activities* for the accounting requirements for such loans.

Accounting policy choice

12.2   An entity shall choose to apply either:

(a)   the provisions of both Section 11 and Section 12 in full; or

(b)   the **recognition** and **measurement** provisions of IAS 39 *Financial Instruments: Recognition and Measurement* (as adopted for use in the EU), the disclosure requirements of Sections 11 and 12 and the presentation requirements of paragraphs 11.38A or 12.25B; or

(c)   the recognition and measurement provisions of IFRS 9 *Financial Instruments* and/or IAS 39 (as amended following the publication of IFRS 9) subject to the restriction in paragraph 12.2A, the disclosure requirements of Sections 11 and 12 and the presentation requirements of paragraph 11.38A or 12.25B;

to account for all of its financial instruments. Where an entity chooses (b) or (c) it applies the scope of the relevant standard to its financial instruments. An entity's choice of (a), (b) or (c) is an **accounting policy** choice. Paragraphs 10.8 to 10.14 contain requirements for determining when a change in accounting policy is appropriate, how such a change should be accounted for and what information should be disclosed about the change in accounting policy.

12.2A   An entity, including an entity that is not a company, that has made the accounting policy choice in paragraph 12.2(c) to apply the recognition and measurement provisions of IFRS 9 shall depart from those provisions of IFRS 9 as follows:

A financial asset that is not permitted by the **Small Companies Regulations**, the **Regulations, the Small LLP Regulations** or the **LLP Regulations** to be measured at **fair value** through **profit or loss** shall be measured at **amortised cost** in accordance with paragraphs 5.4.1 to 5.4.4 of IFRS 9.

Scope of Section 12

12.3   Section 12 applies to all financial instruments except the following:

(a)   Those covered by Section 11.

(b) Investments in **subsidiaries** (see Section 9 *Consolidated and Separate Financial Statements*), **associates** (see Section 14 *Investments in Associates*) and **joint ventures** (see Section 15 *Investments in Joint Ventures*).

(c) Employers' rights and obligations under employee benefit plans (see Section 28 *Employee Benefits*).

(d) **Insurance contracts** (including **reinsurance contracts**) that the entity issues and reinsurance contracts that the entity holds (see FRS 103 *Insurance Contracts*).

(e) Financial instruments that meet the definition of an entity's own **equity** and the equity component of **compound financial instruments** issued by the reporting entity that contain both a **liability** and an equity component (see Section 22 *Liabilities and Equity*).

(f) **Leases** (see Section 20 *Leases*) unless the lease could, as a result of non-typical contractual terms, result in a loss to the lessor or the lessee.

(g) Contracts for contingent consideration in a **business combination** (see Section 19 *Business Combinations and Goodwill*). This exemption applies only to the acquirer.

(h) Any forward contract between an acquirer and a selling shareholder to buy or sell an acquiree that will result in a business combination at a future **acquisition date**. The term of the forward contract should not exceed a reasonable period normally necessary to obtain any required approvals and to complete the transaction.

(i) Financial instruments, contracts and obligations to which Section 26 *Share-based Payment* applies, except for contracts within the scope of paragraph 12.5.

(j) Financial instruments issued by an entity with a **discretionary participation feature** (see FRS 103).

(k) Reimbursement assets accounted for in accordance with Section 21 *Provisions and Contingencies*.

(l) **Financial guarantee contracts** (see Section 21).

A reporting entity that issues the financial instruments set out in (d) or (j) or holds the financial instruments set out in (d) is required by paragraph 1.6 to apply FRS 103 to those financial instruments.

12.4   Most contracts to buy or sell a non-financial item such as a commodity, **inventory**, or **property, plant and equipment** are excluded from this section because they are not financial instruments. However, this section applies to all contracts that impose risks on the buyer or seller that are not typical of contracts to buy or sell non-financial items. For example, this section applies to contracts that, as a result of its contractual terms, could result in a loss to the buyer or seller that is unrelated to changes in the price of the non-financial item, changes in foreign exchange rates, or a default by one of the counterparties.

12.5   In addition to the contracts described in paragraph 12.4, this section applies to contracts to buy or sell non-financial items if the contract can be settled net in **cash** or another financial instrument, or by exchanging financial instruments as if the contracts were financial instruments, with the following exception: contracts that were entered into and continue to be held for the purpose of the receipt or delivery of a non-financial item in accordance with the entity's expected purchase, sale or usage requirements are not financial instruments for the purposes of this section.

Initial recognition of financial assets and liabilities

12.6   An entity shall recognise a financial asset or a financial liability only when the entity becomes a party to the contractual provisions of the instrument.

Initial measurement

12.7   When a financial asset or financial liability is recognised initially, an entity shall measure it at its fair value, which is normally the transaction price (including **transaction costs** except in the initial measurement of financial assets and liabilities that are measured at fair value through profit or loss). If payment for an asset is deferred beyond normal business terms or is financed at a rate of interest that is not a market rate, the entity shall initially measure the asset at the **present value** of the future payments discounted at a market rate of interest for a similar debt instrument.

Subsequent measurement

12.8   At the end of each **reporting period**, an entity shall measure all financial instruments within the scope of Section 12 at fair value and recognise changes in fair value in profit or loss, except as follows:

(a)   investments in equity instruments that are not **publicly traded** and whose fair value cannot otherwise be measured reliably and contracts linked to such instruments that, if exercised, will result in delivery of such instruments, shall be measured at cost less impairment;

(b)   hedging instruments in a designated hedging relationship accounted for in accordance with paragraph 12.23; and

(c)   financial instruments that are not permitted by the Small Company Regulations, the Regulations, the Small LLP Regulations or the LLP Regulations to be measured at fair value through profit or loss shall be measured at amortised cost in accordance with paragraphs 11.15 to 11.20.

12.9   If a reliable measure of fair value is no longer available for an equity instrument (or a contract linked to such an instrument) that is not publicly traded but is measured at fair value through profit or loss, its fair value at the last date the instrument was reliably measurable is treated as the cost of the instrument. The entity shall measure the instrument at this cost amount less impairment until a reliable measure of fair value becomes available.

Fair value

12.10   An entity shall apply the guidance on fair value in paragraphs 11.27 to 11.32 to fair value measurements in accordance with this section as well as for fair value measurements in accordance with Section 11.

12.11   The fair value of a financial liability that is due on demand is not less than the amount payable on demand, discounted from the first date that the amount could be required to be paid.

12.12   An entity shall not include transaction costs in the initial measurement of financial assets and liabilities that will be measured subsequently at fair value through profit or loss.

Impairment of financial instruments measured at cost or amortised cost

12.13   An entity shall apply the guidance on impairment of a financial instrument measured at cost in paragraphs 11.21 to 11.26 to financial instruments measured at cost less impairment in accordance with this section.

Derecognition of a financial asset or financial liability

12.14   An entity shall apply the **derecognition** requirements in paragraphs 11.33 to 11.38 to financial assets and financial liabilities to which this section applies.

Hedge accounting

12.15   A hedging relationship consists of a hedging instrument and a hedged item. Provided the qualifying conditions in paragraph 12.18 are met, an entity may apply hedge accounting.

Hedged items

12.16   A hedged item can be a recognised **asset** or liability, an unrecognised **firm commitment**, a **highly probable forecast transaction** or a **net investment in a foreign operation**, or a component of any such item, provided the item is reliably measurable.

12.16A For hedge accounting purposes, only assets, liabilities, firm commitments or a highly probable forecast transaction with a party external to the reporting entity can be a hedged item. Hedge accounting can be applied to transactions between entities in the same **group** only in the **individual financial statements** of those entities, except for:

   (a)   transactions with subsidiaries, where the subsidiaries are not consolidated in the **consolidated financial statements**;

   (b)   the foreign currency risk of intragroup **monetary items** that result in an exposure to foreign exchange **gains** or losses that are not fully eliminated on consolidation in accordance with Section 30 *Foreign Currency Translation*; and

   (c)   the foreign currency risk of highly probable forecast intragroup transactions, provided the transactions are denominated in a currency other than the **functional currency** of the entity entering into the transactions and the foreign currency risk affects consolidated profit or loss.

12.16B A group of items, including components of items, can be an eligible hedged item provided that all of the following conditions are met:

   (a)   it consists of items that are individually eligible hedged items;

   (b)   the items in the group share the same risk;

   (c)   the items in the group are managed together on a group basis for risk management purposes; and

   (d)   it does not include items with offsetting risk positions.

12.16C A component of an item comprises less than the entire fair value change or **cash flow** variability of an item. The following components of an item (including combinations thereof) may be a hedged item:

   (a)   changes in the cash flows or fair value attributable to a separately identifiable and reliably measureable specific risk or risks, including cash flow and fair value changes above or below a specified price or other variable;

(b)   one or more selected contractual cash flows; or

(c)   a specified part of the nominal amount of an item.

Hedging instruments

12.17   An instrument may be a hedging instrument provided all of the following conditions are met:

(a)   it is a financial instrument measured at fair value through profit or loss;

(b)   it is a contract with a party external to the reporting entity (ie external to the group or individual entity that is being reported on); and

(c)   it is not a written option, except as described in paragraph 12.17C.

12.17A   An instrument (or a combination of such instruments) meeting the conditions of paragraph 12.17, may only be a hedging instrument:

(a)   in its entirety; or

(b)   a proportion of such an instrument or a proportion of a combination of such instruments, eg 50 per cent of the nominal amount of the instrument.

12.17B   For a hedge of foreign currency risk, the foreign currency risk component of a financial instrument, provided that it is not a financial instrument as described in paragraph 11.6(b), may be a hedging instrument.

12.17C   A written option is not a hedging instrument unless the written option is an offset to or is combined with a purchased option and the effect of the offset or combination is not a net written option. An example of a combination of a written and a purchased option that is not a net written option is a zero cost interest rate collar.

Conditions for hedge accounting

12.18   An entity may apply hedge accounting to a hedging relationship from the date all of the following conditions are met:

(a)   the hedging relationship consists only of a hedging instrument and a hedged item as described in paragraphs 12.16 to 12.17C;

(b)   the hedging relationship is consistent with the entity's risk management objectives for undertaking hedges;

(c)   there is an economic relationship between the hedged item and the hedging instrument;

(d)   the entity has documented the hedging relationship so that the risk being hedged, the hedged item and the hedging instrument are clearly identified; and

(e)   the entity has determined and documented causes of hedge ineffectiveness.

12.18A   An economic relationship between a hedged item and hedging instrument exists when the entity expects that the values of the hedged item and hedging instrument will typically move in opposite directions in response to movements in the same risk, which is the hedged risk.

Accounting for qualifying hedging relationships

12.19   There are three types of hedging relationships:

(a)   fair value hedge: a hedge of the exposure to changes in fair value of a recognised asset or liability or an unrecognised firm commitment, or a component of any such item, that are attributable to a particular risk and could affect profit or loss;

(b)   cash flow hedge: a hedge of the exposure to variability in cash flows that is attributable to a particular risk associated with all, or a component of, a recognised asset or liability (such as all or some future interest payments on variable rate debt) or a highly probable forecast transaction, and could affect profit or loss; and

(c)   hedge of a net investment in a foreign operation.

12.19A   A hedge of the foreign currency risk of an unrecognised firm commitment may be accounted for as a fair value hedge or as a cash flow hedge.

Fair value hedges

12.20   A fair value hedge shall be accounted for as follows from the date the conditions in paragraph 12.18 are met:

(a)   the gain or loss on the hedging instrument shall be recognised in profit or loss; and

(b)   the **hedging gain or loss** on the hedged item shall adjust the carrying amount of the hedged item (if applicable) and be recognised in profit or loss. When a hedged item is an unrecognised firm commitment, the cumulative hedging gain or loss on the hedged item is recognised as an asset or liability with a corresponding gain or loss recognised in profit or loss.

12.21   When an unrecognised firm commitment to acquire an asset or assume a liability is the hedged item, the initial carrying amount of the asset or liability that results from the entity meeting the firm commitment is adjusted to include the cumulative hedging gain or loss of the hedged item that was recognised in the statement of financial position.

12.22   Any adjustment arising from paragraph 12.20(b) shall be amortised to profit or loss if the hedged item is a financial instrument measured at amortised cost. Amortisation may begin as soon as an adjustment exists and shall begin no later than when the hedged item ceases to be adjusted for hedging gains and losses. The amortisation is based on a recalculated effective interest rate at the date amortisation begins.

Cash flow hedges

12.23   A cash flow hedge shall be accounted for as follows from the date the conditions in paragraph 12.18 are met:

(a)   the separate component of equity associated with the hedged item (cash flow hedge reserve) is adjusted to the lower of the following (in absolute amounts):

(i)   the cumulative gain or loss on the hedging instrument from the date the conditions of paragraph 12.18 are met; and

(ii)   the cumulative change in fair value on the hedged item (ie the present value of the cumulative change of expected future cash flows) from the date the conditions of paragraph 12.18 are met;

(b)   the portion of the gain or loss on the hedging instrument that is determined to be an effective hedge (ie the portion that is offset by the change in the cash flow hedge reserve calculated in accordance with (a)) shall be recognised in **other comprehensive income**;

(c)   any remaining gain or loss on the hedging instrument (or any gain or loss required to balance the change in the cash flow hedge reserve calculated in accordance with (a)), is hedge ineffectiveness that shall be recognised in profit or loss; and

(d) the amount that has been accumulated in the cash flow hedge reserve in accordance with (a) shall be accounted for as follows:

    (i) if a hedged forecast transaction subsequently results in the recognition of a non-financial asset or non-financial liability, or a hedged forecast transaction for a non-financial asset or non-financial liability becomes a firm commitment for which fair value hedge accounting is applied, the entity shall remove that amount from the cash flow hedge reserve and include it directly in the initial cost or other carrying amount of the asset or liability;

    (ii) for cash flow hedges other than those covered by (i), that amount shall be reclassified from the cash flow hedge reserve to profit or loss in the same period or periods during which the hedged expected future cash flows affect profit or loss (for example, in the periods that interest income or interest expense is recognised or when a forecast sale occurs); and

    (iii) if the amount is a loss, and all or part of that loss is not expected to be recovered, the amount of the loss not expected to be recovered shall be reclassified to profit or loss immediately.

Hedges of a net investment in a foreign operation

12.24 Hedges of a net investment in a foreign operation, including a hedge of a monetary item that is accounted for as part of the net investment (see Section 30), shall be accounted for similarly to cash flow hedges from the date the conditions of paragraph 12.18 are met:

(a) the portion of the gain or loss on the hedging instrument that is determined to be an effective hedge shall be recognised in other comprehensive income (see paragraphs 12.23(a) and (b)); and

(b) the ineffective portion shall be recognised in profit or loss.

The cumulative gain or loss on the hedging instrument relating to the effective portion of the hedge that has been accumulated in equity shall not be reclassified from equity to profit or loss on disposal or partial disposal of the foreign operation.

Discontinuing hedge accounting

12.25 The entity may discontinue hedge accounting provided the entity has documented its election.

The entity shall discontinue hedge accounting when:

(a) the hedging instrument has expired, is sold, terminated or exercised; or

(b) the conditions for hedge accounting in paragraph 12.18 are no longer met.

In all cases, hedge accounting shall be discontinued prospectively.

12.25A In a fair value hedge, any adjustment arising from paragraph 12.20(b) is dealt with in accordance with paragraph 12.22.

In a cash flow hedge, if the hedged future cash flows are no longer expected to occur, the amount that has been accumulated in the cash flow hedge reserve in accordance with paragraph 12.23(a) shall be reclassified from the cash flow hedge reserve to profit or loss immediately. If the hedged future cash flows are still expected to occur (for example a future cash flow that is no longer highly probable may still be expected to occur), the cumulative gain or loss in the cash flow hedge reserve is dealt with in accordance with paragraph 12.23(d).

In a net investment hedge, in accordance with paragraph 12.24, the amount that has been accumulated in equity is not reclassified to profit or loss.

Presentation

12.25B A financial asset and a financial liability shall be offset and the net amount presented in the **statement of financial position** when, and only when, an entity:

(a) currently has a legally enforceable right to set off the recognised amounts; and

(b) intends either to settle on a net basis, or to realise the asset and settle the liability simultaneously.

Disclosures

12.26 An entity applying this section shall make all of the disclosures required in Section 11 incorporating in those disclosures, financial instruments that are within the scope of this section as well as those within the scope of Section 11. For financial instruments in the scope of this section that are not held as part of a trading portfolio and are not **derivative** instruments, an entity shall provide additional disclosures as set out in paragraph 11.48A. In addition, if the entity uses hedge accounting, it shall make the additional disclosures in paragraphs 12.27 to 12.29A.

12.27 An entity shall disclose the following separately for each type of hedging relationship described in paragraph 12.19:

(a) a description of the hedge;

(b) a description of the financial instruments designated as hedging instruments and their fair values at the **reporting date**; and

(c) the nature of the risks being hedged, including a description of the hedged item.

* 12.28 If an entity uses hedge accounting for a fair value hedge it shall disclose the following:

(a) the amount of the change in fair value of the hedging instrument recognised in profit or loss for the period; and

(b) the amount of the change in fair value of the hedged item recognised in profit or loss for the period.

12.29 If an entity uses hedge accounting for a cash flow hedge it shall disclose the following:

(a) the periods when the cash flows are expected to occur and when they are expected to affect profit or loss;

(b) a description of any forecast transaction for which hedge accounting had previously been used, but which is no longer expected to occur;

* (c) the amount of the change in fair value of the hedging instrument that was recognised in other comprehensive income during the period;

* (d) the amount, if any, that was reclassified from equity to profit or loss for the period; and

* (e) the amount, if any, of any excess of the fair value of the hedging instrument over the change in the fair value of the expected cash flows that was recognised in profit or loss for the period.

12.29A If an entity uses hedge accounting for a net investment in a foreign operation it shall disclose separately the amounts recognised in other comprehensive income in accordance with paragraph 12.24(a) and the amounts recognised in profit or loss in accordance with paragraph 12.24(b).

Appendix to Section 12

Examples of hedge accounting

This appendix accompanies, but is not part of, Section 12. It provides guidance for applying the requirements of paragraphs 12.15 to 12.25A.

Example 1

Fair value hedge accounting – Hedge of forward foreign currency risk of an unrecognised firm commitment

In accordance with paragraph 12.19A, a hedge of the foreign currency risk of an unrecognised firm commitment may be accounted for as a cash flow or fair value hedge. This example illustrates fair value hedge accounting.

12A.1   On 9 June 20X5 an entity enters into a purchase agreement with a third party over a non-financial asset in a foreign currency (FC) for FC515,000. On the same day, the entity enters into a forward currency contract to buy FC500,000 for CU1,000,000. Under the purchase agreement, the non-financial asset will be delivered and paid for on 30 March 20X6, the same day the forward currency contract is required to be settled.

In this example the hedged item is the total of the commitment of FC515,000 and the hedging instrument is the forward contract to buy FC500,000. Since the nominal amounts of the two contracts do not match, hedge ineffectiveness arises. It should be noted that in practice an entity could avoid ineffectiveness arising for this reason by identifying an amount of FC500,000 of the total commitment as the hedged item in accordance with paragraph 12.16C.

For simplification, this example disregards other sources of ineffectiveness, eg counter party credit risk associated with the forward currency contract.

The entity's financial year ends on 31 December.

This example assumes that the qualifying conditions for hedge accounting in paragraph 12.18 are met from 9 June 20X5.

The table below sets out the applicable forward exchange rates, the fair value of the forward currency contract (the hedging instrument) and the hedging gains/losses on the purchase commitment (the hedged item) on the relevant dates. This example ignores the effects of discounting.

	9 Jun 20X5	**31 Dec 20X5**	**30 Mar 20X6**
Forward exchange rate (CU:FC)	2:1	2.2:1	2.16:1
Forward currency contract (hedging instrument)			
Fair value	nil	FC500,000 x CU0.2:FC = CU100,000	FC500,000 x CU0.16:FC = CU80,000[†]
Fair value change	nil	CU100,000 – 0 = CU100,000	CU80,000 – CU100,000 = (CU20,000)
Purchase commitment (hedged item)			
Cumulative hedging (loss)[‡]	nil	(FC515,000) x CU0.2:FC = (CU103,000)	(FC515,000) x CU0.16:FC = (CU82,400)
Hedging (loss)/ gain	nil	(CU103,000) – 0 = (CU103,000)	(CU82,400) – (CU103,000) = CU20,600

Key to table:

[†]: This is the fair value of the contract prior to settlement.
[‡]: In accordance with paragraph 12.20(b), the commitment is fair valued only for the hedged risk, which in this example is the forward exchange rate risk.

12A.2 Hedge accounting:

Note that there are no hedge accounting entries on 9 June 20X5.

31 December 20X5

(1)   In accordance with paragraph 12.20(a) the fair value gain of CU100,000 on the forward currency contract is recognised in profit or loss.

(2)   In accordance with paragraph 12.20(b) the cumulative hedging loss of CU103,000 on the commitment is recorded as a liability with a corresponding loss recognised in profit or loss.

Accounting entries:

Ref		Debit	Credit
(1)	Forward currency contract	CU100,000	
	Profit or loss		CU100,000
(2)	Profit or loss	CU103,000	
	Hedged item (commitment)		CU103,000

30 March 20X6

(1) In accordance with paragraph 12.20(a) the fair value loss of CU20,000 on the forward currency contract is recognised in profit or loss.

(2) In accordance with paragraph 12.20(b) the hedging gain on the commitment of CU20,600 is recognised in profit or loss with a corresponding adjustment to the recognised liability from CU103,000 to CU82,400.

(3) In accordance with paragraph 12.21 the non-financial asset's carrying amount is adjusted to include the cumulative hedging loss on the hedged item of CU82,400.

Note A: For illustrative purposes the accounting entry in respect of the settlement of the forward currency contract in cash for CU80,000 is shown below.

Note B: For illustrative purposes the accounting entry for the purchase of the non-financial asset at the applicable spot rate of FC2.16:CU for CU1,112,400 (settled in cash) is shown below.

Accounting entries:

Ref		Debit	Credit
(1)	Profit or loss	CU20,000	
	Forward currency contract		CU20,000
(2)	Hedged item (commitment)	CU20,600	
	Profit or loss		CU20,600
(3)	Hedged item (commitment)	CU82,400	
	Property, plant and equipment (PP&E)		CU82,400
(A)	Cash	CU80,000	
	Forward currency contract		CU80,000
(B)	Property, plant and equipment (PP&E)	CU1,112,400	
	Cash		CU1,112,400

Example 2

Cash flow hedge accounting – Hedge of variability in cash flows in a floating rate loan due to interest rate risk

This example illustrates the accounting for a cash flow hedge of interest rate risk associated with a floating rate loan. The entity borrows money at a floating rate and enters into an interest rate swap with the effect of paying a fixed rate overall.

12A.3 On 1 January 20X5, an entity borrows CU10,000,000 from a bank at a floating rate of 3-month LIBOR plus 2.5 per cent. The interest is payable annually in arrears on 31 December. The loan is repayable on 31 December 20X7.

On 1 January 20X5 the entity also enters into an interest rate swap with a third party, under which it receives 6-month LIBOR and pays a fixed rate of interest of 4.5 per cent. The notional amount of the swap is CU10,000,000. The swap is settled annually in arrears on 31 December and expires on 31 December 20X7.

The LIBOR rates on the loan and the interest rate swap are reset and fixed annually in advance on 31 December based on the expected LIBOR rates applicable at that time. Note that in practice the loan and swap interest rates would be reset more frequently than assumed for the purpose of simplification in this example.

The entity hedges the variability of the interest rate payments on the bank loan based on 3-month LIBOR. It should be noted that because the entity receives interest based on 6-month LIBOR under the interest rate swap, ineffectiveness will arise because the expected cash flows of the hedged item and the hedging instrument differ. The fair value of the interest rate swap may be affected by other factors that cause ineffectiveness, for example counter party credit risk, but these have been disregarded in this example.

There are no transaction costs.

The entity's financial year ends on 31 December.

This example assumes that the qualifying conditions for hedge accounting in paragraph 12.18 are met from 1 January 20X5.

The table in paragraph 12A.5 summarises the impact of hedge accounting on the interest rate swap, profit or loss and other comprehensive income.

The table below sets out the applicable LIBOR rates, interest payments and swap settlements. The fair values of the interest rate swap and the hedged item shown in the table are shown for illustrative purposes only.

Note that in practice, when forecasted variable interest rate payments are the hedged item, the fair value of a hypothetical swap, that would be expected to perfectly offset the hedged cash flows, is used as a proxy of the fair value of the hedged item. The hypothetical derivative in this scenario is a fixed to floating interest rate swap with terms that match those of the loan and a fixed rate of 4.3 per cent, which for the purpose of this example, is the interest rate where the fair value of the hypothetical swap is nil at the inception of the hedging relationship.

	1 Jan 20X5	31 Dec 20X5	31 Dec 20X6	31 Dec 20X7
Actual 3-month LIBOR	4.3%	5%	3%	n/a
Actual 6-month LIBOR	4.5%	4.9%	3.2%	n/a
Interest payments based on 3-month LIBOR	n/a	CU10m x (4.3% + 2.5%) = CU680,000	CU10m x (5% + 2.5%) = CU750,000	CU10m x (3% + 2.5%) = CU550,000
Interest rate swap (hedging instrument)				
Fair value	nil	CU78,000	(CU89,000)[†]	(CU130,000)[‡]
Fair value change	nil	CU78,000 – 0 = CU78,000	(CU89,000) – CU78,000 = (CU167,000)	(CU130,000) – (CU40,000)[§] – (CU89,000) = (CU1,000)
Swap settlement receipts/ (payments) based on 6-month LIBOR	n/a	CU10m x (4.5% – 4.5%) = nil	CU10m x (4.9% – 4.5%) = CU40,000	CU10m * (3.2% – 4.5%) = (CU130,000)
Hedged item				
Fair value	nil	(CU137,000)	CU59,000	CU130,000

Key to table:

[†]: This valuation is determined before the receipt of the cash settlement of CU40,000 due on 31 December 20X6.

[‡]: This valuation is determined before the payment of the cash settlement of CU130,000 due on 31 December 20X7.

[§]: CU40,000 is the settlement of the interest rate swap as at 31 December 20X6 which affects the fair value of the swap, but is not included in the fair value of the swap at 31 December 20X6 of CU89,000.

12A.4 Hedge accounting:

31 December 20X5

(1) In accordance with paragraph 12.23(a), the cash flow hedge reserve is adjusted to the lower of (in absolute amounts) the cumulative gain on the hedging instrument (ie the interest rate swap), which equals its fair value, of CU78,000 and the cumulative change in fair value of the hedged item, which equals its fair value of (CU137,000).

In accordance with paragraph 12.23(b), the gain of CU78,000 on the interest rate swap is recognised in other comprehensive income.

(2) The fixed interest element on the hypothetical swap is CU430,000, the same amount as the variable rate component. The variability of the 3-month LIBOR did therefore not affect profit or loss during the period. The reclassification adjustment in accordance with paragraph 12.23(d)(ii) is nil. (Note that no accounting entry is shown below.)

Note A: For illustrative purposes the accounting entry for interest payments is shown below. Note that in practice the accrual and payment of interest may be recorded in separate accounting entries.

Accounting entries:

Note that the accounting entries shown are only those relevant to demonstrate the effects of hedge accounting. In practice other accounting entries would be required, eg an entry to recognise the loan liability.

Ref		Debit	Credit
(1)	Interest rate swap	CU78,000	
	Other comprehensive income		CU78,000
(A)	Profit or loss	CU680,000	
	Cash		CU680,000

31 December 20X6

(1) In accordance with paragraph 12.23(a), the cash flow hedge reserve is adjusted to the lower of (in absolute amounts) the cumulative loss on the hedging instrument (ie the interest rate swap) which equals its fair value of (CU89,000) and the cumulative change in fair value of the hedged item, which equals its fair value of CU59,000. The cash flow hedge reserve moves from CU78,000 to (CU59,000), a change of (CU137,000).

In accordance with paragraph 12.23(b), a loss of CU137,000 on the interest rate swap is recognised in other comprehensive income, as this part of the loss is fully off-set by the change in the cash flow hedge reserve. The remainder of the loss on the interest rate swap of CU30,000 is recognised in profit or loss, as required by paragraph 12.23(c).

(2) The fixed interest element on the hypothetical swap is CU430,000, whilst the variable rate component is CU500,000. The variability of the 3-month LIBOR affects profit or loss during the period by CU70,000. Accordingly, the reclassification adjustment in accordance with paragraph 12.23(d)(ii) is CU70,000.

Note A: For illustrative purposes the accounting entry for interest payments is shown below. Note that in practice the accrual and payment of interest may be recorded in separate accounting entries.

Note B: For illustrative purposes the accounting entry for the settlement of the swap is shown below.

Accounting entries:

Ref		Debit	Credit
(1)	Other comprehensive income	CU137,000	
	Profit or loss	CU30,000	
	Interest rate swap		CU167,000
(2)	Other comprehensive income	CU70,000	
	Profit or loss		CU70,000
(A)	Profit or loss	CU750,000	
	Cash		CU750,000
(B)	Cash	CU40,000	
	Interest rate swap		CU40,000

31 December 20X7

(1) In accordance with paragraph 12.23(a), the cash flow hedge reserve is adjusted to the lower of (in absolute amounts) the cumulative loss on the hedging instrument (ie the interest rate swap) which equals the fair value of (CU130,000) and the cumulative change in fair value of the hedged item, which equals its fair value of CU130,000.

The cash flow hedge reserve moves from (CU129,000) to (CU130,000), a change of (CU1,000). In accordance with paragraph 12.23(b), the loss of CU1,000 on the interest rate swap is recognised in other comprehensive income.

(2) The fixed interest element on the hypothetical swap is CU430,000, whilst the variable rate component is CU300,000. The variability of the 3-month LIBOR affects profit or loss during the period by (CU130,000). Accordingly, the reclassification adjustment in accordance with paragraph 12.23(d)(ii) is (CU130,000).

Note A: For illustrative purposes the accounting entry for interest payments is shown below. Note that in practice the accrual and payment of interest may be recorded in separate accounting entries.

Note B: For illustrative purposes the accounting entry for the settlement of the swap is shown below.

Accounting entries:

Ref		Debit	Credit
(1)	Other comprehensive income	CU1,000	
	Interest rate swap		CU1,000
(2)	Profit or loss	CU130,000	
	Other comprehensive income		CU130,000
(A)	Profit or loss	CU550,000	
	Cash		CU550,000
(B)	Interest rate swap	CU130,000	
	Cash		CU130,000

12A.5 The table below summarises the effects of the accounting entries shown in paragraph 12A.4 on the interest rate swap, profit or loss and other comprehensive income.

Description	Interest rate swap	Other comprehensive income	Profit or loss
31 December 20X5			
Opening balance	**nil**	**nil**[†]	–
Interest on the loan			CU680,000
Interest rate swap fair value movement	CU78,000	(CU78,000)	–
Closing balance	**CU78,000**	**(CU78,000)**[†]	–
31 December 20X6			
Opening balance	**CU78,000**	**(CU78,000)**[†]	–
Interest on the loan			CU750,000
Interest rate swap fair value movement	(CU167,000)	CU137,000	CU30,000
Settlement receipt interest rate swap	(40,000)	–	–
Reclassification from cash flow hedge reserve	–	CU70,000	(CU70,000)
Closing balance	**(CU129,000)**	**CU129,000**[†]	–
31 December 20X7			
Opening balance	**(CU129,000)**	**CU129,000**[†]	–
Interest on the loan			CU550,000
Interest rate swap movement	(1,000)	1,000	–
Settlement payment interest rate swap	CU130,000	–	–
Reclassification from cash flow hedge reserve	–	(CU130,000)	CU130,000
Closing balance	**nil**	**nil**[†]	–

Key to table:

[†]:   This is the balance of the cash flow hedge reserve.

Example 3

Hedge accounting: Net investment in a foreign operation

This example illustrates the accounting for a net investment hedge in the consolidated financial statements. The entity has a foreign operation and hedges its exposure to foreign currency risk in the foreign operation by the use of a foreign currency loan.

12A.6   On 1 April 20X5 an entity with functional currency CU acquires an investment in an overseas subsidiary (with functional currency FC) at a cost of FC1,200,000. On the same day the entity takes out a loan with a third party of FC1,200,000 to finance the investment. This example disregards the effects of interest or other transaction costs associated with the loan.

This example assumes that the carrying amount of the investment denominated in FC is impaired below FC1,200,000 as presented in the table below, which causes ineffectiveness.

The entity's financial year ends on 31 December.

This example assumes that the qualifying conditions for hedge accounting in paragraph 12.18 are met from 1 April 20X5.

The table below sets out the applicable exchange rates, the carrying amount of the loan and the foreign exchange gains and losses on the loan as determined in accordance with Section 30, as well as the retranslation differences on the foreign investment recognised in other comprehensive income in accordance with Section 30.

	1 Apr 20X5	**31 Dec 20X5**	**31 Dec 20X6**
Spot exchange rate CU:FC	0.35:1	0.3:1	0.45:1
Loan (hedging instrument)			
Carrying amount under Section 30	(FC1,200,000) x CU0.35:FC = (CU420,000)	(FC1,200,000) x CU0.3:FC = (CU360,000)	(FC1,200,000) x CU0.45:FC = (CU540,000)
Cumulative gain/(loss)	nil	(CU360,000) – (CU420,000) = CU60,000	(CU540,000) – (CU420,000) = (CU120,000)
Gain/(loss)	nil	(CU360,000) – (CU420,000) = CU60,000	(CU540,000) – (CU360,000) = (CU180,000)

	1 April 20X5	31 December 20X5	31 December 20X6
Investment in foreign operation (hedged item)			
Retranslation difference in accordance with Section 30	nil	(CU55,000)[†]	CU157,500[‡]
Cumulative retranslation differences	nil	(CU55,000) – 0 = (CU55,000)	CU157,500 + (CU55,000) = CU102,500

Key to table:

[†]: This is the exchange difference referred to in paragraph 30.20 which is recognised in other comprehensive income. The amount under paragraph 30.20(a) is CU5,000 and under paragraph 30.20(b) (CU60,000). The calculation is based on the translation of the FC200,000 loss at the average rate of 0.325CU:FC.

[‡]: This is the exchange difference referred to in paragraph 30.20 which is recognised in other comprehensive income. The amount under paragraph 30.20(a) is CU7,500 and under paragraph 30.20(b) CU150,000. The calculation is based on the translation of the FC100,000 profit at the average rate of 0.375CU:FC.

12A.7 Hedge accounting:

31 December 20X5

A component of equity is adjusted to the lower of (in absolute amounts) the cumulative exchange gain on the loan of CU60,000 and the cumulative retranslation difference on the net investment of (CU55,000).

In accordance with paragraph 12.24(a), a gain of CU55,000 on the loan is recognised in other comprehensive income. The remainder of the gain of CU5,000 is recognised in profit or loss, as required by paragraph 12.24(b).

Accounting entry:

Note that only the accounting entry in relation to hedge accounting as described in paragraph 12.24 is shown. Other accounting entries in relation to the loan and the investment in the foreign operation would be required in practice.

	Debit	Credit
Loan	CU60,000	
Other comprehensive income		CU55,000
Profit or loss		CU5,000

31 December 20X6

A component of equity is adjusted to the lower of (in absolute amounts) the cumulative exchange loss on the loan of CU120,000 and the cumulative exchange difference on the net investment of CU102,500.

The amount recorded in equity changes from CU55,000 to (CU102,500), a change of (CU157,500). In accordance with paragraph 12.24(a) a loss of CU157,500 on the loan is recognised in other comprehensive income. The remainder of the loss of CU22,500 is recorded in profit or loss, as required by paragraph 12.24(b).

Accounting entry:

	Debit	Credit
Other comprehensive income	CU157,500	
Profit or loss	CU22,500	
Loan		CU180,000

Section 13
Inventories

Scope of this section

13.1   This section sets out the principles for recognising and measuring **inventories**. Inventories are **assets**:

(a)   held for sale in the ordinary course of business;

(b)   in the process of production for such sale; or

(c)   in the form of materials or supplies to be consumed in the production process or in the rendering of services.

13.2   This section applies to all inventories, except:

(a)   work in progress arising under **construction contracts**, including directly related service contracts (see Section 23 *Revenue*);

(b)   **financial instruments** (see Section 11 *Basic Financial Instruments* and Section 12 *Other Financial Instruments Issues*); and

(c)   **biological assets** related to **agricultural activity** and **agricultural produce** at the point of harvest (see Section 34 *Specialised Activities*).

13.3   Other than the disclosure requirements in paragraph 13.22, this section does not apply to the **measurement** of inventories at **fair value less costs to sell** through **profit or loss** at each **reporting date**. Inventories shall not be measured at fair value less costs to sell unless it is a more relevant measure of the entity's **performance** because the entity operates in an **active market** where sale can be achieved at published prices, and inventory is a store of readily realisable value.

Measurement of inventories

13.4   An entity shall measure inventories at the lower of **cost** and estimated selling price less costs to complete and sell.

13.4A   **Inventories held for distribution at no or nominal consideration** shall be measured at the lower of cost adjusted, when applicable, for any loss of **service potential** and replacement cost.

Cost of inventories

13.5   An entity shall include in the cost of inventories all costs of purchase, costs of conversion and other costs incurred in bringing the inventories to their present location and condition.

13.5A   Where inventories are acquired through a **non-exchange transaction**, their cost shall be measured at their **fair value** as at the date of acquisition. For **public benefit entities** and entities within a **public benefit entity group**, this requirement only applies to inventories that are recognised as a result of the requirements for incoming resources from non-exchange transactions as prescribed in Section 34 *Specialised Activities*.

Costs of purchase

13.6   The costs of purchase of inventories comprise the purchase price, import duties and other taxes (other than those subsequently recoverable by the entity from the taxing authorities), and transport, handling and other costs directly attributable to the acquisition of finished goods, materials and services. Trade discounts, rebates and other similar items are deducted in determining the costs of purchase.

13.7   An entity may purchase inventories on deferred settlement terms. In some cases, the arrangement effectively contains an unstated financing element, for example, a difference between the purchase price for normal credit terms and the deferred settlement amount. In these cases, the difference is recognised as interest expense over the period of the financing and is not added to the cost of the inventories unless the inventory is a **qualifying asset** (see Section 25 *Borrowing Costs*) and the entity adopts a policy of capitalisation of borrowing costs.

Costs of conversion

13.8   The costs of conversion of inventories include costs directly related to the units of production, such as direct labour. They also include a systematic allocation of fixed and variable production overheads that are incurred in converting materials into finished goods. Fixed production overheads are those indirect costs of production that remain relatively constant regardless of the volume of production, such as **depreciation** and maintenance of factory buildings and equipment, and the cost of factory management and administration. Variable production overheads are those indirect costs of production that vary directly, or nearly directly, with the volume of production, such as indirect materials and indirect labour.

13.8A   Production overheads include the costs for obligations (recognised and measured in accordance with Section 21 *Provisions and Contingencies*) for dismantling, removing and restoring a site on which an item of **property, plant and equipment** is located that are incurred during the **reporting period** as a consequence of having used that item of property, plant and equipment to produce inventory during that period.

Allocation of production overheads

13.9   An entity shall allocate fixed production overheads to the costs of conversion on the basis of the normal capacity of the production facilities. Normal capacity is the production expected to be achieved on average over a number of periods or seasons under normal circumstances, taking into account the loss of capacity resulting from planned maintenance. The actual level of production may be used if it approximates normal capacity. The amount of fixed overhead allocated to each unit of production is not increased as a consequence of low production or idle plant. Unallocated overheads are recognised as an **expense** in the period in which they are incurred. In periods of abnormally high production, the amount of fixed overhead allocated to each unit of production is decreased so that inventories are not measured above cost. Variable production overheads are allocated to each unit of production on the basis of the actual use of the production facilities.

Joint products and by-products

13.10   A production process may result in more than one product being produced simultaneously. This is the case, for example, when joint products are produced or when there is a main product and a by-product. When the costs of raw materials or conversion of each product are not separately identifiable, an entity shall allocate them between the products on a rational and consistent basis. The allocation may be based, for example, on the relative sales value of each product either at the stage in the production process when the products become separately identifiable, or at the completion of production. Most by-products, by their nature, are immaterial. When this is the case, the entity shall measure them at selling price less costs to complete and sell and deduct this amount from the cost of the main product. As a result, the **carrying amount** of the main product is not materially different from its cost.

Other costs included in inventories

13.11   An entity shall include other costs in the cost of inventories only to the extent that they are incurred in bringing the inventories to their present location and condition.

13.12   [Not used]

Costs excluded from inventories

13.13   Examples of costs excluded from the cost of inventories and recognised as expenses in the period in which they are incurred are:

(a)   abnormal amounts of wasted materials, labour or other production costs;

(b)   storage costs, unless those costs are necessary during the production process before a further production stage;

(c)   administrative overheads that do not contribute to bringing inventories to their present location and condition; and

(d)   selling costs.

Cost of inventories of a service provider

13.14   To the extent that service providers have inventories, they measure them at the costs of their production. These costs consist primarily of the labour and other costs of personnel directly engaged in providing the service, including supervisory personnel, and attributable overheads. Labour and other costs relating to sales and general administrative personnel are not included but are recognised as expenses in the period in which they are incurred. The cost of inventories of a service provider does not include profit margins or non-attributable overheads that are often factored into prices charged by service providers.

Cost of agricultural produce harvested from biological assets

13.15   Section 34 requires that inventories comprising agricultural produce that an entity has harvested from its biological assets should be measured on initial **recognition,** at the point of harvest, at either their fair value less estimated costs to sell or the lower of cost and estimated selling price less costs to complete and sell. This becomes the cost of the inventories at that date for application of this section.

Techniques for measuring cost, such as standard costing, retail method and most recent purchase price

13.16   An entity may use techniques such as the standard cost method, the retail method or most recent purchase price for measuring the cost of inventories if the result approximates cost. Standard costs take into account normal levels of materials and supplies, labour, efficiency and capacity utilisation. They are regularly reviewed and, if necessary, revised in the light of current conditions. The retail method measures cost by reducing the sales value of the inventory by the appropriate percentage gross margin.

Cost formulas

13.17 An entity shall measure the cost of inventories of items that are not ordinarily interchangeable and goods or services produced and segregated for specific projects by using specific identification of their individual costs.

13.18 An entity shall measure the cost of inventories, other than those dealt with in paragraph 13.17, by using the first-in, first-out (FIFO) or weighted average cost formula. An entity shall use the same cost formula for all inventories having a similar nature and use to the entity. For inventories with a different nature or use, different cost formulas may be justified. The last-in, first-out method (LIFO) is not permitted by this FRS.

Impairment of inventories

13.19 Paragraphs 27.2 to 27.4 require an entity to assess at the end of each reporting period whether any inventories are impaired, ie the carrying amount is not fully recoverable (eg because of damage, obsolescence or declining selling prices). If an item (or group of items) of inventory is impaired, those paragraphs require the entity to measure the inventory at its selling price less costs to complete and sell, and to recognise an **impairment loss**. Those paragraphs also require a reversal of a prior impairment in some circumstances.

Recognition as an expense

13.20 When inventories are sold, the entity shall recognise the carrying amount of those inventories as an expense in the period in which the related **revenue** is recognised.

13.20A When inventories held for distribution at no or nominal consideration are distributed, the carrying amount of those inventories shall be recognised as an expense.

13.21 Some inventories may be allocated to other asset accounts, for example, inventory used as a component of self-constructed property, plant or equipment. Inventories allocated to another asset in this way are accounted for subsequently in accordance with the section of this FRS relevant to that type of asset.

Disclosures

13.22 An entity shall disclose the following:

(a) the **accounting policies** adopted in measuring inventories, including the cost formula used;

(b) the total carrying amount of inventories and the carrying amount in classifications appropriate to the entity;

(c) the amount of inventories recognised as an expense during the period;

(d) impairment losses recognised or reversed in profit or loss in accordance with Section 27; and

* (e) the total carrying amount of inventories pledged as security for **liabilities**.

Section 14
Investments in Associates

Scope of this section

14.1 This section applies to accounting for **associates** in **consolidated financial statements**. This section also applies to accounting for investments in associates in the **individual financial statements** of an investor that is not a **parent**. An entity that is a parent shall account for its investments in associates in its **separate financial statements** in accordance with paragraphs 9.26 and 9.26A, as appropriate.

Associates defined

14.2 An associate is an entity, including an unincorporated entity such as a partnership, over which the investor has **significant influence** and that is neither a **subsidiary** nor an interest in a **joint venture**.

14.3 Significant influence is the power to participate in the financial and operating policy decisions of the associate but is not **control** or **joint control** over those policies.

    (a) If an investor holds, directly or indirectly (eg through subsidiaries), 20 per cent or more of the voting power of the associate, it is presumed that the investor has significant influence, unless it can be clearly demonstrated that this is not the case.

    (b) Conversely, if the investor holds, directly or indirectly (eg through subsidiaries), less than 20 per cent of the voting power of the associate, it is presumed that the investor does not have significant influence, unless such influence can be clearly demonstrated.

    (c) A substantial or majority ownership by another investor does not preclude an investor from having significant influence.

Measurement—accounting policy election

14.4 An investor that is not a parent but that has an investment in one or more associates shall, in its individual financial statements, account for all of its investments in associates using either:

    (a) the cost model in accordance with paragraphs 14.5 to 14.6;

    (b) [not used]

    (c) the fair value model in accordance with paragraphs 14.9 to 14.10A; or

    (d) at fair value with changes in fair value recognised in profit or loss (paragraphs 11.27 to 11.32 provide guidance on fair value).

14.4A An investor that is a parent shall, in its consolidated financial statements, account for all of its investments in associates using the equity method in accordance with paragraph 14.8, except as required by paragraph 14.4B.

14.4B Where an investor is a parent and has an associate that is **held as part of an investment portfolio**, the associate shall be measured at **fair value** with changes in fair value recognised in **profit or loss** in the consolidated financial statements.

Cost model

14.5   An investor that is not a parent, that chooses to adopt the cost model, shall measure its investments in associates at cost less any accumulated **impairment losses** recognised in accordance with Section 27 *Impairment of Assets*.

14.6   The investor shall recognise dividends and other distributions received from the investment as **income** without regard to whether the distributions are from accumulated profits of the associate arising before or after the date of acquisition.

14.7   [Not used]

Equity method

14.8   Under the equity method of accounting, an equity investment is initially recognised at the transaction price (including **transaction costs**) and is subsequently adjusted to reflect the investor's share of the profit or loss, **other comprehensive income** and **equity** of the associate.

(a)   *Distributions and other adjustments to carrying amount.* Distributions received from the associate reduce the **carrying amount** of the investment. Adjustments to the carrying amount may also be required as a consequence of changes in the associate's equity arising from items of other comprehensive income.

(b)   *Potential voting rights.* Although potential voting rights are considered in deciding whether significant influence exists, an investor shall measure its share of profit or loss and other comprehensive income of the associate and its share of changes in the associate's equity on the basis of present ownership interests. Those measurements shall not reflect the possible exercise or conversion of potential voting rights.

(c)   *Implicit goodwill and fair value adjustments.* On acquisition of the investment in an associate, an investor shall account for any difference (whether positive or negative) between the cost of acquisition and the investor's share of the fair values of the net identifiable assets of the associate in accordance with paragraphs 19.22 to 19.24. An investor shall adjust its share of the associate's profits or losses after acquisition to account for additional **depreciation** or **amortisation** of the associate's depreciable or amortisable assets (including **goodwill**) on the basis of the excess of their fair values over their carrying amounts at the time the investment was acquired.

(d)   *Impairment.* If there is an indication that an investment in an associate may be impaired, an investor shall test the entire carrying amount of the investment for impairment in accordance with Section 27 as a single **asset**. Any goodwill included as part of the carrying amount of the investment in the associate is not tested separately for impairment but, rather, as part of the test for impairment of the investment as a whole.

(e)   *Investor's transactions with associates.* The investor shall eliminate unrealised profits and losses resulting from upstream (associate to investor) and downstream (investor to associate) transactions to the extent of the investor's interest in the associate. Unrealised losses on such transactions may provide evidence of an impairment of the asset transferred.

(f)   *Date of associate's financial statements.* In applying the equity method, the investor shall use the **financial statements** of the associate as of the same date as the financial statements of the investor unless it is **impracticable** to do so. If it is impracticable, the investor shall use the most recent available financial statements of the associate, with adjustments made for the effects of any significant transactions or events occurring between the accounting period ends.

(g) *Associate's accounting policies.* If the associate uses **accounting policies** that differ from those of the investor, the investor shall adjust the associate's financial statements to reflect the investor's accounting policies for the purpose of applying the equity method unless it is impracticable to do so.

(h) *Losses in excess of investment.* If an investor's share of losses of an associate equals or exceeds the carrying amount of its investment in the associate, the investor shall discontinue recognising its share of further losses. After the investor's interest is reduced to zero, the investor shall recognise additional losses by a **provision** (see Section 21 *Provisions and Contingencies*) only to the extent that the investor has incurred legal or **constructive obligations** or has made payments on behalf of the associate. If the associate subsequently reports profits, the investor shall resume recognising its share of those profits only after its share of the profits equals the share of losses not recognised.

(i) *Discontinuing the equity method.* An investor shall cease using the equity method from the date that significant influence ceases and, provided the associate does not become a subsidiary in accordance with *Section 19 Business Combinations and Goodwill* or a joint venture in accordance with Section 15 *Investments in Joint Ventures*, shall account for the investment as follows:

(i) If the investor loses significant influence over an associate as a result of a full or partial disposal, it shall derecognise that associate and recognise in profit or loss the difference between the proceeds from the disposal and the carrying amount of the investment in the associate relating to the proportion disposed of or lost at the date significant influence is lost. The investor shall account for any retained interest using Section 11 *Basic Financial Instruments* or Section 12 *Other Financial Instruments Issues*, as appropriate. The carrying amount of the investment at the date that it ceases to be an associate shall be regarded as its cost on initial **measurement** as a **financial asset**; and

(ii) If an investor loses significant influence for reasons other than a partial disposal of its investment, the investor shall regard the carrying amount of the investment at that date as a new cost basis and shall account for the investment using Sections 11 or 12, as appropriate.

The gain or loss arising on the disposal shall also include those amounts that have been recognised in **other comprehensive income** in relation to that associate, where those amounts are required to be reclassified to profit or loss upon disposal in accordance with other sections of this FRS. Amounts that are not required to be reclassified to profit or loss upon disposal of the related assets or liabilities in accordance with other sections of this FRS shall be transferred directly to retained earnings.

Fair value model

14.9 When an investment in an associate is recognised initially, an investor that is not a parent, that chooses to adopt the fair value model, shall measure it at the transaction price.

14.10 At each reporting date, an investor that is not a parent, that chooses to adopt the fair value model, shall measure its investments in associates at fair value, with changes in fair value recognised in other comprehensive income in accordance with paragraphs 17.15E and 17.15F, using the fair value guidance in paragraphs 11.27 to 11.32. An investor using the fair value model shall use the cost model for any investment in an associate for which it is impracticable to measure fair value reliably without undue cost or effort.

14.10A The investor shall recognise dividends and other distributions received from the investment as income without regard to whether the distributions are from accumulated profits of the associate arising before or after the date of acquisition.

Presentation in individual and consolidated financial statements

14.11 Unless otherwise required under the Regulations, an investor shall classify investments in associates as **fixed assets**.

Disclosures in individual and consolidated financial statements

14.12 The financial statements shall disclose:

(a) the accounting policy for investments in associates;

(b) the carrying amount of investments in associates; and

(c) the fair value of investments in associates accounted for using the equity method for which there are published price quotations.

14.13 For investments in associates accounted for in accordance with the cost model, an investor shall disclose the amount of dividends and other distributions recognised as income.

14.14 For investments in associates accounted for in accordance with the equity method, an investor shall disclose separately its share of the profit or loss of such associates and its share of any **discontinued operations** of such associates.

14.15 For investments in associates accounted for in accordance with the fair value model, an investor shall make the disclosures required by paragraphs 11.43 and 11.44.

14.15A The individual financial statements of an investor that is not a parent shall disclose summarised financial information about the investments in the associates, along with the effect of including those investments as if they had been accounted for using the equity method. Investing entities that are exempt from preparing consolidated financial statements, or would be exempt if they had subsidiaries, are exempt from this requirement.

Section 15
Investments in Joint Ventures

Scope of this section

15.1   This section applies to accounting for **joint ventures** in **consolidated financial statements**, for investments in joint ventures in the **individual financial statements** of a **venturer** that is not a **parent**, and for investment in **jointly controlled operations** and **jointly controlled assets** in the **separate financial statements** of a venturer that is a parent. A venturer that is a parent shall account for interests in **jointly controlled entities** in its **separate financial statements** in accordance with paragraphs 9.26 and 9.26A, as appropriate.

Joint ventures defined

15.2   **Joint control** is the contractually agreed sharing of **control** over an economic activity, and exists only when the strategic financial and operating decisions relating to the activity require the unanimous consent of the parties sharing control (the venturers).

15.3   A joint venture is a contractual arrangement whereby two or more parties undertake an economic activity that is subject to joint control. Joint ventures can take the form of jointly controlled operations, jointly controlled assets, or jointly controlled entities.

Jointly controlled operations

15.4   The operation of some joint ventures involves the use of the **assets** and other resources of the venturers rather than the establishment of a corporation, partnership or other entity, or a financial structure that is separate from the venturers themselves. Each venturer uses its own **property, plant and equipment** and carries its own **inventories**. It also incurs its own **expenses** and **liabilities** and raises its own finance, which represent its own obligations. The joint venture activities may be carried out by the venturer's employees alongside the venturer's similar activities. The joint venture agreement usually provides a means by which the **revenue** from the sale of the joint product and any expenses incurred in common are shared among the venturers.

15.5   In respect of its interests in jointly controlled operations, a venturer shall recognise in its **financial statements**:

     (a)   the assets that it controls and the liabilities that it incurs; and

     (b)   the expenses that it incurs and its share of the **income** that it earns from the sale of goods or services by the joint venture.

Jointly controlled assets

15.6   Some joint ventures involve the joint control, and often the joint ownership, by the venturers of one or more assets contributed to, or acquired for the purpose of, the joint venture and dedicated to the purposes of the joint venture.

15.7   In respect of its interest in a jointly controlled asset, a venturer shall recognise in its financial statements:

(a)   its share of the jointly controlled assets, classified according to the nature of the assets;

(b)   any liabilities that it has incurred;

(c)   its share of any liabilities incurred jointly with the other venturers in relation to the joint venture;

(d)   any income from the sale or use of its share of the output of the joint venture, together with its share of any expenses incurred by the joint venture; and

(e)   any expenses that it has incurred in respect of its interest in the joint venture.

Jointly controlled entities

15.8   A jointly controlled entity is a joint venture that involves the establishment of a corporation, partnership or other entity in which each venturer has an interest. The entity operates in the same way as other entities, except that a contractual arrangement between the venturers establishes joint control over the economic activity of the entity.

Measurement—accounting policy election

15.9   A venturer that is not a parent but has one or more interests in jointly controlled entities shall, in its individual financial statements, account for all of its interests in jointly controlled entities using either:

(a)   the cost model in accordance with paragraphs 15.10 to 15.11;

(b)   [not used]

(c)   the fair value model in accordance with paragraphs 15.14 to 15.15A; or

(d)   at fair value with changes in fair value recognised in profit or loss (paragraphs 11.27 to 11.32 provide guidance on fair value).

15.9A   A venturer that is a parent shall, in its consolidated financial statements, account for all of its investments in jointly controlled entities using the equity method in accordance with paragraph 15.13, except as required by paragraph 15.9B.

15.9B   A venture that is a parent, shall measure its investments in jointly controlled entities **held as part of an investment portfolio** at **fair value** with changes in fair value recognised in **profit or loss** in the consolidated financial statements.

Cost model

15.10   A venturer that is not a parent, that chooses to adopt the cost model, shall measure its investments in jointly controlled entities, at cost less any accumulated **impairment losses** recognised in accordance with Section 27 *Impairment of Assets*.

15.11   The venturer shall recognise distributions received from the investment as income without regard to whether the distributions are from accumulated profits of the jointly controlled entity arising before or after the date of acquisition.

15.12   [Not used]

Equity method

15.13 A venturer shall measure its investments in jointly controlled entities by the equity method using the procedures in accordance with paragraph 14.8 (substituting 'joint control' where that paragraph refers to 'significant influence', and 'jointly controlled entity' where that paragraph refers to 'associate').

Fair value model

15.14 When an investment in a jointly controlled entity is recognised initially, a venturer that is not a parent, that chooses to adopt the fair value model, shall measure it at the transaction price.

15.15 At each reporting date, a venturer that is not a parent, that chooses to adopt the fair value model, shall measure its investments in jointly controlled entities at fair value using the fair value guidance in paragraphs 11.27 to 11.32. Changes in fair value shall be recognised in accordance with paragraphs 17.15E and 17.15F. A venturer using the fair value model shall use the cost model for any investment in a jointly controlled entity for which it is **impracticable** to measure fair value reliably without undue cost or effort.

15.15A The venturer shall recognise dividends and other distributions received from the investment as income without regard to whether the distributions are from accumulated profits of the jointly controlled entity arising before or after the date of acquisition.

Transactions between a venturer and a joint venture

15.16 When a venturer contributes or sells assets to a joint venture, **recognition** of any portion of a **gain** or loss from the transaction shall reflect the substance of the transaction. While the assets are retained by the joint venture, and provided the venturer has transferred the significant risks and rewards of ownership, the venturer shall recognise only that portion of the gain or loss that is attributable to the interests of the other venturers. The venturer shall recognise the full amount of any loss when the contribution or sale provides evidence of an impairment loss.

15.17 When a venturer purchases assets from a joint venture, the venturer shall not recognise its share of the profits of the joint venture from the transaction until it resells the assets to an independent party. A venturer shall recognise its share of the losses resulting from these transactions in the same way as profits except that losses shall be recognised immediately when they represent an impairment loss.

If investor does not have joint control

15.18 An investor in a joint venture that does not have joint control shall account for that investment in accordance with Section 11 *Basic Financial Instruments* or Section 12 *Other Financial Instruments Issues* or, if it has **significant influence** in the joint venture, in accordance with Section 14 *Investments in Associates*.

Disclosures in individual and consolidated financial statements

15.19 The financial statements shall disclose the following:

(a) the **accounting policy** for recognising investments in jointly controlled entities;

(b) the **carrying amount** of investments in jointly controlled entities;

(c)   the fair value of investments in jointly controlled entities accounted for using the equity method for which there are published price quotations; and

* (d)   the aggregate amount of its commitments relating to joint ventures, including its share in the capital commitments that have been incurred jointly with other venturers, as well as its share of the capital commitments of the joint ventures themselves.

15.20   For jointly controlled entities accounted for in accordance with the equity method, the venturer shall disclose separately its share of the profit or loss of such investments and its share of any **discontinued operations** of such jointly controlled entities.

15.21   For jointly controlled entities accounted for in accordance with the fair value model, the venturer shall make the disclosures required by paragraphs 11.43 and 11.44.

15.21A   The individual financial statements of a venturer that is not a parent shall disclose summarised financial information about the investments in the jointly controlled entities, along with the effect of including those investments as if they had been accounted for using the equity method. Investing entities that are exempt from preparing consolidated financial statements, or would be exempt if they had subsidiaries, are exempt from this requirement.

Section 16
Investment Property

Scope of this section

16.1   This section applies to accounting for investments in land or buildings that meet the definition of **investment property** in paragraph 16.2 and some property interests held by a lessee under an **operating lease** (see paragraph 16.3) that are treated like investment property. Only investment property whose **fair value** can be measured reliably without undue cost or effort on an on-going basis is accounted for in accordance with this section at fair value through **profit or loss**. All other investment property is accounted for as **property, plant and equipment** using the cost model in Section 17 *Property, Plant and Equipment* and remains within the scope of Section 17 unless a reliable measure of fair value becomes available and it is expected that fair value will be reliably measurable on an on-going basis.

Definition and initial recognition of investment property

16.2   Investment property is property (land or a building, or part of a building, or both) held by the owner or by the lessee under a **finance lease** to earn rentals or for capital appreciation or both, rather than for:

   (a)   use in the production or supply of goods or services or for administrative purposes; or

   (b)   sale in the ordinary course of business.

16.3   A property interest that is held by a lessee under an operating lease may be classified and accounted for as investment property using this section if, and only if, the property would otherwise meet the definition of an investment property and the lessee can measure the fair value of the property interest without undue cost or effort on an on-going basis. This classification alternative is available on a property-by-property basis.

16.3A   Property held primarily for the provision of social benefits, eg social housing held by a **public benefit entity**, shall not be classified as investment property and shall be accounted for as property, plant and equipment in accordance with Section 17.

16.4   Mixed use property shall be separated between investment property and property, plant and equipment. However, if the fair value of the investment property component cannot be measured reliably without undue cost or effort, the entire property shall be accounted for as property, plant and equipment in accordance with Section 17.

Measurement at initial recognition

16.5   An entity shall measure investment property at its cost at initial **recognition**. The cost of a purchased investment property comprises its purchase price and any directly attributable expenditure such as legal and brokerage fees, property transfer taxes and other transaction costs. If payment is deferred beyond normal credit terms, the cost is the **present value** of all future payments. An entity shall determine the cost of a self-constructed investment property in accordance with paragraphs 17.10 to 17.14.

16.6   The initial cost of a property interest held under a **lease** and classified as an investment property shall be as prescribed for a finance lease by paragraphs 20.9 and 20.10, even if the lease would otherwise be classified as an operating lease if it was in the scope of Section 20 *Leases*. In other words, the **asset** is recognised at the lower of the fair value of the property and the present value of the **minimum lease payments**. An equivalent amount is recognised as a **liability** in accordance with paragraphs 20.9 and 20.10. Any premium paid for a lease is treated as part of the minimum lease payments for this purpose, and is therefore included in the cost of the asset, but is excluded from the liability.

Measurement after recognition

16.7   Investment property whose fair value can be measured reliably without undue cost or effort shall be measured at fair value at each **reporting date** with changes in fair value recognised in profit or loss. If a property interest held under a lease is classified as investment property, the item accounted for at fair value is that interest and not the underlying property. Paragraphs 11.27 to 11.32 provide guidance on determining fair value. An entity shall account for all other investment property as property, plant and equipment using the cost model in Section 17.

Transfers

16.8   If a reliable measure of fair value is no longer available without undue cost or effort for an item of investment property measured using the fair value model, the entity shall thereafter account for that item as property, plant and equipment in accordance with Section 17 until a reliable measure of fair value becomes available. The **carrying amount** of the investment property on that date becomes its cost under Section 17. Paragraph 16.10(e)(iii) requires disclosure of this change. It is a change of circumstances and not a change in **accounting policy**.

16.9   Other than as required by paragraph 16.8, an entity shall transfer a property to, or from, investment property only when the property first meets, or ceases to meet, the definition of investment property.

Disclosures

16.10   An entity shall disclose the following for all investment property accounted for at fair value through profit or loss (paragraph 16.7):

* (a)   the methods and significant assumptions applied in determining the fair value of investment property;

(b)   the extent to which the fair value of investment property (as measured or disclosed in the **financial statements**) is based on a valuation by an independent valuer who holds a recognised and relevant professional qualification and has recent experience in the location and class of the investment property being valued. If there has been no such valuation, that fact shall be disclosed;

* (c)   the existence and amounts of restrictions on the realisability of investment property or the remittance of **income** and proceeds of disposal;

* (d)   contractual obligations to purchase, construct or develop investment property or for repairs, maintenance or enhancements; and

* (e)   a reconciliation between the carrying amounts of investment property at the beginning and end of the period, showing separately:

(i)   additions, disclosing separately those additions resulting from acquisitions through **business combinations**;

* (ii)   net gains or losses from fair value adjustments;

        (iii)   transfers to property, plant and equipment when a reliable measure of fair value is no longer available without undue cost or effort (see paragraph 16.8);

        (iv)   transfers to and from **inventories** and owner-occupied property; and

        (v)   other changes.

        This reconciliation need not be presented for prior periods.

16.11   In accordance with Section 20 *Leases*, an entity shall provide all relevant disclosures required in that section about leases into which it has entered.

Section 17
Property, Plant and Equipment

Scope

17.1   This section applies to the accounting for **property, plant and equipment** and to **investment property** whose **fair value** cannot be measured reliably without undue cost or effort. Section 16 *Investment Property* applies to investment property whose fair value can be measured reliably without undue cost or effort.

17.2   Property, plant and equipment are tangible assets that:

(a)   are held for use in the production or supply of goods or services, for rental to others, or for administrative purposes; and

(b)   are expected to be used during more than one period;

17.3   Property, plant and equipment does not include:

(a)   **biological assets** related to **agricultural activity** (see Section 34 *Specialised Activities*) or **heritage assets** (see Section 34); or

(b)   mineral rights and mineral reserves, such as oil, natural gas and similar non-regenerative resources (see Section 34).

Recognition

17.4   An entity shall apply the **recognition** criteria in paragraph 2.27 in determining whether to recognise an item of property, plant or equipment. Therefore, the entity shall recognise the cost of an item of property, plant and equipment as an **asset** if, and only if:

(a)   it is **probable** that future economic benefits associated with the item will flow to the entity; and

(b)   the cost of the item can be measured reliably.

17.5   Spare parts and servicing equipment are usually carried as **inventory** and recognised in **profit or loss** as consumed. However, major spare parts and stand-by equipment are property, plant and equipment when an entity expects to use them during more than one period. Similarly, if the spare parts and servicing equipment can be used only in connection with an item of property, plant and equipment, they are considered property, plant and equipment.

17.6   Parts of some items of property, plant and equipment may require replacement at regular intervals (eg the roof of a building). An entity shall add to the **carrying amount** of an item of property, plant and equipment the cost of replacing part of such an item when that cost is incurred if the replacement part is expected to provide incremental future benefits to the entity. The carrying amount of those parts that are replaced is derecognised in accordance with paragraphs 17.27 to 17.30. Paragraph 17.16 provides that if the major components of an item of property, plant and equipment have significantly different patterns of consumption of economic benefits, an entity shall allocate the initial cost of the asset to its major components and depreciate each such component separately over its **useful life**.

17.7   A condition of continuing to operate an item of property, plant and equipment (eg a bus) may be performing regular major inspections for faults regardless of whether parts of the item are replaced. When each major inspection is performed, its cost is recognised in the carrying amount of the item of property, plant and equipment as a replacement if the recognition criteria are satisfied. Any remaining carrying amount of the cost of the previous major inspection (as distinct from physical parts) is derecognised. This is done regardless of whether the cost of the previous major inspection was identified in the transaction in which the item was acquired or constructed. If necessary, the estimated cost of a future similar inspection may be used as an indication of what the cost of the existing inspection component was when the item was acquired or constructed.

17.8   Land and buildings are separable assets, and an entity shall account for them separately, even when they are acquired together.

Measurement at initial recognition

17.9   An entity shall measure an item of property, plant and equipment at initial recognition at its cost.

Elements of cost

17.10   The cost of an item of property, plant and equipment comprises all of the following:

(a)   Its purchase price, including legal and brokerage fees, import duties and non-refundable purchase taxes, after deducting trade discounts and rebates.

(b)   Any costs directly attributable to bringing the asset to the location and condition necessary for it to be capable of operating in the manner intended by management. These can include the costs of site preparation, initial delivery and handling, installation and assembly, and testing of functionality.

(c)   The initial estimate of the costs, recognised and measured in accordance with Section 21 *Provisions and Contingencies,* of dismantling and removing the item and restoring the site on which it is located, the obligation for which an entity incurs either when the item is acquired or as a consequence of having used the item during a particular period for purposes other than to produce inventories during that period.

(d)   Any **borrowing costs** capitalised in accordance with paragraph 25.2.

17.11   The following costs are not costs of an item of property, plant and equipment, and an entity shall recognise them as an **expense** when they are incurred:

(a)   costs of opening a new facility;

(b)   costs of introducing a new product or service (including costs of advertising and promotional activities);

(c)   costs of conducting business in a new location or with a new class of customer (including costs of staff training); and

(d)   administration and other general overhead costs.

17.12   The **income** and related expenses of incidental operations during construction or development of an item of property, plant and equipment are recognised in profit or loss if those operations are not necessary to bring the item to its intended location and operating condition.

Measurement of cost

17.13   The cost of an item of property, plant and equipment is the cash price equivalent at the recognition date. If payment is deferred beyond normal credit terms, the cost is the **present value** of all future payments.

Exchanges of assets

17.14 An item of property, plant or equipment may be acquired in exchange for a non-monetary asset or assets, or a combination of monetary and non-monetary assets. An entity shall measure the cost of the acquired asset at fair value unless:

(a) the exchange transaction lacks commercial substance; or

(b) the fair value of neither the asset received nor the asset given up is reliably measurable. In that case, the asset's cost is measured at the carrying amount of the asset given up.

Measurement after initial recognition

17.15 An entity shall measure all items of property, plant and equipment after initial recognition using the cost model (in accordance with paragraph 17.15A) or the revaluation model (in accordance with paragraphs 17.15B to 17.15F). Where the revaluation model is selected, this shall be applied to all items of property, plant and equipment in the same class (ie having a similar nature, function or use in the business). An entity shall recognise the costs of day-to-day servicing of an item of property, plant and equipment in profit or loss in the period in which the costs are incurred.

Cost model

17.15A Under the cost model, an entity shall measure an item of property, plant and equipment at cost less any accumulated **depreciation** and any accumulated **impairment losses**.

Revaluation model

17.15B Under the revaluation model, an item of property, plant and equipment whose fair value can be measured reliably shall be carried at a revalued amount, being its fair value at the date of revaluation less any subsequent accumulated depreciation and subsequent accumulated impairment losses. Revaluations shall be made with sufficient regularity to ensure that the carrying amount does not differ materially from that which would be determined using fair value at the end of the **reporting period**.

17.15C The fair value of land and buildings is usually determined from market-based evidence by appraisal that is normally undertaken by professionally qualified valuers. The fair value of items of plant and equipment is usually their market value determined by appraisal. Paragraphs 11.27 to 11.32 provide further guidance on determining fair value.

17.15D If there is no market-based evidence of fair value because of the specialised nature of the item of property, plant and equipment and the item is rarely sold, except as part of a continuing business, an entity may need to estimate fair value using an income or a **depreciated replacement cost** approach.

Reporting gains and losses on revaluations

17.15E If an asset's carrying amount is increased as a result of a revaluation, the increase shall be recognised in **other comprehensive income** and accumulated in **equity**. However, the increase shall be recognised in profit or loss to the extent that it reverses a revaluation decrease of the same asset previously recognised in profit or loss.

17.15F The decrease of an asset's carrying amount as a result of a revaluation shall be recognised in other comprehensive income to the extent of any previously recognised revaluation increase accumulated in equity, in respect of that asset. If a revaluation decrease exceeds the accumulated revaluation gains accumulated in equity in respect of that asset, the excess shall be recognised in **profit or loss**.

Depreciation

17.16 If the major components of an item of property, plant and equipment have significantly different patterns of consumption of economic benefits, an entity shall allocate the initial cost of the asset to its major components and depreciate each such component separately over its useful life. Other assets shall be depreciated over their useful lives as a single asset. There are some exceptions, such as land which generally has an unlimited useful life and therefore is not usually depreciated.

17.17 The depreciation charge for each period shall be recognised in profit or loss unless another section of this FRS requires the cost to be recognised as part of the cost of an asset. For example, the depreciation of manufacturing property, plant and equipment is included in the costs of inventories (see Section 13 *Inventories*).

Depreciable amount and depreciation period

17.18 An entity shall allocate the **depreciable amount** of an asset on a systematic basis over its useful life.

17.19 Factors such as a change in how an asset is used, significant unexpected wear and tear, technological advancement, and changes in market prices may indicate that the **residual value** or useful life of an asset has changed since the most recent annual **reporting date**. If such indicators are present, an entity shall review its previous estimates and, if current expectations differ, amend the residual value, depreciation method or useful life. The entity shall account for the change in residual value, depreciation method or useful life as a change in an accounting estimate in accordance with paragraphs 10.15 to 10.18.

17.20 Depreciation of an asset begins when it is available for use, ie when it is in the location and condition necessary for it to be capable of operating in the manner intended by management. Depreciation of an asset ceases when the asset is derecognised. Depreciation does not cease when the asset becomes idle or is retired from active use unless the asset is fully depreciated. However, under usage methods of depreciation the depreciation charge can be zero while there is no production.

17.21 An entity shall consider all the following factors in determining the useful life of an asset:

(a) The expected usage of the asset. Usage is assessed by reference to the asset's expected capacity or physical output.

(b) Expected physical wear and tear, which depends on operational factors such as the number of shifts for which the asset is to be used and the repair and maintenance programme, and the care and maintenance of the asset while idle.

(c) Technical or commercial obsolescence arising from changes or improvements in production, or from a change in the market demand for the product or service output of the asset.

(d) Legal or similar limits on the use of the asset, such as the expiry dates of related **leases**.

Depreciation method

17.22 An entity shall select a depreciation method that reflects the pattern in which it expects to consume the asset's future economic benefits. The possible depreciation methods include the straight-line method, the diminishing balance method and a method based on usage such as the units of production method.

17.23 If there is an indication that there has been a significant change since the last annual reporting date in the pattern by which an entity expects to consume an asset's future economic benefits, the entity shall review its present depreciation method and, if current expectations differ, change the depreciation method to reflect the new pattern. The entity shall account for the change as a change in an accounting estimate in accordance with paragraphs 10.15 to 10.18.

Impairment

Recognition and measurement of impairment

17.24 At each reporting date, an entity shall apply Section 27 *Impairment of Assets* to determine whether an item or group of items of property, plant and equipment is impaired and, if so, how to recognise and measure the impairment loss. That section explains when and how an entity reviews the carrying amount of its assets, how it determines the **recoverable amount** of an asset, and when it recognises or reverses an impairment loss.

Compensation for impairment

17.25 An entity shall include in profit or loss, compensation from third parties for items of property, plant and equipment that were impaired, lost or given up only when the compensation is virtually certain.

Property, plant and equipment held for sale

17.26 Paragraph 27.9(f) states that a plan to dispose of an asset before the previously expected date is an indicator of impairment that triggers the calculation of the asset's recoverable amount for the purpose of determining whether the asset is impaired.

Derecognition

17.27 An entity shall derecognise an item of property, plant and equipment:

(a) on disposal; or

(b) when no future economic benefits are expected from its use or disposal.

17.28 An entity shall recognise the **gain** or loss on the **derecognition** of an item of property, plant and equipment in profit or loss when the item is derecognised (unless Section 20 *Leases* requires otherwise on a sale and leaseback). The entity shall not classify such gains as **revenue**.

17.29 In determining the date of disposal of an item, an entity shall apply the criteria in Section 23 *Revenue* for recognising revenue from the sale of goods. Section 20 applies to disposal by a sale and leaseback.

17.30 An entity shall determine the gain or loss arising from the derecognition of an item of property, plant and equipment as the difference between the net disposal proceeds, if any, and the carrying amount of the item.

Disclosures

17.31   An entity shall disclose the following for each class of property, plant and equipment:

* (a)   the measurement bases used for determining the gross carrying amount;

(b)   the depreciation methods used;

(c)   the useful lives or the depreciation rates used;

* (d)   the gross carrying amount and the accumulated depreciation (aggregated with accumulated impairment losses) at the beginning and end of the reporting period;

* (e)   a reconciliation of the carrying amount at the beginning and end of the reporting period showing separately:

(i)   additions;

(ii)   disposals;

(iii)   acquisitions through **business combinations**;

(iv)   revaluations;

(v)   transfers to or from investment property if a reliable measure of fair value becomes available or unavailable (see paragraph 16.8);

(vi)   impairment losses recognised or reversed in profit or loss in accordance with Section 27 *Impairment of Assets*;

(vii)   depreciation; and

(viii) other changes.

This reconciliation need not be presented for prior periods.

17.32   The entity shall also disclose the following:

* (a)   the existence and carrying amounts of property, plant and equipment to which the entity has restricted title or that is pledged as security for **liabilities**; and

* (b)   the amount of contractual commitments for the acquisition of property, plant and equipment.

17.32A   If items of property, plant and equipment are stated at revalued amounts, the following shall be disclosed:

* (a)   the effective date of the revaluation;

(b)   whether an independent valuer was involved;

* (c)   the methods and significant assumptions applied in estimating the items' fair values; and

* (d)   for each revalued class of property, plant and equipment, the carrying amount that would have been recognised had the assets been carried under the cost model.

Section 18
Intangible Assets other than Goodwill

Scope of this section

18.1 This section applies to accounting for all **intangible assets** other than **goodwill** (see Section 19 *Business Combinations and Goodwill*) and intangible assets held by an entity for sale in the ordinary course of business (see Section 13 *Inventories* and Section 23 *Revenue*).

18.1A This section does not apply to the accounting for **deferred acquisition costs** and intangible assets arising from contracts in the scope of FRS 103 *Insurance Contracts*, except for the disclosure requirements in this section which apply to intangible assets arising from contracts in the scope of FRS 103.

18.2 An intangible asset is an identifiable non-monetary asset without physical substance. Such an **asset** is identifiable when:

(a) it is separable, ie capable of being separated or divided from the entity and sold, transferred, licensed, rented or exchanged, either individually or together with a related contract, asset or **liability**; or

(b) it arises from contractual or other legal rights, regardless of whether those rights are transferable or separable from the entity or from other rights and obligations.

18.3 This section does not apply to the following:

(a) **financial assets** (see Section 11 *Basic Financial Instruments* and Section 12 *Other Financial Instruments Issues*);

(b) **heritage assets** (see Section 34 *Specialised Activities*); or

(c) mineral rights and mineral reserves, such as oil, natural gas and similar non-regenerative resources (see Section 34).

Recognition

General principle for recognising intangible assets

18.4 An entity shall apply the **recognition** criteria in paragraph 2.27 in determining whether to recognise an intangible asset. Therefore, the entity shall recognise an intangible asset as an asset if, and only if:

(a) it is **probable** that the expected future economic benefits that are attributable to the asset will flow to the entity; and

(b) the cost or value of the asset can be measured reliably.

18.5 An entity shall assess the probability of expected future economic benefits using reasonable and supportable assumptions that represent management's best estimate of the economic conditions that will exist over the **useful life** of the asset.

18.6 An entity uses judgement to assess the degree of certainty attached to the flow of future economic benefits that are attributable to the use of the asset on the basis of the evidence available at the time of initial recognition, giving greater weight to external evidence.

18.7 The probability recognition criterion in paragraph 18.4(a) is always considered satisfied for intangible assets that are separately acquired.

Acquisition as part of a business combination

18.8 An intangible asset acquired in a **business combination** is normally recognised as an asset because its **fair value** can be measured with sufficient **reliability**. However, an intangible asset acquired in a business combination is not recognised when it arises from legal or other contractual rights and there is no history or evidence of exchange transactions for the same or similar assets, and otherwise estimating fair value would be dependent on immeasurable variables.

Internally generated intangible assets

18.8A To assess whether an internally generated intangible asset meets the criteria for recognition, an entity classifies the generation of the asset into:

(a) a **research** phase; and

(b) a **development** phase.

18.8B If an entity cannot distinguish the research phase from the development phase of an internal project to create an intangible asset, the entity treats the expenditure on that project as if it were incurred in the research phase only.

18.8C An entity shall recognise expenditure on the following items as an **expense** and shall not recognise such expenditure as intangible assets:

(a) Internally generated brands, logos, publishing titles, customer lists and items similar in substance.

(b) Start-up activities (ie start-up costs), which include establishment costs such as legal and secretarial costs incurred in establishing a legal entity, expenditure to open a new facility or business (ie pre-opening costs) and expenditure for starting new operations or launching new products or processes (ie pre-operating costs).

(c) Training activities.

(d) Advertising and promotional activities (unless it meets the definition of **inventories held for distribution at no or nominal consideration** (see paragraph 13.4A)).

(e) Relocating or reorganising part or all of an entity.

(f) Internally generated goodwill.

18.8D Paragraph 18.8C does not preclude recognising a prepayment as an asset when payment for goods or services has been made in advance of the delivery of the goods or the rendering of the services.

Research phase

18.8E No intangible asset arising from research (or from the research phase of an internal project) shall be recognised. Expenditure on research (or on the research phase of an internal project) shall be recognised as an expense when it is incurred.

18.8F In the research phase of an internal project, an entity cannot demonstrate that an intangible asset exists that will generate probable future economic benefits.

18.8G Examples of research activities are:

(a) Activities aimed at obtaining new knowledge.

(b) The search for, evaluation and final selection of, applications of research findings and other knowledge.

(c) The search for alternatives for materials, devices, products, processes, systems or services.

(d) The formulation, design, evaluation and final selection of possible alternatives for new or improved material, devices, projects, processes, systems or services.

Development phase

18.8H An entity may recognise an intangible asset arising from development (or from the development phase of an internal project) if, and only if, an entity can demonstrate all of the following:

(a) The technical feasibility of completing the intangible asset so that it will be available for use or sale.

(b) Its intention to complete the intangible asset and use or sell it.

(c) Its ability to use or sell the intangible asset.

(d) How the intangible asset will generate probable future economic benefits. Among other things, the entity can demonstrate the existence of a market for the output of the intangible asset or the intangible asset itself or, if it is to be used internally, the usefulness of the intangible asset.

(e) The availability of adequate technical, financial and other resources to complete the development and to use or sell the intangible asset.

(f) Its ability to measure reliably the expenditure attributable to the intangible asset during its development.

18.8I In the development phase of an internal project, an entity can, in some instances, identify an intangible asset and demonstrate that the asset will generate probable future economic benefits. This is because the development phase of a project is further advanced than the research phase.

18.8J Examples of development activities are:

(a) The design, construction and testing of pre-production or pre-use prototypes and models.

(b) The design of tools, jigs, moulds and dies involving new technology.

(c) The design, construction and operation of a pilot plant that is not of a scale economically feasible for commercial production.

(d) The design, construction and testing of a chosen alternative for new or improved materials, devices, products, processes, systems or services.

18.8K Where an entity adopts a policy of capitalising expenditure in the development phase that meets the conditions of paragraph 18.8H, that policy shall be applied consistently to all expenditure that meets the requirements of paragraph 18.8H. Expenditure that does not meet the conditions of paragraph 18.8H is expensed as incurred.

Initial measurement

18.9 An entity shall measure an intangible asset initially at cost.

Separate acquisition

18.10 The cost of a separately acquired intangible asset comprises:

(a) its purchase price, including import duties and non-refundable purchase taxes, after deducting trade discounts and rebates; and

(b)   any directly attributable cost of preparing the asset for its intended use.

Internally generated intangible assets

18.10A   The cost of an internally generated intangible asset for the purpose of paragraph 18.9 is the sum of expenditure incurred from the date when the intangible asset first meets the recognition criteria in paragraphs 18.4 and 18.8H.

18.10B   The cost of an internally generated intangible asset comprises all directly attributable costs necessary to create, produce and prepare the asset to be capable of operating in the manner intended by management. Examples of directly attributable costs are:

(a)   costs of materials and services used or consumed in generating the intangible asset;

(b)   costs of **employee benefits** (as defined in Section 28 *Employee Benefits*) arising from the generation of the intangible asset;

(c)   fees to register a legal right; and

(d)   **amortisation** of patents and licences that are used to generate the intangible asset.

Section 25 *Borrowing Costs* specifies criteria for the recognition of interest as an element of the cost of an internally generated intangible asset.

Acquisition as part of a business combination

18.11   If an intangible asset is acquired in a business combination, the cost of that intangible asset is its fair value at the **acquisition date**.

Acquisition by way of a grant

18.12   If an intangible asset is acquired by way of a grant, the cost of that intangible asset is its fair value at the date the grant is received or receivable in accordance with Section 24 *Government Grants*.

Exchanges of assets

18.13   An intangible asset may be acquired in exchange for a non-monetary asset or assets, or a combination of monetary and non-monetary assets. An entity shall measure the cost of such an intangible asset at fair value unless:

(a)   the exchange transaction lacks commercial substance; or

(b)   the fair value of neither the asset received nor the asset given up is reliably measurable. In that case, the asset's cost is measured at the **carrying amount** of the asset given up.

18.14   [Replaced by paragraph 18.8A]

18.15   [Moved to paragraph 18.8C]

18.16   [Moved to paragraph 18.8D]

Past expenses not to be recognised as an asset

18.17   Expenditure on an intangible item that was initially recognised as an expense shall not be recognised at a later date as part of the cost of an asset.

Measurement after initial recognition

18.18   An entity shall measure intangible assets after initial recognition using the cost model (in accordance with paragraph 18.18A) or the revaluation model (in accordance with paragraphs 18.18B to 18.18H). Where the revaluation model is selected, this shall be applied to all intangible assets in the same class. If an intangible asset in a class of revalued intangible assets cannot be revalued because there is no **active market** for this asset, the asset shall be carried at its cost less any accumulated amortisation and impairment losses.

Cost model

18.18A   Under the cost model, an entity shall measure its assets at cost less any accumulated amortisation and any accumulated **impairment losses**. The requirements for amortisation are set out in paragraphs 18.19 to 18.24.

Revaluation model

18.18B   Under the revaluation model, an intangible asset shall be carried at a revalued amount, being its fair value at the date of revaluation less any subsequent accumulated amortisation and subsequent accumulated impairment losses, provided that the fair value can be determined by reference to an active market. The requirements for amortisation are set out in paragraphs 18.19 to 18.24.

18.18C   The revaluation model does not allow:

(a)   the revaluation of intangible assets that have not previously been recognised as assets; or

(b)   the initial recognition of intangible assets at amounts other than cost.

18.18D   Revaluations shall be made with sufficient regularity to ensure that the carrying amount does not differ materially from that which would be determined using fair value at the end of the **reporting period**.

18.18E   If the fair value of a revalued intangible asset can no longer be determined by reference to an active market in accordance with the requirements of paragraph 18.18B, the carrying amount of the asset shall be its revalued amount at the date of the last revaluation by reference to the active market, less any subsequent accumulated amortisation and any subsequent accumulated impairment losses.

18.18F   The revaluation model is applied after an asset has been initially recognised at cost. However, if only part of the cost of an intangible asset is recognised as an asset because the asset did not meet the criteria for recognition until part of the way through the process (see paragraph 18.10A), the revaluation model may be applied to the whole of that asset.

Reporting gains and losses on revaluations

18.18G   If an asset's carrying amount is increased as a result of a revaluation, the increase shall be recognised in **other comprehensive income** and accumulated in **equity**. However, the increase shall be recognised in **profit or loss** to the extent that it reverses a revaluation decrease of the same asset previously recognised in profit or loss.

18.18H   The decrease of an asset's carrying amount as a result of a revaluation shall be recognised in other comprehensive income to the extent of any previously recognised revaluation increase accumulated in equity, in respect of that asset. If a revaluation decrease exceeds the accumulated revaluation gains recognised in equity in respect of that asset, the excess shall be recognised in profit or loss.

Amortisation over useful life

18.19   For the purpose of this FRS, all intangible assets shall be considered to have a finite useful life. The useful life of an intangible asset that arises from contractual or other legal rights shall not exceed the period of the contractual or other legal rights, but may be shorter depending on the period over which the entity expects to use the asset. If the contractual or other legal rights are conveyed for a limited term that can be renewed, the useful life of the intangible asset shall include the renewal period(s) only if there is evidence to support renewal by the entity without significant cost.

18.20   If, in exceptional cases, an entity is unable to make a reliable estimate of the useful life of an intangible asset, the life shall not exceed 10 years.

Amortisation period and amortisation method

18.21   An entity shall allocate the **depreciable amount** of an intangible asset on a systematic basis over its useful life. The amortisation charge for each period shall be recognised in profit or loss, unless another section of this FRS requires the cost to be recognised as part of the cost of an asset. For example, the amortisation of an intangible asset may be included in the costs of **inventories** or **property, plant and equipment**.

18.22   Amortisation begins when the intangible asset is available for use, ie when it is in the location and condition necessary for it to be usable in the manner intended by management. Amortisation ceases when the asset is derecognised. The entity shall choose an amortisation method that reflects the pattern in which it expects to consume the asset's future economic benefits. If the entity cannot determine that pattern reliably, it shall use the straight-line method.

Residual value

18.23   An entity shall assume that the **residual value** of an intangible asset is zero unless:

    (a)   there is a commitment by a third party to purchase the asset at the end of its useful life; or

    (b)   there is an active market for the asset and:

        (i)   residual value can be determined by reference to that market; and

        (ii)   it is probable that such a market will exist at the end of the asset's useful life.

Review of amortisation period and amortisation method

18.24   Factors such as a change in how an intangible asset is used, technological advancement, and changes in market prices may indicate that the residual value or useful life of an intangible asset has changed since the most recent annual **reporting date**. If such indicators are present, an entity shall review its previous estimates and, if current expectations differ, amend the residual value, amortisation method or useful life. The entity shall account for the change in residual value, amortisation method or useful life as a change in an accounting estimate in accordance with paragraphs 10.15 to 10.18.

Recoverability of the carrying amount—impairment losses

18.25   To determine whether an intangible asset is impaired, an entity shall apply Section 27 *Impairment of Assets*. That section explains when and how an entity reviews the carrying amount of its assets, how it determines the **recoverable amount** of an asset, and when it recognises or reverses an impairment loss.

Retirements and disposals

18.26   An entity shall derecognise an intangible asset, and shall recognise a **gain** or loss in profit or loss:

(a)   on disposal; or

(b)   when no future economic benefits are expected from its use or disposal.

Disclosures

18.27   An entity shall disclose the following for each class of intangible assets:

* (a)   the useful lives or the amortisation rates used and the reasons for choosing those periods;

(b)   the amortisation methods used;

* (c)   the gross carrying amount and any accumulated amortisation (aggregated with accumulated impairment losses) at the beginning and end of the reporting period;

(d)   the line item(s) in the **statement of comprehensive income** (or in the **income statement**, if presented) in which any amortisation of intangible assets is included; and

* (e)   a reconciliation of the carrying amount at the beginning and end of the reporting period showing separately:

(i)   additions, indicating separately those from internal development and those acquired separately;

(ii)   disposals;

(iii)   acquisitions through business combinations;

(iv)   revaluations;

(v)   amortisation;

(vi)   impairment losses; and

(vii)   other changes.

This reconciliation need not be presented for prior periods.

18.28   An entity shall also disclose:

(a)   a description, the carrying amount and remaining amortisation period of any individual intangible asset that is **material** to the entity's **financial statements**;

(b)   for intangible assets acquired by way of a grant and initially recognised at fair value (see paragraph 18.12):

(i)   the fair value initially recognised for these assets; and

(ii)   their carrying amounts.

* (c)   the existence and carrying amounts of intangible assets to which the entity has restricted title or that are pledged as security for liabilities; and

* (d)   the amount of contractual commitments for the acquisition of intangible assets.

18.29   An entity shall disclose the aggregate amount of research and development expenditure recognised as an expense during the period (ie the amount of expenditure incurred internally on research and development that has not been capitalised as an intangible asset or as part of the cost of another asset that meets the recognition criteria in this FRS).

18.29A   If intangible assets are accounted for at revalued amounts, an entity shall disclose the following:

* (a)   the effective date of the revaluation;

(b)   whether an independent valuer was involved;

* (c)   the methods and significant assumptions applied in estimating the assets' fair values; and

* (d)   for each revalued class of intangible assets, the carrying amount that would have been recognised had the assets been carried under the cost model.

Section 19
Business Combinations and Goodwill

Scope of this section

19.1   This section applies to accounting for **business combinations**. It provides guidance on identifying the acquirer, measuring the cost of the business combination, and allocating that cost to the **assets** acquired and **liabilities** and **provisions** for **contingent liabilities** assumed. It also addresses accounting for **goodwill** both at the time of a business combination and subsequently.

19.2   This section specifies the accounting for all business combinations except:

     (a)   the formation of a **joint venture**; and

     (b)   acquisition of a group of assets that does not constitute a **business**.

PBE19.2A   In addition, **public benefit entities** shall consider the requirements of Section 34 *Specialised Activities* in accounting for **public benefit entity combinations**.

Business combinations defined

19.3   A business combination is the bringing together of separate entities or businesses into one reporting entity. The result of nearly all business combinations is that one entity, the acquirer, obtains **control** of one or more other businesses, the acquiree. The **acquisition date** is the date on which the acquirer obtains control of the acquiree.

19.4   A business combination may be structured in a variety of ways for legal, taxation or other reasons. It may involve the purchase by an entity of the **equity** of another entity, the purchase of all the net assets of another entity, the assumption of the liabilities of another entity, or the purchase of some of the net assets of another entity that together form one or more businesses.

19.5   A business combination may be effected by the issue of equity instruments, the transfer of **cash**, **cash equivalents** or other assets, or a mixture of these. The transaction may be between the shareholders of the combining entities or between one entity and the shareholders of another entity. It may involve the establishment of a new entity to control the combining entities or net assets transferred, or the restructuring of one or more of the combining entities.

Purchase method

19.6   All business combinations shall be accounted for by applying the purchase method, except for:

     (a)   **group reconstructions** which may be accounted for by using the merger accounting method (see paragraphs 19.27 to 19.33); and

     (b)   public benefit entity **combinations that are in substance a gift** or that are a **merger** which shall be accounted for in accordance with Section 34 *Specialised Activities*.

19.7   Applying the purchase method involves the following steps:

     (a)   identifying an acquirer;

     (b)   measuring the cost of the business combination; and

(c) allocating, at the acquisition date, the cost of the business combination to the assets acquired and liabilities and provisions for contingent liabilities assumed.

Identifying the acquirer

19.8 An acquirer shall be identified for all business combinations accounted for by applying the purchase method. The acquirer is the combining entity that obtains control of the other combining entities or businesses.

19.9 Control is the power to govern the financial and operating policies of an entity or business so as to obtain benefits from its activities. Control of one entity by another is described in Section 9 *Consolidated and Separate Financial Statements*.

19.10 Although it may sometimes be difficult to identify an acquirer, there are usually indications that one exists. For example:

(a) If the **fair value** of one of the combining entities is significantly greater than that of the other combining entity, the entity with the greater fair value is likely to be the acquirer.

(b) If the business combination is effected through an exchange of voting ordinary equity instruments for cash or other assets, the entity giving up cash or other assets is likely to be the acquirer.

(c) If the business combination results in the management of one of the combining entities being able to dominate the selection of the management team of the resulting combined entity, the entity whose management is able so to dominate is likely to be the acquirer.

Cost of a business combination

19.11 The acquirer shall measure the cost of a business combination as the aggregate of:

(a) the fair values, at the acquisition date, of assets given, liabilities incurred or assumed, and equity instruments issued by the acquirer, in exchange for control of the acquiree; plus

(b) any costs directly attributable to the business combination.

19.11A Where control is achieved following a series of transactions, the cost of the business combination is the aggregate of the fair values of the assets given, liabilities assumed and equity instruments issued by the acquirer at the date of each transaction in the series.

Adjustments to the cost of a business combination contingent on future events

19.12 When a business combination agreement provides for an adjustment to the cost of the combination contingent on future events, the acquirer shall include the estimated amount of that adjustment in the cost of the combination at the acquisition date if the adjustment is **probable** and can be measured reliably.

19.13 However, if the potential adjustment is not recognised at the acquisition date but subsequently becomes probable and can be measured reliably, the additional consideration shall be treated as an adjustment to the cost of the combination.

Allocating the cost of a business combination to the assets acquired and liabilities and contingent liabilities assumed

19.14 The acquirer shall, at the acquisition date, allocate the cost of a business combination by recognising the acquiree's identifiable assets and liabilities and a provision for those contingent liabilities (that satisfy the **recognition** criteria in paragraph 19.20) at their fair values at that date, except for the items specified in paragraphs 19.15A to 19.15C. Any difference between the cost of the business combination and the acquirer's interest in the net amount of the identifiable assets, liabilities and provisions for contingent liabilities so recognised shall be accounted for in accordance with paragraphs 19.22 to 19.24.

19.15   Except for the items specified in paragraphs 19.15A to 19.15C, the acquirer shall recognise separately the acquiree's identifiable assets, liabilities and contingent liabilities at the acquisition date only if they satisfy the following criteria at that date:

(a)   In the case of an asset other than an **intangible asset**, it is probable that any associated future economic benefits will flow to the acquirer, and its fair value can be measured reliably.

(b)   In the case of a liability other than a contingent liability, it is probable that an outflow of resources will be required to settle the obligation, and its fair value can be measured reliably.

(c)   In the case of an intangible asset or a contingent liability, its fair value can be measured reliably.

19.15A   The acquirer shall recognise and measure a **deferred tax asset** or **liability** arising from the assets acquired and liabilities assumed in accordance with Section 29 *Income Tax.*

19.15B   The acquirer shall recognise and measure a liability (or asset, if any) related to the acquiree's employee benefit arrangements in accordance with Section 28 *Employee Benefits.*

19.15C   The acquirer shall recognise and measure a share-based payment in accordance with Section 26 *Share-based Payment.*

19.16   The acquirer's **statement of comprehensive income** shall incorporate the acquiree's profits or losses after the acquisition date by including the acquiree's **income** and **expenses** based on the cost of the business combination to the acquirer. For example, depreciation expense included after the acquisition date in the acquirer's statement of comprehensive income that relates to the acquiree's depreciable assets shall be based on the fair values of those depreciable assets at the acquisition date, ie their cost to the acquirer.

19.17   Application of the purchase method starts from the acquisition date, which is the date on which the acquirer obtains control of the acquiree. Because control is the power to govern the financial and operating policies of an entity or business so as to obtain benefits from its activities, it is not necessary for a transaction to be closed or finalised at law before the acquirer obtains control. All pertinent facts and circumstances surrounding a business combination shall be considered in assessing when the acquirer has obtained control.

19.18   In accordance with paragraph 19.14, the acquirer recognises separately only the identifiable assets, liabilities and contingent liabilities of the acquiree that existed at the acquisition date and satisfy the recognition criteria in paragraph 19.15 (except for the items specified in paragraphs 19.15A to 19.15C). Therefore:

(a)   the acquirer shall recognise liabilities for terminating or reducing the activities of the acquiree as part of allocating the cost of the combination only to the extent that the acquiree has, at the acquisition date, an existing liability for restructuring recognised in accordance with Section 21 *Provisions and Contingencies*; and

(b)   the acquirer, when allocating the cost of the combination, shall not recognise liabilities for future losses or other costs expected to be incurred as a result of the business combination.

19.19   If the initial accounting for a business combination is incomplete by the end of the **reporting period** in which the combination occurs, the acquirer shall recognise in its **financial statements** provisional amounts for the items for which the accounting is incomplete. Within twelve months after the acquisition date, the acquirer shall retrospectively adjust the provisional amounts recognised as assets and liabilities at the acquisition date (ie account for them as if they were made at the acquisition date) to reflect new information obtained. Beyond twelve months after the acquisition date, adjustments to the initial accounting for a business combination shall be recognised only to correct a **material error** in accordance with Section 10 *Accounting Policies, Estimates and Errors*.

Contingent liabilities

19.20   Paragraph 19.15(c) specifies that the acquirer recognises separately a provision for a contingent liability of the acquiree only if its fair value can be measured reliably. If its fair value cannot be measured reliably:

(a)   there is a resulting effect on the amount recognised as goodwill or the amount accounted for in accordance with paragraph 19.24; and

(b)   the acquirer shall disclose the information about that contingent liability as required by Section 21.

19.21   After their initial recognition, the acquirer shall measure contingent liabilities that are recognised separately in accordance with paragraph 19.15(c) at the higher of:

(a)   the amount that would be recognised in accordance with Section 21; and

(b)   the amount initially recognised less amounts previously recognised as **revenue** in accordance with Section 23 *Revenue*.

Goodwill

19.22   The acquirer shall, at the acquisition date:

(a)   recognise goodwill acquired in a business combination as an asset; and

(b)   initially measure that goodwill at its cost, being the excess of the cost of the business combination over the acquirer's interest in the net amount of the identifiable assets, liabilities and contingent liabilities recognised and measured in accordance with paragraphs 19.15, 19.15A to 19.15C.

19.23   After initial recognition, the acquirer shall measure goodwill acquired in a business combination at cost less accumulated **amortisation** and accumulated **impairment losses**:

(a)   An entity shall follow the principles in paragraphs 18.19 to 18.24 for amortisation of goodwill. Goodwill shall be considered to have a finite **useful life**, and shall be amortised on a systematic basis over its life. If, in exceptional cases, an entity is unable to make a reliable estimate of the useful life of goodwill, the life shall not exceed 10 years.

(b)   An entity shall follow Section 27 *Impairment of Assets* for recognising and measuring the impairment of goodwill.

Excess over cost of acquirer's interest in the net fair value of acquiree's identifiable assets, liabilities and contingent liabilities

19.24 If the acquirer's interest in the net amount of the identifiable assets, liabilities and provisions for contingent liabilities recognised in accordance with paragraph 19.14 exceeds the cost of the business combination (also referred to as 'negative goodwill'), the acquirer shall:

(a) Reassess the identification and **measurement** of the acquiree's assets, liabilities and provisions for contingent liabilities and the measurement of the cost of the combination.

(b) Recognise and separately disclose the resulting excess on the face of the **statement of financial position** on the acquisition date, immediately below goodwill, and followed by a subtotal of the net amount of goodwill and the excess.

(c) Recognise subsequently the excess up to the fair value of non-monetary assets acquired in profit or loss in the periods in which the non-monetary assets are recovered. Any excess exceeding the fair value of non-monetary assets acquired shall be recognised in profit or loss in the periods expected to be benefited.

Disclosures

For business combinations effected during the reporting period

19.25 For each business combination, excluding any group reconstructions, that was effected during the period, the acquirer shall disclose the following:

(a) the names and descriptions of the combining entities or businesses;

(b) the acquisition date;

(c) the percentage of voting equity instruments acquired;

(d) the cost of the combination and a description of the components of that cost (such as cash, equity instruments and debt instruments);

(e) the amounts recognised at the acquisition date for each class of the acquiree's assets, liabilities and contingent liabilities, including goodwill;

(f) [not used]

* (g) the useful life of goodwill, and if this cannot be reliably estimated, supporting reasons for the period chosen; and

(h) the periods in which the excess recognised in accordance with paragraph 19.24 will be recognised in profit or loss.

19.25A The acquirer shall disclose, separately for each material business combination that occurred during the reporting period, the amounts of revenue and profit or loss of the acquiree since the acquisition date included in the consolidated statement of comprehensive income for the reporting period. The disclosure may be provided in aggregate for business combinations that occurred during the reporting period which, individually, are not material.

For all business combinations

* 19.26 An acquirer shall disclose a reconciliation of the **carrying amount** of goodwill at the beginning and end of the reporting period, showing separately:

(a) changes arising from new business combinations;

(b) amortisation;

(c) impairment losses;

(d) disposals of previously acquired businesses; and

(e) other changes.

This reconciliation need not be presented for prior periods.

19.26A An acquirer shall disclose a reconciliation of the carrying amount of the excess recognised in accordance with paragraph 19.24 at the beginning and end of the reporting period, showing separately:

(a) changes arising from new business combinations;

(b) amounts recognised in profit or loss in accordance with paragraph 19.24(c);

(c) disposals of previously acquired businesses; and

(d) other changes.

This reconciliation need not be presented for prior periods.

Group reconstructions

19.27 Group reconstructions may be accounted for by using the merger accounting method provided:

(a) the use of the merger accounting method is not prohibited by company law or other relevant legislation;

(b) the ultimate equity holders remain the same, and the rights of each equity holder, relative to the others, are unchanged; and

(c) no **non-controlling interest** in the net assets of the **group** is altered by the transfer.

Applicability to various structures of business combinations

19.28 The provisions of paragraphs 19.29 to 19.33, which are explained by reference to an acquirer or issuing entity that issues shares as consideration for the transfer to it of shares in the other parties to the combination, should also be read so as to apply to other arrangements that achieve similar results.

Merger accounting method

19.29 With the merger accounting method the carrying values of the assets and liabilities of the parties to the combination are not required to be adjusted to fair value, although appropriate adjustments shall be made to achieve uniformity of **accounting policies** in the combining entities.

19.30 The results and cash flows of all the combining entities shall be brought into the financial statements of the combined entity from the beginning of the financial year in which the combination occurred, adjusted so as to achieve uniformity of accounting policies. The comparative information shall be restated by including the **total comprehensive income** for all the combining entities for the previous reporting period and their statement of financial position for the previous **reporting date**, adjusted as necessary to achieve uniformity of accounting policies.

19.31 The difference, if any, between the nominal value of the shares issued plus the fair value of any other consideration given, and the nominal value of the shares received in exchange shall be shown as a movement on other reserves in the **consolidated**

financial statements. Any existing balances on the share premium account or capital redemption reserve of the new subsidiary shall be brought in by being shown as a movement on other reserves. These movements shall be shown in the **statement of changes in equity**.

19.32   Merger expenses are not to be included as part of this adjustment, but shall be charged to the statement of comprehensive income as part of profit or loss of the combined entity at the effective date of the group reconstruction.

Disclosures

19.33   For each group reconstruction, that was effected during the period, the combined entity shall disclose the following:

(a)   the names of the combining entities (other than the reporting entity);

(b)   whether the combination has been accounted for as an acquisition or a merger; and

(c)   the date of the combination.

Section 20
Leases

Scope of this section

20.1 This section covers accounting for all **leases** other than:

(a) leases to explore for or use minerals, oil, natural gas and similar non-regenerative resources (see Section 34 *Specialised Activities*);

(b) licensing agreements for such items as motion picture films, video recordings, plays, manuscripts, patents and copyrights (see Section 18 *Intangible Assets other than Goodwill*);

(c) **measurement** of property held by lessees that is accounted for as **investment property** and measurement of investment property provided by lessors under **operating leases** (see Section 16 *Investment Property*);

(d) measurement of **biological assets** held by lessees under **finance leases** and biological assets provided by lessors under operating leases (see Section 34); and

(e) leases that could lead to a loss to the lessor or the lessee as a result of non-typical contractual terms (see paragraph 12.3(f)).

(f) [not used]

20.2 This section applies to agreements that transfer the right to use **assets** even though substantial services by the lessor may be called for in connection with the operation or maintenance of such assets. This section does not apply to agreements that are contracts for services that do not transfer the right to use assets from one contracting party to the other.

20.3 Some arrangements do not take the legal form of a lease but convey rights to use assets in return for payments. Examples of arrangements in which one entity (the supplier) may convey a right to use an asset to another entity (the purchaser), often together with related services, may include outsourcing arrangements, telecommunication contracts that provide rights to capacity and take-or-pay contracts.

20.3A Determining whether an arrangement is, or contains, a lease shall be based on the substance of the arrangement and requires an assessment of whether:

(a) fulfilment of the arrangement is dependent on the use of a specific asset or assets. Although a specific asset may be explicitly identified in an arrangement, it is not the subject of a lease if fulfilment of the arrangement is not dependent on the use of the specified asset. An asset is implicitly specified if, for example, the supplier owns or leases only one asset with which to fulfil the obligation and it is not economically feasible or practicable for the supplier to perform its obligation through the use of alternative assets; and

(b) the arrangement conveys a right to use the asset. This will be the case where the arrangement conveys to the purchaser the right to control the use of the underlying asset.

Classification of leases

20.4 A lease is classified as a finance lease if it transfers substantially all the risks and rewards incidental to ownership. A lease is classified as an operating lease if it does not transfer substantially all the risks and rewards incidental to ownership.

20.5   Whether a lease is a finance lease or an operating lease depends on the substance of the transaction rather than the form of the contract. Examples of situations that individually or in combination would normally lead to a lease being classified as a finance lease are:

(a)   the lease transfers ownership of the asset to the lessee by the end of the **lease term**;

(b)   the lessee has the option to purchase the asset at a price that is expected to be sufficiently lower than the **fair value** at the date the option becomes exercisable for it to be reasonably certain, at the **inception of the lease**, that the option will be exercised;

(c)   the lease term is for the major part of the economic life of the asset even if title is not transferred;

(d)   at the inception of the lease the **present value** of the **minimum lease payments** amounts to at least substantially all of the fair value of the leased asset; and

(e)   the leased assets are of such a specialised nature that only the lessee can use them without major modifications.

20.6   Indicators of situations that individually or in combination could also lead to a lease being classified as a finance lease are:

(a)   if the lessee can cancel the lease, the lessor's losses associated with the cancellation are borne by the lessee;

(b)   **gains** or losses from the fluctuation in the **residual value** of the leased asset accrue to the lessee (eg in the form of a rent rebate equalling most of the sales proceeds at the end of the lease); and

(c)   the lessee has the ability to continue the lease for a secondary period at a rent that is substantially lower than market rent.

20.7   The examples and indicators in paragraphs 20.5 and 20.6 are not always conclusive. If it is clear from other features that the lease does not transfer substantially all risks and rewards incidental to ownership, the lease is classified as an operating lease. For example, this may be the case if ownership of the asset is transferred to the lessee at the end of the lease for a variable payment equal to the asset's then fair value, or if there are **contingent rents**, as a result of which the lessee does not have substantially all risks and rewards incidental to ownership.

20.8   Lease classification is made at the inception of the lease and is not changed during the term of the lease unless the lessee and the lessor agree to change the provisions of the lease (other than simply by renewing the lease), in which case the lease classification shall be re-evaluated.

Financial statements of lessees: finance leases

Initial recognition

20.9   At the **commencement of the lease term**, a lessee shall recognise its rights of use and obligations under finance leases as assets and **liabilities** in its **statement of financial position** at amounts equal to the fair value of the leased asset or, if lower, the present value of the minimum lease payments, determined at the inception of the lease. Any initial direct costs of the lessee (incremental costs that are directly attributable to negotiating and arranging a lease) are added to the amount recognised as an asset.

20.10 The present value of the minimum lease payments shall be calculated using the **interest rate implicit in the lease**. If this cannot be determined, the **lessee's incremental borrowing rate** shall be used.

Subsequent measurement

20.11 A lessee shall apportion minimum lease payments between the finance charge and the reduction of the outstanding liability using the **effective interest method** (see paragraphs 11.15 to 11.20). The lessee shall allocate the finance charge to each period during the lease term so as to produce a constant periodic rate of interest on the remaining balance of the liability. A lessee shall charge contingent rents as **expenses** in the periods in which they are incurred.

20.12 A lessee shall depreciate an asset leased under a finance lease in accordance with Section 17 *Property, Plant and Equipment*. If there is no reasonable certainty that the lessee will obtain ownership by the end of the lease term, the asset shall be fully depreciated over the shorter of the lease term and its **useful life**. A lessee shall also assess at each **reporting date** whether an asset leased under a finance lease is impaired (see Section 27 *Impairment of Assets*).

Disclosures

20.13 A lessee shall make the following disclosures for finance leases:

(a) for each **class of asset**, the net **carrying amount** at the end of the **reporting period**;

(b) the total of future minimum lease payments at the end of the reporting period, for each of the following periods:

(i) not later than one year;

(ii) later than one year and not later than five years; and

(iii) later than five years; and

(c) a general description of the lessee's significant leasing arrangements including, for example, information about contingent rent, renewal or purchase options and escalation clauses, subleases, and restrictions imposed by lease arrangements.

20.14 In addition, the requirements for disclosure about assets in accordance with Sections 17 and 27 apply to lessees for assets leased under finance leases.

Financial statements of lessees: operating leases

Recognition and measurement

20.15 A lessee shall recognise lease payments under operating leases (excluding costs for services such as insurance and maintenance) as an expense over the lease term on a straight-line basis unless either:

(a) another systematic basis is representative of the time pattern of the user's benefit, even if the payments are not on that basis; or

(b) the payments to the lessor are structured to increase in line with expected general inflation (based on published indexes or statistics) to compensate for the lessor's expected inflationary cost increases. If payments to the lessor vary because of factors other than general inflation, then this condition (b) is not met.

> **Example of applying paragraph 20.15(b):**
>
> X operates in a jurisdiction in which the consensus forecast by local banks is that the general price level index, as published by the government, will increase by an average of 10 per cent annually over the next five years. X leases some office space from Y for five years under an operating lease. The lease payments are structured to reflect the expected 10 per cent annual general inflation over the five-year term of the lease as follows:
>
> Year 1   CU100,000
>
> Year 2   CU110,000
>
> Year 3   CU121,000
>
> Year 4   CU133,000
>
> Year 5   CU146,000
>
> X recognises annual rent expense equal to the amounts owed to the lessor as shown above. If the escalating payments are not clearly structured to compensate the lessor for expected inflationary cost increases based on published indexes or statistics, then X recognises annual rent expense on a straight-line basis: CU122,000 each year (sum of the amounts payable under the lease divided by five years).

20.15A   A lessee shall recognise the aggregate benefit of **lease incentives** as a reduction to the expense recognised in accordance with paragraph 20.15 over the lease term, on a straight-line basis unless another systematic basis is representative of the time pattern of the lessee's benefit from the use of the leased asset. Any costs incurred by the lessee (for example costs for termination of a pre-existing lease, relocation or leasehold improvements) shall be accounted for in accordance with the applicable section of this FRS.

20.15B   Where an operating lease becomes an **onerous contract** an entity shall also apply Section 21 *Provisions and Contingencies.*

Disclosures

* 20.16   A lessee shall make the following disclosures for operating leases:

(a)   the total of future minimum lease payments under non-cancellable operating leases for each of the following periods:

(i)   not later than one year;

(ii)   later than one year and not later than five years; and

(iii) later than five years; and

(b)   lease payments recognised as an expense.

(c)   [not used]

Financial statements of lessors: finance leases

Initial recognition and measurement

20.17   A lessor shall recognise assets held under a finance lease in its statement of financial position and present them as a receivable at an amount equal to the net investment in the lease. The **net investment in a lease** is the lessor's **gross investment in the lease** discounted at the interest rate implicit in the lease. The gross investment in the lease is the aggregate of:

(a)   the minimum lease payments receivable by the lessor under a finance lease; and

(b)   any unguaranteed residual value accruing to the lessor.

20.18   For finance leases other than those involving manufacturer or dealer lessors, initial direct costs (costs that are incremental and directly attributable to negotiating and arranging a lease) are included in the initial measurement of the finance lease receivable and reduce the amount of **income** recognised over the lease term.

Subsequent measurement

20.19   The **recognition** of finance income shall be based on a pattern reflecting a constant periodic rate of return on the lessor's net investment in the finance lease. Lease payments relating to the period, excluding costs for services, are applied against the gross investment in the lease to reduce both the principal and the unearned finance income. If there is an indication that the estimated unguaranteed residual value used in computing the lessor's gross investment in the lease has changed significantly, the income allocation over the lease term is revised, and any reduction in respect of amounts accrued is recognised immediately in **profit or loss**.

Manufacturer or dealer lessors

20.20   Manufacturers or dealers often offer to customers the choice of either buying or leasing an asset. A finance lease of an asset by a manufacturer or dealer lessor gives rise to two types of income:

(a)   profit or loss equivalent to the profit or loss resulting from an outright sale of the asset being leased, at normal selling prices, reflecting any applicable volume or trade discounts; and

(b)   finance income over the lease term.

20.21   The sales **revenue** recognised at the commencement of the lease term by a manufacturer or dealer lessor is the fair value of the asset or, if lower, the present value of the minimum lease payments accruing to the lessor, computed at a market rate of interest. The cost of sale recognised at the commencement of the lease term is the cost, or carrying amount if different, of the leased asset less the present value of the unguaranteed residual value. The difference between the sales revenue and the cost of sale is the selling profit, which is recognised in accordance with the entity's policy for outright sales.

20.22   If artificially low rates of interest are quoted, selling profit shall be restricted to that which would apply if a market rate of interest were charged. Costs incurred by manufacturer or dealer lessors in connection with negotiating and arranging a lease shall be recognised as an expense when the selling profit is recognised.

Disclosures

20.23   A lessor shall make the following disclosures for finance leases:

(a)   a reconciliation between the gross investment in the lease at the end of the reporting period, and the present value of minimum lease payments receivable at the end of the reporting period. In addition, a lessor shall disclose the gross investment in the lease and the present value of minimum lease payments receivable at the end of the reporting period, for each of the following periods:

(i)   not later than one year;

      (ii)   later than one year and not later than five years; and

      (iii) later than five years;

  (b)   unearned finance income;

  (c)   the unguaranteed residual values accruing to the benefit of the lessor;

  (d)   the accumulated allowance for uncollectible minimum lease payments receivable;

  (e)   contingent rents recognised as income in the period; and

  (f)   a general description of the lessor's significant leasing arrangements, including, for example, information about contingent rent, renewal or purchase options and escalation clauses, subleases, and restrictions imposed by lease arrangements.

Financial statements of lessors: operating leases

Recognition and measurement

20.24   A lessor shall present assets subject to operating leases in its statement of financial position according to the nature of the asset.

20.25   A lessor shall recognise lease income from operating leases (excluding amounts for services such as insurance and maintenance) in profit or loss on a straight-line basis over the lease term, unless either:

  (a)   another systematic basis is representative of the time pattern of the lessee's benefit from the leased asset, even if the receipt of payments is not on that basis; or

  (b)   the payments to the lessor are structured to increase in line with expected general inflation (based on published indexes or statistics) to compensate for the lessor's expected inflationary cost increases. If payments to the lessor vary according to factors other than inflation, then condition (b) is not met.

20.25A A lessor shall recognise the aggregate cost of lease incentives as a reduction to the income recognised in accordance with paragraph 20.25 over the lease term on a straight-line basis, unless another systematic basis is representative of the time pattern over which the lessor's benefit from the leased asset is diminished.

20.26   A lessor shall recognise as an expense, costs, including **depreciation**, incurred in earning the lease income. The depreciation policy for depreciable leased assets shall be consistent with the lessor's normal depreciation policy for similar assets.

20.27   A lessor shall add to the carrying amount of the leased asset any initial direct costs it incurs in negotiating and arranging an operating lease and shall recognise such costs as an expense over the lease term on the same basis as the lease income.

20.28   To determine whether a leased asset has become impaired, a lessor shall apply Section 27.

20.29   A manufacturer or dealer lessor does not recognise any selling profit on entering into an operating lease because it is not the equivalent of a sale.

Disclosures

20.30   A lessor shall disclose the following for operating leases:

(a)   the future minimum lease payments under non-cancellable operating leases for each of the following periods:

(i)   not later than one year;

(ii)   later than one year and not later than five years; and

(iii)   later than five years;

(b)   total contingent rents recognised as income; and

(c)   a general description of the lessor's significant leasing arrangements, including, for example, information about contingent rent, renewal or purchase options and escalation clauses, and restrictions imposed by lease arrangements.

20.31   In addition, the requirements for disclosure about assets in accordance with Sections 17 and 27 apply to lessors for assets provided under operating leases.

Sale and leaseback transactions

20.32   A sale and leaseback transaction involves the sale of an asset and the leasing back of the same asset. The lease payment and the sale price are usually interdependent because they are negotiated as a package. The accounting treatment of a sale and leaseback transaction depends on the type of lease.

Sale and leaseback transaction results in a finance lease

20.33   If a sale and leaseback transaction results in a finance lease, the seller-lessee shall not recognise immediately, as income, any excess of sales proceeds over the carrying amount. Instead, the seller-lessee shall defer such excess and amortise it over the lease term.

Sale and leaseback transaction results in an operating lease

20.34   If a sale and leaseback transaction results in an operating lease, and it is clear that the transaction is established at fair value, the seller-lessee shall recognise any profit or loss immediately. If the sale price is below fair value, the seller-lessee shall recognise any profit or loss immediately unless the loss is compensated for by future lease payments at below market price. In that case the seller-lessee shall defer and amortise such loss in proportion to the lease payments over the period for which the asset is expected to be used. If the sale price is above fair value, the seller-lessee shall defer the excess over fair value and amortise it over the period for which the asset is expected to be used.

Disclosures

20.35   Disclosure requirements for lessees and lessors apply equally to sale and leaseback transactions. The required description of significant leasing arrangements includes description of unique or unusual provisions of the agreement or terms of the sale and leaseback transactions.

Section 21
Provisions and Contingencies

Scope of this section

21.1 This section applies to all **provisions** (ie **liabilities** of uncertain timing or amount), **contingent liabilities** and **contingent assets** except those provisions covered by other sections of this FRS. Where those other sections contain no specific requirements to deal with contracts that have become onerous, this section applies to those contracts.

21.1A This section applies to **financial guarantee contracts** unless:

(a) an entity has chosen to apply IAS 39 *Financial Instruments: Recognition and Measurement* and/or IFRS 9 *Financial Instruments* to its **financial instruments** (see paragraphs 11.2 and 12.2); or

(b) an entity has elected under FRS 103 *Insurance Contracts* to continue the application of insurance contract accounting.

21.1B This section does not apply to financial instruments (including loan commitments) that are within the scope of Section 11 *Basic Financial Instruments* and 12 *Other Financial Instruments Issues*. This section does not apply to **insurance contracts** (including **reinsurance contracts**) that an entity issues and reinsurance contracts that the entity holds, or financial instruments issued by an entity with a **discretionary participation feature** that are within the scope of FRS 103 *Insurance Contracts*.

21.2 The requirements in this section do not apply to executory contracts unless they are **onerous contracts**. Executory contracts are contracts under which neither party has performed any of its obligations or both parties have partially performed their obligations to an equal extent.

21.3 The word 'provision' is sometimes used in the context of such items as **depreciation**, impairment of **assets**, and uncollectible receivables. Those are adjustments of the **carrying amounts** of assets, rather than **recognition** of liabilities, and therefore are not covered by this section.

Initial recognition

21.4 An entity shall recognise a provision only when:

(a) the entity has an obligation at the **reporting date** as a result of a past event;

(b) it is **probable** (ie more likely than not) that the entity will be required to transfer economic benefits in settlement; and

(c) the amount of the obligation can be estimated reliably.

21.5 The entity shall recognise the provision as a liability in the **statement of financial position** and shall recognise the amount of the provision as an **expense**, unless another section of this FRS requires the cost to be recognised as part of the cost of an asset such as **inventories** or **property, plant and equipment**.

21.6 The condition in paragraph 21.4(a) means that the entity has no realistic alternative to settling the obligation. This can happen when the entity has a legal obligation that can be enforced by law or when the entity has a **constructive obligation** because the past event (which may be an action of the entity) has created valid expectations in other parties that the entity will discharge the obligation. Obligations that will arise from the entity's future actions (ie the future conduct of its business) do not satisfy the condition in paragraph 21.4(a), no matter how likely they are to occur and even if they are contractual. To illustrate, because of commercial pressures or legal requirements, an entity may intend or need to carry out expenditure to operate in a particular way in the future (for example, by fitting smoke filters in a particular type of factory). Because the entity can avoid the future expenditure by its future actions, for example by changing its method of operation or selling the factory, it has no present obligation for that future expenditure and no provision is recognised.

Initial measurement

21.7 An entity shall measure a provision at the best estimate of the amount required to settle the obligation at the reporting date. The best estimate is the amount an entity would rationally pay to settle the obligation at the end of the **reporting period** or to transfer it to a third party at that time.

(a) When the provision involves a large population of items, the estimate of the amount reflects the weighting of all possible outcomes by their associated probabilities. The provision will therefore be different depending on whether the probability of a loss of a given amount is, for example, 60 per cent or 90 per cent. Where there is a continuous range of possible outcomes, and each point in that range is as likely as any other, the mid-point of the range is used.

(b) When the provision arises from a single obligation, the individual most likely outcome may be the best estimate of the amount required to settle the obligation. However, even in such a case, the entity considers other possible outcomes. When other possible outcomes are either mostly higher or mostly lower than the most likely outcome, the best estimate will be a higher or lower amount.

When the effect of the time value of money is **material**, the amount of a provision shall be the **present value** of the amount expected to be required to settle the obligation. The discount rate (or rates) shall be a pre-tax rate (or rates) that reflect(s) current market assessments of the time value of money and risks specific to the liability. The risks specific to the liability shall be reflected either in the discount rate or in the estimation of the amounts required to settle the obligation, but not both.

21.8 An entity shall exclude **gains** from the expected disposal of assets from the **measurement** of a provision.

21.9 When some or all of the amount required to settle a provision may be reimbursed by another party (eg through an insurance claim), the entity shall recognise the reimbursement as a separate asset only when it is virtually certain that the entity will receive the reimbursement on settlement of the obligation. The amount recognised for the reimbursement shall not exceed the amount of the provision. The reimbursement receivable shall be presented in the statement of financial position as an asset and shall not be offset against the provision. In the **statement of comprehensive income** (or in the **income statement**, if presented) the expense relating to a provision may be presented net of the amount recognised for a reimbursement.

Subsequent measurement

21.10 An entity shall charge against a provision only those expenditures for which the provision was originally recognised.

21.11 An entity shall review provisions at each reporting date and adjust them to reflect the current best estimate of the amount that would be required to settle the obligation at that reporting date. Any adjustments to the amounts previously recognised shall be recognised in **profit or loss** unless the provision was originally recognised as part of the cost of an asset (see paragraph 21.5). When a provision is measured at the present value of the amount expected to be required to settle the obligation, the unwinding of the discount shall be recognised as a finance cost in profit or loss in the period it arises.

Onerous contracts

21.11A   If an entity has an **onerous contract**, the present obligation under the contract shall be recognised and measured as a provision (see Example 2 of the Appendix to this section).

Future operating losses

21.11B   Provisions shall not be recognised for future operating losses (see Example 1 of the Appendix to this section).

Restructuring

21.11C   A **restructuring** gives rise to a constructive obligation only when an entity:

    (a)   has a detailed formal plan for the restructuring identifying at least:

        (i)   the business or part of a business concerned;

        (ii)   the principal locations affected;

        (iii) the location, function, and approximate number of employees who will be compensated for terminating their services;

        (iv)   the expenditures that will be undertaken; and

        (v)   when the plan will be implemented; and

    (b)   has raised a valid expectation in those affected that it will carry out the restructuring by starting to implement that plan or announcing its main features to those affected by it.

21.11D   An entity recognises a provision for restructuring costs only when it has a legal or constructive obligation at the reporting date to carry out the restructuring.

Contingent liabilities

21.12   A contingent liability is either a possible but uncertain obligation or a present obligation that is not recognised because it fails to meet one or both of the conditions (b) and (c) in paragraph 21.4. An entity shall not recognise a contingent liability as a liability, except for provisions for contingent liabilities of an acquiree in a **business combination** (see paragraphs 19.20 and 19.21). Disclosure of a contingent liability is required by paragraph 21.15 unless the possibility of an outflow of resources is remote. When an entity is jointly and severally liable for an obligation, the part of the obligation that is expected to be met by other parties is treated as a contingent liability.

Contingent assets

21.13   An entity shall not recognise a contingent asset as an asset. Disclosure of a contingent asset is required by paragraph 21.16 when an inflow of economic benefits is probable. However, when the flow of future economic benefits to the entity is virtually certain, then the related asset is not a contingent asset, and its recognition is appropriate.

Disclosures

Disclosures about provisions

21.14   For each class of provision, an entity shall disclose the following:

(a)   a reconciliation showing:

(i)   the carrying amount at the beginning and end of the period;

(ii)   additions during the period, including adjustments that result from changes in measuring the discounted amount;

(iii) amounts charged against the provision during the period; and

(iv)   unused amounts reversed during the period;

(b)   a brief description of the nature of the obligation and the expected amount and timing of any resulting payments;

(c)   an indication of the uncertainties about the amount or timing of those outflows; and

(d)   the amount of any expected reimbursement, stating the amount of any asset that has been recognised for that expected reimbursement.

Comparative information for prior periods is not required.

Disclosures about contingent liabilities

* 21.15   Unless the possibility of any outflow of resources in settlement is remote, an entity shall disclose, for each class of contingent liability at the reporting date, a brief description of the nature of the contingent liability and, when practicable:

(a)   an estimate of its financial effect, measured in accordance with paragraphs 21.7 to 21.11;

(b)   an indication of the uncertainties relating to the amount or timing of any outflow; and

(c)   the possibility of any reimbursement.

If it is **impracticable** to make one or more of these disclosures, that fact shall be stated.

Disclosures about contingent assets

21.16   If an inflow of economic benefits is probable (more likely than not) but not virtually certain, an entity shall disclose a description of the nature of the contingent assets at the end of the reporting period, and, when practicable, an estimate of their financial effect, measured using the principles set out in paragraphs 21.7 to 21.11. If it is impracticable to make this disclosure, that fact shall be stated.

Prejudicial disclosures

21.17   In extremely rare cases, disclosure of some or all of the information required by paragraphs 21.14 to 21.16 can be expected to prejudice seriously the position of the entity in a dispute with other parties on the subject matter of the provision, contingent liability or contingent asset. In such cases, an entity need not disclose all of the information required by those paragraphs insofar as it relates to the dispute, but shall disclose at least the following.

In relation to provisions, the following information shall be given:

(a) a table showing the reconciliation required by paragraph 21.14(a) in aggregate, including the source and application of any amounts transferred to or from provisions during the reporting period;

(b) particulars of each provision in any case where the amount of the provision is material; and

(c) the fact that, and reason why, the information required by paragraph 21.14 has not been disclosed.

In relation to contingent liabilities, the following information shall be given:

(a) particulars and the total amount of any contingent liabilities (excluding those which arise out of insurance contracts) that are not included in the statement of financial position;

(b) the total amount of contingent liabilities which are undertaken on behalf of or for the benefit of:

(i) any **parent** or fellow **subsidiary** of the entity;

(ii) any subsidiary of the entity; or

(iii) any entity in which the reporting entity has a participating interest,

shall each be stated separately; and

(c) the fact that, and reason why, the information required by paragraph 21.15 has not been disclosed.

In relation to contingent assets, the entity shall disclose the general nature of the dispute, together with the fact that, and reason why, the information required by paragraph 21.16 has not been disclosed.

Disclosure about financial guarantee contracts

21.17A An entity shall disclose the nature and business purpose of the financial guarantee contracts it has issued. If applicable, an entity shall also provide the disclosures required by paragraphs 21.14 and 21.15.

Appendix to Section 21

Examples of recognising and measuring provisions

This appendix accompanies, but is not part of, Section 21. It provides guidance for applying the requirements of Section 21 in recognising and measuring provisions.

All of the entities in the examples in this appendix have 31 December as their reporting date. In all cases, it is assumed that a reliable estimate can be made of any outflows expected. In some examples the circumstances described may have resulted in impairment of the assets; this aspect is not dealt with in the examples. References to 'best estimate' are to the present value amount, when the effect of the time value of money is material.

Example 1 Future operating losses

21A.1   An entity determines that it is probable that a segment of its operations will incur future operating losses for several years.

Present obligation as a result of a past obligating event: There is no past event that obliges the entity to pay out resources.

Conclusion: The entity does not recognise a provision for future operating losses. Expected future losses do not meet the definition of a liability. The expectation of future operating losses may be an indicator that one or more assets are impaired (see Section 27 *Impairment of Assets*).

Example 2 Onerous contracts

21A.2   An onerous contract is one in which the unavoidable costs of meeting the obligations under the contract exceed the economic benefits expected to be received under it. The unavoidable costs under a contract reflect the least net cost of exiting from the contract, which is the lower of the cost of fulfilling it and any compensation or penalties arising from failure to fulfil it. For example, an entity may be contractually required under an operating lease to make payments to lease an asset for which it no longer has any use.

Present obligation as a result of a past obligating event: The entity is contractually required to pay out resources for which it will not receive commensurate benefits.

Conclusion: If an entity has a contract that is onerous, the entity recognises and measures the present obligation under the contract as a provision.

Example 3 Restructurings

21A.3   [Moved to paragraph 21.11C]

Example 4 Warranties

21A.4   A manufacturer gives warranties at the time of sale to purchasers of its product. Under the terms of the contract for sale, the manufacturer undertakes to make good, by repair or replacement, manufacturing defects that become apparent within three years from the date of sale. On the basis of experience, it is probable (ie more likely than not) that there will be some claims under the warranties.

Present obligation as a result of a past obligating event: The obligating event is the sale of the product with a warranty, which gives rise to a legal obligation.

An outflow of resources embodying economic benefits in settlement: Probable for the warranties as a whole.

Conclusion: The entity recognises a provision for the best estimate of the costs of making good under the warranty products sold before the reporting date.

Illustration of calculations:

In 20X0, goods are sold for CU1,000,000. Experience indicates that 90 per cent of products sold require no warranty repairs; 6 per cent of products sold require minor repairs costing 30 per cent of the sale price; and 4 per cent of products sold require major repairs or replacement costing 70 per cent of sale price. Therefore estimated warranty costs are:

CU1,000,000 × 90% × 0 =	CU0
CU1,000,000 × 6% × 30% =	CU18,000
CU1,000,000 × 4% × 70% =	CU28,000
Total	CU46,000

The expenditures for warranty repairs and replacements for products sold in 20X0 are expected to be made 60 per cent in 20X1, 30 per cent in 20X2, and 10 per cent in 20X3, in each case at the end of the period. Because the estimated cash flows already reflect the probabilities of the cash outflows, and assuming there are no other risks or uncertainties that must be reflected, to determine the present value of those cash flows the entity uses a 'risk-free' discount rate based on government bonds with the same term as the expected cash outflows (6 per cent for one-year bonds and 7 per cent for two-year and three-year bonds). Calculation of the present value, at the end of 20X0, of the estimated cash flows related to the warranties for products sold in 20X0 is as follows:

Year		Expected cash payments (CU)	Discount rate	Discount factor	Present value (CU)
1	60% × CU46,000	27,600	6%	0.9434 (at 6% for 1 year)	26,038
2	30% × CU46,000	13,800	7%	0.8734 (at 7% for 2 years)	12,053
3	10% × CU46,000	4,600	7%	0.8163 (at 7% for 3 years)	3,755
Total					41,846

The entity will recognise a warranty obligation of CU41,846 at the end of 20X0 for products sold in 20X0.

Example 5 Refunds policy

21A.5 A retail store has a policy of refunding purchases by dissatisfied customers, even though it is under no legal obligation to do so. Its policy of making refunds is generally known.

Present obligation as a result of a past obligating event: The obligating event is the sale of the product, which gives rise to a constructive obligation because the conduct of the store has created a valid expectation on the part of its customers that the store will refund purchases.

An outflow of resources embodying economic benefits in settlement: Probable that a proportion of goods will be returned for refund.

Conclusion: The entity recognises a provision for the best estimate of the amount required to settle the refunds.

Example 6 Closure of a division: no implementation before end of reporting period

21A.6   On 12 December 20X0 the board of an entity decided to close down a division. Before the end of the reporting period (31 December 20X0) the decision was not communicated to any of those affected and no other steps were taken to implement the decision.

Present obligation as a result of a past obligating event: There has been no obligating event, and so there is no obligation.

Conclusion: The entity does not recognise a provision.

Example 7 Closure of a division: communication and implementation before end of reporting period

21A.7   On 12 December 20X0 the board of an entity decided to close a division making a particular product. On 20 December 20X0 a detailed plan for closing the division was agreed by the board, letters were sent to customers warning them to seek an alternative source of supply, and redundancy notices were sent to the staff of the division.

Present obligation as a result of a past obligating event: The obligating event is the communication of the decision to the customers and employees, which gives rise to a constructive obligation from that date, because it creates a valid expectation that the division will be closed.

An outflow of resources embodying economic benefits in settlement: Probable.

Conclusion: The entity recognises a provision at 31 December 20X0 for the best estimate of the costs that would be incurred to close the division at the reporting date.

Example 8 Staff retraining as a result of changes in the income tax system

21A.8   The government introduces changes to the income tax system. As a result of those changes, an entity in the financial services sector will need to retrain a large proportion of its administrative and sales workforce in order to ensure continued compliance with tax regulations. At the end of the reporting period, no retraining of staff has taken place.

Present obligation as a result of a past obligating event: The tax law change does not impose an obligation on an entity to do any retraining. An obligating event for recognising a provision (the retraining itself) has not taken place.

Conclusion: The entity does not recognise a provision.

Example 9 A court case

21A.9   A customer has sued Entity X, seeking damages for injury the customer allegedly sustained from using a product sold by Entity X. Entity X disputes liability on grounds that the customer did not follow directions in using the product. Up to the date the board authorised the financial statements for the year to 31 December 20X1 for issue, the entity's lawyers advise that it is probable that the entity will not be found liable. However, when the entity prepares the financial statements for the year to 31 December 20X2, its lawyers advise that, owing to developments in the case, it is now probable that the entity will be found liable.

(a)   At 31 December 20X1

Present obligation as a result of a past obligating event: On the basis of the evidence available when the financial statements were approved, there is no obligation as a result of past events.

Conclusion: No provision is recognised. The matter is disclosed as a contingent liability unless the probability of any outflow is regarded as remote.

(b)   At 31 December 20X2

Present obligation as a result of a past obligating event: On the basis of the evidence available, there is a present obligation. The obligating event is the sale of the product to the customer.

An outflow of resources embodying economic benefits in settlement: Probable.

Conclusion: A provision is recognised at the best estimate of the amount to settle the obligation at 31 December 20X2, and the expense is recognised in profit or loss. It is not a correction of an error in 20X1 because, on the basis of the evidence available when the 20X1 financial statements were approved, a provision should not have been recognised at that time.

Section 22
Liabilities and Equity

Scope of this section

22.1   This section establishes principles for classifying **financial instruments** as either **liabilities** or **equity** and deals with the accounting for **compound financial instruments**. It also addresses the issue of equity instruments and distributions to individuals or other parties acting in their capacity as investors in equity instruments (ie in their capacity as **owners**) and the accounting for purchases of own equity. This section also deals with the accounting for **non-controlling interests** in **consolidated financial statements**. Section 26 *Share-based Payment* addresses accounting for a transaction in which the entity receives goods or services (including employee services) as consideration for its equity instruments (including shares or **share options**) from employees and other vendors acting in their capacity as vendors of goods and services.

22.2   This section shall be applied to all types of financial instruments except:

(a)   Investments in **subsidiaries**, **associates** and **joint ventures** that are accounted for in accordance with Section 9 *Consolidated and Separate Financial Statements*, Section 14 *Investments in Associates* or Section 15 *Investments in Joint Ventures*.

(b)   Employers' rights and obligations under employee benefit plans, to which Section 28 *Employee Benefits* applies.

(c)   Contracts for contingent consideration in a **business combination** (see Section 19 *Business Combinations and Goodwill*). This exemption applies only to the acquirer.

(d)   Financial instruments, contracts and obligations under **share-based payment transactions** to which Section 26 applies, except that paragraphs 22.3 to 22.6 shall be applied to **treasury shares** issued, purchased, sold, transferred or cancelled in connection with employee share option plans, employee share purchase plans, and all other share-based payment arrangements.

(e)   **Insurance contracts** (including **reinsurance contracts**) that an entity issues and reinsurance contracts that it holds (see FRS 103 *Insurance Contracts*).

(f)   Financial instruments with a **discretionary participation feature** that an entity issues (see FRS 103).

(g)   **Financial guarantee contracts** (see Section 21 *Provisions and Contingencies*).

A reporting entity that issues the financial instruments set out in (e) and (f) or holds the financial instruments set out (e) is required by paragraph 1.6 to apply FRS 103 to those financial instruments.

Classification of an instrument as liability or equity

22.3   Equity is the residual interest in the **assets** of an entity after deducting all its liabilities. Equity includes investments by the owners of the entity, plus additions to those investments earned through profitable operations and retained for use in the entity's operations, minus reductions to owners' investments as a result of unprofitable operations and distributions to owners.

A **financial liability** is any liability that is:

(a) a contractual obligation:

    (i) to deliver **cash** or another **financial asset** to another entity; or

    (ii) to exchange financial assets or financial liabilities with another entity under conditions that are potentially unfavourable to the entity; or

(b) a contract that will or may be settled in the entity's own equity instruments and:

    (i) under which the entity is or may be obliged to deliver a variable number of the entity's own equity instruments; or

    (ii) which will or may be settled other than by the exchange of a fixed amount of cash or another financial asset for a fixed number of the entity's own equity instruments. For this purpose the entity's own equity instruments do not include instruments that are themselves contracts for the future receipt or delivery of the entity's own equity instruments.

22.3A A financial instrument, where the issuer does not have the unconditional right to avoid settling in cash or by delivery of another financial asset (or otherwise to settle it in such a way that it would be a financial liability) and where settlement is dependent on the occurrence or non-occurrence of uncertain future events beyond the control of the issuer and the holder, is a financial liability of the issuer unless:

(a) the part of the contingent settlement provision that could require settlement in cash or another financial asset (or otherwise in such a way that it would be a financial liability) is not genuine;

(b) the issuer can be required to settle the obligation in cash or another financial asset (or otherwise to settle it in such a way that it would be a financial liability) only in the event of liquidation of the issuer; or

(c) the instrument has all the features and meets the conditions in paragraph 22.4.

22.4 Some financial instruments that meet the definition of a liability are classified as equity because they represent the residual interest in the net assets of the entity:

(a) A puttable instrument is a financial instrument that gives the holder the right to sell that instrument back to the issuer for cash or another financial asset or is automatically redeemed or repurchased by the issuer on the occurrence of an uncertain future event or the death or retirement of the instrument holder. A puttable instrument that has all of the following features is classified as an equity instrument:

    (i) It entitles the holder to a pro rata share of the entity's net assets in the event of the entity's liquidation. The entity's net assets are those assets that remain after deducting all other claims on its assets.

    (ii) The instrument is in the class of instruments that is subordinate to all other classes of instruments.

    (iii) All financial instruments in the class of instruments that is subordinate to all other classes of instruments have identical features.

    (iv) Apart from the contractual obligation for the issuer to repurchase or redeem the instrument for cash or another financial asset, the instrument does not include any contractual obligation to deliver cash or another financial asset to another entity, or to exchange financial assets or financial liabilities with another entity under conditions that are potentially unfavourable to the entity, and it is not a contract that will or may be settled in the entity's own equity instruments as set out in paragraph 22.3(b) of the definition of a financial liability.

        (v)   The total expected **cash flows** attributable to the instrument over the life of the instrument are based substantially on the **profit or loss**, the change in the recognised net assets or the change in the **fair value** of the recognised and unrecognised net assets of the entity over the life of the instrument (excluding any effects of the instrument).

    (b)   Instruments, or components of instruments, that are subordinate to all other classes of instruments are classified as equity if they impose on the entity an obligation to deliver to another party a pro rata share of the net assets of the entity only on liquidation.

22.5   The following are examples of instruments that are either classified as liabilities or equity:

    (a)   An instrument of the type described in paragraph 22.4(b) is classified as a liability if the distribution of net assets on liquidation is subject to a maximum amount (a ceiling). For example, if on liquidation the holders of the instrument receive a pro rata share of the net assets, but this amount is limited to a ceiling and the excess net assets are distributed to a charity organisation or the government, the instrument is not classified as equity.

    (b)   A puttable instrument is classified as equity if, when the put option is exercised, the holder receives a pro rata share of the net assets of the entity determined by:

        (i)   dividing the entity's net assets on liquidation into units of equal amounts; and

        (ii)   multiplying that amount by the number of the units held by the financial instrument holder.

    However, if the holder is entitled to an amount measured on some other basis the instrument is classified as a liability.

    (c)   An instrument is classified as a liability if it obliges the entity to make payments to the holder before liquidation, such as a mandatory dividend.

    (d)   A puttable instrument that is classified as equity in a subsidiary's **financial statements** is classified as a liability in the consolidated financial statements.

    (e)   A preference share that provides for mandatory redemption by the issuer for a fixed or determinable amount at a fixed or determinable future date, or gives the holder the right to require the issuer to redeem the instrument at or after a particular date for a fixed or determinable amount, is a financial liability.

22.6   Members' shares in co-operative entities and similar instruments are equity if:

    (a)   the entity has an unconditional right to refuse redemption of the members' shares; or

    (b)   redemption is unconditionally prohibited by local law, regulation or the entity's governing charter.

Original issue of shares or other equity instruments

22.7   An entity shall recognise the issue of shares or other equity instruments as equity when it issues those instruments and another party is obliged to provide cash or other resources to the entity in exchange for the instruments.

    (a)   [Not used]

    (b)   If the entity receives the cash or other resources before the equity instruments are issued, and the entity cannot be required to repay the cash or other resources received, the entity shall recognise the corresponding increase in equity to the extent of consideration received.

(c) To the extent that the equity instruments have been subscribed for but not issued (or called up), and the entity has not yet received the cash or other resources, the entity shall not recognise an increase in equity.

22.8 An entity shall measure the equity instruments at the fair value of the cash or other resources received or receivable, net of direct costs of issuing the equity instruments. If payment is deferred and the time value of money is **material**, the initial **measurement** shall be on a **present value** basis.

22.9 An entity shall account for the **transaction costs** of an equity transaction as a deduction from equity, net of any related income tax benefit.

22.10 How the increase in equity arising on the issue of shares or other equity instruments is presented in the **statement of financial position** is determined by applicable laws. For example, the par value (or other nominal value) of shares and the amount paid in excess of par value may be presented separately.

Exercise of options, rights and warrants

22.11 An entity shall apply the principles in paragraphs 22.7 to 22.10 to equity issued by means of exercise of options, rights, warrants and similar equity instruments.

Capitalisation or bonus issues of shares and share splits

22.12 A capitalisation or bonus issue (sometimes referred to as a stock dividend) is the issue of new shares to shareholders in proportion to their existing holdings. For example, an entity may give its shareholders one dividend or bonus share for every five shares held. A share split (sometimes referred to as a stock split) is the dividing of an entity's existing shares into multiple shares. For example, in a share split, each shareholder may receive one additional share for each share held. In some cases, the previously outstanding shares are cancelled and replaced by new shares. Capitalisation and bonus issues and share splits do not change total equity. An entity shall reclassify amounts within equity as required by applicable laws.

Convertible debt or similar compound financial instruments

22.13 On issuing convertible debt or similar compound financial instruments that contain both a liability and an equity component, an entity shall allocate the proceeds between the liability component and the equity component. To make the allocation, the entity shall first determine the amount of the liability component as the fair value of a similar liability that does not have a conversion feature or similar associated equity component. The entity shall allocate the residual amount as the equity component. Transaction costs shall be allocated between the debt component and the equity component on the basis of their relative fair values.

22.14 The entity shall not revise the allocation in a subsequent period.

22.15 In periods after the instruments were issued, the entity shall account for the liability component as a financial instrument in accordance with Section 11 *Basic Financial Instruments* or Section 12 *Other Financial Instruments Issues* as appropriate. The appendix to this section illustrates the issuer's accounting for convertible debt where the liability component is a basic financial instrument.

Treasury shares

22.16 Treasury shares are the equity instruments of an entity that have been issued and subsequently reacquired by the entity. An entity shall deduct from equity the fair value of the consideration given for the treasury shares. The entity shall not recognise a **gain** or loss in profit or loss on the purchase, sale, transfer or cancellation of treasury shares.

Distributions to owners

22.17 An entity shall reduce equity for the amount of distributions to its owners (holders of its equity instruments).

22.18 An entity shall disclose the fair value of any non-cash assets that have been distributed to its owners during the **reporting period**, except when the non-cash assets are ultimately controlled by the same parties both before and after the distribution.

Non-controlling interest and transactions in shares of a consolidated subsidiary

22.19 In the consolidated financial statements, a non-controlling interest in the net assets of a subsidiary is included in equity. An entity shall treat changes in a parent's controlling interest in a subsidiary that do not result in a loss of **control** as transactions with equity holders in their capacity as equity holders. Accordingly, the **carrying amount** of the non-controlling interest shall be adjusted to reflect the change in the parent's interest in the subsidiary's net assets. Any difference between the amount by which the non-controlling interest is so adjusted and the fair value of the consideration paid or received, if any, shall be recognised directly in equity and attributed to equity holders of the parent. An entity shall not recognise a gain or loss on these changes. Also, an entity shall not recognise any change in the carrying amounts of assets (including goodwill) or liabilities as a result of such transactions.

Appendix to Section 22

Example of the issuer's accounting for convertible debt

The appendix accompanies, but is not part of, Section 22. It provides guidance for applying the requirements of paragraphs 22.13 to 22.15.

On 1 January 20X5 an entity issues 500 convertible bonds. The bonds are issued at par with a face value of CU100 per bond and are for a five-year term, with no transaction costs. The total proceeds from the issue are CU50,000. Interest is payable annually in arrears at an annual interest rate of 4 per cent. Each bond is convertible, at the holder's discretion, into 25 ordinary shares at any time up to maturity. At the time the bonds are issued, the market interest rate for similar debt that does not have the conversion option is 6 per cent.

When the instrument is issued, the liability component must be valued first, and the difference between the total proceeds on issue (which is the fair value of the instrument in its entirety) and the fair value of the liability component is assigned to the equity component. The fair value of the liability component is calculated by determining its present value using the discount rate of 6 per cent. The calculations and journal entries are illustrated below:

	CU
Proceeds from the bond issue (A)	50,000
Present value of principal at the end of five years (see calculations below)	37,363
Present value of interest payable annually in arrears for five years	8,425
Present value of liability, which is the fair value of liability component (B)	45,788
Residual, which is the fair value of the equity component (A) – (B)	4,212

The issuer of the bonds makes the following journal entry at issue on 1 January 20X5:

Dr Cash	CU50,000	
Cr Financial Liability – Convertible bond		CU45,788
Cr Equity		CU4,212

The CU4,212 represents a discount on issue of the bonds, so the entry could also be shown 'gross':

Dr Cash	CU50,000	
Dr Financial Liability – Convertible bond discount	CU4,212	
Cr Financial Liability – Convertible bond		CU50,000
Cr Equity		CU4,212

After issue, the issuer will amortise the bond discount according to the following table:

	(a) Interest payment	(b) Total interest expense = 6% x (e)	(c) Amortisation of bond discount = (b) – (a)	(d) Bond discount = (d) – (c)	(e) Net liability = 50,000 – (d)
	CU	CU	CU	CU	CU
1/1/20X5				4,212	45,788
31/12/20X5	2,000	2,747	747	3,465	46,535
31/12/20X6	2,000	2,792	792	2,673	47,327
31/12/20X7	2,000	2,840	840	1,833	48,167
31/12/20X8	2,000	2,890	890	943	49,057
31/12/20X9	2,000	2,943	943	0	50,000
Totals	10,000	14,212	4,212		

At the end of 20X5, the issuer would make the following journal entry:

Dr Interest expense	CU2,747	
Cr Bond discount		CU747
Cr Cash		CU2,000

Calculations

Present value of principal of CU50,000 at 6 per cent

$CU50,000/(1.06)^5 = 37,363$

Present value of the interest annuity of CU2,000 (= CU50,000 × 4 per cent) payable at the end of each of five years

The CU2,000 annual interest payments are an annuity: a cash flow stream with a limited number (n) of periodic payments (C), receivable at dates 1 to n. To calculate the present value of this annuity, future payments are discounted by the periodic rate of interest (i) using the following formula:

$PV = C/i \times [1 - 1/(1+i)^n]$

Therefore, the present value of the CU2,000 interest payments is $(2,000/.06) \times [1 - [(1/1.06)^5]$ $= 8,425$

This is equivalent to the sum of the present values of the five individual CU2,000 payments, as follows:

	CU
Present value of interest payment at 31 December 20X5 = 2,000/1.06	1,887
Present value of interest payment at 31 December 20X6 = $2,000/1.06^2$	1,780
Present value of interest payment at 31 December 20X7 = $2,000/1.06^3$	1,679
Present value of interest payment at 31 December 20X8 = $2,000/1.06^4$	1,584
Present value of interest payment at 31 December 20X9 = $2,000/1.06^5$	1,495
Total	8,425

Yet another way to calculate this is to use a table of present value of an ordinary annuity in arrears, five periods, interest rate of 6 per cent per period. (Such tables are easily found on the Internet.) The present value factor is 4.2124. Multiplying this by the annuity payment of CU2,000 determines the present value of CU8,425.

Section 23
Revenue

Scope of this section

23.1   This section shall be applied in accounting for **revenue** arising from the following transactions and events:

(a)   the sale of goods (whether produced by the entity for the purpose of sale or purchased for resale);

(b)   the rendering of services;

(c)   **construction contracts** in which the entity is the contractor; and

(d)   the use by others of entity assets yielding interest, royalties or dividends.

23.2   Revenue or other income arising from some transactions and events is dealt with in other sections of this FRS:

(a)   lease agreements (see Section 20 *Leases*);

(b)   dividends and other income arising from investments that are accounted for using the equity method (see Section 14 *Investments in Associates* and Section 15 *Investments in Joint Ventures*);

(c)   changes in the **fair value** of **financial assets** and **financial liabilities** or their disposal (see Section 11 *Basic Financial Instruments* and Section 12 *Other Financial Instruments Issues*);

(d)   changes in the fair value of **investment property** (see Section 16 *Investment Property*);

(e)   initial **recognition** and changes in the fair value of **biological assets** related to **agricultural activity** (see Section 34 *Specialised Activities*); and

(f)   initial recognition of **agricultural produce** (see Section 34).

23.2A   This section excludes revenue or other income arising from transactions and events dealt with in FRS 103 *Insurance Contracts*.

Measurement of revenue

23.3   An entity shall measure revenue at the fair value of the consideration received or receivable. The fair value of the consideration received or receivable takes into account the amount of any trade discounts, prompt settlement discounts and volume rebates allowed by the entity.

23.4   An entity shall include in revenue only the gross inflows of economic benefits received and receivable by the entity on its own account. An entity shall exclude from revenue all amounts collected on behalf of third parties such as sales taxes, goods and services taxes and value added taxes. In an agency relationship, an entity (the **agent**) shall include in revenue only the amount of its commission. The amounts collected on behalf of the **principal** are not revenue of the entity.

Deferred payment

23.5   When the inflow of **cash** or **cash equivalents** is deferred, and the arrangement constitutes in effect a financing transaction, the fair value of the consideration is the **present value** of all future receipts determined using an **imputed rate of interest**. A financing transaction arises when, for example, an entity provides interest-free credit to the buyer or accepts a note receivable bearing a below-market interest rate from the buyer as consideration for the sale of goods. The imputed rate of interest is the more clearly determinable of either:

(a) the prevailing rate for a similar instrument of an issuer with a similar credit rating; or

(b) a rate of interest that discounts the nominal amount of the instrument to the current cash sales price of the goods or services.

An entity shall recognise the difference between the present value of all future receipts and the nominal amount of the consideration as interest revenue in accordance with paragraphs 23.28 and 23.29 and Section 11.

Exchanges of goods or services

23.6   An entity shall not recognise revenue:

(a) when goods or services are exchanged for goods or services that are of a similar nature and value; or

(b) when goods or services are exchanged for dissimilar goods or services but the transaction lacks commercial substance.

23.7   An entity shall recognise revenue when goods are sold or services are exchanged for dissimilar goods or services in a transaction that has commercial substance. In that case, the entity shall measure the transaction:

(a) at the fair value of the goods or services received adjusted by the amount of any cash or cash equivalents transferred;

(b) if the amount under (a) cannot be measured reliably, then at the fair value of the goods or services given up adjusted by the amount of any cash or cash equivalents transferred; or

(c) if the fair value of neither the goods or services received nor the goods or services given up can be measured reliably, then at the **carrying amount** of the goods or services given up adjusted by the amount of any cash or cash equivalents transferred.

Identification of the revenue transaction

23.8   An entity usually applies the revenue recognition criteria in this section separately to each transaction. However, an entity applies the recognition criteria to the separately identifiable components of a single transaction when necessary to reflect the substance of the transaction. For example, an entity applies the recognition criteria to the separately identifiable components of a single transaction when the selling price of a product includes an identifiable amount for subsequent servicing. Conversely, an entity applies the recognition criteria to two or more transactions together when they are linked in such a way that the commercial effect cannot be understood without reference to the series of transactions as a whole. For example, an entity applies the recognition criteria to two or more transactions together when it sells goods and, at the same time, enters into a separate agreement to repurchase the goods at a later date, thus negating the substantive effect of the transaction.

23.9   Sometimes, as part of a sales transaction, an entity grants its customer a loyalty award that the customer may redeem in the future for free or discounted goods or services. In this case, in accordance with paragraph 23.8, the entity shall account for the award credits as a separately identifiable component of the initial sales transaction. The entity shall allocate the fair value of the consideration received or receivable in respect of the initial sale between the award credits and the other components of the sale. The consideration allocated to the award credits shall be measured by reference to their fair value, ie the amount for which the award credits could be sold separately.

Sale of goods

23.10   An entity shall recognise revenue from the sale of goods when all the following conditions are satisfied:

(a)   the entity has transferred to the buyer the significant risks and rewards of ownership of the goods;

(b)   the entity retains neither continuing managerial involvement to the degree usually associated with ownership nor effective control over the goods sold;

(c)   the amount of revenue can be measured reliably;

(d)   it is **probable** that the economic benefits associated with the transaction will flow to the entity; and

(e)   the costs incurred or to be incurred in respect of the transaction can be measured reliably.

23.11   The assessment of when an entity has transferred the significant risks and rewards of ownership to the buyer requires an examination of the circumstances of the transaction. In most cases, the transfer of the risks and rewards of ownership coincides with the transfer of the legal title or the passing of possession to the buyer. This is the case for most retail sales. In other cases, the transfer of risks and rewards of ownership occurs at a time different from the transfer of legal title or the passing of possession.

23.12   An entity does not recognise revenue if it retains significant risks and rewards of ownership. Examples of situations in which the entity may retain the significant risks and rewards of ownership are:

(a)   when the entity retains an obligation for unsatisfactory performance not covered by normal warranties;

(b)   when the receipt of the revenue from a particular sale is contingent on the buyer selling the goods;

(c)   when the goods are shipped subject to installation and the installation is a significant part of the contract that has not yet been completed; and

(d)   when the buyer has the right to rescind the purchase for a reason specified in the sales contract, or at the buyer's sole discretion without any reason, and the entity is uncertain about the probability of return.

23.13   If an entity retains only an insignificant risk of ownership, the transaction is a sale and the entity recognises the revenue. For example, a seller recognises revenue when it retains the legal title to the goods solely to protect the collectability of the amount due. Similarly an entity recognises revenue when it offers a refund if the customer finds the goods faulty or is not satisfied for other reasons, and the entity can estimate the returns reliably. In such cases, the entity recognises a **provision** for returns in accordance with Section 21 *Provisions and Contingencies*.

Rendering of services

23.14   When the outcome of a transaction involving the rendering of services can be estimated reliably, an entity shall recognise revenue associated with the transaction by reference to the stage of completion of the transaction at the end of the **reporting period** (sometimes referred to as the percentage of completion method). The outcome of a transaction can be estimated reliably when all the following conditions are satisfied:

(a)   the amount of revenue can be measured reliably;

(b)   it is probable that the economic benefits associated with the transaction will flow to the entity;

(c)   the stage of completion of the transaction at the end of the reporting period can be measured reliably; and

(d)   the costs incurred for the transaction and the costs to complete the transaction can be measured reliably.

Paragraphs 23.21 to 23.27 provide guidance for applying the percentage of completion method.

23.15   When services are performed by an indeterminate number of acts over a specified period of time, an entity recognises revenue on a straight-line basis over the specified period unless there is evidence that some other method better represents the stage of completion. When a specific act is much more significant than any other act, the entity postpones recognition of revenue until the significant act is executed.

23.16   When the outcome of the transaction involving the rendering of services cannot be estimated reliably, an entity shall recognise revenue only to the extent of the **expenses** recognised that are recoverable.

Construction contracts

23.17   When the outcome of a construction contract can be estimated reliably, an entity shall recognise contract revenue and contract costs associated with the construction contract as revenue and expenses respectively by reference to the stage of completion of the contract activity at the end of the reporting period (often referred to as the percentage of completion method). Reliable estimation of the outcome requires reliable estimates of the stage of completion, future costs and collectability of billings. Paragraphs 23.21 to 23.27 provide guidance for applying the percentage of completion method.

23.18   The requirements of this section are usually applied separately to each construction contract. However, in some circumstances, it is necessary to apply this section to the separately identifiable components of a single contract or to a group of contracts together in order to reflect the substance of a contract or a group of contracts.

23.19   When a contract covers a number of **assets**, the construction of each asset shall be treated as a separate construction contract when:

(a)   separate proposals have been submitted for each asset;

(b)   each asset has been subject to separate negotiation, and the contractor and customer are able to accept or reject that part of the contract relating to each asset; and

(c)   the costs and revenues of each asset can be identified.

23.20   A group of contracts, whether with a single customer or with several customers, shall be treated as a single construction contract when:

(a)   the group of contracts is negotiated as a single package;

(b)   the contracts are so closely interrelated that they are, in effect, part of a single project with an overall profit margin; and

(c)   the contracts are performed concurrently or in a continuous sequence.

Percentage of completion method

23.21   This method is used to recognise revenue from rendering services (see paragraphs 23.14 to 23.16) and from construction contracts (see paragraphs 23.17 to 23.20). An entity shall review and, when necessary, revise the estimates of revenue and costs as the service transaction or construction contract progresses.

23.22   An entity shall determine the stage of completion of a transaction or contract using the method that measures most reliably the work performed. Possible methods include:

(a)   the proportion that costs incurred for work performed to date bear to the estimated total costs. Costs incurred for work performed to date do not include costs relating to future activity, such as for materials or prepayments;

(b)   surveys of work performed; and

(c)   completion of a physical proportion of the contract work or the completion of a proportion of the service contract.

Progress payments and advances received from customers often do not reflect the work performed.

23.23   An entity shall recognise costs that relate to future activity on the transaction or contract, such as for materials or prepayments, as an asset if it is probable that the costs will be recovered.

23.24   An entity shall recognise as an expense immediately any costs whose recovery is not probable.

23.25   When the outcome of a construction contract cannot be estimated reliably:

(a)   an entity shall recognise revenue only to the extent of contract costs incurred that it is probable will be recoverable; and

(b)   the entity shall recognise contract costs as an expense in the period in which they are incurred.

23.26   When it is probable that total contract costs will exceed total contract revenue on a construction contract, the expected loss shall be recognised as an expense immediately, with a corresponding provision for an **onerous contract** (see Section 21).

23.27   If the collectability of an amount already recognised as contract revenue is no longer probable, the entity shall recognise the uncollectible amount as an expense rather than as an adjustment of the amount of contract revenue.

Interest, royalties and dividends

23.28   An entity shall recognise revenue arising from the use by others of entity assets yielding interest, royalties and dividends on the bases set out in paragraph 23.29 when:

(a)   it is probable that the economic benefits associated with the transaction will flow to the entity; and

(b)   the amount of the revenue can be measured reliably.

23.29   An entity shall recognise revenue on the following bases:

(a)   Interest shall be recognised using the **effective interest method** as described in paragraphs 11.15 to 11.20. When calculating the **effective interest rate**, an entity shall include any related fees, finance charges paid or received (such as 'points'), **transaction costs** and other premiums or discounts.

(b)   Royalties shall be recognised on an **accrual basis** in accordance with the substance of the relevant agreement.

(c)   Dividends shall be recognised when the shareholder's right to receive payment is established.

Disclosures

General disclosures about revenue

23.30   An entity shall disclose:

(a)   the **accounting policies** adopted for the recognition of revenue, including the methods adopted to determine the stage of completion of transactions involving the rendering of services; and

(b)   the amount of each category of revenue recognised during the period, showing separately, at a minimum, revenue arising from:

(i)   the sale of goods;

(ii)   the rendering of services;

(iii)   interest;

(iv)   royalties;

(v)   dividends;

(vi)   commissions;

(vii)   grants; and

(viii)   any other significant types of revenue.

Disclosures relating to revenue from construction contracts

23.31   An entity shall disclose the following:

(a)   the amount of contract revenue recognised as revenue in the period;

(b)   the methods used to determine the contract revenue recognised in the period; and

(c)   the methods used to determine the stage of completion of contracts in progress.

23.32   An entity shall present:

   (a)   the gross amount due from customers for contract work, as an asset; and

   (b)   the gross amount due to customers for contract work, as a **liability**.

Appendix to Section 23

Examples of revenue recognition under the principles in Section 23

This appendix accompanies, but is not part of, Section 23. It provides guidance for applying the requirements of Section 23 in recognising revenue.

23A.1   The following examples focus on particular aspects of a transaction and are not a comprehensive discussion of all the relevant factors that might influence the recognition of revenue. The examples generally assume that the amount of revenue can be measured reliably, it is probable that the economic benefits will flow to the entity and the costs incurred or to be incurred can be measured reliably.

Sale of goods

23A.2   The law in different countries may cause the recognition criteria in Section 23 to be met at different times. In particular, the law may determine the point in time at which the entity transfers the significant risks and rewards of ownership. Therefore, the examples in this appendix need to be read in the context of the laws relating to the sale of goods in the country in which the transaction takes place.

Example 1 'Bill and hold' sales, in which delivery is delayed at the buyer's request but the buyer takes title and accepts billing

23A.3   The seller recognises revenue when the buyer takes title, provided:

(a)   it is probable that delivery will be made;

(b)   the item is on hand, identified and ready for delivery to the buyer at the time the sale is recognised;

(c)   the buyer specifically acknowledges the deferred delivery instructions; and

(d)   the usual payment terms apply.

Revenue is not recognised when there is simply an intention to acquire or manufacture the goods in time for delivery.

Example 2 Goods shipped subject to conditions: installation and inspection

23A.4   The seller normally recognises revenue when the buyer accepts delivery, and installation and inspection are complete. However, revenue is recognised immediately upon the buyer's acceptance of delivery when:

(a)   the installation process is simple, for example the installation of a factory-tested television receiver that requires only unpacking and connection of power and antennae; or

(b)   the inspection is performed only for the purposes of final determination of contract prices, for example, shipments of iron ore, sugar or soya beans.

Example 3 Goods shipped subject to conditions: on approval when the buyer has negotiated a limited right of return

23A.5   If there is uncertainty about the possibility of return, the seller recognises revenue when the shipment has been formally accepted by the buyer or the goods have been delivered and the time period for rejection has elapsed.

Example 4 Goods shipped subject to conditions: consignment sales under which the recipient (buyer) undertakes to sell the goods on behalf of the shipper (seller)

23A.6   The shipper recognises revenue when the goods are sold by the recipient to a third party.

Example 5 Goods shipped subject to conditions: cash on delivery sales

23A.7   The seller recognises revenue when delivery is made and cash is received by the seller or its agent.

Example 6 Layaway sales under which the goods are delivered only when the buyer makes the final payment in a series of instalments

23A.8   The seller recognises revenue from such sales when the goods are delivered. However, when experience indicates that most such sales are consummated, revenue may be recognised when a significant deposit is received, provided the goods are on hand, identified and ready for delivery to the buyer.

Example 7 Orders when payment (or partial payment) is received in advance of delivery for goods not currently held in inventory, for example, the goods are still to be manufactured or will be delivered direct to the buyer from a third party

23A.9   The seller recognises revenue when the goods are delivered to the buyer.

Example 8 Sale and repurchase agreements (other than swap transactions) under which the seller concurrently agrees to repurchase the same goods at a later date, or when the seller has a call option to repurchase, or the buyer has a put option to require the repurchase, by the seller, of the goods

23A.10   For a sale and repurchase agreement on an asset other than a financial asset, the seller must analyse the terms of the agreement to ascertain whether, in substance, the risks and rewards of ownership have been transferred to the buyer. If they have been transferred, the seller recognises revenue. When the seller has retained the risks and rewards of ownership, even though legal title has been transferred, the transaction is a financing arrangement and does not give rise to revenue. For a sale and repurchase agreement on a financial asset, the derecognition provisions of Section 11 apply.

Example 9 Sales to intermediate parties, such as distributors, dealers or others for resale

23A.11   The seller generally recognises revenue from such sales when the risks and rewards of ownership have been transferred. However, when the buyer is acting, in substance, as an agent, the sale is treated as a consignment sale.

Example 10 Subscriptions to publications and similar items

23A.12   When the items involved are of similar value in each time period, the seller recognises revenue on a straight-line basis over the period in which the items are dispatched. When the items vary in value from period to period, the seller recognises revenue on the basis of the sales value of the item dispatched in relation to the total estimated sales value of all items covered by the subscription.

Example 11 Instalment sales, under which the consideration is receivable in instalments

23A.13   The seller recognises revenue attributable to the sales price, exclusive of interest, at the date of sale. The sale price is the present value of the consideration, determined by discounting the instalments receivable at the imputed rate of interest. The seller recognises the interest element as revenue using the effective interest method.

Example 12 Agreements for the construction of real estate

23A.14 An entity that undertakes the construction of real estate, directly or through subcontractors, and enters into an agreement with one or more buyers before construction is complete, shall account for the agreement using the percentage of completion method, only if:

(a) the buyer is able to specify the major structural elements of the design of the real estate before construction begins and/or specify major structural changes once construction is in progress (whether it exercises that ability or not); or

(b) the buyer acquires and supplies construction materials and the entity provides only construction services.

23A.15 If the entity is required to provide services together with construction materials in order to perform its contractual obligation to deliver real estate to the buyer, the agreement shall be accounted for as the sale of goods. In this case, the buyer does not obtain control or the significant risks and rewards of ownership of the work in progress in its current state as construction progresses. Rather, the transfer occurs only on delivery of the completed real estate to the buyer.

Example 13 Sale with customer loyalty award

23A.16 An entity sells product A for CU100. Purchasers of product A get an award credit enabling them to buy product B for CU10. The normal selling price of product B is CU18. The entity estimates that 40 per cent of the purchasers of product A will use their award to buy product B at CU10. The normal selling price of product A, after taking into account discounts that are usually offered but that are not available during this promotion, is CU95.

23A.17 The fair value of the award credit is 40 per cent $\times$ [CU18 – CU10] = CU3.20. The entity allocates the total revenue of CU100 between product A and the award credit by reference to their relative fair values of CU95 and CU3.20 respectively. Therefore:

(a) Revenue for product A is CU100 $\times$ [CU95 / (CU95 + CU3.20)] = CU96.74

(b) Revenue for product B is CU100 $\times$ [CU3.20 / (CU95 + CU3.20)] = CU3.26

Rendering of services

Example 14 Installation fees

23A.18 The seller recognises installation fees as revenue by reference to the stage of completion of the installation, unless they are incidental to the sale of a product, in which case they are recognised when the goods are sold.

Example 15 Servicing fees included in the price of the product

23A.19 When the selling price of a product includes an identifiable amount for subsequent servicing (eg after sales support and product enhancement on the sale of software), the seller defers that amount and recognises it as revenue over the period during which the service is performed. The amount deferred is that which will cover the expected costs of the services under the agreement, together with a reasonable profit on those services.

Example 16 Advertising commissions

23A.20 Media commissions are recognised when the related advertisement or commercial appears before the public. Production commissions are recognised by reference to the stage of completion of the project.

Example 17 Insurance agency commissions

23A.21 Insurance agency commissions received or receivable that do not require the agent to render further service are recognised as revenue by the agent on the effective commencement or renewal dates of the related policies. However, when it is probable that the agent will be required to render further services during the life of the policy, the agent defers the commission, or part of it, and recognises it as revenue over the period during which the policy is in force.

Example 17A Financial services fees

23A.21A The recognition of revenue for financial service fees depends on the purposes for which the fees are assessed and the basis of accounting for any associated financial instrument. The description of fees for financial services may not be indicative of the nature and substance of the services provided. Therefore it is necessary to distinguish between fees that are an integral part of the effective interest rate of a financial instrument, fees that are earned as services are provided, and fees that are earned on the execution of a significant act.

Example 18 Admission fees

23A.22 The seller recognises revenue from artistic performances, banquets and other special events when the event takes place. When a subscription to a number of events is sold, the seller allocates the fee to each event on a basis that reflects the extent to which services are performed at each event.

Example 19 Tuition fees

23A.23 The seller recognises revenue over the period of instruction.

Example 20 Initiation, entrance and membership fees

23A.24 Revenue recognition depends on the nature of the services provided. If the fee permits only membership, and all other services or products are paid for separately, or if there is a separate annual subscription, the fee is recognised as revenue when no significant uncertainty about its collectability exists. If the fee entitles the member to services or publications to be provided during the membership period, or to purchase goods or services at prices lower than those charged to non-members, it is recognised on a basis that reflects the timing, nature and value of the benefits provided.

Franchise fees

23A.25 Franchise fees may cover the supply of initial and subsequent services, equipment and other tangible assets, and know-how. Accordingly, franchise fees are recognised as revenue on a basis that reflects the purpose for which the fees were charged. The following methods of franchise fee recognition are appropriate.

Example 21 Franchise fees: Supplies of equipment and other tangible assets

23A.26 The franchisor recognises the fair value of the assets sold as revenue when the items are delivered or title passes.

Example 22 Franchise fees: Supplies of initial and subsequent services

23A.27   The franchisor recognises fees for the provision of continuing services, whether part of the initial fee or a separate fee, as revenue as the services are rendered. When the separate fee does not cover the cost of continuing services together with a reasonable profit, part of the initial fee, sufficient to cover the costs of continuing services and to provide a reasonable profit on those services, is deferred and recognised as revenue as the services are rendered.

23A.28   The franchise agreement may provide for the franchisor to supply equipment, inventories, or other tangible assets at a price lower than that charged to others or a price that does not provide a reasonable profit on those sales. In these circumstances, part of the initial fee, sufficient to cover estimated costs in excess of that price and to provide a reasonable profit on those sales, is deferred and recognised over the period the goods are likely to be sold to the franchisee. The balance of an initial fee is recognised as revenue when performance of all the initial services and other obligations required of the franchisor (such as assistance with site selection, staff training, financing and advertising) has been substantially accomplished.

23A.29   The initial services and other obligations under an area franchise agreement may depend on the number of individual outlets established in the area. In this case, the fees attributable to the initial services are recognised as revenue in proportion to the number of outlets for which the initial services have been substantially completed.

23A.30   If the initial fee is collectible over an extended period and there is a significant uncertainty that it will be collected in full, the fee is recognised as cash instalments are received.

Example 23 Franchise fees: Continuing franchise fees

23A.31   Fees charged for the use of continuing rights granted by the agreement, or for other services provided during the period of the agreement, are recognised as revenue as the services are provided or the rights used.

Example 24 Franchise fees: Agency transactions

23A.32   Transactions may take place between the franchisor and the franchisee that, in substance, involve the franchisor acting as agent for the franchisee. For example, the franchisor may order supplies and arrange for their delivery to the franchisee at no profit. Such transactions do not give rise to revenue.

Example 25 Fees from the development of customised software

23A.33   The software developer recognises fees from the development of customised software as revenue by reference to the stage of completion of the development, including completion of services provided for post-delivery service support.

Interest, royalties and dividends

Example 26 Licence fees and royalties

23A.34   The licensor recognises fees and royalties paid for the use of an entity's assets (such as trademarks, patents, software, music copyright, record masters and motion picture films) in accordance with the substance of the agreement. As a practical matter, this may be on a straight-line basis over the life of the agreement, for example, when a licensee has the right to use specified technology for a specified period of time.

23A.35 An assignment of rights for a fixed fee or non-refundable guarantee under a non-cancellable contract that permits the licensee to exploit those rights freely and the licensor has no remaining obligations to perform is, in substance, a sale. An example is a licensing agreement for the use of software when the licensor has no obligations after delivery. Another example is the granting of rights to exhibit a motion picture film in markets in which the licensor has no control over the distributor and expects to receive no further revenues from the box office receipts. In such cases, revenue is recognised at the time of sale.

23A.36 In some cases, whether or not a licence fee or royalty will be received is contingent on the occurrence of a future event. In such cases, revenue is recognised only when it is probable that the fee or royalty will be received, which is normally when the event has occurred.

Section 24
Government Grants

Scope of this section

24.1   This section specifies the accounting for all **government grants**. A government grant is assistance by government in the form of a transfer of resources to an entity in return for past or future compliance with specified conditions relating to the **operating activities** of the entity.

24.2   Government grants exclude those forms of government assistance that cannot reasonably have a value placed upon them and transactions with government that cannot be distinguished from the normal trading transactions of the entity.

24.3   This section does not cover government assistance that is provided for an entity in the form of benefits that are available in determining **taxable profit (tax loss)**, or are determined or limited on the basis of income tax liability. Examples of such benefits are income tax holidays, investment tax credits, accelerated depreciation allowances and reduced income tax rates. Section 29 *Income Tax* covers accounting for taxes based on **income**.

Recognition and measurement

24.3A   Government grants, including non-monetary grants shall not be recognised until there is reasonable assurance that:

(a)   the entity will comply with the conditions attaching to them; and

(b)   the grants will be received.

24.4   An entity shall recognise grants either based on the performance model or the accrual model. This policy choice shall be applied on a class-by-class basis.

24.5   An entity shall measure grants at the **fair value** of the **asset** received or receivable.

24.5A   Where a grant becomes repayable it shall be recognised as a **liability** when the repayment meets the definition of a liability.

Performance model

24.5B   An entity applying the performance model shall recognise grants as follows:

(a)   A grant that does not impose specified future **performance-related conditions** on the recipient is recognised in income when the grant proceeds are received or receivable.

(b)   A grant that imposes specified future performance-related conditions on the recipient is recognised in income only when the performance-related conditions are met.

(c)   Grants received before the **revenue recognition** criteria are satisfied are recognised as a liability.

Accrual model

24.5C   An entity applying the accrual model shall classify grants either as a grant relating to revenue or a grant relating to assets.

24.5D   Grants relating to revenue shall be recognised in income on a systematic basis over the periods in which the entity recognises the related costs for which the grant is intended to compensate.

24.5E   A grant that becomes receivable as compensation for **expenses** or losses already incurred or for the purpose of giving immediate financial support to the entity with no future related costs shall be recognised in income in the period in which it becomes receivable.

24.5F   Grants relating to assets shall be recognised in income on a systematic basis over the expected **useful life** of the asset.

24.5G   Where part of a grant relating to an asset is deferred it shall be recognised as deferred income and not deducted from the **carrying amount** of the asset.

Disclosures

24.6   An entity shall disclose the following:

   (a)   the **accounting policy** adopted for grants in accordance with paragraph 24.4;

   (b)   the nature and amounts of grants recognised in the **financial statements**;

   (c)   unfulfilled conditions and other contingencies attaching to grants that have been recognised in income; and

   (d)   an indication of other forms of government assistance from which the entity has directly benefited.

24.7   For the purpose of the disclosure required by paragraph 24.6(d), government assistance is action by government designed to provide an economic benefit specific to an entity or range of entities qualifying under specified criteria. Examples include free technical or marketing advice, the provision of guarantees, and loans at nil or low interest rates.

Section 25
Borrowing Costs

Scope of this section

25.1   This section specifies the accounting for **borrowing costs**. Borrowing costs are interest and other costs that an entity incurs in connection with the borrowing of funds. Borrowing costs include:

(a)   interest expense calculated using the **effective interest method** as described in Section 11 *Basic Financial Instruments*;

(b)   finance charges in respect of **finance leases** recognised in accordance with Section 20 *Leases*; and

(c)   exchange differences arising from foreign currency borrowings to the extent that they are regarded as an adjustment to interest costs.

Recognition

25.2   An entity may adopt a policy of capitalising borrowing costs that are directly attributable to the acquisition, construction or production of a **qualifying asset** as part of the cost of that **asset**. Where an entity adopts a policy of capitalisation of borrowing costs, it shall be applied consistently to a class of qualifying assets. Where an entity does not adopt a policy of capitalising borrowing costs, all borrowing costs shall be recognised as an **expense** in **profit or loss** in the period in which they are incurred.

25.2A   The borrowing costs that are directly attributable to the acquisition, construction or production of a qualifying asset are those borrowing costs that would have been avoided if the expenditure on the qualifying asset had not been made.

25.2B   To the extent that an entity borrows funds specifically for the purpose of obtaining a qualifying asset, the entity shall determine the amount of borrowing costs eligible for capitalisation as the actual borrowing costs incurred on that borrowing during the period less any investment income on the temporary investment of those borrowings.

25.2C   To the extent that funds applied to obtain a qualifying asset form part of the entity's general borrowings, the amount of borrowing costs eligible for capitalisation are determined by applying a capitalisation rate to the expenditure on that asset. For this purpose the expenditure on the asset is the average **carrying amount** of the asset during the period, including borrowing costs previously capitalised. The capitalisation rate used in an accounting period shall be the weighted average of rates applicable to the entity's general borrowings that are outstanding during the period. This excludes borrowings by the entity that are specifically for the purpose of obtaining other qualifying assets. The amount of borrowing costs that an entity capitalises during a period shall not exceed the amount of borrowing costs it incurred during that period.

25.2D   An entity shall:

(a)   capitalise borrowing costs as part of the cost of a qualifying asset from the point when it first incurs both expenditure on the asset and borrowing costs, and undertakes activities necessary to prepare the asset for its intended use or sale;

(b)   suspend capitalisation during extended periods where active development of the asset has paused; and

(c)   cease capitalisation when substantially all the activities necessary to prepare the qualifying asset for its intended use or sale are complete.

Disclosures

25.3   Paragraph 5.5 sets out the presentation requirements for items of profit or loss, including interest payable. Paragraph 11.48(b) requires disclosure of total interest expense (using the effective interest method) for **financial liabilities** that are not at fair value through profit or loss. When a policy of capitalising borrowing costs is not adopted, this section does not require any additional disclosure.

25.3A   Where a policy of capitalisation is adopted, an entity shall disclose:

   * (a)   the amount of borrowing costs capitalised in the period; and

     (b)   the capitalisation rate used.

Section 26
Share-based Payment

Scope of this section

26.1 This section specifies the accounting for all **share-based payment transactions** including:

(a) **equity-settled share-based payment transactions**, in which the entity:

(i) receives goods or services as consideration for its own equity instruments (including shares or **share options**); or

(ii) receives goods or services but has no obligation to settle the transaction with supplier;

(b) **cash-settled share-based payment transactions**, in which the entity acquires goods or services by incurring a **liability** to transfer **cash** or other assets to the supplier of those goods or services for amounts that are based on the price (or value) of the entity's shares or other equity instruments of the entity or another group entity; and

(c) transactions in which the entity receives or acquires goods or services and the terms of the arrangement provide either the entity or the supplier of those goods or services with a choice of whether the entity settles the transaction in cash (or other assets) or by issuing equity instruments.

26.1A A share-based payment transaction may be settled by another group entity (or a shareholder of any group entity) on behalf of the entity receiving or acquiring the goods or services. Paragraph 26.1 also applies to an entity that:

(a) receives goods or services when another entity in the same group (or shareholder of any group entity) has the obligation to settle the share-based payment transaction; or

(b) has an obligation to settle a share-based payment transaction when another entity in the same group receives the goods or services

unless the transaction is clearly for a purpose other than payment for goods or services supplied to the entity receiving them.

26.2 Cash-settled share-based payment transactions include share appreciation rights. For example, an entity might grant share appreciation rights to employees as part of their remuneration package, whereby the employees will become entitled to a future cash payment (rather than an equity instrument), based on the increase in the entity's share price from a specified level over a specified period of time. Or an entity might grant to its employees a right to receive a future cash payment by granting to them a right to shares (including shares to be issued upon the exercise of share options) that are redeemable, either mandatorily (eg upon cessation of employment) or at the employee's option.

Recognition

26.3 An entity shall recognise the goods or services received or acquired in a share-based payment transaction when it obtains the goods or as the services are received. The entity shall recognise a corresponding increase in **equity** if the goods or services were received in an equity-settled share-based payment transaction, or a liability if the goods or services were acquired in a cash-settled share-based payment transaction.

26.4   When the goods or services received or acquired in a share-based payment transaction do not qualify for **recognition** as assets, the entity shall recognise them as **expenses**.

Recognition when there are vesting conditions

26.5   If the share-based payments granted to employees **vest** immediately, the employee is not required to complete a specified period of service before becoming unconditionally entitled to those share-based payments. In the absence of evidence to the contrary, the entity shall presume that services rendered by the employee as consideration for the share-based payments have been received. In this case, on **grant date** the entity shall recognise the services received in full, with a corresponding increase in equity or liabilities.

26.6   If the share-based payments do not vest until the employee completes a specified period of service, the entity shall presume that the services to be rendered by the counterparty as consideration for those share-based payments will be received in the future, during the vesting period. The entity shall account for those services as they are rendered by the employee during the vesting period, with a corresponding increase in equity or liabilities.

Measurement of equity-settled share-based payment transactions

Measurement principle

26.7   For equity-settled share-based payment transactions, an entity shall measure the goods or services received, and the corresponding increase in equity, at the **fair value** of the goods or services received, unless that fair value cannot be estimated reliably. If the entity cannot estimate reliably the fair value of the goods or services received, the entity shall measure their value, and the corresponding increase in equity, by reference to the fair value of the equity instruments granted measured in accordance with paragraphs 26.10 and 26.11. To apply this requirement to transactions with employees and others providing similar services, the entity shall measure the fair value of the services received by reference to the fair value of the equity instruments granted, because typically it is not possible to estimate reliably the fair value of the services received.

26.8   For transactions with employees (including others providing similar services), the fair value of the equity instruments shall be measured at grant date. For transactions with parties other than employees, the measurement date is the date when the entity obtains the goods or the counterparty renders service.

26.9   A grant of equity instruments might be conditional on employees satisfying specified vesting conditions related to service or performance. An example of a vesting condition relating to service is where a grant of shares or share options is conditional on the employee remaining in the entity's employ for a specified period of time. Examples of vesting conditions relating to performance are where a grant of shares or share options is conditional on the entity achieving a specified growth in profit (an example of a non-market condition) or a specified increase in the entity's share price (an example of a **market condition**). All vesting conditions related solely to employee service or to a non-market performance condition shall be taken into account when estimating the number of equity instruments expected to vest. Subsequently, the entity shall revise that estimate, if necessary, if new information indicates that the number of equity instruments expected to vest differs from previous estimates. On the vesting date, the entity shall revise the estimate to equal the number of equity instruments that ultimately vested. All market conditions and non-vesting conditions shall be taken into account when estimating the fair value of the shares or share options at the measurement date, with no subsequent adjustment irrespective of the outcome of the market or non-vesting condition, provided that all other vesting conditions are satisfied.

Shares

26.10 An entity shall measure the fair value of shares (and the related goods or services received) using the following three-tier measurement hierarchy:

(a) If an observable market price is available for the equity instruments granted, use that price.

(b) If an observable market price is not available, measure the fair value of equity instruments granted using entity-specific observable market data such as:

    (i) a recent transaction in the entity's shares; or

    (ii) a recent independent fair valuation of the entity or its principal assets.

(c) If an observable market price is not available and obtaining a reliable **measurement** of fair value under (b) is **impracticable**, indirectly measure the fair value of the shares using a valuation method that uses market data to the greatest extent practicable to estimate what the price of those equity instruments would be on the grant date in an arm's length transaction between knowledgeable, willing parties. The entity's directors shall use their judgement to apply a generally accepted valuation methodology for valuing equity instruments that is appropriate to the circumstances of the entity.

Share options and equity-settled share appreciation rights

26.11 An entity shall measure the fair value of share options and equity-settled share appreciation rights (and the related goods or services received) using the following three-tier measurement hierarchy:

(a) If an observable market price is available for the equity instruments granted, use that price.

(b) If an observable market price is not available, measure the fair value of share options and share appreciation rights granted using entity-specific observable market data such as for a recent transaction in the share options.

(c) If an observable market price is not available and obtaining a reliable measurement of fair value under (b) is impracticable, indirectly measure the fair value of share options or share appreciation rights using an alternative valuation methodology such as an option pricing model. The inputs for an option pricing model (such as the weighted average share price, exercise price, expected volatility, option life, expected dividends and the risk-free interest rate) shall use market data to the greatest extent possible. Paragraph 26.10 provides guidance on determining the fair value of the shares used in determining the weighted average share price. The entity shall derive an estimate of expected volatility consistent with the valuation methodology used to determine the fair value of the shares.

Modifications to the terms and conditions on which equity instruments were granted

26.12   If an entity modifies the vesting conditions in a manner that is beneficial to the employee, for example, by reducing the exercise price of an option or reducing the vesting period or by modifying or eliminating a performance condition, the entity shall take the modified vesting conditions into account in accounting for the share-based payment transaction, as follows:

(a)   If the modification increases the fair value of the equity instruments granted (or increases the number of equity instruments granted) measured immediately before and after the modification, the entity shall include the incremental fair value granted in the measurement of the amount recognised for services received as consideration for the equity instruments granted. The incremental fair value granted is the difference between the fair value of the modified equity instrument and that of the original equity instrument, both estimated as at the date of the modification. If the modification occurs during the vesting period, the incremental fair value granted is included in the measurement of the amount recognised for services received over the period from the modification date until the date when the modified equity instruments vest, in addition to the amount based on the grant date fair value of the original equity instruments, which is recognised over the remainder of the original vesting period.

(b)   If the modification reduces the total fair value of the share-based payment arrangement, or apparently is not otherwise beneficial to the employee, the entity shall nevertheless continue to account for the services received as consideration for the equity instruments granted as if that modification had not occurred.

Cancellations and settlements

26.13   An entity shall account for a cancellation or settlement of an equity-settled share-based payment award as an acceleration of vesting, and therefore shall recognise immediately the amount that otherwise would have been recognised for services received over the remainder of the vesting period.

Cash-settled share-based payment transactions

26.14   For cash-settled share-based payment transactions, an entity shall measure the goods or services acquired and the liability incurred at the fair value of the liability. Until the liability is settled, the entity shall remeasure the fair value of the liability at each **reporting date** and at the date of settlement, with any changes in fair value recognised in **profit or loss** for the period.

Share-based payment transactions with cash alternatives

26.15   Some share-based payment transactions give either the entity or the counterparty a choice of settling the transaction in cash (or other assets) or by the transfer of equity instruments.

26.15A   When the entity has a choice of settlement of the transaction in cash (or other assets) or by the transfer of equity instruments, the entity shall account for the transaction as a wholly equity-settled share-based payment transaction in accordance with paragraphs 26.7 to 26.13 unless:

(a)   the choice of settlement in equity instruments has no commercial substance (eg because the entity is legally prohibited from issuing shares); or

(b)   the entity has a past practice or a stated policy of settling in cash, or generally settles in cash whenever the counterparty asks for cash settlement.

In circumstances (a) and (b) the entity shall account for the transaction as a wholly cash-settled transaction in accordance with paragraph 26.14.

26.15B   When the counterparty has a choice of settlement of the transaction in cash (or other assets) or by the transfer of equity instruments, the entity shall account for the transaction as a wholly cash-settled share-based payment transaction in accordance with paragraph 26.14 unless:

(a)   the choice of settlement in cash (or other assets) has no commercial substance because the cash settlement amount (or value of the other assets) bears no relationship to, and is likely to be lower in value than, the fair value of the equity instruments.

In circumstance (a) the entity shall account for the transaction as a wholly equity-settled transaction in accordance with paragraphs 26.7 to 26.13.

Group plans

26.16   If a share-based payment award is granted by an entity to the employees of one or more members in the **group**, the members are permitted, as an alternative to the treatment set out in paragraphs 26.3 to 26.15, to recognise and measure the share-based payment expense on the basis of a reasonable allocation of the expense for the group.

Government-mandated plans

26.17   Some jurisdictions have programmes established under law by which equity investors (such as employees) are able to acquire equity without providing goods or services that can be specifically identified (or by providing goods or services that are clearly less than the fair value of the equity instruments granted). This indicates that other consideration has been or will be received (such as past or future employee services). These are equity-settled share-based payment transactions within the scope of this section. The entity shall measure the unidentifiable goods or services received (or to be received) as the difference between the fair value of the share-based payment and the fair value of any identifiable goods or services received (or to be received) measured at the grant date.

Disclosures

26.18   An entity shall disclose the following information about the nature and extent of share-based payment arrangements that existed during the period:

(a)   A description of each type of share-based payment arrangement that existed at any time during the period, including the general terms and conditions of each arrangement, such as vesting requirements, the maximum term of options granted, and the method of settlement (eg whether in cash or equity). An entity with substantially similar types of share-based payment arrangements may aggregate this information.

(b)   The number and weighted average exercise prices of share options for each of the following groups of options:

(i)   outstanding at the beginning of the period;

(ii)   granted during the period;

(iii)   forfeited during the period;

(iv)   exercised during the period;

(v) expired during the period;

(vi) outstanding at the end of the period; and

(vii) exercisable at the end of the period.

26.19 For equity-settled share-based payment arrangements, an entity shall disclose information about how it measured the fair value of goods or services received or the value of the equity instruments granted. If a valuation methodology was used, the entity shall disclose the method and its reason for choosing it.

26.20 For cash-settled share-based payment arrangements, an entity shall disclose information about how the liability was measured.

26.21 For share-based payment arrangements that were modified during the period, an entity shall disclose an explanation of those modifications.

26.22 If the entity is part of a group share-based payment plan, and it recognises and measures its share-based payment expense on the basis of a reasonable allocation of the expense recognised for the group, it shall disclose that fact and the basis for the allocation (see paragraph 26.16).

26.23 An entity shall disclose the following information about the effect of share-based payment transactions on the entity's profit or loss for the period and on its **financial position**:

(a) the total expense recognised in profit or loss for the period; and

(b) the total **carrying amount** at the end of the period for liabilities arising from share-based payment transactions.

Section 27
Impairment of Assets

Objective and scope

27.1 An **impairment loss** occurs when the **carrying amount** of an **asset** exceeds its **recoverable amount**. This section shall be applied in accounting for the impairment of all assets other than the following, for which other sections of this FRS establish impairment requirements:

(a) assets arising from **construction contracts** (see Section 23 *Revenue*);

(b) **deferred tax assets** (see Section 29 *Income Tax*);

(c) assets arising from **employee benefits** (see Section 28 *Employee Benefits*);

(d) **financial assets** within the scope of Section 11 *Basic Financial Instruments* or Section 12 *Other Financial Instruments Issues*;

(e) **investment property** measured at **fair value** (see Section 16 *Investment Property*); and

(f) **biological assets** related to **agricultural activity** measured at fair value less estimated costs to sell (see Section 34 *Specialised Activities*).

27.1A This section shall not apply in accounting for the impairment of **deferred acquisition costs** and **intangible assets** arising from contracts within the scope of FRS 103 *Insurance Contracts*.

Impairment of inventories

Selling price less costs to complete and sell

27.2 An entity shall assess at each **reporting date** whether any **inventories** are impaired. The entity shall make the assessment by comparing the carrying amount of each item of inventory (or group of similar items – see paragraph 27.3) with its selling price less costs to complete and sell. If an item of inventory (or group of similar items) is impaired, the entity shall reduce the carrying amount of the inventory (or the group) to its selling price less costs to complete and sell. That reduction is an impairment loss and it is recognised immediately in **profit or loss**.

27.3 If it is **impracticable** to determine the selling price less costs to complete and sell for inventories item by item, the entity may group items of inventory relating to the same product line that have similar purposes or end uses and are produced and marketed in the same geographical area for the purpose of assessing impairment.

Reversal of impairment

27.4 An entity shall make a new assessment of selling price less costs to complete and sell at each subsequent reporting date. When the circumstances that previously caused inventories to be impaired no longer exist or when there is clear evidence of an increase in selling price less costs to complete and sell because of changed economic circumstances, the entity shall reverse the amount of the impairment (ie the reversal is limited to the amount of the original impairment loss) so that the new carrying amount is the lower of the cost and the revised selling price less costs to complete and sell.

General principles

27.5   If, and only if, the recoverable amount of an asset is less than its carrying amount, the entity shall reduce the carrying amount of the asset to its recoverable amount. That reduction is an impairment loss. Paragraphs 27.11 to 27.20A provide guidance on measuring recoverable amount.

27.6   An entity shall recognise an impairment loss immediately in profit or loss, unless the asset is carried at a revalued amount in accordance with another section of this FRS (for example, in accordance with the revaluation model in Section 17 *Property, Plant and Equipment*). Any impairment loss of a revalued asset shall be treated as a revaluation decrease in accordance with that other section.

Indicators of impairment

27.7   An entity shall assess at each reporting date whether there is any indication that an asset may be impaired. If any such indication exists, the entity shall estimate the recoverable amount of the asset. If there is no indication of impairment, it is not necessary to estimate the recoverable amount.

27.8   If it is not possible to estimate the recoverable amount of the individual asset, an entity shall estimate the recoverable amount of the **cash-generating unit** to which the asset belongs. This may be the case because measuring recoverable amount requires forecasting **cash flows**, and sometimes individual assets do not generate cash flows by themselves. An asset's cash-generating unit is the smallest identifiable group of assets that includes the asset and generates cash inflows that are largely independent of the cash inflows from other assets or groups of assets.

27.9   In assessing whether there is any indication that an asset may be impaired, an entity shall consider, as a minimum, the following indications:

External sources of information

(a)   During the period, an asset's market value has declined significantly more than would be expected as a result of the passage of time or normal use.

(b)   Significant changes with an adverse effect on the entity have taken place during the period, or will take place in the near future, in the technological, market, economic or legal environment in which the entity operates or in the market to which an asset is dedicated.

(c)   Market interest rates or other market rates of return on investments have increased during the period, and those increases are likely to affect materially the discount rate used in calculating an asset's **value in use** and decrease the asset's **fair value less costs to sell**.

(d)   The carrying amount of the net assets of the entity is more than the estimated fair value of the entity as a whole (such an estimate may have been made, for example, in relation to the potential sale of part or all of the entity).

Internal sources of information

(e)   Evidence is available of obsolescence or physical damage of an asset.

(f)   Significant changes with an adverse effect on the entity have taken place during the period, or are expected to take place in the near future, in the extent to which, or manner in which, an asset is used or is expected to be used. These changes include the asset becoming idle, plans to discontinue or restructure the operation to which an asset belongs, plans to dispose of an asset before the previously expected date, and reassessing the **useful life** of an asset as finite rather than indefinite.

(g) Evidence is available from internal reporting that indicates that the economic performance of an asset is, or will be, worse than expected. In this context economic performance includes operating results and cash flows.

27.10　If there is an indication that an asset may be impaired, this may indicate that the entity should review the remaining useful life, the **depreciation (amortisation)** method or the **residual value** for the asset and adjust it in accordance with the section of this FRS applicable to the asset (eg Section 17 *Property, Plant and Equipment* and Section 18 *Intangible Assets other than Goodwill*), even if no impairment loss is recognised for the asset.

Measuring recoverable amount

27.11　The recoverable amount of an asset or a cash-generating unit is the higher of its fair value less costs to sell and its value in use. If it is not possible to estimate the recoverable amount of an individual asset, references to an asset in paragraphs 27.12 to 27.20A should be read as references also to an asset's cash-generating unit.

27.12　It is not always necessary to determine both an asset's fair value less costs to sell and its value in use. If either of these amounts exceeds the asset's carrying amount, the asset is not impaired and it is not necessary to estimate the other amount.

27.13　If there is no reason to believe that an asset's value in use materially exceeds its fair value less costs to sell, the asset's fair value less costs to sell may be used as its recoverable amount. This will often be the case for an asset that is held for disposal.

Fair value less costs to sell

27.14　Fair value less costs to sell is the amount obtainable from the sale of an asset in an arm's length transaction between knowledgeable, willing parties, less the costs of disposal. The best evidence of the fair value less costs to sell of an asset is a price in a binding sale agreement in an arm's length transaction or a market price in an **active market**. If there is no binding sale agreement or active market for an asset, fair value less costs to sell is based on the best information available to reflect the amount that an entity could obtain, at the reporting date, from the disposal of the asset in an arm's length transaction between knowledgeable, willing parties, after deducting the costs of disposal. In determining this amount, an entity considers the outcome of recent transactions for similar assets within the same industry.

27.14A　When determining an asset's fair value less costs to sell, consideration shall be given to any restrictions imposed on that asset. Costs to sell shall also include the cost of obtaining relaxation of a restriction where necessary in order to enable the asset to be sold. If a restriction would also apply to any potential purchaser of an asset, the fair value of the asset may be lower than that of an asset whose use is not restricted.

Value in use

27.15　Value in use is the **present value** of the future cash flows expected to be derived from an asset. This present value calculation involves the following steps:

(a) estimating the future cash inflows and outflows to be derived from continuing use of the asset and from its ultimate disposal; and

(b) applying the appropriate discount rate to those future cash flows.

27.16   The following elements shall be reflected in the calculation of an asset's value in use:

(a)   an estimate of the future cash flows the entity expects to derive from the asset;

(b)   expectations about possible variations in the amount or timing of those future cash flows;

(c)   the time value of money, represented by the current market risk-free rate of interest;

(d)   the price for bearing the uncertainty inherent in the asset; and

(e)   other factors, such as illiquidity, that market participants would reflect in pricing the future cash flows the entity expects to derive from the asset.

27.17   In measuring value in use, estimates of future cash flows shall include:

(a)   projections of cash inflows from the continuing use of the asset;

(b)   projections of cash outflows that are necessarily incurred to generate the cash inflows from continuing use of the asset (including cash outflows to prepare the asset for use) and can be directly attributed, or allocated on a reasonable and consistent basis, to the asset; and

(c)   net cash flows, if any, expected to be received (or paid) for the disposal of the asset at the end of its useful life in an arm's length transaction between knowledgeable, willing parties.

The entity may wish to use any recent financial budgets or forecasts to estimate the cash flows, if available. To estimate cash flow projections beyond the period covered by the most recent budgets or forecasts an entity may wish to extrapolate the projections based on the budgets or forecasts using a steady or declining growth rate for subsequent years, unless an increasing rate can be justified.

27.18   Estimates of future cash flows shall not include:

(a)   cash inflows or outflows from **financing activities**; or

(b)   income tax receipts or payments.

27.19   Future cash flows shall be estimated for the asset in its current condition. Estimates of future cash flows shall not include estimated future cash inflows or outflows that are expected to arise from:

(a)   a future restructuring to which an entity is not yet committed; or

(b)   improving or enhancing the asset's performance.

27.20   The discount rate (rates) used in the present value calculation shall be a pre-tax rate (rates) that reflect(s) current market assessments of:

(a)   the time value of money; and

(b)   the risks specific to the asset for which the future cash flow estimates have not been adjusted.

The discount rate (rates) used to measure an asset's value in use shall not reflect risks for which the future cash flow estimates have been adjusted, to avoid double-counting.

27.20A   For assets held for their **service potential**, a cash flow driven valuation (such as value in use) may not be appropriate. In these circumstances **value in use (in respect of assets held for their service potential)** is determined by the present value of the asset's remaining service potential plus the net amount the entity will receive from its disposal. In some cases this may be taken to be costs avoided by possession of the asset. Therefore, **depreciated replacement cost**, may be a suitable measurement model but other approaches may be used where more appropriate.

Recognising and measuring an impairment loss for a cash-generating unit

27.21 An impairment loss shall be recognised for a cash-generating unit if, and only if, the recoverable amount of the unit is less than the carrying amount of the unit. The impairment loss shall be allocated to reduce the carrying amount of the assets of the unit in the following order:

(a) first, to reduce the carrying amount of any **goodwill** allocated to the cash-generating unit; and

(b) then, to the other assets of the unit pro rata on the basis of the carrying amount of each asset in the cash-generating unit.

27.22 However, an entity shall not reduce the carrying amount of any asset in the cash-generating unit below the highest of:

(a) its fair value less costs to sell (if determinable);

(b) its value in use (if determinable); and

(c) zero.

27.23 Any excess amount of the impairment loss that cannot be allocated to an asset because of the restriction in paragraph 27.22 shall be allocated to the other assets of the unit pro rata on the basis of the carrying amount of those other assets.

Additional requirements for impairment of goodwill

27.24 Goodwill, by itself, cannot be sold. Nor does it generate cash flows to an entity that are independent of the cash flows of other assets. As a consequence, the fair value of goodwill cannot be measured directly. Therefore, the fair value of goodwill must be derived from **measurement** of the fair value of the cash-generating unit(s) of which the goodwill is a part.

27.25 For the purpose of impairment testing, goodwill acquired in a **business combination** shall, from the **acquisition date**, be allocated to each of the acquirer's cash-generating units that are expected to benefit from the synergies of the combination, irrespective of whether other assets or **liabilities** of the acquiree are assigned to those units.

27.26 Part of the recoverable amount of a cash-generating unit is attributable to the **non-controlling interest** in goodwill. For the purpose of impairment testing of a non-wholly-owned cash-generating unit with goodwill, the carrying amount of that unit is notionally adjusted, before being compared with its recoverable amount, by grossing up the carrying amount of goodwill allocated to the unit to include the goodwill attributable to the non-controlling interest. This notionally adjusted carrying amount is then compared with the recoverable amount of the unit to determine whether the cash-generating unit is impaired.

27.27 If goodwill cannot be allocated to individual cash-generating units (or groups of cash-generating units) on a non-arbitrary basis, then for the purposes of testing goodwill the entity shall test the impairment of goodwill by determining the recoverable amount of either:

(a) the acquired entity in its entirety, if the goodwill relates to an acquired entity that has not been integrated. Integrated means the acquired **business** has been restructured or dissolved into the reporting entity or other **subsidiaries**; or

(b) the entire group of entities, excluding any entities that have not been integrated, if the goodwill relates to an entity that has been integrated.

In applying this paragraph, an entity will need to separate goodwill into goodwill relating to entities that have been integrated and goodwill relating to entities that have not been integrated. Also the entity shall follow the requirements for cash-generating units in this section when calculating the recoverable amount of, and allocating impairment losses and reversals to assets belonging to, the acquired entity or group of entities.

Reversal of an impairment loss

27.28 An impairment loss recognised for goodwill shall not be reversed in a subsequent period.

27.29 For all assets other than goodwill, if and only if the reasons for the impairment loss have ceased to apply, an impairment loss shall be reversed in a subsequent period. An entity shall assess at each reporting date whether there is any indication that an impairment loss recognised in prior periods may no longer exist or may have decreased. Indications that an impairment loss may have decreased or may no longer exist are generally the opposite of those set out in paragraph 27.9. If any such indication exists, the entity shall determine whether all or part of the prior impairment loss should be reversed. The procedure for making that determination will depend on whether the prior impairment loss on the asset was based on:

(a) the recoverable amount of that individual asset (see paragraph 27.30); or

(b) the recoverable amount of the cash-generating unit to which the asset belongs (see paragraph 27.31).

Reversal where recoverable amount was estimated for an individual impaired asset

27.30 When the prior impairment loss was based on the recoverable amount of the individual impaired asset, the following requirements apply:

(a) The entity shall estimate the recoverable amount of the asset at the current reporting date.

(b) If the estimated recoverable amount of the asset exceeds its carrying amount, the entity shall increase the carrying amount to recoverable amount, subject to the limitation described in (c) below. That increase is a reversal of an impairment loss. The entity shall recognise the reversal immediately in profit or loss unless the asset is carried at revalued amount in accordance with another section of this FRS (for example, the revaluation model in Section 17 *Property, plant and equipment*). Any reversal of an impairment loss of a revalued asset shall be treated as a revaluation increase in accordance with the relevant section of this FRS.

(c) The reversal of an impairment loss shall not increase the carrying amount of the asset above the carrying amount that would have been determined (net of amortisation or depreciation) had no impairment loss been recognised for the asset in prior years.

(d) After a reversal of an impairment loss is recognised, the entity shall adjust the depreciation (amortisation) charge for the asset in future periods to allocate the asset's revised carrying amount, less its residual value (if any), on a systematic basis over its remaining useful life.

Reversal when recoverable amount was estimated for a cash-generating unit

27.31   When the original impairment loss was based on the recoverable amount of the cash-generating unit to which the asset, including goodwill belongs, the following requirements apply:

(a)   The entity shall estimate the recoverable amount of that cash-generating unit at the current reporting date.

(b)   If the estimated recoverable amount of the cash-generating unit exceeds its carrying amount, that excess is a reversal of an impairment loss. The entity shall allocate the amount of that reversal to the assets of the unit, except for goodwill, pro rata with the carrying amounts of those assets, subject to the limitation described in (c) below. Those increases in carrying amounts shall be treated as reversals of impairment losses and recognised immediately in profit or loss unless an asset is carried at revalued amount in accordance with another section of this FRS (for example, the revaluation model in Section 17 *Property, plant and equipment*). Any reversal of an impairment loss of a revalued asset shall be treated as a revaluation increase in accordance with the relevant section of this FRS.

(c)   In allocating a reversal of an impairment loss for a cash-generating unit, the reversal shall not increase the carrying amount of any asset above the lower of:

(i)   its recoverable amount; and

(ii)   the carrying amount that would have been determined (net of amortisation or depreciation) had no impairment loss been recognised for the asset in prior periods.

(d)   Any excess amount of the reversal of the impairment loss that cannot be allocated to an asset because of the restriction in (c) above shall be allocated pro rata to the other assets of the cash-generating unit, except for goodwill.

(e)   After a reversal of an impairment loss is recognised, if applicable, the entity shall adjust the depreciation (amortisation) charge for each asset in the cash-generating unit in future periods to allocate the asset's revised carrying amount, less its residual value (if any), on a systematic basis over its remaining useful life.

Disclosures

27.32   An entity shall disclose the following for each **class of assets** indicated in paragraph 27.33:

* (a)   the amount of impairment losses recognised in profit or loss during the period and the line item(s) in the **statement of comprehensive income** (or in the **income statement**, if presented) in which those impairment losses are included; and

* (b)   the amount of reversals of impairment losses recognised in profit or loss during the period and the line item(s) in the statement of comprehensive income (or in the income statement, if presented) in which those impairment losses are reversed.

27.33   An entity shall disclose the information required by paragraph 27.32 for each of the following classes of asset:

(a)   inventories;

(b)   **property, plant and equipment** (including investment property accounted for by the cost method);

      (c)   goodwill;

      (d)   **intangible assets** other than goodwill;

      (e)   investments in **associates**; and

      (f)   investments in **joint ventures**.

27.33A An entity shall disclose a description of the events and circumstances that led to the **recognition** or reversal of the impairment loss.

Section 28
Employee Benefits

Scope of this section

28.1 **Employee benefits** are all forms of consideration given by an entity in exchange for service rendered by employees, including directors and management. This section applies to all employee benefits, except for **share-based payment transactions**, which are covered by Section 26 *Share-based Payment*. Employee benefits covered by this section will be one of the following four types:

    (a) short-term employee benefits, which are employee benefits (other than **termination benefits**) that are expected to be settled wholly before twelve months after the end of the **reporting period** in which the employees render the related service;

    (b) **post-employment benefits**, which are employee benefits (other than termination benefits and short-term employee benefits) that are payable after the completion of employment;

    (c) other long-term employee benefits, which are all employee benefits, other than short-term employee benefits, post-employment benefits and termination benefits; or

    (d) termination benefits, which are employee benefits provided in exchange for the termination of an employee's employment as a result of either:

        (i) an entity's decision to terminate an employee's employment before the normal retirement date; or

        (ii) an employee's decision to accept voluntary redundancy in exchange for those benefits.

28.2 [Not used]

General recognition principle for all employee benefits

28.3 An entity shall recognise the cost of all employee benefits to which its employees have become entitled as a result of service rendered to the entity during the reporting period:

    (a) As a **liability**, after deducting amounts that have been paid either directly to the employees or as a contribution to an employee benefit fund[12]. If the amount paid exceeds the obligation arising from service before the **reporting date**, an entity shall recognise that excess as an asset to the extent that the prepayment will lead to a reduction in future payments or a cash refund.

    (b) As an **expense**, unless another section of this FRS requires the cost to be recognised as part of the cost of an asset such as **inventories** (for example in accordance with paragraph 13.8) or **property, plant and equipment** (in accordance with paragraph 17.10).

---

[12] Contributions to an employee benefit fund that is an intermediate payment arrangement shall be accounted for in accordance with paragraphs 9.33 to 9.38, and as a result if the employer is a sponsoring entity the assets and liabilities of the intermediary will be accounted for by the sponsoring entity as an extension of its own business. In which case the payment to the employee benefit fund does not extinguish the liability of the employer.

Examples

28.4   Short-term employee benefits include items such as the following, if expected to be settled wholly before 12 months after the end of the annual reporting period in which the employees render the related service:

(a)   wages, salaries and social security contributions;

(b)   paid annual leave and paid sick leave;

(c)   profit-sharing and bonuses; and

(d)   non-monetary benefits (such as medical care, housing, cars and free or subsidised goods or services) for current employees.

Measurement of short-term benefits generally

28.5   When an employee has rendered service to an entity during the reporting period, the entity shall measure the amounts recognised in accordance with paragraph 28.3 at the undiscounted amount of short-term employee benefits expected to be paid in exchange for that service.

Recognition and measurement: Short-term compensated absences

28.6   An entity may compensate employees for absence for various reasons including annual leave and sick leave. Some short-term compensated absences accumulate—they can be carried forward and used in future periods if the employee does not use the current period's entitlement in full. Examples include annual leave and sick leave. An entity shall recognise the expected cost of **accumulating compensated absences** when the employees render service that increases their entitlement to future compensated absences. The entity shall measure the expected cost of accumulating compensated absences at the undiscounted additional amount that the entity expects to pay as a result of the unused entitlement that has accumulated at the end of the reporting period. The entity shall present this amount as falling due within one year at the reporting date.

28.7   An entity shall recognise the cost of other (non-accumulating) compensated absences when the absences occur. The entity shall measure the cost of non-accumulating compensated absences at the undiscounted amount of salaries and wages paid or payable for the period of absence.

Recognition: Profit-sharing and bonus plans

28.8   An entity shall recognise the expected cost of profit-sharing and bonus payments only when:

(a)   the entity has a present legal or **constructive obligation** to make such payments as a result of past events (this means that the entity has no realistic alternative but to make the payments); and

(b)   a reliable estimate of the obligation can be made.

Post-employment benefits: Distinction between defined contribution plans and defined benefit plans

28.9   Post-employment benefits include, for example:

(a)   retirement benefits, such as pensions; and

(b)   other post-employment benefits, such as post-employment life insurance and post-employment medical care.

Arrangements whereby an entity provides post-employment benefits are **post-employment benefit plans**. An entity shall apply this section to all such arrangements whether or not they involve the establishment of a separate entity to receive contributions and to pay benefits. In some cases, these arrangements are imposed by law rather than by action of the entity. In some cases, these arrangements arise from actions of the entity even in the absence of a formal, documented plan.

28.10   Post-employment benefit plans are classified as either **defined contribution plans** or **defined benefit plans**, depending on their principal terms and conditions:

(a)   Defined contribution plans are post-employment benefit plans under which an entity pays fixed contributions into a separate entity (a fund) and has no legal or constructive obligation to pay further contributions or to make direct benefit payments to employees if the fund does not hold sufficient assets to pay all employee benefits relating to employee service in the current and prior periods. Thus, the amount of the post-employment benefits received by the employee is determined by the amount of contributions paid by an entity (and perhaps also the employee) to a post-employment benefit plan or to an insurer, together with investment returns arising from the contributions.

(b)   Defined benefit plans are post-employment benefit plans other than defined contribution plans. Under defined benefit plans, the entity's obligation is to provide the agreed benefits to current and former employees, and actuarial risk (that benefits will cost more or less than expected) and investment risk (that returns on assets set aside to fund the benefits will differ from expectations) are borne, in substance, by the entity. If actuarial or investment experience is worse than expected, the entity's obligation may be increased, and vice versa if actuarial or investment experience is better than expected.

Multi-employer plans and state plans

28.11   **Multi-employer plans** and **state plans** are classified as defined contribution plans or defined benefit plans on the basis of the terms of the plan, including any constructive obligation that goes beyond the formal terms. However, if sufficient information is not available to use defined benefit accounting for a multi-employer plan that is a defined benefit plan, an entity shall account for the plan in accordance with paragraphs 28.13 and 28.13A as if it was a defined contribution plan and make the disclosures required by paragraphs 28.40 and 28.40A. An entity shall account for a state plan in the same way as for a multi-employer plan.

28.11A Where an entity participates in a defined benefit plan, which is a multi-employer plan that in accordance with paragraph 28.11 is accounted for as if the plan were a defined contribution plan, and the entity has entered into an agreement with the multi-employer plan that determines how the entity will fund a deficit, the entity shall recognise a liability for the contributions payable that arise from the agreement (to the extent that they relate to the deficit) and the resulting expense in **profit or loss** in accordance with paragraphs 28.13 and 28.13A.

Insured benefits

28.12   An entity may pay insurance premiums to fund a post-employment benefit plan. The entity shall treat such a plan as a defined contribution plan unless the entity has a legal or constructive obligation either:

(a)   to pay the employee benefits directly when they become due; or

(b)   to pay further amounts if the insurer does not pay all future employee benefits relating to employee service in the current and prior periods.

A constructive obligation could arise indirectly through the plan, through the mechanism for setting future premiums, or through a **related party** relationship with the insurer. If the entity retains such a legal or constructive obligation, the entity shall treat the plan as a defined benefit plan.

Post-employment benefits: Defined contribution plans

Recognition and measurement

28.13   An entity shall recognise the contribution payable for a period:

(a)   As a liability, after deducting any amount already paid. If contribution payments exceed the contribution due for service before the reporting date, an entity shall recognise that excess as an asset to the extent that the prepayment will lead to a reduction in future payments or a cash refund.

(b)   As an expense, unless another section of this FRS requires the cost to be recognised as part of the cost of an asset such as inventories or property, plant and equipment.

28.13A   When contributions to a defined contribution plan (or a defined benefit plan which, in accordance with paragraph 28.11, is accounted for as a defined contribution plan) are not expected to be settled wholly within 12 months after the end of the reporting period in which the employees render the related service, the liability shall be measured at the **present value** of the contributions payable using the methodology for selecting a discount rate specified in paragraph 28.17. The unwinding of the discount shall be recognised as a finance cost in profit or loss in the period in which it arises.

Post-employment benefits: Defined benefit plans

Recognition

28.14   In applying the general **recognition** principle in paragraph 28.3 to defined benefit plans, an entity shall recognise:

(a)   a liability for its obligations under defined benefit plans net of **plan assets**—its 'net defined benefit liability' (see paragraphs 28.15 to 28.22); and

(b)   the net change in that liability during the period as the cost of its defined benefit plans during the period (see paragraphs 28.23 to 28.27).

Measurement of the net defined benefit liability

28.15   An entity shall measure the net defined benefit liability for its obligations under defined benefit plans at the net total of the following amounts:

(a)   the present value of its obligations under defined benefit plans (its **defined benefit obligation**) at the reporting date (paragraphs 28.16 to 28.21A provide guidance for measuring this obligation); minus

(b) the **fair value** at the reporting date of plan assets (if any) out of which the obligations are to be settled. Paragraphs 11.27 to 11.32 establish requirements for determining the fair values of those plan assets, except that, if the asset is an insurance policy that exactly matches the amount and timing of some or all of the benefits payable under the plan, the fair value of the asset is deemed to be the present value of the related obligation.

28.15A   Where an entity has measured its defined benefit obligation using the **projected unit credit method** (including the use of appropriate **actuarial assumptions**), as set out in paragraph 28.18, it shall not recognise any additional liabilities to reflect differences between these assumptions and those used for the most recent actuarial valuation of the plan for funding purposes. For the avoidance of doubt, no additional liabilities shall be recognised in respect of an agreement with the defined benefit plan to fund a deficit (such as a schedule of contributions).

Inclusion of both vested and unvested benefits

28.16   The present value of an entity's obligations under defined benefit plans at the reporting date shall reflect the estimated amount of benefit that employees have earned in return for their service in the current and prior periods, including benefits that are not yet **vested** (see paragraph 28.26) and including the effects of benefit formulas that give employees greater benefits for later years of service. This requires the entity to determine how much benefit is attributable to the current and prior periods on the basis of the plan's benefit formula and to make estimates (actuarial assumptions) about demographic variables (such as employee turnover and mortality) and financial variables (such as future increases in salaries and medical costs) that influence the cost of the benefit. The actuarial assumptions shall be unbiased (neither imprudent nor excessively conservative), mutually compatible, and selected to lead to the best estimate of the future **cash flows** that will arise under the plan.

Discounting

28.17   An entity shall measure its defined benefit obligation on a discounted present value basis. The entity shall determine the rate used to discount the future payments by reference to market yields at the reporting date on high quality corporate bonds. In countries with no deep market in such bonds, the entity shall use the market yields (at the reporting date) on government bonds. The currency and term of the corporate bonds or government bonds shall be consistent with the currency and estimated period of the future payments.

Actuarial valuation method

28.18   An entity shall use the projected unit credit method to measure its defined benefit obligation and the related expense. If defined benefits are based on future salaries, the projected unit credit method requires an entity to measure its defined benefit obligations on a basis that reflects estimated future salary increases. Additionally, the projected unit credit method requires an entity to make various actuarial assumptions in measuring the defined benefit obligation, including discount rates, employee turnover, mortality, and (for defined benefit medical plans) medical cost trend rates.

28.19   [Not used]

28.20   This FRS does not require an entity to engage an independent actuary to perform the comprehensive actuarial valuation needed to calculate its defined benefit obligation. Nor does it require that a comprehensive actuarial valuation must be done annually. In the periods between comprehensive actuarial valuations, if the principal actuarial assumptions have not changed significantly the defined benefit obligation can be measured by adjusting the prior period measurement for changes in employee demographics such as number of employees and salary levels.

Plan introductions, changes, curtailments and settlements

28.21   If a defined benefit plan has been introduced or the benefits have changed in the current period, the entity shall increase or decrease its net defined benefit liability to reflect the change, and shall recognise the increase (decrease) as an expense (**income**) in measuring **profit or loss** in the current reporting period.

28.21A If a defined benefit plan has been curtailed (ie benefits or group of covered employees are reduced) or settled (the relevant part of the employer's obligation is completely discharged) in the current period, the defined benefit obligation shall be decreased or eliminated, and the entity shall recognise the resulting **gain** or loss in profit or loss in the current period.

Defined benefit plan asset

28.22   If the present value of the defined benefit obligation at the reporting date is less than the fair value of plan assets at that date, the plan has a surplus. An entity shall recognise a plan surplus as a defined benefit plan asset only to the extent that it is able to recover the surplus either through reduced contributions in the future or through refunds from the plan.

Cost of a defined benefit plan

28.23   An entity shall recognise the cost of a defined benefit plan, except to the extent that another section of this FRS requires part or all of the cost to be recognised as part of the cost of an asset, as follows:

(a)   the change in the net defined benefit liability arising from employee service rendered during the reporting period in profit or loss;

(b)   net interest on the net defined benefit liability during the reporting period in profit or loss;

(c)   the cost of plan introductions, benefit changes, curtailments and settlements in profit or loss (see paragraphs 28.21 and 28.21A); and

(d)   remeasurement of the net defined benefit liability in **other comprehensive income**.

Some defined benefit plans require employees or third parties to contribute to the cost of the plan. Contributions by employees reduce the cost of the benefits to the entity.

28.24   The net interest on the net defined benefit liability shall be determined by multiplying the net defined benefit liability by the discount rate in paragraph 28.17, both as determined at the start of the annual reporting period, taking account of any changes in the net defined benefit liability during the period as a result of contribution and benefit payments.

28.24A The net interest on the net defined benefit liability can be viewed as comprising interest cost on the defined benefit obligation and interest income on plan assets excluding the effect of any surplus that is not recoverable in accordance with paragraph 28.22.

28.24B Interest income on plan assets, excluding the effect of any surplus that is not recoverable in accordance with paragraph 28.22, is a component of the return on plan assets, and is determined by multiplying the fair value of the plan assets by the discount rate specified in paragraph 28.17 both as determined at the start of the annual reporting period, taking account of any changes in the plan assets held during the period as a result of contribution and benefit payments. The difference between the interest income on plan assets and the return on plan assets is included in the remeasurement of the net defined benefit liability.

28.25   Remeasurement of the net defined benefit liability comprises:

(a)   **actuarial gains and losses**;

(b)   the return on plan assets, excluding amounts included in net interest on the net defined benefit liability; and

(c)   any change in the amount of a defined benefit plan surplus that is not recoverable (see paragraph 28.22), excluding amounts included in net interest on the net defined benefit liability.

28.25A   Remeasurement of the net defined benefit liability recognised in other comprehensive income shall not be reclassified to profit or loss in a subsequent period.

28.26   Employee service gives rise to an obligation under a defined benefit plan even if the benefits are conditional on future employment (in other words, they are not yet vested). Employee service before the vesting date gives rise to a constructive obligation because, at each successive reporting date, the amount of future service that an employee will have to render before becoming entitled to the benefit is reduced. In measuring its defined benefit obligation, an entity considers the probability that some employees may not satisfy vesting requirements. Similarly, although some post-employment benefits (such as post-employment medical benefits) become payable only if a specified event occurs when an employee is no longer employed (such as an illness), an obligation is created when the employee renders service that will provide entitlement to the benefit if the specified event occurs. The probability that the specified event will occur affects the **measurement** of the obligation, but does not determine whether the obligation exists.

28.27   If defined benefits are reduced for amounts that will be paid to employees under government-sponsored plans, an entity shall measure its defined benefit obligations on a basis that reflects the benefits payable under the government plans, but only if:

(a)   those plans were enacted before the reporting date; or

(b)   past history, or other reliable evidence, indicates that those state benefits will change in some predictable manner, for example, in line with future changes in general price levels or general salary levels.

Reimbursements

28.28   If an entity is virtually certain that another party will reimburse some or all of the expenditure required to settle a defined benefit obligation, the entity shall recognise its right to reimbursement as a separate asset. An entity shall treat that asset in the same way as plan assets.

Other long-term employee benefits

28.29   Other long-term employee benefits include items such as the following, if not expected to be settled wholly before 12 months after the end of the annual reporting period in which the employees render the related service:

(a)   long-term paid absences such as long-service or sabbatical leave;

(b)   other long-service benefits;

(c)   long-term disability benefits;

(d) profit-sharing and bonuses; and

(e) deferred remuneration.

28.30 An entity shall recognise a liability for other long-term employee benefits measured at the net total of the following amounts:

(a) the present value of the benefit obligation at the reporting date (calculated using the methodology for selecting a discount rate in paragraph 28.17); minus

(b) the fair value at the reporting date of plan assets (if any) out of which the obligations are to be settled directly.

An entity shall recognise the change in the liability in profit or loss, except to the extent that this FRS requires or permits their inclusion in the cost of an asset.

Termination benefits

28.31 An entity may be committed, by legislation, by contractual or other agreements with employees or their representatives or by a constructive obligation based on business practice, custom or a desire to act equitably, to make payments (or provide other benefits) to employees when it terminates their employment. Such payments are termination benefits.

Recognition

28.32 Because termination benefits do not provide an entity with future economic benefits, an entity shall recognise them as an expense in profit or loss immediately.

28.33 When an entity recognises termination benefits, the entity may also have to account for a curtailment of retirement benefits or other employee benefits.

28.34 An entity shall recognise termination benefits as a liability and an expense only when the entity is demonstrably committed either:

(a) to terminate the employment of an employee or group of employees before the normal retirement date; or

(b) to provide termination benefits as a result of an offer made in order to encourage voluntary redundancy.

28.35 An entity is demonstrably committed to a termination only when the entity has a detailed formal plan for the termination[13] and is without realistic possibility of withdrawal from the plan.

Measurement

28.36 An entity shall measure termination benefits at the best estimate of the expenditure that would be required to settle the obligation at the reporting date. In the case of an offer made to encourage voluntary redundancy, the measurement of termination benefits shall be based on the number of employees expected to accept the offer.

28.37 When termination benefits are due more than 12 months after the end of the reporting period, they shall be measured at their discounted present value using the methodology for selecting a discount rate specified in paragraph 28.17.

---

[13] An example of the features of a detailed formal plan for restructuring, which may include termination benefits, is given in paragraph 21.11C.

Group plans

28.38   Where an entity participates in a defined benefit plan that shares risks between entities under common control it shall obtain information about the plan as a whole measured in accordance with this FRS on the basis of assumptions that apply to the plan as a whole. If there is a contractual agreement or stated policy for charging the net defined benefit cost of a defined benefit plan as a whole measured in accordance with this FRS to individual group entities, the entity shall, in its **individual financial statements**, recognise the net defined benefit cost of a defined benefit plan so charged. If there is no such agreement or policy, the net defined benefit cost of a defined benefit plan shall be recognised in the individual financial statements of the group entity which is legally responsible for the plan. The other group entities shall, in their individual financial statements, recognise a cost equal to their contribution payable for the period.

Disclosures

Disclosures about short-term employee benefits

28.39   This section does not require specific disclosures about short-term employee benefits.

Disclosures about defined contribution plans

28.40   An entity shall disclose the amount recognised in profit or loss as an expense for defined contribution plans.

28.40A   If an entity treats a defined benefit multi-employer plan as a defined contribution plan because sufficient information is not available to use defined benefit accounting (see paragraph 28.11) it shall:

* (a)   disclose the fact that it is a defined benefit plan and the reason why it is being accounted for as a defined contribution plan, along with any available information about the plan's surplus or deficit and the implications, if any, for the entity;

* (b)   include a description of the extent to which the entity can be liable to the plan for other entities' obligations under the terms and conditions of the multi-employer plan; and

  (c)   disclose how any liability recognised in accordance with paragraph 28.11A has been determined.

Disclosures about defined benefit plans

28.41   An entity shall disclose the following information about defined benefit plans (except for any defined multi-employer benefit plans that are accounted for as a defined contribution plan in accordance with paragraphs 28.11 and 28.11A, for which the disclosures in paragraphs 28.40 and 28.40A apply instead). If an entity has more than one defined benefit plan, these disclosures may be made in aggregate, separately for each plan, or in such groupings as are considered to be the most useful:

  (a)   A general description of the type of plan, including **funding** policy. This includes the amount and timing of the future payments to be made by the entity under any agreement with the defined benefit plan to fund a deficit (such as a schedule of contributions).

  (b)   [Not used]

  (c)   [Not used]

(d) The date of the most recent comprehensive actuarial valuation and, if it was not as of the reporting date, a description of the adjustments that were made to measure the defined benefit obligation at the reporting date.

(e) A reconciliation of opening and closing balances for each of the following:

    (i) the defined benefit obligation;

    (ii) the fair value of plan assets; and

    (iii) any reimbursement right recognised as an asset.

(f) Each of the reconciliations in paragraph 28.41(e) shall show each of the following, if applicable:

    (i) the change in the defined benefit liability arising from employee service rendered during the reporting period in profit or loss;

    (ii) interest income or expense;

    (iii) remeasurement of the defined benefit liability, showing separately actuarial gains and losses and the return on plan assets less amounts included in (ii) above; and

    (iv) plan introductions, changes, curtailments and settlements.

(g) The total cost relating to defined benefit plans for the period, disclosing separately the amounts:

    (i) recognised in profit or loss as an expense; and

    (ii) included in the cost of an asset.

(h) For each major class of plan assets, which shall include, but is not limited to, equity instruments, debt instruments, property, and all other assets, the percentage or amount that each major class constitutes of the fair value of the total plan assets at the reporting date.

(i) The amounts included in the fair value of plan assets for:

    (i) each class of the entity's own **financial instruments**; and

    (ii) any property occupied by, or other assets used by, the entity.

(j) The return on plan assets.

(k) The principal actuarial assumptions used, including, when applicable:

    (i) the discount rates;

    (ii) [not used]

    (iii) the expected rates of salary increases;

    (iv) medical cost trend rates; and

    (v) any other **material** actuarial assumptions used.

The reconciliations in (e) and (f) above need not be presented for prior periods.

28.41A If an entity participates in a defined benefit plan that shares risks between entities under common control (see paragraph 28.38) it shall disclose the following information:

(a) The contractual agreement or stated policy for charging the cost of a defined benefit plan or the fact that there is no policy.

(b) The policy for determining the contribution to be paid by the entity.

(c) If the entity accounts for an allocation of the net defined benefit cost, all the information required in paragraph 28.41.

* (d) If the entity accounts for the contributions payable for the period, the information about the plan as a whole required by paragraph 28.41(a), (d), (h) and (i).

This information can be disclosed by cross-reference to disclosures in another group entity's **financial statements** if:

(i) that group entity's financial statements separately identify and disclose the information required about the plan; and

(ii) that group entity's financial statements are available to users of the financial statements on the same terms as the financial statements of the entity and at the same time as, or earlier than, the financial statements of the entity.

Disclosures about other long-term benefits

28.42 For each category of other long-term benefits that an entity provides to its employees, the entity shall disclose the nature of the benefit, the amount of its obligation and the extent of funding at the reporting date.

Disclosures about termination benefits

28.43 For each category of termination benefits that an entity provides to its employees, the entity shall disclose the nature of the benefit, its **accounting policy**, and the amount of its obligation and the extent of funding at the reporting date.

28.44 When there is uncertainty about the number of employees who will accept an offer of termination benefits, a **contingent liability** exists. Section 21 *Provisions and Contingencies* requires an entity to disclose information about its contingent liabilities unless the possibility of an outflow in settlement is remote.

Section 29
Income Tax

Scope of this section

29.1 For the purpose of this FRS, **income tax** includes all domestic and foreign taxes that are based on **taxable profit**. Income tax also includes taxes, such as withholding taxes, that are payable by a **subsidiary**, **associate** or **joint venture** on distributions to the reporting entity.

29.2 This section covers accounting for income tax. It requires an entity to recognise the current and future tax consequences of transactions and other events that have been recognised in the **financial statements**. These recognised tax amounts comprise **current tax** and **deferred tax**. Current tax is tax payable (refundable) in respect of the taxable profit (tax loss) for the current period or past **reporting periods**. Deferred tax represents the future tax consequences of transactions and events recognised in the financial statements of the current and previous periods. This section also requires that deferred tax is recognised in respect of **assets** (other than **goodwill**) and **liabilities** recognised as a result of a **business combination**.

29.2A This section also covers accounting for value added tax (VAT) and other similar sales taxes, which are not income taxes.

Recognition and measurement of current tax

29.3 An entity shall recognise a current tax liability for tax payable on taxable profit for the current and past periods. If the amount of tax paid for the current and past periods exceeds the amount of tax payable for those periods, the entity shall recognise the excess as a current tax asset.

29.4 An entity shall recognise a current tax asset for the benefit of a tax loss that can be carried back to recover tax paid in a previous period.

29.5 An entity shall measure a current tax liability (asset) at the amount of tax it expects to pay (recover) using the tax rates and laws that have been enacted or **substantively enacted** by the **reporting date**.

Recognition of deferred tax

Timing differences

29.6 Deferred tax shall be recognised in respect of all **timing differences** at the reporting date, except as otherwise required by paragraphs 29.7 to 29.9 and 29.11 below. Timing differences are differences between taxable profits and **total comprehensive income** as stated in the financial statements that arise from the inclusion of **income** and **expenses** in tax assessments in periods different from those in which they are recognised in financial statements.

29.7 Unrelieved tax losses and other **deferred tax assets** shall be recognised only to the extent that it is **probable** that they will be recovered against the reversal of **deferred tax liabilities** or other future taxable profits (the very existence of unrelieved tax losses is strong evidence that there may not be other future taxable profits against which the losses will be relieved).

29.8   Deferred tax shall be recognised when the tax allowances for the cost of a **fixed asset** are received before or after the **depreciation** of the fixed asset is recognised in **profit or loss**. If and when all conditions for retaining the tax allowances have been met, the deferred tax shall be reversed.

29.9   Deferred tax shall be recognised when income or expenses from a subsidiary, associate, branch, or interest in joint venture have been recognised in the financial statements, and will be assessed to or allowed for tax in a future period, except where:

(a)   the reporting entity is able to control the reversal of the timing difference; and

(b)   it is probable that the timing difference will not reverse in the foreseeable future.

Such timing differences may arise, for example, where there are undistributed profits in a subsidiary, associate, branch or interest in a joint venture.

Permanent differences

29.10   **Permanent differences** arise because certain types of **income** and expenses are non-taxable or disallowable, or because certain tax charges or allowances are greater or smaller than the corresponding income or expense in the financial statements. Deferred tax shall not be recognised on permanent differences except for circumstances set out in paragraph 29.11.

Business combinations

29.11   When the amount that can be deducted for tax for an asset (other than goodwill) that is recognised in a business combination is less (more) than the value at which it is recognised, a deferred tax liability (asset) shall be recognised for the additional tax that will be paid (avoided) in respect of that difference. Similarly, a deferred tax asset (liability) shall be recognised for the additional tax that will be avoided (paid) because of a difference between the value at which a liability is recognised and the amount that will be assessed for tax. The amount attributed to goodwill shall be adjusted by the amount of deferred tax recognised.

Measurement of deferred tax

29.12   An entity shall measure a deferred tax liability (asset) using the tax rates and laws that have been enacted or substantively enacted by the reporting date that are expected to apply to the reversal of the timing difference except for the cases dealt with in paragraphs 29.15 and 29.16 below.

29.13   When different tax rates apply to different levels of taxable profit, an entity shall measure deferred tax expense (income) and related deferred tax liabilities (assets) using the average enacted or substantively enacted rates that it expects to be applicable to the taxable profit (tax loss) of the periods in which it expects the deferred tax asset to be realised or the deferred tax liability to be settled.

29.14   In some jurisdictions, income taxes are payable at a higher or lower rate if part or all of the profit or retained earnings is paid out as a dividend to shareholders of the entity. In other jurisdictions, income taxes may be refundable or payable if part or all of the profit or retained earnings is paid out as a dividend to shareholders of the entity. In both of those circumstances, an entity shall measure current and deferred taxes at the tax rate applicable to undistributed profits until the entity recognises a liability to pay a dividend. When the entity recognises a liability to pay a dividend, it shall recognise the resulting current or deferred tax liability (asset), and the related **tax expense** (income).

29.15   Deferred tax relating to a non-depreciable asset that is measured using the revaluation model in Section 17 *Property, Plant and Equipment* shall be measured using the tax rates and allowances that apply to the sale of the asset.

29.16   Deferred tax relating to **investment property** that is measured at **fair value** in accordance with Section 16 *Investment Property* shall be measured using the tax rates and allowances that apply to sale of the asset, except for investment property that has a limited **useful life** and is held within a business model whose objective is to consume substantially all of the economic benefits embodied in the property over time.

Measurement of both current and deferred tax

29.17   An entity shall not discount current or deferred tax assets and liabilities.

Withholding tax on dividends

29.18   When an entity pays dividends to its shareholders, it may be required to pay a portion of the dividends to taxation authorities on behalf of shareholders. Outgoing dividends and similar amounts payable shall be recognised at an amount that includes any withholding tax but excludes other taxes, such as attributable tax credits.

29.19   Incoming dividends and similar income receivable shall be recognised at an amount that includes any withholding tax but excludes other taxes, such as attributable tax credits. Any withholding tax suffered shall be shown as part of the tax charge.

Value Added Tax ('VAT') and other similar sales taxes

29.20   **Turnover** shown in profit or loss shall exclude VAT and other similar sales taxes on taxable outputs and VAT imputed under the flat rate VAT scheme. Expenses shall exclude recoverable VAT and other similar recoverable sales taxes. Irrecoverable VAT allocable to fixed assets and to other items disclosed separately in the financial statements shall be included in their cost where practicable and **material**.

Presentation

Allocation in comprehensive income and equity

29.21   An entity shall present changes in a current tax liability (asset) and changes in a deferred tax liability (asset) as tax expense (income) with the exception of those changes arising on the initial **recognition** of a business combination which shall be dealt with in accordance with paragraph 29.11.

29.22   An entity shall present tax expense (income) in the same component of **total comprehensive income** (ie continuing or **discontinued operations**, and profit or loss or **other comprehensive income**) or **equity** as the transaction or other event that resulted in the tax expense (income).

Presentation in the statement of financial position

29.23   An entity shall present deferred tax liabilities within provisions for liabilities and deferred tax assets within debtors.

Offsetting

29.24   An entity shall offset current tax assets and current tax liabilities, if and only if, it has a legally enforceable right to set off the amounts and it intends either to settle on a net basis or to realise the asset and settle the liability simultaneously.

29.24A An entity shall offset deferred tax assets and deferred tax liabilities if, and only if:

   (a) the entity has a legally enforceable right to set off current tax assets against current tax liabilities; and

   (b) the deferred tax assets and deferred tax liabilities relate to income taxes levied by the same taxation authority on either the same taxable entity or different taxable entities which intend either to settle current tax liabilities and assets on a net basis, or to realise the assets and settle the liabilities simultaneously, in each future period in which significant amounts of deferred tax liabilities or assets are expected to be settled or recovered.

Disclosures

29.25   An entity shall disclose information that enables users of its financial statements to evaluate the nature and financial effect of the current and deferred tax consequences of recognised transactions and other events.

29.26   An entity shall disclose separately the major components of tax expense (income). Such components of tax expense (income) may include:

   (a) current tax expense (income);

   (b) any adjustments recognised in the period for current tax of prior periods;

   (c) the amount of deferred tax expense (income) relating to the origination and reversal of timing differences;

   (d) the amount of deferred tax expense (income) relating to changes in tax rates or the imposition of new taxes;

   (e) adjustments to deferred tax expense (income) arising from a change in the tax status of the entity or its shareholders; and

   (f) the amount of tax expense (income) relating to changes in **accounting policies** and **material errors** (see Section 10 *Accounting Policies, Estimates and Errors*).

29.27   An entity shall disclose the following separately:

 * (a) the aggregate current and deferred tax relating to items that are recognised as items of other comprehensive income or equity;

   (b) a reconciliation between:

      (i)   the tax expense (income) included in profit or loss; and

      (ii) the profit or loss on ordinary activities before tax multiplied by the applicable tax rate;

   (c) the amount of the net reversal of deferred tax assets and deferred tax liabilities expected to occur during the year beginning after the **reporting period** together with a brief explanation for the expected reversal;

   (d) an explanation of changes in the applicable tax rate(s) compared with the previous reporting period;

(e) the amount of deferred tax liabilities and deferred tax assets at the end of the reporting period for each type of timing difference and the amount of unused tax losses and tax credits;

(f) the expiry date, if any, of timing differences, unused tax losses and unused tax credits; and

(g) in the circumstances described in paragraph 29.14, an explanation of the nature of the potential income tax consequences that would result from the payment of dividends to its shareholders.

Section 30
Foreign Currency Translation

Scope of this section

30.1   An entity can conduct foreign activities in two ways. It may have transactions in foreign currencies or it may have **foreign operations**. In addition, an entity may present its **financial statements** in a foreign currency. This section prescribes how to include foreign currency transactions and foreign operations in the financial statements of an entity and how to translate financial statements into a **presentation currency**. Hedge accounting of foreign currency items is dealt with in Section 12 *Other Financial Instruments Issues*.

Functional currency

30.2   Each entity shall identify its **functional currency**. An entity's functional currency is the currency of the primary economic environment in which the entity operates.

30.3   The primary economic environment in which an entity operates is normally the one in which it primarily generates and expends **cash**. Therefore, the following are the most important factors an entity considers in determining its functional currency:

   (a)   the currency:

      (i)   that mainly influences sales prices for goods and services (this will often be the currency in which sales prices for its goods and services are denominated and settled); and

      (ii) of the country whose competitive forces and regulations mainly determine the sales prices of its goods and services; and

   (b)   the currency that mainly influences labour, material and other costs of providing goods or services (this will often be the currency in which such costs are denominated and settled).

30.4   The following factors may also provide evidence of an entity's functional currency:

   (a)   the currency in which funds from **financing activities** (issuing debt and equity instruments) are generated; and

   (b)   the currency in which receipts from **operating activities** are usually retained.

30.5   The following additional factors are considered in determining the functional currency of a foreign operation, and whether its functional currency is the same as that of the reporting entity (the reporting entity, in this context, being the entity that has the foreign operation as its **subsidiary**, branch, **associate** or **joint venture**):

   (a)   Whether the activities of the foreign operation are carried out as an extension of the reporting entity, rather than being carried out with a significant degree of autonomy. An example of the former is when the foreign operation only sells goods imported from the reporting entity and remits the proceeds to it. An example of the latter is when the operation accumulates cash and other **monetary items**, incurs **expenses**, generates **income** and arranges borrowings, all substantially in its local currency.

   (b)   Whether transactions with the reporting entity are a high or a low proportion of the foreign operation's activities.

   (c)   Whether **cash flows** from the activities of the foreign operation directly affect the cash flows of the reporting entity and are readily available for remittance to it.

(d) Whether cash flows from the activities of the foreign operation are sufficient to service existing and normally expected debt obligations without funds being made available by the reporting entity.

Reporting foreign currency transactions in the functional currency

Initial recognition

30.6 A foreign currency transaction is a transaction that is denominated or requires settlement in a foreign currency, including transactions arising when an entity:

(a) buys or sells goods or services whose price is denominated in a foreign currency;

(b) borrows or lends funds when the amounts payable or receivable are denominated in a foreign currency; or

(c) otherwise acquires or disposes of **assets**, or incurs or settles **liabilities**, denominated in a foreign currency.

30.7 An entity shall record a foreign currency transaction, on initial **recognition** in the functional currency, by applying to the foreign currency amount the spot exchange rate between the functional currency and the foreign currency at the date of the transaction.

30.8 The date of a transaction is the date on which the transaction first qualifies for recognition in accordance with this FRS. For practical reasons, a rate that approximates the actual rate at the date of the transaction is often used, for example, an average rate for a week or a month might be used for all transactions in each foreign currency occurring during that period. However, if exchange rates fluctuate significantly, the use of the average rate for a period is inappropriate.

Reporting at the end of the subsequent reporting periods

30.9 At the end of each **reporting period**, an entity shall:

(a) translate foreign currency monetary items using the **closing rate**;

(b) translate non-monetary items that are measured in terms of historical cost in a foreign currency using the exchange rate at the date of the transaction; and

(c) translate non-monetary items that are measured at **fair value** in a foreign currency using the exchange rates at the date when the fair value was determined.

30.10 An entity shall recognise, in **profit or loss** in the period in which they arise, exchange differences arising on the settlement of monetary items or on translating monetary items at rates different from those at which they were translated on initial recognition during the period or in previous periods, except as described in paragraph 30.13.

30.11 When another section of this FRS requires a **gain** or loss on a non-monetary item to be recognised in **other comprehensive income**, an entity shall recognise any exchange component of that gain or loss in other comprehensive income. Conversely, when a gain or loss on a non-monetary item is recognised in profit or loss, an entity shall recognise any exchange component of that gain or loss in profit or loss.

Net investment in a foreign operation

30.12 An entity may have a monetary item that is receivable from or payable to a foreign operation. An item for which settlement is neither planned nor likely to occur in the foreseeable future is, in substance, a part of the entity's net investment in that foreign operation, and is accounted for in accordance with paragraph 30.13. Such monetary items may include long-term receivables or loans. They do not include trade receivables or trade payables.

30.13 Exchange differences arising on a monetary item that forms part of a reporting entity's **net investment in a foreign operation** shall be recognised in profit or loss in the **separate financial statements** of the reporting entity or the **individual financial statements** of the foreign operation, as appropriate. In the financial statements that include the foreign operation and the reporting entity (eg **consolidated financial statements** when the foreign operation is a subsidiary), such exchange differences shall be recognised in other comprehensive income and accumulated in **equity**. They shall not be recognised in profit or loss on disposal of the net investment.

Change in functional currency

30.14 When there is a change in an entity's functional currency, the entity shall apply the translation procedures applicable to the new functional currency prospectively from the date of the change.

30.15 As noted in paragraphs 30.2 to 30.5, the functional currency of an entity reflects the underlying transactions, events and conditions that are relevant to the entity. Accordingly, once the functional currency is determined, it can be changed only if there is a change to those underlying transactions, events and conditions. For example, a change in the currency that mainly influences the sales prices of goods and services may lead to a change in an entity's functional currency.

30.16 The effect of a change in functional currency is accounted for prospectively. In other words, an entity translates all items into the new functional currency using the exchange rate at the date of the change. The resulting translated amounts for non-monetary items are treated as their historical cost.

Use of a presentation currency other than the functional currency

Translation to the presentation currency

30.17 An entity may present its financial statements in any currency (or currencies). If the presentation currency differs from the entity's functional currency, the entity shall translate its items of income and expense and **financial position** into the presentation currency. For example, when a **group** contains individual entities with different functional currencies, the items of income and expense and financial position of each entity are expressed in a common currency so that consolidated financial statements may be presented.

30.18 An entity whose functional currency is not the currency of a hyperinflationary economy shall translate its results and financial position into a different presentation currency using the following procedures:

(a) assets and liabilities for each **statement of financial position** presented (ie including comparatives) shall be translated at the closing rate at the date of that statement of financial position;

(b) income and expenses for each **statement of comprehensive income** (ie including comparatives) shall be translated at exchange rates at the dates of the transactions; and

(c) all resulting exchange differences shall be recognised in other comprehensive income.

30.19   For practical reasons, an entity may use a rate that approximates the exchange rates at the dates of the transactions, for example an average rate for the period to translate income and expense items. However, if exchange rates fluctuate significantly, the use of the average rate for a period is inappropriate.

30.20   The exchange differences referred to in paragraph 30.18(c) result from:

(a)   translating income and expenses at the exchange rates at the dates of the transactions and assets and liabilities at the closing rate; and

(b)   translating the opening net assets at a closing rate that differs from the previous closing rate.

When the exchange differences relate to a foreign operation that is consolidated but not wholly-owned, accumulated exchange differences arising from translation and attributable to the **non-controlling interest** are allocated to, and recognised as part of, non-controlling interest in the consolidated statement of financial position.

30.21   An entity whose functional currency is the currency of a hyperinflationary economy shall adjust its results and financial position using the procedures specified in Section 31 *Hyperinflation* before applying the requirements of this section.

Translation of a foreign operation into the investor's presentation currency

30.22   In incorporating the assets, liabilities, income and expenses of a foreign operation with those of the reporting entity, the entity shall follow normal consolidation procedures, such as the elimination of intragroup balances and intragroup transactions of a subsidiary (see Section 9 *Consolidated and Separate Financial Statements*) and the translation procedures set out in paragraphs 30.17 to 30.21. An intragroup monetary asset (or liability), whether short-term or long-term, cannot be eliminated against the corresponding intragroup liability (or asset) without showing the results of currency fluctuations in the consolidated financial statements. This is because the monetary item represents a commitment to convert one currency into another and exposes the reporting entity to a gain or loss through currency fluctuations. Accordingly, in the consolidated financial statements, a reporting entity continues to recognise such an exchange difference in profit or loss or, if it arises from the circumstances described in paragraph 30.13, the entity shall recognise it in other comprehensive income.

30.23   Any **goodwill** arising on the acquisition of a foreign operation and any fair value adjustments to the **carrying amounts** of assets and liabilities arising on the acquisition of that foreign operation shall be treated as assets and liabilities of the foreign operation. Thus, they shall be expressed in the functional currency of the foreign operation and shall be translated at the closing rate in accordance with paragraph 30.18.

Disclosures

30.24   In paragraphs 30.26 and 30.27, references to functional currency apply, in the case of a group, to the functional currency of the **parent**.

30.25   An entity shall disclose the following:

(a)   the amount of exchange differences recognised in profit or loss during the period, except for those arising on **financial instruments** measured at fair value through profit or loss in accordance with Sections 11 *Basic Financial Instruments* and Section 12.

(b)   the amount of exchange differences arising during the period and classified in equity at the end of the period.

30.26   An entity shall disclose the currency in which the financial statements are presented. When the presentation currency is different from the functional currency, an entity shall state that fact and shall disclose the functional currency and the reason for using a different presentation currency.

30.27   When there is a change in the functional currency of either the reporting entity or a significant foreign operation, the entity shall disclose that fact and the reason for the change in functional currency.

Section 31
Hyperinflation

Scope of this section

31.1   This section applies to an entity whose **functional currency** is the currency of a hyperinflationary economy. It requires such an entity to prepare **financial statements** that have been adjusted for the effects of hyperinflation.

Hyperinflationary economy

31.2   This section does not establish an absolute rate at which an economy is deemed hyperinflationary. An entity shall make that judgement by considering all available information including, but not limited to, the following possible indicators of hyperinflation:

(a)   The general population prefers to keep its wealth in non-monetary assets or in a relatively stable foreign currency. Amounts of local currency held are immediately invested to maintain purchasing power.

(b)   The general population regards monetary amounts not in terms of the local currency but in terms of a relatively stable foreign currency. Prices may be quoted in that currency.

(c)   Sales and purchases on credit take place at prices that compensate for the expected loss of purchasing power during the credit period, even if the period is short.

(d)   Interest rates, wages and prices are linked to a price index.

(e)   The cumulative inflation rate over three years is approaching, or exceeds, 100 per cent.

Measuring unit in the financial statements

31.3   All amounts in the financial statements of an entity whose functional currency is the currency of a hyperinflationary economy shall be stated in terms of the measuring unit current at the end of the **reporting period**. The comparative information for the previous period required by paragraph 3.14, and any information presented in respect of earlier periods, shall also be stated in terms of the measuring unit current at the **reporting date**.

31.4   The restatement of financial statements in accordance with this section requires the use of a general price index that reflects changes in general purchasing power. In most economies there is a recognised general price index, normally produced by the government, that entities will follow.

Procedures for restating historical cost financial statements

Statement of financial position

31.5   **Statement of financial position** amounts not expressed in terms of the measuring unit current at the end of the reporting period are restated by applying a general price index.

31.6   **Monetary items** are not restated because they are expressed in terms of the measuring unit current at the end of the reporting period. Monetary items are money held and items to be received or paid in money.

31.7   **Assets** and **liabilities** linked by agreement to changes in prices, such as index-linked bonds and loans, are adjusted in accordance with the agreement and presented at this adjusted amount in the restated statement of financial position.

31.8   All other assets and liabilities are non-monetary:

(a)   Some non-monetary items are carried at amounts current at the end of the reporting period, such as net realisable value and **fair value**, so they are not restated. All other non-monetary assets and liabilities are restated.

(b)   Most non-monetary items are carried at cost or cost less **depreciation**; hence they are expressed at amounts current at their date of acquisition. The restated cost, or cost less depreciation, of each item is determined by applying to its historical cost and accumulated depreciation the change in a general price index from the date of acquisition to the end of the reporting period.

(c)   The restated amount of a non-monetary item is reduced, in accordance with Section 27 *Impairment of Assets*, when it exceeds its **recoverable amount**.

31.9   At the beginning of the first period of application of this section, the components of **equity**, except retained earnings, are restated by applying a general price index from the dates the components were contributed or otherwise arose. Restated retained earnings are derived from all the other amounts in the restated statement of financial position.

31.10   At the end of the first period and in subsequent periods, all components of owners' equity are restated by applying a general price index from the beginning of the period or the date of contribution, if later. The changes for the period in owners' equity are disclosed in accordance with Section 6 *Statement of Changes in Equity and Statement of Income and Retained Earnings*.

Statement of comprehensive income and income statement

31.11   All items in the **statement of comprehensive income** (and in the **income statement**, if presented) shall be expressed in terms of the measuring unit current at the end of the reporting period. Therefore, all amounts need to be restated by applying the change in the general price index from the dates when the items of **income** and **expenses** were initially recognised in the financial statements. If general inflation is approximately even throughout the period, and the items of income and expense arose approximately evenly throughout the period, an average rate of inflation may be appropriate.

Statement of cash flows

31.12   An entity shall express all items in the **statement of cash flows** in terms of the measuring unit current at the end of the reporting period.

Gain or loss on net monetary position

31.13   In a period of inflation, an entity holding an excess of monetary assets over monetary liabilities loses purchasing power, and an entity with an excess of monetary liabilities over monetary assets gains purchasing power, to the extent the assets and liabilities are not linked to a price level. An entity shall include in **profit or loss** the **gain** or loss on the net monetary position. An entity shall offset the adjustment to those assets and liabilities linked by agreement to changes in prices made in accordance with paragraph 31.7 against the gain or loss on net monetary position.

Economies ceasing to be hyperinflationary

31.14   When an economy ceases to be hyperinflationary and an entity discontinues the preparation and presentation of financial statements prepared in accordance with this section, it shall treat the amounts expressed in the **presentation currency** at the end of the previous reporting period as the basis for the **carrying amounts** in its subsequent financial statements.

Disclosures

31.15   An entity to which this section applies shall disclose the following:

(a)   the fact that financial statements and other prior period data have been restated for changes in the general purchasing power of the functional currency;

(b)   the identity and level of the price index at the reporting date and changes during the current reporting period and the previous reporting period; and

(c)   amount of gain or loss on monetary items.

Section 32
Events after the End of the Reporting Period

Scope of this section

32.1 This section defines events after the end of the **reporting period** and sets out principles for recognising, measuring and disclosing those events.

Events after the end of the reporting period defined

32.2 Events after the end of the reporting period are those events, favourable and unfavourable, that occur between the end of the reporting period and the date when the **financial statements** are authorised for issue. There are two types of events:

(a) those that provide evidence of conditions that existed at the end of the reporting period (adjusting events after the end of the reporting period); and

(b) those that are indicative of conditions that arose after the end of the reporting period (non-adjusting events after the end of the reporting period).

32.3 Events after the end of the reporting period include all events up to the date when the financial statements are authorised for issue, even if those events occur after the public announcement of **profit or loss** or other selected financial information.

Recognition and measurement

Adjusting events after the end of the reporting period

32.4 An entity shall adjust the amounts recognised in its financial statements, including related disclosures, to reflect adjusting events after the end of the reporting period.

32.5 The following are examples of adjusting events after the end of the reporting period that require an entity to adjust the amounts recognised in its financial statements, or to recognise items that were not previously recognised:

(a) The settlement after the end of the reporting period of a court case that confirms that the entity had a present obligation at the end of the reporting period. The entity adjusts any previously recognised **provision** related to this court case in accordance with Section 21 *Provisions and Contingencies* or recognises a new provision. The entity does not merely disclose a **contingent liability**. Rather, the settlement provides additional evidence to be considered in determining the provision that should be recognised at the end of the reporting period in accordance with Section 21.

(b) The receipt of information after the end of the reporting period indicating that an **asset** was impaired at the end of the reporting period, or that the amount of a previously recognised **impairment loss** for that asset needs to be adjusted. For example:

(i) the bankruptcy of a customer that occurs after the end of the reporting period usually confirms that a loss existed at the end of the reporting period on a trade receivable and that the entity needs to adjust the **carrying amount** of the trade receivable; and

(ii) the sale of **inventories** after the end of the reporting period may give evidence about their selling price at the end of the reporting period for the purpose of assessing impairment at that date.

(c) The determination after the end of the reporting period of the cost of assets purchased, or the proceeds from assets sold, before the end of the reporting period.

(d) The determination after the end of the reporting period of the amount of profit-sharing or bonus payments, if the entity had a legal or **constructive obligation** at the end of the reporting period to make such payments as a result of events before that date (see Section 28 *Employee Benefits*).

(e) The discovery of fraud or **errors** that show that the financial statements are incorrect.

Non-adjusting events after the end of the reporting period

32.6 An entity shall not adjust the amounts recognised in its financial statements to reflect non-adjusting events after the end of the reporting period.

32.7 Examples of non-adjusting events after the end of the reporting period include:

(a) A decline in market value of investments between the end of the reporting period and the date when the financial statements are authorised for issue. The decline in market value does not normally relate to the condition of the investments at the end of the reporting period, but reflects circumstances that have arisen subsequently. Therefore, an entity does not adjust the amounts recognised in its financial statements for the investments. Similarly, the entity does not update the amounts disclosed for the investments as at the end of the reporting period, although it may need to give additional disclosure in accordance with paragraph 32.10.

(b) An amount that becomes receivable as a result of a favourable judgement or settlement of a court case after the **reporting date** but before the financial statements are authorised for issued. This would be a **contingent asset** at the reporting date (see paragraph 21.13), and disclosure may be required by paragraph 21.16. However, agreement on the amount of damages for a judgement that was reached before the reporting date, but was not previously recognised because the amount could not be measured reliably, may constitute an adjusting event.

Further examples of non-adjusting events are set out in paragraph 32.11.

Going concern

32.7A An entity shall not prepare its financial statements on a **going concern** basis if management determines after the reporting period either that it intends to liquidate the entity or to cease trading, or that it has no realistic alternative but to do so.

32.7B Deterioration in operating results and **financial position** after the reporting period may indicate a need to consider whether the going concern assumption is still appropriate. If the going concern assumption is no longer appropriate, the effect is so pervasive that this section requires a fundamental change in the basis of accounting, rather than an adjustment to the amounts recognised within the original basis of accounting and therefore the disclosure requirements of paragraph 3.9 apply.

Dividends

32.8 If an entity declares dividends to holders of its equity instruments after the end of the reporting period, the entity shall not recognise those dividends as a **liability** at the end of the reporting period because no obligation exists at that time. The amount of the dividend may be presented as a segregated component of retained earnings at the end of the reporting period.

Date of authorisation for issue

32.9   An entity shall disclose the date when the financial statements were authorised for issue and who gave that authorisation. If the entity's **owners** or others have the power to amend the financial statements after issue, the entity shall disclose that fact.

Non-adjusting events after the end of the reporting period

* 32.10   An entity shall disclose the following for each category of non-adjusting event after the end of the reporting period:

(a)   the nature of the event; and

(b)   an estimate of its financial effect or a statement that such an estimate cannot be made.

* 32.11   The following are examples of non-adjusting events after the end of the reporting period that would generally result in disclosure. The disclosures will reflect information that becomes known after the end of the reporting period but before the financial statements are authorised for issue:

(a)   a major **business combination** or disposal of a major **subsidiary**;

(b)   announcement of a plan to discontinue an operation;

(c)   major purchases of assets, disposals or plans to dispose of assets, or expropriation of major assets by government;

(d)   the destruction of a major production plant by a fire;

(e)   announcement, or commencement of the implementation, of a major restructuring;

(f)   issues or repurchases of an entity's debt or equity instruments;

(g)   abnormally large changes in asset prices or foreign exchange rates;

(h)   changes in tax rates or tax laws enacted or announced that have a significant effect on current and **deferred tax assets and liabilities**;

(i)   entering into significant commitments or contingent liabilities, for example, by issuing significant guarantees; and

(j)   commencement of major litigation arising solely out of events that occurred after the end of the reporting period.

Section 33
Related Party Disclosures

Scope of this section

33.1 This section requires an entity to include in its **financial statements** the disclosures necessary to draw attention to the possibility that its **financial position** and **profit or loss** have been affected by the existence of **related parties** and by transactions and outstanding balances with such parties.

33.1A Disclosures need not be given of transactions entered into between two or more members of a **group**, provided that any **subsidiary** which is a party to the transaction is wholly owned by such a member.

Related party defined

33.2 A related party is a person or entity that is related to the entity that is preparing its financial statements (the reporting entity).

    (a) A person or a **close member of that person's family** is related to a reporting entity if that person:

        (i) has **control** or **joint control** over the reporting entity;

        (ii) has **significant influence** over the reporting entity; or

        (iii) is a member of the **key management personnel** of the reporting entity or of a **parent** of the reporting entity.

    (b) An entity is related to a reporting entity if any of the following conditions apply:

        (i) the entity and the reporting entity are members of the same group (which means that each parent, subsidiary and fellow subsidiary is related to the others).

        (ii) one entity is an **associate** or **joint venture** of the other entity (or an associate or joint venture of a member of a group of which the other entity is a member).

        (iii) both entities are joint ventures of the same third party.

        (iv) one entity is a joint venture of a third entity and the other entity is an associate of the third entity.

        (v) the entity is a **post-employment benefit plan** for the benefit of employees of either the reporting entity or an entity related to the reporting entity. If the reporting entity is itself such a plan, the sponsoring employers are also related to the reporting entity.

        (vi) the entity is controlled or jointly controlled by a person identified in (a).

        (vii) a person identified in (a)(i) has significant influence over the entity or is a member of the key management personnel of the entity (or of a parent of the entity).

        (viii) the entity, or any member of a group of which it is a part, provides key management personnel services to the reporting entity or to the parent of the reporting entity.

33.3 In considering each possible related party relationship, an entity shall assess the substance of the relationship and not merely the legal form.

33.4   In the context of this FRS, the following are not related parties:

(a)   Two entities simply because they have a director or other member of key management personnel in common or because a member of key management personnel of one entity has significant influence over the other entity.

(b)   Two **venturers** simply because they share joint control over a joint venture.

(c)   Any of the following simply by virtue of their normal dealings with an entity (even though they may affect the freedom of action of an entity or participate in its decision-making process):

(i)   providers of finance;

(ii)   trade unions;

(iii)   public utilities; and

(iv)   government departments and agencies.

(d)   A customer, supplier, franchisor, distributor or general agent with whom an entity transacts a significant volume of business, merely by virtue of the resulting economic dependence.

33.4A   In the definition of a related party, an associate includes subsidiaries of the associate and a joint venture includes subsidiaries of the joint venture. Therefore, for example, an associate's subsidiary and the investor that has significant influence over the associate are related to each other.

Disclosures

Disclosure of parent-subsidiary relationships

* 33.5   Relationships between a parent and its subsidiaries shall be disclosed irrespective of whether there have been **related party transactions**. An entity shall disclose the name of its parent and, if different, the ultimate controlling party. If neither the entity's parent nor the ultimate controlling party produces financial statements available for public use, the name of the next most senior parent that does so (if any) shall also be disclosed.

Disclosure of key management personnel compensation

33.6   Key management personnel are those persons having authority and responsibility for planning, directing and controlling the activities of the entity, directly or indirectly, including any director (whether executive or otherwise) of that entity. Compensation includes all **employee benefits** (as defined in Section 28 *Employee Benefits*) including those in the form of share-based payments (see Section 26 *Share-based Payment*). Employee benefits include all forms of consideration paid, payable or provided by the entity, or on behalf of the entity (eg by its parent or by a shareholder), in exchange for services rendered to the entity. It also includes such consideration paid on behalf of a parent of the entity in respect of goods or services provided to the entity.

33.7   An entity shall disclose key management personnel compensation in total.

Disclosure of related party transactions

33.8   A related party transaction is a transfer of resources, services or obligations between a reporting entity and a related party, regardless of whether a price is charged. Examples of related party transactions that are common to entities within the scope of this FRS include, but are not limited to:

(a)   transactions between an entity and its principal **owner(s)**;

(b)   transactions between an entity and another entity when both entities are under the common control of a single entity or person; and

(c)   transactions in which an entity or person that controls the reporting entity incurs **expenses** directly that otherwise would have been borne by the reporting entity.

* 33.9   If an entity has related party transactions, it shall disclose the nature of the related party relationship as well as information about the transactions, outstanding balances and commitments necessary for an understanding of the potential effect of the relationship on the financial statements. Those disclosure requirements are in addition to the requirements in paragraph 33.7 to disclose key management personnel compensation. At a minimum, disclosures shall include:

(a)   The amount of the transactions.

(b)   The amount of outstanding balances and:

(i)   their terms and conditions, including whether they are secured, and the nature of the consideration to be provided in settlement; and

* (ii)   details of any guarantees given or received.

(c)   Provisions for uncollectible receivables related to the amount of outstanding balances.

(d)   The expense recognised during the period in respect of bad or doubtful debts due from related parties.

Such transactions could include purchases, sales, or transfers of goods or services, **leases**, guarantees and settlements by the entity on behalf of the related party or vice versa.

33.10   An entity shall make the disclosures required by paragraph 33.9 separately for each of the following categories:

(a)   entities with control, joint control or significant influence over the entity;

(b)   entities over which the entity has control, joint control or significant influence;

(c)   key management personnel of the entity or its parent (in the aggregate);

(d)   entities that provide key management personnel services to the entity; and

(e)   other related parties.

33.11   An entity is exempt from the disclosure requirements of paragraph 33.9 in relation to:

(a)   a **state** (a national, regional or local government) that has control, joint control or significant influence over the reporting entity; and

(b)   another entity that is a related party because the same state has control, joint control or significant influence over both the reporting entity and the other entity.

However, the entity must still disclose a parent-subsidiary relationship as required by paragraph 33.5.

33.12   The following are examples of transactions that shall be disclosed if they are with a related party:

(a)   purchases or sales of goods (finished or unfinished);

(b)   purchases or sales of property and other **assets**;

(c)   rendering or receiving of services;

(d)   leases;

(e)   transfers of **research** and **development**;

(f)   transfers under licence agreements;

(g)   transfers under finance arrangements (including loans and equity contributions in **cash** or in kind);

(h)   provision of guarantees or collateral;

(i)   settlement of **liabilities** on behalf of the entity or by the entity on behalf of another party; and

(j)   participation by a parent or subsidiary in a **defined benefit plan** that shares risks between group entities.

33.13   An entity shall not state that related party transactions were made on terms equivalent to those that prevail in arm's length transactions unless such terms can be substantiated.

* 33.14   An entity may disclose items of a similar nature in the aggregate except when separate disclosure is necessary for an understanding of the effects of related party transactions on the financial statements of the entity.

Section 34
Specialised Activities

Scope of this section

34.1   This section sets out the financial reporting requirements for entities applying this FRS involved in the following types of specialised activities:

(a)   Agriculture (see paragraphs 34.2 to 34.10A);

(b)   Extractive Activities (see paragraphs 34.11 to 34.11C);

(c)   Service Concession Arrangements (see paragraphs 34.12 to 34.16A);

(d)   Financial Institutions (see paragraphs 34.17 to 34.33);

(e)   Retirement Benefit Plans: Financial Statements (see paragraphs 34.34 to 34.48);

(f)   Heritage Assets (see paragraphs 34.49 to 34.56);

(g)   Funding Commitments (see paragraphs 34.57 to 34.63);

(h)   Incoming Resources from Non-Exchange Transactions (see paragraphs 34.64 to 34.74);

(i)   Public Benefit Entity Combinations (see paragraphs 34.75 to 34.86); and

(j)   Public Benefit Entity Concessionary Loans (see paragraphs 34.87 to 34.97).

Agriculture

34.2   An entity using this FRS that is engaged in **agricultural activity** shall determine an **accounting policy** for each class of **biological asset** and its related **agricultural produce.**

Recognition

34.3   An entity shall recognise a biological asset or an item of agricultural produce when, and only when:

(a)   the entity controls the **asset** as a result of past events;

(b)   it is **probable** that future economic benefits associated with the asset will flow to the entity; and

(c)   the **fair value** or cost of the asset can be measured reliably.

Measurement

34.3A   For each class of biological asset and its related agricultural produce an entity shall choose as its accounting policy either:

(a)   the fair value model set out in paragraphs 34.4 to 34.7A; or

(b)   the cost model set out in paragraphs 34.8 to 34.10A.

34.3B   If an entity has chosen the fair value model for a class of biological asset and its related agricultural produce, it shall not subsequently change its accounting policy to the cost model.

Measurement – fair value model

34.4 An entity applying the fair value model shall measure a biological asset on initial **recognition** and at each **reporting date** at its **fair value less costs to sell**. Changes in fair value less costs to sell shall be recognised in **profit or loss**.

34.5 Agricultural produce harvested from an entity's biological assets shall be measured at the point of harvest at its fair value less costs to sell. Such **measurement** is the cost at that date when applying Section 13 *Inventories* or another applicable section of this FRS.

34.6 In determining fair value, an entity shall consider the following:

(a) If an **active market** exists for a biological asset or agricultural produce in its present location and condition, the quoted price in that market is the appropriate basis for determining the fair value of that asset. If an entity has access to different active markets, the entity shall use the price existing in the market that it expects to use.

(b) If an active market does not exist, an entity uses one or more of the following, when available, in determining fair value:

(i) the most recent market transaction price, provided that there has not been a significant change in economic circumstances between the date of that transaction and the end of the **reporting period**;

(ii) market prices for similar assets with adjustment to reflect differences; and

(iii) sector benchmarks such as the value of an orchard expressed per export tray, bushel, or hectare, and the value of cattle expressed per kilogram of meat.

(c) In some cases, the information sources listed in (b) may suggest different conclusions as to the fair value of a biological asset or an item of agricultural produce. An entity considers the reasons for those differences, to arrive at the most reliable estimate of fair value within a relatively narrow range of reasonable estimates.

(d) In some circumstances, fair value may be readily determinable even though market determined prices or values are not available for a biological asset in its present condition. An entity shall consider whether the **present value** of expected net cash flows from the asset discounted at a current market determined rate results in a reliable measure of fair value.

34.6A If the fair value of a biological asset cannot be measured reliably, the entity shall apply the cost model to that biological asset in accordance with paragraphs 34.8 and 34.10A until such time that the fair value can be reliably measured.

Disclosures – fair value model

34.7 An entity shall disclose the following for each class of biological asset measured using the fair value model:

(a) A description of each class of biological asset.

* (b) The methods and significant assumptions applied in determining the fair value of each class of biological asset.

* (c) A reconciliation of changes in the **carrying amount** of each class of biological asset between the beginning and the end of the current period. The reconciliation shall include:

* (i) the **gain** or loss arising from changes in fair value less costs to sell;

(ii) increases resulting from purchases;

(iii) decreases attributable to sales;

(iv) decreases resulting from harvest;

(v) increases resulting from **business combinations**; and

(vi) other changes.

This reconciliation need not be presented for prior periods.

34.7A   If an entity measures any individual biological assets at cost in accordance with paragraph 34.6A, it shall explain why fair value cannot be reliably measured. If the fair value of such a biological asset becomes reliably measurable during the current period an entity shall explain why fair value has become reliably measurable and the effect of the change.

34.7B   An entity shall disclose the methods and significant assumptions applied in determining the fair value at the point of harvest of each class of agricultural produce.

Measurement – cost model

34.8   An entity applying the cost model shall measure biological assets at cost less any accumulated **depreciation** and any accumulated **impairment losses**.

34.9   In applying the cost model, agricultural produce harvested from an entity's biological assets shall be measured at the point of harvest at either:

(a) the lower of cost and estimated selling price less costs to complete and sell; or

(b) its fair value less costs to sell. Any gain or loss arising on initial recognition of agricultural produce at fair value less costs to sell shall be included in profit or loss for the period in which it arises.

Such measurement is the cost at that date when applying Section 13 or another applicable section of this FRS.

Disclosures – cost model

34.10   An entity shall disclose the following for each class of biological asset measured using the cost model:

(a) a description of each class of biological asset;

(b) [not used]

(c) the depreciation method used;

(d) the useful lives or the depreciation rates used; and

* (e) a reconciliation of changes in the carrying amount of each class of biological asset between the beginning and the end of the current period. The reconciliation shall include:

(i) increases resulting from purchases;

(ii) decreases attributable to sales;

(iii) decreases resulting from harvest;

(iv) increases resulting from business combinations;

(v) impairment losses recognised or reversed in profit or loss in accordance with Section 27 *Impairment of Assets;* and

(vi) other changes.

This reconciliation need not be presented for prior periods.

34.10A An entity shall disclose, for any agricultural produce measured at fair value less costs to sell, the methods and significant assumptions applied in determining the fair value at the point of harvest of each class of agricultural produce.

Extractive Activities

34.11 An entity using this FRS that is engaged in the exploration for and/or evaluation of mineral resources (extractive activities) shall apply the requirements of IFRS 6 *Exploration for and Evaluation of Mineral Resources.*

34.11A When applying the requirements of IFRS 6, references made to other IFRSs within that standard shall be taken to be references to the relevant section or paragraph within this FRS.

34.11B Notwithstanding the requirements of paragraph 34.11A, when applying paragraph 21 of IFRS 6, a **cash-generating unit** or group of cash-generating units shall be no larger than an **operating segment** and the reference to IFRS 8 *Operating Segments* shall be ignored.

34.11C On first-time adoption of this FRS if it is not practical to apply a particular requirement of paragraph 18 of IFRS 6 to previous comparative amounts, an entity shall disclose that fact.

Service Concession Arrangements

34.12 A **service concession arrangement** is an arrangement whereby a public sector body, or a **public benefit entity** (the grantor) contracts with a private sector entity (the operator) to construct (or upgrade), operate and maintain **infrastructure assets** for a specified period of time (concession period). The operator is paid for its services over the period of the arrangement. A common feature of a service concession arrangement is the public service nature of the obligation undertaken by the operator, whereby the arrangement contractually obliges the operator to provide services to, or on behalf of, the grantor for the benefit of the public.

34.12A Specifically an arrangement is a service concession arrangement when the following conditions apply:

(a) the grantor controls or regulates what services the operator must provide using the infrastructure assets, to whom, and at what price; and

(b) the grantor controls, through ownership, beneficial entitlement or otherwise, any significant **residual interest** in the assets at the end of the term of the arrangement.

Where the infrastructure assets have no significant **residual value** at the end of the term of the arrangement (ie the arrangement is for its entire useful life), then the arrangement shall be accounted for as a service concession if the conditions in (a) are met.

For the purpose of condition (b), the grantor's control over any significant residual interest should both restrict the operator's practical ability to sell or pledge the infrastructure assets and give the grantor a continuing right of use throughout the concession period.

34.12B A service concession arrangement shall be accounted for in accordance with the requirements of paragraphs 34.12E to 34.16A.

34.12C A service concession arrangement may contain a group of contracts and sub-arrangements as elements of the service concession arrangement as a whole. Such an arrangement shall be treated as a whole when the group of contracts and sub-arrangements are linked in such a way that the commercial effect cannot be understood without reference to them as a whole. Accordingly, the contractual terms of certain contracts or arrangements may meet both the scope requirements of paragraphs 34.12 and 34.12A, and Section 20 *Leases*. Where this is the case, the requirements of this section shall prevail.

34.12D Where an arrangement does not meet the requirements of paragraphs 34.12 and 34.12A, it shall be accounted for in accordance with Section 17 *Property, Plant and Equipment*, Section 18 *Intangible Assets other than Goodwill*, Section 20 or Section 23 *Revenue*, based on the nature of the arrangement.

Accounting by grantors – Finance lease liability model

34.12E The infrastructure assets shall be recognised as **assets** of the grantor together with a **liability** for its obligations under the service concession arrangement.

34.12F The grantor shall initially recognise the infrastructure assets and associated liability in accordance with paragraphs 20.9 and 20.10. If as a result of applying paragraphs 20.9 and 20.10 the grantor has not recognised a liability to make payments to the operator, it shall not recognise the infrastructure assets.

34.12G The liability shall be recognised as a finance lease liability and subsequently accounted for in accordance with paragraph 20.11.

34.12H The infrastructure assets shall be recognised as **property, plant and equipment** or as **intangible assets**, as appropriate, and subsequently accounted for in accordance with Section 17 or Section 18.

Accounting by operators

Treatment of the operator's rights over the infrastructure

34.12I Infrastructure assets shall not be recognised as property, plant and equipment by the operator because the contractual service arrangement does not convey the right to control the use of the public service assets to the operator. The operator has access to operate the infrastructure to provide the public service on behalf of the grantor in accordance with the terms specified in the arrangement.

Recognition and measurement of consideration

34.13 There are two principal categories of service concession arrangements:

(a) In one, the operator receives a **financial asset** – an unconditional contractual right to receive a specified or determinable amount of **cash** or another financial asset from, or at the direction of, the grantor in return for constructing (or upgrading) the infrastructure assets, and then operating and maintaining the asset for a specified period of time. This category includes guarantees by the grantor to pay for any shortfall between amounts received from users of the public service and specified or determinable amounts.

(b) In the other, the operator receives an **intangible asset** – a right to charge for use of the infrastructure assets that it constructs (or upgrades) and then operates and maintains for a specified period of time. A right to charge users is not an unconditional right to receive cash because the amounts are contingent on the extent to which the public uses the service.

Sometimes, a single arrangement may contain both types: to the extent that the grantor has given an unconditional guarantee of payment for the construction (or upgrade) of the infrastructure assets, the operator has a financial asset; to the extent that the operator receives a right to charge the public for using the service the operator has an intangible asset.

Accounting – financial asset model

34.14 The operator shall recognise a financial asset to the extent that it has an unconditional contractual right to receive cash or another financial asset from, or at the direction of, the grantor for the construction (or upgrade) services. The operator shall initially recognise the financial asset at fair value for the consideration received or receivable, based on the fair value of the construction (or upgrade) services provided. Thereafter, it shall account for the financial asset in accordance with Section 11 *Basic Financial Instruments* and Section 12 *Other Financial Instruments Issues*.

Accounting – intangible asset model

34.15 The operator shall recognise an intangible asset to the extent that it receives a right (a licence) to charge users of the public service. The operator shall initially recognise the intangible asset at fair value for the consideration received or receivable, based on the fair value of the construction (or upgrade) services provided. Thereafter, it shall account for the intangible asset in accordance with Section 18.

Operating services

34.16 The operator shall account for **revenue** in accordance with Section 23 for the operating services it performs.

Borrowing costs

34.16A **Borrowing costs** attributable to the arrangement shall be recognised as an **expense**, in accordance with Section 25 *Borrowing Costs*, in the period in which they are incurred unless the operator has an intangible asset. In this case borrowing costs attributable to the arrangement may be capitalised in accordance with Section 25 where a policy of capitalisation has been adopted in accordance with that section.

Financial Institutions

34.17 A **financial institution** (other than a **retirement benefit plan**) applying this FRS shall, in addition to the disclosure requirements in Section 11 *Basic Financial Instruments* and Section 12 *Other Financial Instruments Issues*, provide the disclosures in paragraphs 34.19 to 34.33. The disclosures in paragraphs 34.19 to 34.33 are required to be provided in:

(a) the **individual financial statements** of a financial institution (other than a retirement benefit plan); and

(b) the **consolidated financial statements** of a **group** containing a financial institution (other than a retirement benefit plan) when the **financial instruments** held by the financial institution are **material** to the group. Where this is the case, the disclosures apply regardless of whether the principal activity of the group is being a financial institution or not. The disclosures in paragraphs 34.19 to 34.33 only need to be given in respect of financial instruments held by entities within the group that are financial institutions (other than retirement benefit plans).

34.18 A retirement benefit plan shall provide the disclosures in paragraphs 34.35 to 34.48 of this FRS.

Disclosures

Significance of financial instruments for financial position and performance

34.19   A financial institution shall disclose information that enables users of its **financial statements** to evaluate the significance of financial instruments for its **financial position** and **performance**.

34.20   A financial institution shall disclose a disaggregation of the **statement of financial position** line item by class of financial instrument. A class is a grouping of financial instruments that is appropriate to the nature of the information disclosed and that takes into account the characteristics of those financial instruments.

Impairment

34.21   Where a financial institution uses a separate allowance account to record impairments, it shall disclose a reconciliation of changes in that account during the period for each class of **financial asset**.

Fair value

34.22   For financial instruments held at **fair value** in the statement of financial position, a financial institution shall disclose for each class of financial instrument, an analysis of the level in the fair value hierarchy (as set out in paragraph 11.27) into which the fair value measurements are categorised.

Nature and extent of risks arising from financial instruments

34.23   A financial institution shall disclose information that enables users of its financial statements to evaluate the nature and extent of **credit risk**, **liquidity risk** and **market risk** arising from financial instruments to which the financial institution is exposed at the end of the **reporting period**.

34.24   For each type of risk arising from financial instruments, a financial institution shall disclose:

(a)   the exposures to risk and how they arise;

(b)   its objectives, policies and processes for managing the risk and the methods used to measure the risk; and

(c)   any changes in (a) or (b) from the previous period.

Credit risk

34.25   A financial institution shall disclose by class of financial instrument:

(a)   The amount that best represents its maximum exposure to credit risk at the end of the reporting period. This disclosure is not required for financial instruments whose **carrying amount** best represents the maximum exposure to credit risk.

(b)   A description of collateral held as security and of other credit enhancements, and the extent to which these mitigate credit risk.

(c)   The amount by which any related credit **derivatives** or similar instruments mitigate that maximum exposure to credit risk.

(d)   Information about the credit quality of **financial assets** that are neither past due nor impaired.

34.26   A financial institution shall provide, by class of financial asset, an analysis of:

(a)   the age of financial assets that are past due as at the end of the reporting period but not impaired; and

(b)   the financial assets that are individually determined to be impaired as at the end of the reporting period, including the factors the financial institution considered in determining that they are impaired.

34.27   When a financial institution obtains financial or non-financial assets during the period by taking possession of collateral it holds as security or calling on other credit enhancements (eg guarantees), and such **assets** meet the **recognition** criteria in other sections, a financial institution shall disclose:

(a)   the nature and carrying amount of the assets obtained; and

(b)   when the assets are not readily convertible into **cash**, its policies for disposing of such assets or for using them in its operations.

Liquidity risk

34.28   A financial institution shall provide a maturity analysis for **financial liabilities** that shows the remaining contractual maturities at undiscounted amounts separated between derivative and non-derivative financial liabilities.

Market risk

34.29   A financial institution shall provide a sensitivity analysis for each type of market risk (eg interest rate risk, currency risk, other price risk) it is exposed to, showing the impact on **profit or loss** and **equity**. Details of the methods and assumptions used should be provided.

34.30   If a financial institution prepares a sensitivity analysis, such as value-at-risk, that reflects interdependencies between risk variables (eg interest rates and exchange rates) and uses it to manage **financial risks**, it may use that sensitivity analysis instead.

Capital

34.31   A financial institution shall disclose information that enables users of its financial statements to evaluate the entity's objectives, policies and processes for managing capital. A financial institution shall disclose the following:

(a)   Qualitative information about its objectives, policies and processes for managing capital, including:

(i)   a description of what it manages as capital;

(ii)   when an entity is subject to externally imposed capital requirements, the nature of those requirements and how those requirements are incorporated into the management of capital; and

(iii)   how it is meeting its objectives for managing capital.

(b)   Summary quantitative data about what it manages as capital. Some entities regard some financial liabilities (eg some forms of subordinated debt) as part of capital. Other entities regard capital as excluding some components of equity (eg components arising from cash flow hedges).

(c)   Any changes in (a) and (b) from the previous period.

(d)   Whether during the period it complied with any externally imposed capital requirements to which it is subject.

(e) When the entity has not complied with such externally imposed capital requirements, the consequences of such non-compliance.

A financial institution bases these disclosures on the information provided internally to **key management personnel**.

34.32 A financial institution may manage capital in a number of ways and be subject to a number of different capital requirements. For example, a conglomerate may include entities that undertake insurance activities and banking activities and those entities may operate in several jurisdictions. When an aggregate disclosure of capital requirements and how capital is managed would not provide useful information or would distort a financial statement user's understanding of the financial institution's capital resources, the financial institution shall disclose separate information for each capital requirement to which the entity is subject.

Reporting cash flows on a net basis

34.33 A financial institution that presents a statement of cash flow in accordance with Section 7 *Statement of Cash Flows* may report cash flows arising from each of the following activities on a net basis:

(a) cash receipts and payments for the acceptance and repayment of deposits with a fixed maturity date;

(b) the placement of deposits with and withdrawal of deposits from other financial institutions; and

(c) cash advances and loans made to customers and the repayment of those advances and loans.

This paragraph does not impose a requirement to produce a cash flow statement.

Retirement Benefit Plans: Financial Statements

34.34 An entity applying this FRS that is a **retirement benefit plan** shall also apply the requirements of paragraphs 34.35 to 34.48. A retirement benefit plan may be a **defined benefit plan**, a **defined contribution plan**, or have both defined benefit and defined contribution elements. The **financial statements** shall distinguish between defined benefit and defined contribution elements, where **material**.

Requirements applicable to both defined benefit plans and defined contribution plans

34.35 A retirement benefit plan need not comply with the requirements of paragraph 3.17. The financial statements of a retirement benefit plan shall contain as part of the financial statements:

(a) a statement of changes in **net assets available for benefits** (which can also be called a Fund Account) (see paragraph 34.37);

(b) a statement of net assets available for benefits (see paragraph 34.38); and

(c) **notes**, comprising a summary of significant **accounting policies** and other explanatory information.

34.36 At each **reporting date**, the net assets available for benefits shall be measured in accordance with paragraph 28.15(b). Changes in fair value shall be recognised in the statements of changes in net assets available for benefits.

Statement of changes in net assets available for benefits (Fund Account)

34.37 The financial statements of a retirement benefit plan, whether defined contribution or defined benefit, shall present the following in the statement of changes in net assets available for benefits:

(a) employer contributions;

(b) employee contributions;

(c) investment income such as interest and dividends;

(d) other income;

(e) benefits paid or payable (analysed, for example, as retirement, death and disability benefits, and lump sum payments);

(f) administrative expenses;

(g) other expenses;

(h) taxes on income;

(i) profits and losses on disposal of investments and changes in value of investments; and

(j) transfers from and to other plans.

Statement of net assets available for benefits

34.38 The financial statements of a retirement benefit plan, whether defined contribution or defined benefit, shall present the following in the statement of net assets available for benefits:

(a) **assets** at the end of the period suitably classified; and

(b) **liabilities** other than the actuarial **present value** of promised retirement benefits.

The basis of valuation of assets shall be presented in the notes to the financial statements.

Disclosures

Assets other than financial instruments held at fair value

34.39 Where a retirement benefit plan holds assets other than financial instruments at fair value in accordance with paragraph 34.36, it shall apply the disclosure requirements of the relevant section of this FRS, for example in relation to **investment property** it shall provide the disclosures required by paragraph 16.10.

Significance of financial instruments for financial position and performance

34.40 A retirement benefit plan shall disclose information that enables users of its financial statements to evaluate the significance of financial instruments for its **financial position** and **performance**.

34.41 A retirement benefit plan shall disclose a disaggregation of the statement of net assets available for benefits by class of financial instrument. A class is a grouping of financial instruments that is appropriate to the nature of the information disclosed and that takes into account the characteristics of those financial instruments.

Fair value

34.42   For financial instruments held at fair value in the statement of net assets available for benefits, a retirement benefit plan shall disclose for each class of financial instrument, an analysis of the level in the fair value hierarchy (as set out in paragraph 11.27) into which the fair value measurements are categorised.

Nature and extent of risks arising from financial instruments

34.43   A retirement benefit plan shall disclose information that enables users of its financial statements to evaluate the nature and extent of **credit risk** and **market risk** arising from financial instruments to which the retirement benefit plan is exposed at the end of the **reporting period**.

34.44   For each type of credit and market risk arising from financial instruments, a retirement benefit plan shall disclose:

(a)   the exposures to risk and how they arise;

(b)   its objectives, policies and processes for managing the risk and the methods used to measure the risk; and

(c)   any changes in (a) or (b) from the previous period.

In relation to credit risk, a retirement benefit plan shall, in addition, provide the disclosures set out in paragraphs 34.45 and 34.46.

Credit risk

34.45   A retirement benefit plan shall disclose by class of financial instrument:

(a)   The amount that best represents its maximum exposure to credit risk at the end of the reporting period. This disclosure is not required for financial instruments whose **carrying amount** best represents the maximum exposure to credit risk.

(b)   A description of collateral held as security and of other credit enhancements, and the extent to which these mitigate credit risk.

(c)   The amount by which any related credit **derivatives** or similar instruments mitigate that maximum exposure to credit risk.

(d)   Information about the credit quality of financial assets that are neither past due nor impaired.

34.46   When a retirement benefit plan obtains financial or non-financial assets during the period by taking possession of collateral it holds as security or calling on other credit enhancements (eg guarantees), and such assets meet the **recognition** criteria in other sections, a retirement benefit plan shall disclose:

(a)   the nature and carrying amount of the assets obtained; and

(b)   when the assets are not readily convertible into **cash**, its policies for disposing of such assets or for retaining them.

Defined benefit plans – actuarial liabilities

34.47   A defined benefit plan is not required to recognise a liability in relation to the promised retirement benefits.

34.48   A defined benefit plan shall disclose, in a report alongside the financial statements, information regarding the actuarial present value of promised retirement benefits including:

(a)   a statement of the actuarial present value of promised retirement benefits, based on the most recent valuation of the scheme;

(b)   the date of the most recent valuation of the scheme; and

(c)   the significant actuarial assumptions made and the method used to calculate the actuarial present value of promised retirement benefits.

Heritage Assets

34.49   All **heritage assets** shall be accounted for in accordance with the requirements of paragraphs 34.50 to 34.56. These paragraphs do not apply to **investment property**, **property, plant and equipment** or **intangible assets** which fall within the scope of Section 16 *Investment Properties*, Section 17 *Property, Plant and Equipment* and Section 18 *Intangible Assets other than Goodwill*.

34.50   Works of art and similar objects are sometimes held by commercial entities but are not heritage assets because they are not maintained principally for their contribution to knowledge and culture. These assets shall therefore be accounted for in accordance with Section 17. Heritage assets used by the entity itself, for example historic buildings used for teaching by education establishments, shall also be accounted for in accordance with Section 17. This is based on the view that an operational perspective is likely to be most relevant for most users of **financial statements**. However, entities that use historic buildings and similar assets may wish to consider whether it is appropriate to apply the disclosures required by paragraphs 34.55 and 34.56.

Recognition and measurement

34.51   An entity shall recognise and measure heritage assets in accordance with Section 17 (ie using the cost model or revaluation model), subject to the requirements set out in paragraphs 34.52 to 34.53 below.

34.52   Heritage assets shall be recognised in the **statement of financial position** separately from other assets.

34.53   Where heritage assets have previously been capitalised or are recently purchased, information on the cost or value of the asset will be available. Where this information is not available, and cannot be obtained at a cost which is commensurate with the benefits to users of the financial statements, the assets shall not be recognised in the statement of financial position, but must be disclosed in accordance with the requirements below.

34.54   At each **reporting date**, an entity shall apply Section 27 *Impairment of Assets* to determine whether a heritage asset is impaired and, if so, how to recognise and measure the **impairment loss**. A heritage asset may be impaired, for example where it has suffered physical deterioration, breakage or doubts arise as to its authenticity.

Disclosure

34.55   An entity shall disclose the following for all heritage assets it holds:

(a)   An indication of the nature and scale of heritage assets held by the entity.

(b)   The policy for the acquisition, preservation, management and disposal of heritage assets (including a description of the records maintained by the entity of its collection of heritage assets and information on the extent to which access to the assets is permitted).

(c) The **accounting policies** adopted for heritage assets, including details of the measurement bases used.

(d) For heritage assets that have not been recognised in the statement of financial position, the **notes** to the financial statements shall:

(i) explain the reasons why;

(ii) describe the significance and nature of those assets; and

(iii) disclose information that is helpful in assessing the value of those heritage assets.

* (e) Where heritage assets are recognised in the statement of financial position the following disclosure is required:

(i) the **carrying amount** of heritage assets at the beginning of the **reporting period** and the reporting date, including an analysis between classes or groups of heritage assets recognised at cost and those recognised at valuation; and

* (ii) where assets are recognised at valuation, sufficient information to assist in understanding the valuation being recognised (date of valuation, method used, whether carried out by external valuer and if so their qualification and any significant limitations on the valuation).

* (f) A summary of transactions relating to heritage assets for the reporting period and each of the previous four reporting periods disclosing:

(i) the cost of acquisitions of heritage assets;

(ii) the value of heritage assets acquired by donations;

(iii) the carrying amount of heritage assets disposed of in the period and proceeds received; and

(iv) any impairment recognised in the period.

The summary shall show separately those transactions included in the statement of financial position and those that are not.

(g) In exceptional circumstances where it is **impracticable** to obtain a valuation of heritage assets acquired by donation the reason shall be stated.

Disclosures can be aggregated for groups or classes of heritage assets, provided this does not obscure significant information.

34.56 Where it is impracticable to do so, the disclosures required by paragraph 34.55(f) need not be given for any accounting period earlier than the previous comparable period, and a statement to the effect that it is impracticable shall be made.

Funding Commitments

34.57 An entity that commits to provide resources to other entities shall apply the requirements of paragraphs 34.58 to 34.63 and the accompanying guidance at Appendix A to this section, except for commitments to make a loan to which entities shall apply Section 11 *Basic Financial Instruments* or Section 12 *Other Financial Instruments Issues*, as applicable.

34.58 When applying these paragraphs, the requirements of Section 2 *Concepts and Pervasive Principles* and Section 21 *Provisions and Contingencies* shall also be taken into consideration.

Recognition

34.59 An entity shall recognise a **liability** and, usually, a corresponding **expense**, when it has made a commitment that it will provide resources to another party, if, and only if:

(a) the definition and **recognition** criteria for a liability have been satisfied;

(b) the obligation (which may be a **constructive obligation**) is such that the entity cannot realistically withdraw from it; and

(c) the entitlement of the other party to the resources does not depend on the satisfaction of **performance-related conditions**.

34.60 Commitments that are performance-related will be recognised when those performance-related conditions are met.

Measurement

34.61 An entity shall measure any recognised liability at the **present value** of the resources committed.

Disclosure

* 34.62 An entity that has made a commitment shall disclose the following:

(a) the commitment made;

(b) the time-frame of that commitment;

(c) any performance-related conditions attached to that commitment; and

(d) details of how that commitment will be funded.

34.63 The above disclosures may be made in aggregate, providing that such aggregation does not obscure significant information. However, separate disclosure shall be made for recognised and unrecognised commitments.

Incoming Resources from Non-Exchange Transactions

PBE34.64 The accounting for **government grants** is addressed in Section 24 *Government Grants.*

PBE34.65 Paragraphs PBE34.67 to PBE34.74 and the accompanying guidance at Appendix B to this section apply to other resources received from **non-exchange transactions** by **public benefit entities** or entities within a **public benefit entity group.** A non-exchange transaction is a transaction whereby an entity receives value from another entity without directly giving approximately equal value in exchange or gives value to another entity without directly receiving approximately equal value in exchange.

PBE34.66 Non-exchange transactions include, but are not limited to, donations (of **cash**, goods, and services) and legacies.

Recognition and measurement

PBE34.67 An entity shall recognise receipts of resources from non-exchange transactions as follows:

(a) Transactions that do not impose specified future performance-related conditions on the recipient are recognised in **income** when the resources are received or receivable.

(b) Transactions that do impose specified future performance-related conditions on the recipient are recognised in income only when the performance-related conditions are met.

(c) Where resources are received before the **revenue recognition** criteria are satisfied, a **liability** is recognised.

PBE34.68 The existence of a **restriction** does not prohibit a resource from being recognised in income when receivable.

PBE34.69 When applying the requirements of paragraph PBE34.67, an entity must take into consideration whether the resource can be measured reliably and whether the benefits of recognising the resource outweigh the costs.

PBE34.70 Therefore, where it is not practicable to estimate the value of the resource with sufficient **reliability**, the income shall be included in the financial period when the resource is sold.

PBE34.71 An entity shall recognise a liability for any resource that has previously been received and recognised in income when, as a result of a subsequent failure to meet restrictions or performance-related conditions attached to it, repayment becomes **probable**.

PBE34.72 Donations of services that can be reasonably quantified will usually result in the recognition of income and an **expense**. An **asset** will be recognised only when those services are used for the production of an asset and the services received will be capitalised as part of the cost of that asset.

PBE34.73 An entity shall measure incoming resources from non-exchange transactions as follows:

(a) Donated services and facilities, that would otherwise have been purchased, shall be measured at the value to the entity.

(b) All other incoming resources from non-exchange transactions shall be measured at the **fair value** of the resources received or receivable.

Disclosure

PBE34.74 An entity shall disclose the following:

(a) the nature and amounts of resources receivable from non-exchange transactions recognised in the **financial statements**;

(b) any unfulfilled conditions or other contingencies attaching to resources from non-exchange transactions that have not been recognised in income; and

(c) an indication of other forms of resources from non-exchange transactions from which the entity has benefited.

PBE34.75   Paragraphs PBE34.76 to PBE34.86 apply only to **public benefit entities** for the following categories of **entity combinations** which involve a whole entity or parts of an entity combining with another entity:

(a)   combinations at nil or nominal consideration which are in substance a gift; and

(b)   combinations which meet the definition and criteria of a **merger**.

PBE34.76   Combinations which are determined to be acquisitions shall be accounted for in accordance with Section 19 *Business Combinations and Goodwill*.

Combinations that are in substance a gift

Accounting treatment and disclosure

PBE34.77   A **combination that is in substance a gift** shall be accounted for in accordance with Section 19 except for the matters addressed in paragraphs PBE34.78 and PBE34.79 below.

PBE34.78   Any excess of the **fair value** of the **assets** received over the fair value of the **liabilities** assumed is recognised as a **gain** in **income and expenditure**. This gain represents the gift of the value of one entity to another and shall be recognised as income.

PBE34.79   Any excess of the fair value of the liabilities assumed over the fair value of the assets received is recognised as a loss in income and expenditure. This loss represents the net obligations assumed, for which the receiving entity has not received a financial reward and shall be recognised as an **expense**.

Combinations that are a merger

PBE34.80   Unless it is not permitted by the statutory framework under which a public benefit entity reports, an entity combination that is a merger shall apply merger accounting as prescribed below. If merger accounting is not permitted, an entity combination shall be accounted for as an acquisition in accordance with Section 19.

PBE34.81   Any entity combination:

(a)   which is neither a combination that is in substance a gift nor a merger; or

(b)   for which merger accounting is not permitted by the statutory framework under which the public benefit entity reports

shall be accounted for as an acquisition in accordance with Section 19.

Accounting treatment

PBE34.82   Under merger accounting the carrying value of the assets and liabilities of the parties to the combination are not adjusted to fair value, although adjustments shall be made to achieve uniformity of **accounting policies** across the combining entities.

PBE34.83   The results and **cash flows** of all the combining entities shall be brought into the **financial statements** of the newly formed entity from the beginning of the financial period in which the merger occurs.

PBE34.84   The comparative amounts shall be restated by including the results for all the combining entities for the previous accounting period and their **statement of financial**

positions for the previous **reporting date**. The comparative figures shall be marked as 'combined' figures.

PBE34.85 All costs associated with the merger shall be charged as an expense in the period incurred.

Disclosure

PBE34.86 For each entity combination accounted for as a merger in the **reporting period** the following shall be disclosed in the newly formed entity's financial statements:

(a) the names and descriptions of the combining entities or businesses;

(b) the date of the merger;

(c) an analysis of the principal components of the current year's **total comprehensive income** to indicate:

(i) the amounts relating to the newly formed merged entity for the period after the date of the merger; and

(ii) the amounts relating to each party to the merger up to the date of the merger.

(d) an analysis of the previous year's total comprehensive income between each party to the merger;

(e) the aggregate carrying value of the net assets of each party to the merger at the date of the merger; and

(f) the nature and amount of any significant adjustments required to align accounting policies and an explanation of any further adjustments made to net assets as a result of the merger.

Public Benefit Entity Concessionary Loans

PBE34.87 Paragraphs PBE34.89 to PBE34.97 address the **recognition, measurement** and disclosure of **public benefit entity concessionary loan** arrangements within the **financial statements** of **public benefit entities** or entities within a **public benefit entity group** making or receiving public benefit entity concessionary loans. These paragraphs apply to public benefit entity concessionary loan arrangements only and are not applicable to loans which are at a market rate or to other commercial arrangements.

PBE34.88 Public benefit entity concessionary loans are loans made or received between a public benefit entity or an entity within the public benefit entity group, and another party at below the **prevailing market rate** of interest that are not repayable on demand and are for the purposes of furthering the objectives of the public benefit entity or public benefit entity **parent**.

Accounting treatment

PBE34.89 Entities making or receiving public benefit entity concessionary loans shall use either:

(a) the recognition, measurement and disclosure requirements in Section 11 *Basic Financial Instruments* or Section 12 *Other Financial Instruments Issues* (for example, Section 11 requires initial measurement at **fair value** and subsequent measurement at **amortised cost** using the **effective interest method**); or

(b) the accounting treatment set out in paragraphs PBE34.90 to PBE34.97 below.

A public benefit entity or an entity within a public benefit entity group shall apply the same **accounting policy** to concessionary loans both made and received.

Initial measurement

PBE34.90   A public benefit entity or an entity within a public benefit entity group making or receiving concessionary loans shall initially measure these arrangements at the amount received or paid and recognise them in the **statement of financial position**.

Subsequent measurement

PBE34.91   In subsequent years, the **carrying amount** of concessionary loans in the financial statements shall be adjusted to reflect any accrued interest payable or receivable.

PBE34.92   To the extent that a loan that has been made is irrecoverable, an **impairment loss** shall be recognised in **income and expenditure**.

Presentation and disclosure

PBE34.93   The entity shall present concessionary loans made and concessionary loans received either as a separate line items on the face of the statement of financial position or in the **notes** to the financial statements.

PBE34.94   Concessionary loans shall be presented separately between amounts repayable or receivable within one year and amounts repayable or receivable after more than one year.

PBE34.95   The entity shall disclose in the summary of significant accounting policies the measurement basis used for concessionary loans and any other accounting policies which are relevant to the understanding of these transactions within the financial statements.

PBE34.96   The entity shall disclose the following:

(a)   the terms and conditions of concessionary loan arrangements, for example the interest rate, any security provided and the terms of the repayment; and

(b)   the value of concessionary loans which have been committed but not taken up at the year end.

PBE34.97   Concessionary loans made or received shall be disclosed separately. However multiple loans made or received may be disclosed in aggregate, providing that such aggregation does not obscure significant information.

Appendix A to Section 34

Guidance on funding commitments
(paragraphs 34.57 to 34.63)

This guidance is an integral part of the Standard.

34A.1   Entities often make commitments to provide cash or other resources to other entities. In such a case, it is necessary to determine whether the commitment should be recognised as a liability. The definition of a liability requires that there be a present obligation, and not merely an expectation of a future outflow.

34A.2   A general statement that the entity intends to provide resources to certain classes of potential beneficiaries in accordance with its objectives does not in itself give rise to a liability, as the entity may amend or withdraw its policy, and potential beneficiaries do not have the ability to insist on their fulfilment. Similarly, a promise to provide cash conditional on the receipt of future income in itself may not give rise to a liability where the entity cannot be required to fulfil it if the future income is not received and it is probable that the economic benefits will not be transferred.

34A.3   A liability is recognised only for a commitment that gives the recipient a valid expectation that payment will be made and from which the grantor cannot realistically withdraw. One of the implications of this is that a liability only exists where the commitment has been communicated to the recipient.

34A.4   Commitments are not recognised if they are subject to performance-related conditions. In such a case, the entity is required to fulfil its commitment only when the performance-related conditions are met and no liability exists until that time.

34A.5   A commitment may contain conditions that are not performance-related conditions. For example, a requirement to provide an annual financial report to the grantor may serve mainly as an administrative tool because failure to comply would not release the grantor from its commitment. This may be distinguished from a requirement to submit a detailed report for review and consideration by the grantor of how funds will be utilised in order to secure payment. A mere restriction on the specific purpose for which funds are to be used does not in itself constitute a performance-related condition.

34A.6   For funding commitments that are not recognised, it is important that full and informative disclosures are made of their existence and of the sources of funding for these unrecognised commitments.

Appendix B to Section 34

Guidance on incoming resources from non-exchange transactions (paragraphs 34.64 to 34.74)

This guidance is an integral part of the Standard.

Recognition

PBE34B.1   The receipt of resources will usually result in an entity recognising an asset and corresponding income for the fair value of resources when those resources become received or receivable. Instances when this may differ include where:

   (a)   an entity received those resources in the form of services (see paragraphs PBE34B.8 to PBE34B.12); or

   (b)   there are performance-related conditions attached to the resources, which have yet to be fulfilled (see paragraphs PBE34B.13 to PBE34B.14).

PBE34B.2   Resources shall only be recognised when the fair value of the incoming resources can be measured reliably.

PBE34B.3   The concepts of materiality (see paragraph 2.6), and balance between benefit and cost (see paragraph 2.13) should be considered when deciding which resources received shall be recognised in the financial statements.

PBE34B.4   When it is impracticable to recognise resources from non-exchange transactions, the income is recognised in the period in which the resources are sold or distributed. The most common example is that of high volume, low value second-hand goods donated for resale.

Legacies

PBE34B.5   Donations in the form of legacies are recognised when it is probable that the legacy will be received and its value can be measured reliably. These criteria will normally be met following probate once the executor(s) of the estate has established that there are sufficient assets in the estate, after settling liabilities, to pay the legacy.

PBE34B.6   Evidence that the executor(s) has determined that a payment can be made, may arise on the agreement of the estate's accounts or notification that payment will be made. Where notification is received after the year-end but it is clear that the executor(s) has agreed prior to the year-end that the legacy can be paid, the legacy is accrued in the financial statements. The certainty and measurability of the receipt may be affected by subsequent events such as valuations and disputes.

PBE34B.7   Entities that are in receipt of numerous immaterial legacies for which individual identification would be burdensome may take a portfolio approach.

Services

PBE34B.8   Donated services that can be reasonably quantified shall be recognised in the financial statements when they are received.

PBE34B.9   Donated services that are consumed immediately are usually recognised as an expense. However, there may be circumstances when a service is used in the production of an asset, for example erecting a building. In these cases, the associated donated service (eg plumbing and electrical services) would be recognised as a part of the cost of that asset.

PBE34B.10 Donated services that can be reasonably quantified include donated facilities, such as office accommodation, services that would otherwise have been purchased and services usually provided by an individual or an entity as part of their trade or profession for a fee.

PBE34B.11 It is expected that contributions made by volunteers cannot be reasonably quantified and therefore these services shall not be recognised.

PBE34B.12 Paragraph PBE34.74(c) requires an entity to disclose other forms of resources from non-exchange transactions from which the entity has benefited. This will include the disclosure of unrecognised volunteer services.

Performance-related conditions

PBE34B.13 Some resources are given with performance-related conditions attached which require the recipient to use the resources to provide a specified level of service in order to be entitled to retain the resources. An entity will not recognise income from those resources until these performance-related conditions have been met.

PBE34B.14 However, some requirements are stated so broadly that they do not actually impose a performance-related condition on the recipient. In these cases the recipient will recognise income on receipt of the transfer of resources.

Measurement

PBE34B.15 Paragraph PBE34.73(a) requires donated services and facilities to be measured at the value to the entity. This requirement only applies to those services and facilities that would otherwise have been purchased by the entity. The value placed on these services and facilities should be the estimated value to the entity of the service or facility received, this will be the price the entity estimates it would pay in the open market for a service or facility of equivalent utility to the entity.

PBE34B.16 Paragraph PBE34.73(b) requires resources received or receivable, that are not services or facilities, to be measured at their fair value. These fair values are usually the price that the entity would have to pay on the open market for an equivalent resource.

PBE34B.17 When there is no direct evidence of an open market value for an equivalent item a value may be derived from sources such as:

(a) the cost of the item to the donor; or

(b) in the case of goods that are expected to be sold, the estimated resale value (which may reflect the amount actually realised) after deducting the cost to sell the goods.

PBE34B.18 Donated services are recognised as income and an equivalent amount shall be recognised as an expense in income and expenditure, unless the expense can be capitalised as part of the cost of an asset.

Section 35
Transition to this FRS

Scope of this section

35.1   This section applies to a **first-time adopter of this FRS**, regardless of whether its previous accounting framework was **EU-adopted IFRS** or another set of generally accepted accounting principles (GAAP) such as its national accounting standards, or another framework such as the local income tax basis.

35.2   Notwithstanding the requirements in paragraphs 35.3 and 35.4, an entity that has applied **FRS 102** in a previous **reporting period**, but whose most recent previous annual **financial statements** did not contain an explicit and unreserved statement of compliance with this FRS, must either apply this section or else apply FRS 102 retrospectively in accordance with Section 10 *Accounting Policies, Changes in Estimates and Errors* as if the entity had never stopped applying this FRS.

First-time adoption

35.3   A first-time adopter of this FRS shall apply this section in its first financial statements that conform to this FRS.

35.4   An entity's first financial statements that conform to this FRS are the first financial statements[14] in which the entity makes an explicit and unreserved statement in those financial statements of compliance with this FRS. Financial statements prepared in accordance with this FRS are an entity's first such financial statements if, for example, the entity:

(a)   did not present financial statements for previous periods;

(b)   presented its most recent previous financial statements under previous UK and Republic of Ireland requirements that are therefore not consistent with this FRS in all respects; or

(c)   presented its most recent previous financial statements in conformity with EU-adopted IFRS.

35.5   Paragraph 3.17 defines a complete set of financial statements.

35.6   Paragraph 3.14 requires an entity to disclose, in a complete set of financial statements, comparative information in respect of the preceding period for all amounts presented in the financial statements, as well as specified comparative narrative and descriptive information. An entity may present comparative information in respect of more than one preceding period. Therefore, an entity's **date of transition** to this FRS is the beginning of the earliest period for which the entity presents full comparative information in accordance with this FRS in its first financial statements that comply with this FRS.

---

[14] This excludes interim financial statements.

Procedures for preparing financial statements at the date of transition

35.7   Except as provided in paragraphs 35.9 to 35.11B, an entity shall, in its opening **statement of financial position** as of its date of transition to this FRS (ie the beginning of the earliest period presented):

(a)   recognise all **assets** and **liabilities** whose **recognition** is required by this FRS;

(b)   not recognise items as assets or liabilities if this FRS does not permit such recognition;

(c)   reclassify items that it recognised under its previous financial reporting framework as one type of asset, liability or component of **equity**, but are a different type of asset, liability or component of equity under this FRS; and

(d)   apply this FRS in measuring all recognised assets and liabilities.

This section does not require the opening statement of financial position to be presented.

35.8   The **accounting policies** that an entity uses in its opening statement of financial position under this FRS may differ from those that it used for the same date using its previous financial reporting framework. The resulting adjustments arise from transactions, other events or conditions before the date of transition to this FRS. Therefore, an entity shall recognise those adjustments directly in retained earnings (or, if appropriate, another category of equity) at the date of transition to this FRS.

35.9   On first-time adoption of this FRS, an entity shall not retrospectively change the accounting that it followed under its previous financial reporting framework for any of the following transactions:

(a)   *Derecognition of financial assets and financial liabilities*:
Financial assets and liabilities derecognised under an entity's previous accounting framework before the date of transition shall not be recognised upon adoption of this FRS. Conversely, for financial assets and liabilities that would have been derecognised under this FRS in a transaction that took place before the date of transition, but that were not derecognised under an entity's previous accounting framework, an entity may choose:

(i)   to derecognise them on adoption of this FRS; or

(ii)   to continue to recognise them until disposed of or settled.

(b)   [Not used]

(c)   *Accounting estimates.*

(d)   *Discontinued operations.*

(e)   *Measuring non-controlling interests*:
The requirements:

(i)   to allocate **profit or loss** and **total comprehensive income** between non-controlling interest and **owners** of the **parent**;

(ii)   for accounting for changes in the parent's ownership interest in a subsidiary that do not result in a loss of control; and

(iii)   for accounting for a loss of control over a subsidiary

shall be applied prospectively from the date of transition to this FRS (or from such earlier date as this FRS is applied to restate **business combinations**—see paragraph 35.10(a)).

35.10　An entity may use one or more of the following exemptions in preparing its first financial statements that conform to this FRS:

(a) **Business combinations, including group reconstructions**

A first-time adopter may elect not to apply Section 19 *Business Combinations and Goodwill* to business combinations that were effected before the date of transition to this FRS. However, if a first-time adopter restates any business combination to comply with Section 19, it shall restate all later business combinations. If a first-time adopter does not apply Section 19 retrospectively, the first-time adopter shall recognise and measure all its assets and liabilities acquired or assumed in a past business combination at the date of transition to this FRS in accordance with paragraphs 35.7 to 35.9 or if applicable, with paragraphs 35.10(b) to (r) except for:

(i) **intangible assets** other than **goodwill** – intangible assets subsumed within goodwill shall not be separately recognised; and

(ii) goodwill – no adjustment shall be made to the carrying value of goodwill.

(b) **Share-based payment transactions**

A first-time adopter is not required to apply Section 26 *Share-based Payment* to equity instruments (including the equity component of share-based payment transactions previously treated as compound instruments) that were granted before the date of transition to this FRS, or to liabilities arising from share-based payment transactions that were settled before the date of transition to this FRS. Except that a first-time adopter previously applying FRS 20 *(IFRS 2) Share-based Payment* or IFRS 2 *Share-based Payment* shall, in relation to equity instruments (including the equity component of share-based payment transactions previously treated as compound instruments) that were granted before the date of transition to this FRS, apply either FRS 20/IFRS 2 (as applicable) or Section 26 of this FRS at the date of transition.

In addition, for a small entity that first adopts this FRS for an accounting period that commences before 1 January 2017, this exemption is extended to equity instruments that were granted before the start of the first reporting period that complies with this FRS, provided that the small entity did not previously apply FRS 20 or IFRS 2.

A small entity that chooses to apply this exemption shall provide disclosures in accordance with paragraph 1AC.31.

(c) **Fair value as deemed cost**

A first-time adopter may elect to measure an:

(i) item of **property, plant and equipment**;

(ii) **investment property**; or

(iii) intangible asset which meets the recognition criteria and the criteria for revaluation in Section 18 *Intangible Assets other than Goodwill*

on the date of transition to this FRS at its **fair value** and use that fair value as its **deemed cost** at that date.

(d) **Revaluation as deemed cost**

A first-time adopter may elect to use a previous GAAP revaluation of an:

(i) item of property, plant and equipment;

(ii) investment property; or

(iii) intangible asset which meets the recognition criteria and the criteria for revaluation in Section 18 at, or before, the date of transition to this FRS as its deemed cost at the revaluation date.

(e)   [Not used]

(f)   *Individual and separate financial statements*

When an entity prepares individual or **separate financial statements**, paragraphs 9.26, 14.4 and 15.9 require the entity to account for its investments in **subsidiaries**, **associates**, and **jointly controlled entities** either at cost less impairment or at fair value.

If a first-time adopter measures such an investment at cost, it shall measure that investment at one of the following amounts in its individual or separate opening statement of financial position, as appropriate, prepared in accordance with this FRS:

(i)   cost determined in accordance with Section 9 *Consolidated and Separate Financial Statements*, Section 14 *Investments in Associates* or Section 15 *Investments in Joint Ventures*; or

(ii) deemed cost, which shall be the **carrying amount** at the date of transition as determined under the entity's previous GAAP.

(g)   *Compound financial instruments*

Paragraph 22.13 requires an entity to split a **compound financial instrument** into its liability and equity components at the date of issue. A first-time adopter need not separate those two components if the liability component is not outstanding at the date of transition to this FRS.

(h)   [Not used]

(i)   *Service concession arrangements – Accounting by operators*

A first-time adopter is not required to apply paragraphs 34.12I to 34.16A to **service concession arrangements** that were entered into before the date of transition to this FRS. Such service concession arrangements shall continue to be accounted for using the same accounting policies being applied at the date of transition to this FRS.

(j)   *Extractive activities*

A first-time adopter that under a previous GAAP accounted for exploration and development costs for oil and gas properties in the development or production phases, in cost centres that included all properties in a large geographical area may elect to measure oil and gas assets at the date of transition to this FRS on the following basis:

(i)   Exploration and evaluation assets at the amount determined under the entity's previous GAAP.

(ii) Assets in the development or production phases at the amount determined for the cost centre under the entity's previous GAAP. The entity shall allocate this amount to the cost centre's underlying assets pro rata using reserve volumes or reserve values as of that date.

The entity shall test exploration and evaluation assets and assets in the development and production phases for impairment at the date of transition to this FRS in accordance with Section 34 *Specialised Activities* or Section 27 *Impairment of Assets* of this FRS respectively, and if necessary, reduce the amount determined in accordance with (i) or (ii) above. For the purposes of this paragraph, oil and gas assets comprise only those assets used in the exploration, evaluation, development or production of oil and gas.

(k) *Arrangements containing a lease*

A first-time adopter may elect to determine whether an arrangement existing at the date of transition to this FRS contains a **lease** (see paragraph 20.3A) on the basis of facts and circumstances existing at that date, rather than when the arrangement was entered into.

(l) *Decommissioning liabilities included in the cost of property, plant and equipment*

Paragraph 17.10(c) states that the cost of an item of property, plant and equipment includes the initial estimate of the costs of dismantling and removing the item and restoring the site on which it is located, the obligation for which an entity incurs either when the item is acquired or as a consequence of having used the item during a particular period for purposes other than to produce **inventories** during that period. A first-time adopter may elect to measure this component of the cost of an item of property, plant and equipment at the date of transition to this FRS, rather than on the date(s) when the obligation initially arose.

(m) *Dormant companies*

A company within the Companies Act definition of a dormant company may elect to retain its accounting policies for reported assets, liabilities and equity at the date of transition to this FRS until there is any change to those balances or the company undertakes any new transactions.

(n) *Deferred development costs as a deemed cost*

A first-time adopter may elect to measure the carrying amount at the date of transition to this FRS for development costs deferred in accordance with SSAP 13 *Accounting for research and development* as its deemed cost at that date.

(o) *Borrowing costs*

An entity electing to adopt an accounting policy of capitalising **borrowing costs** as part of the cost of a **qualifying asset** may elect to treat the date of transition to this FRS as the date on which capitalisation commences.

(p) *Lease incentives*

A first-time adopter is not required to apply paragraphs 20.15A and 20.25A to **lease incentives** provided the term of the lease commenced before the date of transition to this FRS. The first-time adopter shall continue to recognise any residual benefit or cost associated with these lease incentives on the same basis as that applied at the date of transition to this FRS.

(q) *Public benefit entity combinations*

A first-time adopter may elect not to apply paragraphs PBE34.75 to PBE34.86 relating to **public benefit entity combinations** to combinations that were effected before the date of transition to this FRS. However, if on first-time adoption a **public benefit entity** restates any entity combination to comply with this section, it shall restate all later entity combinations.

(r) *Assets and liabilities of subsidiaries, associates and joint ventures*

If a subsidiary becomes a first-time adopter later than its parent, the subsidiary shall in its financial statements measure its assets and liabilities at either:

(i) the carrying amounts that would be included in the parent's **consolidated financial statements**, based on the parent's date of transition to this FRS, if no adjustments were made for consolidation procedures and for the effects of the business combination in which the parent acquired the subsidiary; or

(ii) the carrying amounts required by the rest of this FRS, based on the subsidiary's date of transition to this FRS. These carrying amounts could differ from those described in (i) when:

(a) the exemptions in this FRS result in measurements that depend on the date of transition to this FRS; or

(b) the accounting policies used in the subsidiary's financial statements differ from those in the consolidated financial statements. For example, the subsidiary may use as its accounting policy the cost model in Section 17 *Property, Plant and Equipment*, whereas the **group** may use the revaluation model.

A similar election is available to an associate or **joint venture** that becomes a first-time adopter later than an entity that has **significant influence** or **joint control** over it.

However, if an entity becomes a first-time adopter later than its subsidiary (or associate or joint venture) the entity shall, in its consolidated financial statements, measure the assets and liabilities of the subsidiary (or associate or joint venture) at the same carrying amounts as in the financial statements of the subsidiary (or associate or joint venture), after adjusting for consolidation (and equity accounting) adjustments and for the effects of the business combination in which the entity acquired the subsidiary (or transaction in which it acquired the associate or joint venture). Similarly, if a parent becomes a first-time adopter for its separate financial statements earlier or later than for its consolidated financial statements, it shall measure its assets and liabilities at the same amounts in both financial statements, except for consolidation adjustments.

(s) *Designation of previously recognised financial instruments*

This FRS permits a financial instrument (provided it meets certain criteria) to be designated on initial recognition as a financial asset or financial liability at fair value through profit or loss. Despite this an entity is permitted to designate, as at the date of transition to this FRS, any financial asset or financial liability at fair value through profit or loss provided the asset or liability meets the criteria in paragraph 11.14(b) at that date.

(t) *Hedge accounting*

(i) *A hedging relationship existing on the date of transition*

A first-time adopter may choose to apply hedge accounting to a hedging relationship of a type described in paragraph 12.19 which exists on the date of transition between a **hedging instrument** and a **hedged item**, provided the conditions of paragraphs 12.18(a) to (c) are met on the date of transition to this FRS and the conditions of paragraphs 12.18(d) and (e) are met no later than the date the first financial statements that comply with this FRS are authorised for issue. This choice applies to each hedging relationship existing on the date of transition.

Hedge accounting as set out in Section 12 *Other Financial Instruments Issues* of this FRS may commence from a date no earlier than the conditions of paragraphs 12.18(a) to (c) are met. In a fair value hedge the cumulative **hedging gain or loss** on the hedged item from the date hedge accounting commenced to the date of transition, shall be recorded in retained earnings (or if appropriate, another category of equity). In a cash flow hedge and net investment hedge, the lower of the following (in absolute amounts) shall be recorded in equity (in respect of cash flow hedges in the cash flow hedge reserve):

(a) the cumulative gain or loss on the hedging instrument from the date hedge accounting commenced to the date of transition; and

(b) the cumulative change in fair value (ie the present value of the cumulative change of expected future cash flows) on the hedged item from the date hedge accounting commenced to the date of transition.

(ii) *A hedging relationship that ceased to exist before the date of transition because the hedging instrument has expired, was sold, terminated or exercised prior to the date of transition*

A first-time adopter may elect not to adjust the carrying amount of an asset or liability for previous GAAP accounting effects of a hedging relationship that has ceased to exist.

A first-time adopter may elect to account for amounts deferred in equity in a cash flow hedge under a previous GAAP, as described in paragraph 12.23(d) from the date of transition. Any amounts deferred in equity in relation to a hedge of a **net investment in a foreign operation** under a previous GAAP shall not be reclassified to profit or loss on disposal or partial disposal of the foreign operation.

(iii) *A hedging relationship that commenced after the date of transition*

A first-time adopter may elect to apply hedge accounting to a hedging relationship of a type described in paragraph 12.19 that commenced after the date of transition between a hedging instrument and a hedged item, starting from the date the conditions of paragraphs 12.18(a) to (c) are met, provided that the conditions of paragraphs 12.18(d) and (e) are met no later than the date the first financial statements that comply with this FRS are authorised for issue.

The choice applies to each hedging relationship that commenced after the date of transition.

(iv) *Entities taking the accounting policy choice under paragraphs 11.2(b) or (c) or paragraphs 12.2(b) or (c) to apply IAS 39 Financial Instruments: Recognition and Measurement or IFRS 9 Financial Instruments*

A first-time adopter adopting an accounting policy set out in paragraphs 11.2(b) or (c) or paragraphs 12.2(b) or (c) shall not apply the transitional provisions of paragraphs (i) to (iii) above. Such a first-time adopter shall apply the transitional requirements applicable to hedge accounting in IFRS 1 *First–time adoption of International Financial Reporting Standards*, paragraphs B4 to B6, except that the designation and documentation of a hedging relationship may be completed after the date of transition, and no later than the date the first financial statements that comply with this FRS are authorised for issue, if the hedging relationship is to qualify for hedge accounting from the date of transition.

A first-time adopter adopting an accounting policy set out in paragraphs 11.2(b) or (c) or paragraphs 12.2(b) or (c) that has entered into a hedging relationship as described in IAS 39 or IFRS 9 in the period between the date of transition and the **reporting date** for the first financial statements that comply with this FRS may elect to apply hedge accounting prospectively from the date all qualifying conditions for hedge accounting in IAS 39 or IFRS 9 are met, except that an entity shall complete the formal designation and documentation of a hedging relationship no later than the date the first financial statements that comply with this FRS are authorised for issue.

(u) *Small entities – fair value measurement of financial instruments*

A small entity that first adopts this FRS for an accounting period that commences before 1 January 2017 need not restate comparative information to comply with the fair value measurement requirements of Section 11 *Basic Financial Instruments* or Section 12, unless those financial instruments were measured at fair value in accordance with the small entity's previous accounting framework.

A small entity that chooses to present comparative information that does not comply with the fair value measurement requirements of Sections 11 and 12 in its first year of adoption:

(a) shall apply its existing accounting policies to the relevant financial instruments in the comparative information and is encouraged to disclose this fact;

(b) shall disclose the accounting policies applied (in accordance with paragraph 1AC.3); and

(c) shall treat any adjustment between the statement of financial position at the comparative period's reporting date and the statement of financial position at the start of the first reporting period that complies with Sections 11 and 12 as an adjustment, in the current reporting period, to opening equity.

(v) **Small entities – financing transactions involving related parties**

A small entity that first adopts this FRS for an accounting period that commences before 1 January 2017 need not restate comparative information to comply with the requirements of paragraph 11.13 only insofar as they related to financing transactions involving **related parties**.

A small entity that chooses to present comparative information that does not comply with the financing transaction requirements of Section 11 in its first year of adoption:

(a) shall apply its existing accounting policies to the relevant financial instruments in the comparative information and is encouraged to disclose this fact;

(b) shall disclose the accounting policies applied (in accordance with paragraph 1AC.3); and

(c) shall treat any adjustment between the statement of financial position at the comparative period's reporting date and the statement of financial position at the start of the first reporting period that complies with paragraph 11.13 as an adjustment, in the current reporting period, to opening equity. The **present value** of the financial asset or financial liability at the start of the first reporting period that complies with this FRS may be determined on the basis of the facts and circumstances existing at that date, rather than when the arrangement was entered into.

35.11   If it is **impracticable** for an entity to restate the opening statement of financial position at the date of transition for one or more of the adjustments required by paragraph 35.7, the entity shall apply paragraphs 35.7 to 35.10 for such adjustments in the earliest period for which it is practicable to do so, and shall identify the data presented for prior periods that are not comparable with data for the period in which it prepares its first financial statements that conform to this FRS. If it is impracticable for an entity to provide any disclosures required by this FRS for any period before the period in which it prepares its first financial statements that conform to this FRS, the omission shall be disclosed.

35.11A Where applicable to the transactions, events or arrangements affected by applying these exemptions, an entity may continue to use the exemptions that are applied at the date of transition to this FRS when preparing subsequent financial statements, until such time when the assets and liabilities associated with those transactions, events or arrangements are derecognised.

35.11B Where there is subsequently a significant change in the circumstances or conditions associated with transactions, events or arrangements that existed at the date of transition, to which an exemption has been applied, an entity shall reassess the appropriateness of applying that exemption in preparing subsequent financial statements in order to maintain **fair presentation** in accordance with Section 3 *Financial Statement Presentation*.

Disclosures

Explanation of transition to this FRS

35.12 An entity shall explain how the transition from its previous financial reporting framework to this FRS affected its reported **financial position** and financial **performance**.

Reconciliations

35.13 To comply with paragraph 35.12, an entity's first financial statements prepared using this FRS shall include:

(a) A description of the nature of each change in accounting policy.

(b) Reconciliations of its equity determined in accordance with its previous financial reporting framework to its equity determined in accordance with this FRS for both of the following dates:

(i) the date of transition to this FRS; and

(ii) the end of the latest period presented in the entity's most recent annual financial statements determined in accordance with its previous financial reporting framework.

(c) A reconciliation of the profit or loss determined in accordance with its previous financial reporting framework for the latest period in the entity's most recent annual financial statements to its profit or loss determined in accordance with this FRS for the same period.

35.14 If an entity becomes aware of **errors** made under its previous financial reporting framework, the reconciliations required by paragraphs 35.13(b) and (c) shall, to the extent practicable, distinguish the correction of those errors from changes in accounting policies.

35.15 If an entity did not present financial statements for previous periods, it shall disclose that fact in its first financial statements that conform to this FRS.

Approval by the FRC

Financial Reporting Standard 102 *The Financial Reporting Standard applicable in the UK and Republic of Ireland* was approved for issue by the Financial Reporting Council on 5 March 2013, following its consideration of the Accounting Council's Advice for this FRS.

Amendments to FRS 102 The Financial Reporting Standard applicable in the UK and Republic of Ireland – Basic financial instruments and Hedge accounting was approved for issue by the Financial Reporting Council on 2 July 2014, following its consideration of the Accounting Council's Advice.

Amendments to FRS 102 The Financial Reporting Standard applicable in the UK and Republic of Ireland – Pension obligations was approved for issue by the Board of the Financial Reporting Council on 25 February 2015, following its consideration of the Accounting Council's Advice.

Amendments to FRS 102 The Financial Reporting Standard applicable in the UK and Republic of Ireland – Small entities and other minor amendments was approved for issue by the Board of the Financial Reporting Council on 1 July 2015, following its consideration of the Accounting Council's Advice.

The Accounting Council's Advice to the FRC to issue FRS 102

Introduction

1   This report provides an overview of the main issues that have been considered by the Accounting Council in advising the Financial Reporting Council (FRC) to issue FRS 102 *The Financial Reporting Standard applicable in the UK and Republic of Ireland*. The FRC, in accordance with the Statutory Auditors (Amendment of Companies Act 2006 and Delegation of Functions etc) Order 2012 (SI 2012/1741), is the prescribed body for issuing accounting standards in the UK. The Foreword to Accounting Standards sets out the application of accounting standards in the Republic of Ireland.

2   In accordance with the *FRC Codes and Standards: procedures*, any proposal to issue, amend or withdraw a code or standard is put to the FRC Board with the full advice of the relevant Councils and/or the Codes & Standards Committee. Ordinarily, the FRC Board will only reject the advice put to it where:

   - it is apparent that a significant group of stakeholders has not been adequately consulted;

   - the necessary assessment of the impact of the proposal has not been completed, including an analysis of costs and benefits;

   - insufficient consideration has been given to the timing or cost of implementation; or

   - the cumulative impact of a number of proposals would make the adoption of an otherwise satisfactory proposal inappropriate.

3   The FRC has established the Accounting Council as the relevant Council to assist it in the setting of accounting standards.

Advice

4   All but one member of the Accounting Council is advising the FRC to issue FRS 102 *The Financial Reporting Standard Applicable in the UK and Republic of Ireland*.

5   One member of the Accounting Council, Edward Beale, does not agree with some aspects of the Accounting Council's advice and his dissenting view is set out in the appendix to the Accounting Council's Advice.

6   FRS 100 *Application of Financial Reporting Requirements* and FRS 101 *Reduced Disclosure Framework* which are also part of this suite of financial reporting standards were issued by the FRC in November 2012. The Accounting Council's advice to the FRC on those standards is contained in those standards.

Background

7   Accounting standards were formerly developed by the Accounting Standards Board (ASB). The ASB commenced its project to update accounting standards in 2002; Appendix V provides a history of the previous consultations and a summary of how the overall proposals have developed.[15]

8   FRS 102 was developed from the IASB's IFRS for SMEs to replace the majority of UK accounting standards in a single volume.

---

[15] References in this section and Appendix V are made to the FRC, ASB or Accounting Council, as appropriate in terms of the time period and context of the reference.

Objective

9 During its consultations on updating accounting standards, the ASB (and subsequently the FRC) gave careful consideration to its objective and the intended effects. In developing the requirements in this FRS, FRS 100 and FRS 101, the overriding objective is:

> To enable users of accounts to receive high-quality understandable financial reporting proportionate to the size and complexity of the entity and users' information needs.

10 In achieving this objective, the Accounting Council decided (and the FRC subsequently adopted this decision) that it should provide succinct financial reporting standards that:

- have consistency with global accounting standards through the application of an IFRS-based solution unless an alternative clearly better meets the overriding objective;

- reflect up-to-date thinking and developments in the way businesses operate and the transactions they undertake;

- balance consistent principles for accounting by all UK and Republic of Ireland entities with practical solutions, based on size, complexity, public interest and users' information needs;

- promote efficiency within groups; and

- are cost-effective to apply.

11 The requirements in this FRS were principally consulted on in four exposure drafts:

- FRED 44 *Financial Reporting Standard for Medium-sized Entitles* issued in October 2010;

- FRED 45 *Financial Reporting Standard for Public Benefit Entities* issued in March 2011;

- FRED 48 *Financial Reporting Standard applicable in the UK and Republic of Ireland* issued in January 2012; and

- Amendment to FRED 48 issued in October 2012.

Consultation with stakeholders

12 The Accounting Council has obtained feedback from stakeholders throughout the project in a variety of ways. Appendix V sets out a history of the consultation on this project. In addition to formal consultation through exposure drafts, and previous consultation papers, feedback has been obtained through an extensive programme of outreach aimed at raising awareness of the proposals and to address the view (held by some) that earlier consultations had not gathered sufficient evidence to support and test its assumptions.

13 The Accounting Council recognised that sometimes stakeholders who will be affected by the outcome of a proposal can be difficult to engage in formal, written consultation. As a result, and in accordance with the principles of Better Regulation it developed an outreach programme that would reach beyond those stakeholders that typically respond to Exposure Drafts.

14 As part of the outreach programme a series of meetings and events took place with lenders to small and medium-sized entities. Lenders noted that financial statements are an important part of their decision-making process when considering providing finance and whilst a decision to provide finance is not based on financial statements alone, they provide useful information and verification to the lender.

15 In addition, a review was made of academic research that addressed the users of small and medium-sized entities' financial statements. The conclusion drawn from the research was that many entities requested financial statements from Companies House when considering whether to trade with another entity. The European Federation of Accountants and Auditors (EFAA) issued in May 2011 a statement that identified the users of financial statements noting who the users of SMEs financial statements are and that information on the public record assists all users of financial statements of SMEs by providing, in an efficient manner, basic information that protects their rights.

16 The Accounting Council considers that the outreach programme, across the project as a whole, has gleaned information from stakeholders who would not normally submit formal responses to a consultation and provided very useful information. The Accounting Council noted that whilst this information was not part of the public record, as formal consultation responses are, it could use the information to assist in finalising the standards, which supplemented the information contained in formal responses.

Consultation with stakeholders carried out by others

17 In addition to the consultation and outreach work carried out by the Accounting Council itself, the Accounting Council notes that some respondents, notably the accountancy institutes, conducted their own outreach amongst their members in determining their responses to the exposure drafts.

Classification of respondents

18 When analysing responses to consultations it has been the Accounting Council's practice to classify respondents into a number of standard categories in order to determine whether similar views are consistently held by a particular category of respondents. This classification is set out in the Feedback Statement that accompanies this FRS.

19 The classification of respondents only allows respondents to be classified to a single category and is based on the main perspective articulated in the response. However, the Accounting Council notes that many people that are interested in financial reporting and respond to consultations have a number of different perspectives, for example those that prepare financial statements often also use the financial statements of customers, suppliers and competitors in making decisions about running their business.

20 Therefore, there is an inherent limitation in the classification of respondents, which tends to underestimate the number of users of financial statements that have responded.

Using the IFRS for SMEs as a basis

21 Set out in Appendix V is a history of previous consultations. The ASB first started to consider the future of UK and Republic of Ireland accounting standards following the EU decision to require consolidated accounts of listed companies to comply with IFRS. The long held view is that there can be no justification for two different sets of accounting standards in the UK. Consequently, throughout the various consultations it has been proposed that the new accounting standards should have consistency with global accounting standards; this has continually been supported by the majority of respondents. Therefore the Accounting Council has proceeded with the project on this basis. The Impact Assessment accompanying this standard sets out alternative strategic options that the Accounting Council considered in framing the project (including UK accounting standards not based on IFRS), but taking into account consultation responses these were rejected. Therefore the Accounting Council developed the standard within the strategic context of an IFRS-based solution.

22 The Accounting Council noted that the IFRS for SMEs:

- is a way of achieving a consistent accounting framework, as it is a simplification of IFRS;

- was developed by the IASB and published in 2009, reflecting more up-to-date thinking and developments than current FRS, especially for financial instruments;

- is a single book setting out clear accounting requirements; and

- is a cost effective way of updating current FRS.

23 The Accounting Council noted that one of the most significant changes being introduced in this standard is the changes to the recognition, measurement and disclosures related to financial instruments. Current FRSs contain limited requirements on accounting for financial instruments for unlisted entities or those that do not apply the fair value accounting rules. Entities use derivatives to manage risk and it is important that financial statements recognise and provide disclosures about the effect of those instruments on the entity's performance and position. The Accounting Council believes that the approach under current FRSs, where derivatives are not recognised, does not adequately reflect the risks arising from financial instruments. FRS 102 will lead to an improvement in accounting for financial instruments.

24 The Accounting Council adopted guidelines for developing this standard from the IFRS for SMEs, and noted that some pragmatism was required in determining when it would be appropriate to diverge from the IFRS for SMEs. The objective is high-quality understandable financial reporting, and the standard needs to work within the legal framework in the UK and Republic of Ireland, including enabling the provisions of company law to be adhered to. The guidelines also balance high-quality understandable financial reporting and cost effective application. The high degree of support from respondents for the strategic thrust of the approach to developing the new standards suggested that respondents were prepared to balance high-quality financial reporting and costs/benefits. The Accounting Council therefore concluded that its objective and guidelines for making changes to the IFRS for SMEs should be:

> In amending the IFRS for SMEs for application in the UK and Republic of Ireland (RoI) the FRC maintains its commitment to:
>
> (a) ensuring high-quality financial reporting by UK and RoI entities applying FRS 102;
>
> (b) operate under an international accounting framework; and
>
> (c) acknowledge that users' preference for consistent financial reporting must be balanced with costs to preparers.
>
> **The guidelines when considering amendments to the IFRS for SMEs are:**
>
> (a) changes should be made to permit accounting treatments that exist in FRSs at the transition date that align with EU-adopted IFRS;
>
> (b) changes should be consistent with EU-adopted IFRS unless a non-IFRS-based solution clearly better meets the objective of providing high-quality understandable financial reporting proportionate to the size and complexity of the entity and the users' information needs. In these cases elements of an IFRS-based solution may nevertheless be retained;
>
> (c) use should be made, where possible, of existing exemptions in company law to avoid gold-plating; and
>
> (d) changes should be made to provide clarification, by reference to EU-adopted IFRS, that will avoid unnecessary diversity in practice.

25 The Accounting Council noted that by providing clarifications within FRS 102 when compared with the IFRS for SMEs it could avoid unnecessary diversity in practice. Similarly, whilst maintaining its commitment to high-quality financial reporting and a global framework, the Accounting Council determined that it should amend the IFRS for SMEs by reference to EU-adopted IFRS.

Amendments made to the IFRS for SMEs in developing FRS 102

26 In developing FRS 102 from the IFRS for SMEs, the Accounting Council advises that a number of amendments should be made to the IFRS for SMEs. The following table identifies the more significant amendments and which of the guidelines were applied in making those amendments. Where an amendment is marked ✓✓ it indicates that the amendment is as a consequence of the decision that the scope of FRS 102 is different from that of the IFRS for SMEs.

Amendment	Guideline				Law
	a)	b)	c)	d)	
Scope					
Elimination of public accountability		✓			
Cross-references to IFRS 8 and IAS 33 for listed entities.				✓✓	
Definition of a financial institution				✓	
Inclusion of public benefit entities		✓			
Presentation					
True and fair override					✓
Statement of financial position					✓
Statement of comprehensive income, including discontinued operations					✓
Statement of changes in equity	✓				
Consolidated financial statements					
Consistency with the Act					✓
ESOPs		✓			
Subsidiaries held exclusively for resale, including in an investment portfolio	✓				
Changes in stake and gains or losses on disposals	✓			✓	✓
Exchanges of businesses for interests in another business (was UITF Abstract 31)				✓	
Accounting policies					
Clarification of when to refer to a SORP in developing accounting policies		✓			

Amendment	Guideline				Law
	a)	b)	c)	d)	
Financial instruments					
Disclosures required by financial institutions (might be considered an expansion of paragraph 11.42 for those entities)				✓✓	
Treatment of loan covenants for determining whether an instrument is basic	✓				
Disclosures for certain financial instruments required by law					✓
Hedge accounting is permitted for a net investment in a foreign operation and in respect of foreign exchange risks in a debt instrument measured at amortised cost	✓	✓			
Borrowing costs may be capitalised in certain circumstances	✓				
Public benefit entities can account for concessionary loans at transaction amount		✓✓			
Fair value option	✓				
Option to apply IAS 39 or IFRS 9 recognition and measurement requirements	✓				
Financial guarantee contracts scoped out of financial instrument accounting		✓			
Property, plant and equipment					
Revaluation	✓				
Intangible assets					
Capitalisation of development costs	✓				
Revaluation after initial recognition	✓				
Where unable to make a reliable estimate of useful life, it should not exceed 5 years.					✓
Business combinations and goodwill					
Permit merger accounting for group reconstructions			✓		
Permit merger accounting by public benefit entities		✓✓			
Where unable to make a reliable estimate of useful life of goodwill, it should not exceed 5 years.					✓
Leases					
Clarification of definitions				✓	

Amendment	Guideline				Law
	a)	b)	c)	d)	
Clarification of scope for 'arrangements that contain a lease'				✓	
Liabilities and equity					
Clarification of whether an instrument is a financial liability or equity in certain circumstances				✓	
Only disclosure required for non-cash distributions to owners		✓			
Grants					
Introduction of accrual method as an option for accounting for government grants	✓				
Share-based payment					
Clarification that option pricing models are not required particularly for unquoted shares				✓	
Share-based payments granted by another group entity				✓	
Employee benefits					
Presentation of the cost of a defined benefit pension is consistent with IAS 19's 2011 amendments.		✓			
Recognition of liability by entities in multi-employer schemes with a schedule of funding for a deficit				✓	
Income tax					
Timing differences plus approach		✓			
Revised disclosure requirements		✓			
Guidance on accounting for VAT				✓	
Related party disclosures					
Disclosure exemption for wholly-owned entities			✓		
Specialised activities					
Agriculture – permit historical cost model for biological assets.		✓			
Extractive industries – refer to IFRS 6	✓				
Service concession arrangements – grantors				✓✓	
Service concession arrangements – operators				✓	
Retirement benefit plans		✓			
Heritage assets		✓			

Amendment	Guideline				Law
	a)	b)	c)	d)	
Funding commitments				✓✓	
PBE – incoming resources from non-exchange transactions (including performance-related conditions and restrictions)		✓✓			

Scope of FRS 102

27　In an earlier consultation the Accounting Council proposed a differential financial reporting system based on three tiers of entities using public accountability as a differentiator, which would have required some entities to apply EU-adopted IFRS that would not otherwise have been required to do so. Several concerns were noted about this; the more significant include:

(a)　the costs for those entities that would be required to apply EU-adopted IFRS could not be justified in relation to the benefit to users of those entities financial statements;

(b)　inconsistencies in the recognition and measurement requirements between EU-adopted IFRS and the proposals at the time for FRS 102 would reduce comparability between entities; and

(c)　the application guidance addressing the definition of public accountability remained unclear despite the guidance being developed further from the Policy Proposal.

28　The Accounting Council wanted to address the concerns from respondents that the costs for those entities that would be required to apply EU-adopted IFRS could not be justified in relation to the benefit to users of those entities' financial statements. As a result it proposed eliminating public accountability as a differentiator and determined that FRS 102 should be applied by entities that were not required to apply EU-adopted IFRS, nor were eligible and chose to apply the FRSSE. Respondents agreed with this approach.

29　As a consequence various entities that are outside the scope of the IFRS for SMEs are within the scope of FRS 102, typically these are financial institutions.

30　The Accounting Council noted that a significant number of public benefit entities apply UK accounting standards, and would be within the scope of FRS 102.

Consequences of the scope of FRS 102

31　As the scope of FRS 102 is wider than the scope of the IFRS for SMEs, there are areas not addressed in the IFRS for SMEs that might be relevant to the broader group of entities applying FRS 102.

32　In considering these areas the Accounting Council reflected on users' needs for additional information relevant to entities that are listed but not on a regulated market, ie those entities that were in part (a) of the definition of public accountability but were not required by EU Regulation to apply EU-adopted IFRS. This identified that earnings per share, operating segments and accounting for insurance contracts were not addressed in the IFRS for SMEs and accounting requirements would need to be set in these areas.

33　The Accounting Council, however, noted that in addressing the needs of this broader group of entities it should not lose sight of its objective to provide succinct financial reporting standards. Consequently, consideration was given to whether entities listed on a non-regulated market could apply EU-adopted IFRS for the areas identified by including cross references to EU-adopted IFRS in FRS 102 rather than setting out the requirements in the FRS itself.

34   The Accounting Council broadly termed as financial institutions those entities that, in accordance with FRED 43 were within the scope of part (b) of the definition of public accountability, (ie entities that hold assets in a fiduciary capacity or take deposits, including credit unions, building societies and investment entities). In considering the users' needs for financial information on financial institutions the Accounting Council noted that FRS 102 set out improvements, from current FRS, for the recognition and measurement of financial instruments, however, it had limited specific disclosure requirements for financial instruments. The Accounting Council decided that if it were to eliminate the definition of public accountability it would need to address the disclosure requirements for financial institutions, noting that financial instruments are central to the business model of these entities and how such entities generate wealth and manage risk.

35   Having identified that it would need to improve the disclosure requirements for financial institutions if it were to remove the definition of public accountability, the Accounting Council sought to find a clear definition of a financial institution. Various options were considered including whether to retain part (b) of the definition of publicly accountable, however this approach was rejected because it did not address the application difficulties raised by respondents to FRED 43.

36   The second option considered was to use the definition in section 467(1) of the Companies Act 2006; one advantage was that this was in part basing the definition on whether the entity was regulated or not.

37   The third option was simply to list the types of entity which should provide additional disclosures for financial instruments. In this regard the Accounting Council gave consideration to its previous accounting standard FRS 13 *Derivatives and Financial Instrument: Disclosures*, which applied a differential disclosure regime depending on the category of entity. On balance the Accounting Council decided that a list of entities provided the clearest approach to determine which entities should be defined as financial institutions. However, the Accounting Council also agreed with some respondents to FRED 48 that a principle behind entities selected for inclusion on the list should be articulated. As a result the Accounting Council added a final item to the list, intended to capture any entities similar to those listed above, which would also add an element of future-proofing to the definition. The Accounting Council advises that a parent entity whose sole activity is to hold investments in other group entities is not a financial institution, but notes that a subsidiary entity engaged solely in treasury activities for the group as a whole is likely to meet the definition of a financial institution.

38   Having undertaken the analysis above, it was concluded that public accountability could be eliminated and FRS 102 could apply to a broader group of entities than the IFRS for SMEs. To address the users' information needs for entities listed on a non-regulated market, FRS 102 includes cross-referencing to EU-adopted IFRS and additional disclosure requirements have been inserted for financial instruments held by financial institutions.

39   The Accounting Council observed that if it were to require a financial institution applying FRS 102 to disclose additional information regarding its financial instruments, it also needed to consider its proposals for reduced disclosures. It decided that financial institutions applying reduced disclosures would not be permitted exemptions from the additional disclosures for financial institutions.

40   The Accounting Council considered whether broadening the scope of FRS 102 would increase the pressure to update the standard (in line with changes being made to full IFRS) more frequently than on a three-year cycle. The Accounting Council agreed that there may be circumstances where FRS 102 would require updating in an interim period

between the three-year cycles, but where this occurred the amendments proposed should be limited.

Presentation

41 The Accounting Council considered feedback to FRED 44 and to the draft case studies prepared by its staff that were posted on its website that addressed the interaction between FRED 44 and the presentation formats required by company law. The Accounting Council noted that there were specific conflicts between the IFRS for SMEs and the formats, specifically the definition of current assets differed between the two sets of requirements.

42 The Accounting Council considered whether to replicate the requirements set out in company law for the information to be presented in the statement of financial position and the income statement, but was concerned that this would add clutter to FRS 102 which was not consistent with its objectives. However, it needed to work within company law and whilst it had encouraged changes to simplify the Accounting Directives it was unlikely such change would take place in the near future. The Accounting Council decided that it should promote only formats already determined in company law. This would have the consequence of all entities being required to comply with the company law formats, promoting consistency amongst all those preparing financial statements intended to give a true and fair view.

43 In amending the IFRS for SMEs to include the Companies Act formats, it was noted that the ASB had had a long-standing policy that company law formats on their own were not sufficient and should be supplemented to highlight a range of important components of financial performance to aid users' understanding of the performance of the entity. Therefore some requirements from FRS 3 *Reporting Financial Performance*, notably covering acquisitions, exceptional items and discontinued operations need to be factored in. The IFRS for SMEs was amended so that FRS 102 includes:

(a) the disclosure of post-acquisition revenue and profit or loss of an acquiree in a business combination in the notes to the financial statements;

(b) no mandatory requirement to disclose an operating profit line but guidance, based on IAS 1 *Presentation of Financial Statements*, on matters to consider where entities choose to present operating profit; and

(c) the inclusion of an explicit requirement to disclose material items.

44 The existing FRS 3 requirement to show separately on the face of the profit and loss account: profits or losses on sale or termination of an operation; costs of a fundamental reorganisation materially affecting the operation and profits; and losses on disposal of fixed assets (all of which would still have to be disclosed where material) has not been included.

45 The Accounting Council advises that, in view of the company law requirement that turnover includes the turnover from discontinued operations, a practical way of presenting this and the post-tax profit or loss on discontinued operations would be for the information about discontinued operations to be presented via a columnar approach. An example illustrating this is set out in FRS 102.

Consolidated financial statements

Definitions of control, parent and subsidiary

46 The Accounting Council notes that the definitions of control, parent and subsidiary included in FRS 102 are consistent with the IFRS for SMEs (and based on EUadopted IFRS prior to the issuing of IFRS 10 *Consolidated Financial Statements*), but differ from

those used in current FRS. Some respondents queried whether the definitions should be based on company law. The Accounting Council rejected this suggestion, but noted that by using the IFRS for SMEs definitions (consistently with its objective and guidelines), it was widening the application of control to include certain special purpose entities within the definition of a group. However, as noted below, the Accounting Council advises that this should not include employee benefit trusts and ESOPs (which should continue to be accounted for as if they are assets and liabilities of the sponsoring entity).

Employee benefit trusts, ESOPs and similar arrangements

47 In clarifying the requirements for consolidation, including considering consistency with company law requirements, the Accounting Council noted that the accounting treatment for employee benefit trusts, ESOPs or similar arrangements would give rise to a change in accounting from current FRS. The removal of UITF Abstract 38 *Accounting for ESOP trusts* would mean that such arrangements would no longer be included in individual financial statements but only in consolidated financial statements. Further, for an entity with such an arrangement, which is not a parent entity, a change in accounting requirements would lead to the preparation of 'group' financial statements where they would otherwise not have been required. Therefore the Accounting Council decided to retain the accounting treatment from UITF Abstract 32 *Employee benefit trusts and other intermediate payment arrangements* which are included in Section 9 *Consolidated and Separate Financial Statements* of FRS 102.

Investment entities exemption from consolidation

48 In September 2011 the IASB issued an exposure draft proposing to exempt qualifying investment entities from consolidating their investments. The accounting requirements were finalised and published as an amendment to IFRS 10 *Consolidated Financial Statements*, IFRS 12 *Disclosure of Interests in Other Entities* and IAS 27 *Separate Financial Statements* in October 2012. The Accounting Council noted that without a similar exemption in FRS 102, investment entities eligible to apply FRS 102, would need to elect to prepare EU-adopted IFRS in order to take advantage of the exemption. The Accounting Council did not consider this to be a logical or meaningful outcome and therefore sought to find a solution.

49 Section 405(3) of the Companies Act sets out the circumstances in which a subsidiary may be excluded from consolidation and the Accounting Council must work within these requirements. Section 405(3) permits a subsidiary to be excluded from consolidation on the following grounds:

(a) severe long-term restrictions substantially hinder the exercise of the rights of the parent company over the assets or management of that subsidiary;

(b) the information necessary for the preparation of group accounts cannot be obtained without disproportion expense or undue delay; or

(c) the interest of the parent company is held exclusively with a view to subsequent resale.

50 Taking into account the IASB's publication of *Investment Entities* (Amendments to IFRS 10, IFRS 12 and IAS 27) in October 2012, the Accounting Council advises that the definition of an interest held exclusively with a view to subsequent resale should include interests held as part of an investment portfolio.

51 FRS 102 permits that subsidiaries excluded from consolidation may be measured at fair value through profit or loss. This is a departure from the requirements of the Companies Act for the overriding purpose of giving a true and fair view in the consolidated financial statements.

Changes in stake and gains or losses on disposals

52 The Accounting Council noted that the requirements of the IFRS for SMEs in relation to changes in stake and gains and losses on disposals were not entirely coherent being based partly on IFRS 3 *Business combinations* (issued 2004) and partly on IFRS 3 *Business combinations* (revised 2008), and further some of the requirements are not consistent with company law provisions on the recognition of unrealised gains.

53 The Accounting Council considered that a coherent model for increases and decreases in stakes held in another entity was required, and that it must be consistent with company law. As a result the requirements of Section 9 *Consolidated and Separate Financial Statements* and Section 19 *Business Combinations and Goodwill* are now based on IFRS 3 (issued 2004), providing an IFRS-based solution that is consistent with company law.

Distribution of non-cash assets to owners

54 The Accounting Council had also been asked to clarify that the distribution of non-cash assets to owners did not apply to distributions within groups. In considering this requirement, the Accounting Council noted a distinction between the disposal of an asset at fair value followed by a distribution to shareholders of the profit, and making a distribution of the asset to shareholders. In its view, a distribution to shareholders does not generate a profit, whereas a disposal does generate a profit that may then be distributed to shareholders. The Accounting Council decided, given it did not support the accounting requirement, to remove the requirement in the IFRS for SMEs to recognise a liability to pay a dividend for a non-cash asset at fair value and to require disclosure of the fair value of the assets distributed to shareholders.

Financial instruments

55 In FREDs 43 and 44 the ASB noted that current FRSs were in need of updating and that they permitted certain transactions not to be recorded. Sections 11 *Basic Financial Instruments* and 12 *Other Financial Instruments Issues* of FRED 44 proposed to address these weaknesses in current FRS. The Accounting Council noted that the IFRS for SMEs has simplified the accounting for financial instruments when compared with IAS 39 *Financial Instruments: Recognition and Measurement*, whilst generally achieving similar accounting. However, there will be areas where those familiar with IAS 39 will need to take care to ensure compliance with FRS 102, for example the hierarchy to be used in determining the fair value of an asset set out in paragraph 11.27 is not the same as the 'fair value hierarchy' set out in IAS 39.

56 The Accounting Council carefully considered the views of respondents to FRED 44 concerning the proposed accounting for financial instruments set out in the FRED.

57 The Accounting Council noted the concern, primarily from the social housing sector, that recognition of derivatives used for hedging purposes at fair value may result in volatility in profit or loss. It considered carefully the requirement to recognise derivatives at fair value but noted that any changes to the financial instrument proposals should be consistent with the guidelines for amending the IFRS for SMEs. The Accounting Council concluded that it would not be consistent with the objective of providing high-quality information, or the guidelines for amending the IFRS for SMEs, to change the recognition requirements for derivatives. Recognition of derivatives, and associated disclosure, will provide relevant information to users about the risks an entity has in relation to its financial instruments.

Impact of the IASB hedge accounting and impairment projects

58 The requirements for hedge accounting and impairment of financial assets in FRS 102 are based on the requirements of IAS 39. The IASB is currently reviewing hedge accounting and impairment requirements (including developing an 'expected loss' model for the recognition of impairments of financial assets) and the Accounting Council is reluctant to propose new accounting requirements in respect of these areas before the IASB's projects are finalised in IFRS 9 *Financial Instruments*. The Accounting Council is concerned that doing so would risk financial instruments requirements in FRS 102 being out of line with both IFRS 9 and IAS 39. Simultaneously, the Accounting Council believes that the next scheduled amendment date for FRS 102 is too far in the future and consequential amendments to FRS 102 may therefore be untimely for entities that would like to apply the new IFRS 9 accounting requirements without undue delay. For that reason the Accounting Council agreed that a proposed amendment to FRS 102 would be issued for public consultation once the IASB has completed the hedge accounting and impairment projects and IFRS 9 has been updated; it is likely that there will be two separate exposure drafts, one addressing each topic. The Accounting Council intends to make amendments to FRS 102 (should the consultation determine this is appropriate) prior its effective date, although the exact timetable of any possible amendment is dependent upon when the IASB completes the impairment and hedge accounting requirements in IFRS 9.

Financial instruments accounting policy choices

59 In order to allow entities applying FRS 102 maximum flexibility, entities have a choice of either:

(a) applying the requirements of Sections 11 and 12 of FRS 102;

(b) applying the recognition and measurement requirements in IAS 39 (as adopted for use in the EU) as the standard applies prior to the application of IFRS 9; or

(c) applying IFRS 9 (as far as it has replaced the requirements in IAS 39) and IAS 39 (as far it remains applicable if IFRS 9 is applied).

By providing these accounting policy choices entities have the flexibility to apply the accounting requirements of IFRS 9 without delay should they wish to do so[16]. Entities that elect to account for financial instruments by applying the requirements of Sections 11 and 12, especially those entities that choose to apply FRS 102 before its effective date, may be required to change their accounting for financial instruments should some of the requirements in Sections 11 and 12 be amended for consistency with the principles of IFRS 9 in respect of hedge and impairment accounting, once those have been determined.

Disclosures by financial institutions

60 Having defined financial institutions, the Accounting Council advises that additional disclosures should be provided for the financial instruments held by these entities. It developed a proportionate set of disclosures for financial institutions, using IFRS 7 *Financial Instruments: Disclosures* as the basis.

Fair value option

61 A number of respondents to FRED 48 noted that bonds within the scope of Section 11 must be measured at amortised cost, even if they are managed on a fair value basis or

---

[16] As FRS 102 is a UK and Republic of Ireland accounting standard, IFRS 9 can be applied through FRS 102 in advance of EU endorsement.

their measurement at amortised cost introduces measurement differences, and suggested that an option to measure such items at fair value should be permitted in FRS 102. The Accounting Council agreed that, consistently with EU-adopted IFRS, an option should be available to designate financial assets and liabilities to be measured at fair value through profit or loss.

Hedge accounting

62   In light of the comments received in response to FREDs 44 and 48, and in order to reduce inconsistencies with EU-adopted IFRS, the Accounting Council advises that hedge accounting of a net investment in a foreign operation in consolidated financial statements be permitted and that entities are permitted to hedge foreign exchange risk arising in a debt instrument measured at amortised cost. Consistently with EU-adopted IFRS the Accounting Council also advises that hedge accounting of a net investment in a foreign operation should not be permitted in the separate financial statements of a parent.

Financial guarantee contracts

63   Respondents to FRED 48 asked for clarification of the accounting requirements for financial guarantee contracts. The accounting for financial guarantee contracts is within the scope of Section 21 *Provisions and Contingencies* unless an entity has chosen to apply IAS 39 and/or IFRS 9, or has an existing accounting policy of insurance contract accounting for financial guarantee contracts and chooses to continue to apply that policy under FRS 103 *Insurance Contracts*.

Group reconstructions

64   The Accounting Council advises that FRS 102 should retain the current accounting permitted by FRS 6 *Acquisitions and mergers* for group reconstructions. The Accounting Council noted that whilst EU-adopted IFRS does not provide accounting requirements for the accounting for business combinations under common control the accounting provided by FRS 6 is well understood and provides useful requirements. It therefore decided to carry forward these requirements into FRS 102. In practice, the Accounting Council does not expect the introduction of FRS 102 to change the accounting for group reconstructions. For example, where a combination is effected by using a newly formed parent company to hold the shares of each of the parties to a combination, the accounting treatment depends on the substance of the business combination being effected.

Leases

65   Leases are accounted for in accordance with the requirements of Section 20 *Leases*, except for those leases falling within the scope of Section 12, which are those that could result in a loss to the lessor or the lessee as a result of non-typical contractual terms, for example those that are unrelated to:

(a)   changes in the price of the leased asset;

(b)   changes in foreign exchange rates; or

(c)   a default by one of the counterparties.

66   The Accounting Council notes that the reference to 'changes in the price of the leased asset' is framed widely and in practice it does not expect many leases to fall within the scope of Section 12.

Grants

67 A number of respondents, particularly from the public benefit entity sector, raised concerns about the proposed changes to the recognition requirements for grants received from government and other bodies. The proposals in FRED 44 based the recognition of income from grants on when an entity fulfilled the performance criteria stipulated in the grant. This would have been a change from both current FRS and EU-adopted IFRS which attempt to match grant income with the related expenditure. The Accounting Council observed that the IFRS for SMEs used an approach not in current EU-adopted IFRSs.

68 The Accounting Council reviewed the concerns of entities noting that it could amend the performance criterion approach to provide application guidance on performance outcome. This approach would require a research project to be undertaken and cause delay to the finalisation of FRS 102. An alternative was to amend the requirements in the IFRS for SMEs so that they were consistent with EU-adopted IFRS and defer a research project on the accounting for grants until after the publication of FRS 102. However, respondents also noted that some entities, mainly in the public benefit entity sector, currently recognised income from grants on the basis of performance criteria and that reverting to the requirements of EU-adopted IFRS (which is similar to current FRS) would introduce a change for these entities. The Accounting Council did not wish to implement a change for entities that might be reversed when it subsequently undertook a research project on grant accounting. It therefore concluded it should allow entities a choice between the accounting requirements of the IFRS for SMEs and those in EU-adopted IFRS.

69 The Accounting Council recognises that the respondents to FRED 44 highlighted an inconsistency in current practice and that the solution in FRS 102 is therefore, an interim solution until completion on a research project is undertaken.

70 Respondents have further commented that as Section 24 *Government Grants* is restricted to government grants, grants received by public benefit entities from other sources will be accounted for in accordance with Section 34 *Specialised Activities: Incoming Resources from Non-Exchange Transactions*, and there is now the possibility that the accounting for grants depends on the source of the grant, rather than whether or not the underlying terms and conditions of the grants differ. Whilst this is not ideal, the Accounting Council advises permitting the accrual model for government grants in accordance with its guidelines for amending the IFRS for SMEs as an interim solution to avoid changes in accounting that might be reversed in the future.

71 For those entities that apply the performance model to capital grants, either as an accounting policy choice for government grants, or through applying Section 34 to grants from other sources, the Accounting Council notes that there may be a change from current accounting practice, which may lead to greater volatility in the income statement. The effect of this volatility can be explained in the notes to the financial statements.

Share-based payment

72 The Accounting Council noted that at present entities in the UK and Republic of Ireland[17] that enter into share-based payment transactions are required to apply FRS 20 (IFRS 2) *Share-based Payment*. However, for unlisted entities it can be difficult to apply option pricing models and therefore the benefits outweigh the costs. As a result the Accounting Council advises that directors apply judgement by using models that are appropriate to the entity's circumstance. The Accounting Council considers that this provides a cost effective way of recognising the cost of share-based payments.

---

[17] Other than those applying the FRSSE.

Employee benefits

73 The Accounting Council noted that the requirements of FRS 17 *Retirement benefits* are broadly consistent with the equivalent requirements of IAS 19 *Employee Benefits*, which form the basis of the IFRS for SMEs in this area, including the principles for the measurement of the net defined benefit liability and the recognition of plan deficits and surpluses. The disclosure requirements of FRS 102 for defined benefit pension plans are reduced when compared with those in FRS 17.

Cost of a defined benefit plan

74 Respondents noted that the presentation requirements for post-employment benefit plans were not clear in FRED 44. Specifically a request was made to clarify where the difference between the actual return on plan assets and expected return on plan assets should be presented. The Accounting Council, in considering this request, noted that the presentation requirements in IAS 19 had been amended in 2011. The amendments to IAS 19 were consistent with the ASB's recommendations in its report following the consultation document *The Financial Reporting of Pensions*. In view of this, the Accounting Council decided to update FRS 102 to be consistent with the revised IAS 19, which requires an entity to recognise the net change in the defined benefit liability as follows:

(a) the change in the defined benefit liability arising from employee service rendered during the reporting period in profit or loss;

(b) net interest on the net defined benefit liability in profit or loss; and

(c) remeasurement of the net defined benefit liability in other comprehensive income.

75 In advising this amendment, the Accounting Council also noted that the accounting requirements in the IFRS for SMEs for group pension plan arrangements were more stringent than those set out in IAS 19 (revised 2011). The Accounting Council therefore decided to update these requirements to be consistent with the IAS 19 (revised 2011).

Group defined benefit pension plans

76 Consistently with IAS 19 (revised 2011), paragraph 28.38 of FRS 102 requires entities participating in a group defined benefit pension plan to recognise the net defined benefit cost in their individual financial statements where a relevant agreement or policy exists. Otherwise the entity that is legally responsible for the group pension plan will recognise the entire net defined benefit cost in its individual financial statements. The Accounting Council noted that although this paragraph only refers explicitly to the cost of the pension plan, the net defined benefit cost is calculated by reference to both the defined benefit obligation and the fair value of plan assets. Therefore paragraph 28.38 does require the recognition of the relevant net defined benefit liability in the individual financial statements of any group entities recognising a net defined benefit cost.

Multi-employer defined benefit plans

77 In October 2012 the FRC issued an exposure draft of proposed amendments to FRED 48, including amendments to Section 28 *Employee Benefits*. These amendments related to multi-employer defined benefit plans that are accounted for as defined contribution plans. The Accounting Council is aware that diversity in accounting practice had arisen in relation to entities who participate in a defined benefit multi-employer plan, who account for that plan as a defined contribution plan and who have entered into a funding agreement for future payments relating to past service liabilities, to recognise a liability in relation to the deficit in the plan in their financial statements.

78   Consistently with the guidelines for amending the IFRS for SMEs, the Accounting Council advises incorporating the relevant requirement from IAS 19 and notes that the IASB's basis for conclusions said that 'In relation to the funding of a deficit, [...] this principle [is] consistent with the recognition of a provision in accordance with IAS 37.'

79   The Accounting Council also advises clarifying the measurement requirements for such a liability. In the circumstances that the entity has entered into a funding agreement for future payments relating to past service it shall recognise those future payments as a liability, discounted using the methodology for selecting a discount rate for post-employment benefit liabilities. The Accounting Council debated whether the discount rate should alternatively be based on the entity's cost of capital, but decided to advise the use of a rate consistent with the methodology used for accounting for other pension liabilities.

80   The Accounting Council noted that some respondents to the exposure draft disagreed with the proposed amendment or requested a delay in implementation, but the Accounting Council believes that where participants in a multi-employer defined benefit pension plan have entered into an agreement to fund a deficit, and have applied defined contribution accounting, a liability exists and its recognition provides useful information to users.

81   Some respondents suggested that FRS 102 should also address situations where a multi-employer pension plan was in surplus, and entered into an agreement to distribute that surplus to the participating employers. Although the Accounting Council noted that this is addressed in IAS 19, it expected that the situation would arise rarely in practice, and considered that entities would be able to determine the appropriate accounting using the principles set out in FRS 102. Therefore it does not advise making an amendment for this.

Income tax

82   In FRED 44 the ASB proposed using the text of IAS 12 *Income Taxes* in place of the IFRS for SMEs section on income tax. The ASB had amended the tax section of the IFRS for SMEs because it had been based on proposals subsequently abandoned by the IASB and therefore the IFRS for SMEs was not consistent with full IFRS. Respondents to the Policy Proposal had not supported retaining the IFRS for SMEs requirements in this area. Respondents to FRED 44 had accepted that the IFRS for SMEs treatment could not be used, but did not support the ASB's proposal to replace the tax section with IAS 12.

83   In developing FRED 48 the ASB considered what would be the most suitable alternative, and took into account the findings of its research work with EFRAG in developing the Discussion Paper *Improving the Financial Reporting of Income Tax* (issued in December 2011), as well as its commitment to an IFRS-based solution and the requirements of FRS 19 *Deferred Tax* from which entities would be transitioning. It set out an alternative approach that based the recognition requirements on timing differences, with additional recognition requirements for certain temporary differences that are not timing differences, which was referred to as a 'timing differences plus' approach. The advantages of this approach seemed to be that it would:

(a)   provide useful information to users of financial statements; and

(b)   provide the simple solution preparers were looking for that was close to current FRS and that would give the same answers as IFRSs in most cases.

84   Most respondents supported the 'timing differences plus' approach, which has therefore been retained in FRS 102.

85   The most significant change to the requirements in current FRS is that the proposed approach requires the recognition of the deferred tax implications of the revaluation of assets. Gains and losses recognised on a revaluation are timing differences and the tax

effects should be recognised. Such a requirement is consistent with IAS 12 and the IFRS for SMEs.

86 Another significant change from current FRS is that discounting of current and deferred tax is not allowed which is consistent with the IFRS for SMEs.

87 Under IAS 12 deferred tax is not generally recognised on the initial recognition of an asset, except that of assets and liabilities arising from a business combination. No specific exception for this is necessary under the 'timing differences plus' approach as no timing difference arises. The proposed treatment is therefore consistent in this respect with IAS 12.

88 A pure timing difference approach does not provide complete consistency with the requirements of IAS 12. In particular, IAS 12 requires that deferred tax is recognised in respect of the difference between the amount recognised on a business combination for assets and liabilities (other than goodwill) and the amount that will be allowed for or assessed to tax in respect of such assets and liabilities. These differences are not timing differences. In order to maintain consistency with IFRS on this major issue, the Accounting Council agreed to supplement the timing difference approach with a requirement to recognise deferred tax on business combinations.

89 However, the 'timing differences plus' approach adopted in FRS 102 does not ensure complete consistency with the requirements of IAS 12. For example FRS 102 does not permit the recognition of deferred tax:

(a) where the tax deduction (or estimated future deduction) for share-based payment exceeds the cumulative amount of the related remuneration expense; and

(b) in some cases, where the tax basis of an asset is changed, for example where legislation changes the amount of future tax relief relating to the asset.

90 The Accounting Council considered, however, that the differences from IAS 12 were likely to be relatively rare and that in such cases the relevance of the information produced in accordance with IAS 12 was unclear.

91 The proposed disclosure requirements have been reviewed in the light of comments on FRED 48. In particular the requirement to disclose differences between the current tax charge and a standard rate of tax for the next three years has been replaced by a requirement to disclose expected net reversals of timing differences for the next year. The requirement to disclose is on a net basis, which takes account of both the reversal of existing timing differences and the origination of new ones. The net basis provides information that is relevant to the entity's future cash flows, and hence is more relevant than disclosure on a gross basis. The Accounting Council considers that the additional benefit of disclosure on a net basis outweighed the cost to preparers of forecasting future new timing differences.

Related party disclosures

92 In response to feedback from respondents, the Accounting Council advises that the company law exemption from disclosing intra-group related party transactions should be included in FRS 102.

93 Some respondents raised the issue of a possible exemption from the disclosure of outstanding balances as well as transactions. However, the Accounting Council noted that there is a separate legal requirement, in relation to the format of the balance sheet which requires disclosure of outstanding balances in aggregate for group undertakings and, separately, for undertakings in which the company has a participating interest. As Section 33 *Related Party Disclosures* requires disclosure in aggregate for a category of

related parties, one of which is 'entities over which the entity has control, joint control or significant influence' this should be met by compliance with the requirements of Section 4 *Statement of Financial Position.* As a result it is not possible to provide an effective exemption from the disclosure of outstanding balances with group undertakings.

Specialised activities

Agriculture

94   The IFRS for SMEs includes guidance for specialised activities including agriculture. The proposed requirements for agriculture are a predominately fair value model and are based on IAS 41 *Agriculture.* Respondents questioned the proposed requirements noting that current FRSs do not set out accounting requirements and although the proposals included an exemption from applying fair value where there is undue cost or effort, the fair value information is inconsistent with the way most agricultural businesses are managed and would not benefit the users of financial statements.

95   The Accounting Council evaluated the comments raised and advises that entities engaged in agricultural activities should be permitted an accounting policy choice for their biological assets, between the cost model and fair value model set out in the IFRS for SMEs.

96   The Accounting Council noted that both the cost model and the fair value model, as set out in the IFRS for SMEs, require agricultural produce to be measured at the point of harvest at fair value less costs to sell. However, it considered that respondents in favour of the cost model would have expected the cost model to mean that both biological assets and agricultural produce would be measured at cost.

97   The Accounting Council noted that agricultural produce should be capable of measurement at fair value without undue cost or effort, and should provide more relevant information to users. However, it noted that respondents argued that agricultural businesses often manage their business on the basis of cost information and advises that agricultural produce should be permitted to be measured at cost. The Accounting Council advises limiting the use of the cost model for agricultural produce to those entities that have chosen the cost model for biological assets; however these entities should also have the option of using the fair value model for agricultural produce.

Extractive activities

98   Respondents noted that the requirements of the IFRS for SMEs in relation to extractive activities were not consistent with IFRS 6 *Exploration for and Evaluation of Mineral Resources*, and the application of the IFRS for SMEs requirements, in conjunction with other elements of FRS 102 would significantly change accounting practices for entities engaged in extractive activities. It would be likely that no assets could be recognised from the costs of exploration activities, yet entities applying EUadopted IFRS would be permitted to recognise such assets.

99   The Accounting Council agreed that entities applying FRS 102 should not be prohibited from applying accounting policies that are available to those entities applying EU-adopted IFRS, and advises that the requirements of IFRS 6 are incorporated into FRS 102 by cross reference.

Service concession arrangements

100 Respondents raised two main issues relating to the accounting for service concession arrangements. The first was that the requirements of the IFRS for SMEs in relation to the accounting by operators had been over-simplified when compared with IFRIC 12 *Service Concession Arrangements.* The Accounting Council agreed and FRS 102 includes

additional clarification of the principles of accounting by operators for service concession arrangements, which were developed from IFRIC 12.

101 The second issue related to grantors, with some respondents noting that grantors might be within the scope of FRS 102. This was addressed in the October 2012 exposure draft of proposed amendments to FRED 48 issued by the FRC.

102 EU-adopted IFRS does not address accounting by grantors of service concession arrangements; grantors are expected to be outside the scope of EU-adopted IFRS. As a result, and consistently with the guidelines for amending the IFRS for SMEs, the Accounting Council sought to develop accounting for grantors that is consistent with the principles underpinning the accounting by operators of service concession arrangements, which is set out in IFRIC 12. The scope of IFRIC 12 is such that the grantor controls the residual interest in the infrastructure asset, and therefore for service concession arrangements meeting the definition in FRS 102, the Accounting Council advises that the grantor recognises its interest in the infrastructure asset usually as property, plant and equipment, with a corresponding liability measured using a finance lease model.

103 The Accounting Council noted that the International Public Sector Accounting Standards Board (IPSASB) has issued a standard IPSAS 32 *Service Concession Arrangements: Grantor*, which includes two models for accounting by the grantor, depending on the terms of the arrangement with the operator. In addition to the finance lease model advised by the Accounting Council, IPSAS 32 includes a 'grant of right to the operator model' which applies to 'user-pays' arrangements. The Accounting Council does not advise the application of this model because it appears to result in the recognition as liabilities of amounts that may not meet the definition of a liability. However, some respondents to the exposure draft suggested that this model should be permitted. The Accounting Council advises that further research should be carried out on the most appropriate accounting for user-pays service concession arrangements, but that this should not delay the issue of FRS 102.

104 The Accounting Council considered whether transitional provisions should be available for grantors. It noted that for some grantors, the proposals would result in recognising assets and liabilities for the infrastructure assets that are not presently recognised. It considered that this provides more relevant information to users, and therefore advises the FRC that transitional provisions should not be available. As a result grantors will not be permitted to apply the transitional exemptions that are available to operators, as set out in FRS 102 paragraph 35.10(i), by analogy.

Retirement benefit plans

105 FRED 43 proposed that retirement benefit plans were publicly accountable and therefore should apply EU-adopted IFRS, but having decided to eliminate the definition of publicly accountable, retirement benefit plans are now within the scope of FRS 102, yet the IFRS for SMEs contains no specific provisions for retirement benefit plans.

106 The Accounting Council considered whether to direct retirement benefit plans to IAS 26 *Accounting and Reporting by Retirement Benefit Plans* and request that the Statement of Recommended Practice (SORP) *Financial Reports of Pension Schemes* be updated to be consistent with IAS 26. This option was, however, rejected based on feedback which suggested that the application of IAS 26 would be difficult for two reasons:

(a) legal accounting and reporting requirements in the UK are different to those in IAS 26; and

(b) IAS 26 itself makes references to other IFRSs and the interaction between these references and FRS 102 would be complicated.

A further complication would arise as the SORP would also provide application guidance for retirement benefit plans.

107 Following this feedback the Accounting Council decided to develop, as part of the specialised activities section, accounting requirements for retirement benefit plans financial statements that could be supplemented by the SORP.

108 In developing the proposals, the Accounting Council considered the issue of whether the financial statements of retirement benefit plans need to provide disclosure regarding the pension liabilities and the related funding of the plan. Following feedback from respondents, the Accounting Council decided that such information should not be recognised in the financial statements, but provided alongside it, as is currently the case.

109 The Accounting Council advises that because of the way in which retirement benefit plans use financial instruments they should be considered to be financial institutions. However, not all of the disclosure requirements for financial institutions are relevant to retirement benefit plans and it will be more user-friendly to have all requirements in one place. Therefore Section 34 sets out all the requirements for retirement benefit plans in one sub-section.

Insurance contracts

110 FRED 48 proposed that entities with insurance contracts should apply IFRS 4 *Insurance Contracts* to those contracts. In addition, insurance-related contracts not meeting the definition of an insurance contract shall usually be accounted for as financial instruments in accordance with Sections 11 and 12.

111 The FRC also has FRS 27 *Life Assurance* in issue. The Accounting Council debated the various options for setting out the requirements for entities engaged in insurance business, and decided that it should advise the FRC to issue a separate accounting standard on insurance contracts, FRS 103 *Insurance Contracts*. An exposure draft of this standard will be available after FRS 102 has been issued, but FRS 102 cross-refers to it. The Accounting Council's Advice to the FRC to issue FRS 103 will be set out in that standard.

Other options available in EU-adopted IFRS

112 Respondents to FRED 44, in general, supported the use of the IFRS for SMEs as a base for a future financial reporting standard in the UK and Republic of Ireland. There were, however, concerns raised that would require careful consideration, most notably the removal of certain accounting treatments (options) that are available in current FRSs and EU-adopted IFRS but were not proposed in FRED 44.

113 Responses from the housing associations particularly focused on how the removal of options might have behavioural implications that the Accounting Council should take into consideration. The housing associations noted that:

(a) the removal of the options would reduce comparability between entities that apply EU-adopted IFRS and those applying FRED 44 for entities operating in the same market, for example entities applying FRED 44 would not be permitted to revalue property, plant and equipment whereas entities applying EU-adopted IFRS could; and

(b) the inability to include borrowing costs as part of the costs of property, plant and equipment may cause some housing associations to breach terms and conditions of current financing arrangements; this gave potential for banks and other lenders to renegotiate existing financing arrangements but at a higher cost of capital.

114 Other respondents noted that removal of the accounting options was potentially an over-simplification for the UK and Republic of Ireland. These respondents noted the IFRS for SMEs had been developed by the IASB for countries that had a less developed financial reporting framework than the UK and Republic of Ireland. They considered that as options existed in current FRSs the simplification had not been justified by the Accounting Council.

115 A further view put forward by respondents was that retaining the options that existed in current FRS would reduce transition costs and ease transition between the different standards and also with EU-adopted IFRS.

116 Application of the guidelines permitted the introduction of accounting options that exist in current FRS and EU-adopted IFRS that respondents had highlighted as reducing comparability. FRS 102 therefore includes accounting options for:

(a) capitalisation of borrowing costs;

(b) revaluation of property, plant and equipment and intangible assets; and

(c) capitalisation of development costs, in certain circumstances.

Providing clarifications in FRS 102

117 Having agreed guidelines that include making amendments to the IFRS for SMEs to provide clarifications, the Accounting Council considered relevant requests from respondents. Some clarifications were made by reference to EU-adopted IFRS (see column (d) of the table at paragraph 26 of the Accounting Council's Advice), others were made by reference to current FRS, for example whether there is an interaction with company law. As a result a number of clarifications have been made, examples include:

(a) disclosure requirements for discontinued operations;

(b) treatment of loan covenants, so that the treatment is consistent with IFRS 9 *Financial Instruments*;

(c) financial instruments that would be equity under IAS 32 *Financial Instruments: Presentation* are not liabilities, when an entity is required to prepare consolidated financial statements;

(d) when an investor that is not a parent but has an investment in one or more associates and/or jointly controlled entities shall account for its investments and/or jointly controlled entities using either cost or fair value;

(e) the presumed life for goodwill, in particular when an entity is otherwise unable to make a reliable estimate shall not be in excess of five years and thereby consistent with company law. The same also applies to intangible assets;

(f) accounting treatment for group share-based payments where the award is granted by the parent or another group entity; and

(g) that option pricing models are not required for the value of shared-based payments, particularly for unquoted shares or share options.

Other matters

118 The Accounting Council considered whether to provide guidance for the term 'undue cost or effort' where respondents had sought clarification. The Accounting Council noted that Section 2 *Concepts and Pervasive Principles* discussed the balance between benefit and cost and that no further clarification was required.

The retention of Urgent Issue Task Force (UITF) Abstracts

119 FREDs 43 and 44 proposed to withdraw all UITF Abstracts except UITF Abstract 43 *The Interpretation of equivalence for the purposes of section 228A of the Companies Act.* Respondents to the FRED proposed that in addition to UITF Abstract 43, other UITF Abstracts should be retained. The Accounting Council gave consideration to this request and noted that rather than retain UITF Abstracts, consistent with its objective to provide succinct financial reporting standards, it should incorporate any guidance into FRS 102.

120 Based on feedback the Accounting Council advises that the following accounting requirements of UITF Abstracts are retained by incorporation, as follows:

UITF Abstract		Action
4	*Presentation of long-term debtors in current assets*	Incorporated into the legal appendix.
31	*Exchange of businesses or other non-monetary assets for an interest in a subsidiary, joint venture or associate*	Additional paragraphs 9.31 and 9.32 are inserted.
32	*Employee benefit trusts and other intermediate payment arrangements*	Additional paragraphs are inserted into Section 9.
43	*The interpretation of equivalence for the purposes of section 228A of the Companies Act 1985*	The guidance has been updated and included as Application Guidance to FRS 100.

121 The Accounting Council decided to advise the withdrawal of UITF Abstract 48 *Accounting implications of the replacement of the retail prices index with the consumer prices index for retirement benefits* as the circumstance it addressed were related to a one time period which has now expired.

Interaction with company law

122 The Accounting Council gave careful consideration to the comments received to its draft legal appendix set out in FREDs 44 and 48. The Accounting Council agreed with respondents' views that the appendix should address entities that are not companies.

123 The Accounting Council also considered whether it should retain, as proposed in FRED 44, accounting options that had been removed because the option conflicted with company law, where an entity that is not a company would not be restricted in the same way as a company. For example, SSAP 4 Accounting for *government grants* contained an option that was not permitted by the company law.

124 The Accounting Council confirmed the position it had taken in developing FRED 44 that options that existed in the IFRS for SMEs, but not permitted by company law, should be removed. This would promote consistency between reporting entities regardless of the legal framework under which they operate.

Public benefit entities (PBEs)

125 The Consultation Paper *Policy Proposal: The Future of UK GAAP* (issued in 2009) set out 10 issues that could be included in a Public Benefit Entities (PBEs) specific standard. However, these 10 issues were refined to six which were deemed to be those most

significant and relevant to the PBE sectors that were not satisfactorily addressed by the IFRS for SMEs. These six issues were:

(a) Concessionary loans;

(b) Property held for the provision of social benefits;

(c) Entity combinations;

(d) Impairment of assets: public benefit considerations;

(e) Funding commitments; and

(f) Incoming resources from non-exchange transactions.

Concessionary loans

126 Paragraphs have been inserted into Section 34 *Specialised Activities* to address the accounting requirements for PBEs making and receiving concessionary loans.

127 There are two main accounting treatments to consider when determining the basis for the measurement of concessionary loans; the amount paid or received, and fair value. This has been the subject of significant discussion and debate by the Accounting Council, taking into account the information that users of PBE accounts may consider useful and the difficulties that may arise for smaller organisations in measuring concessionary loans at fair value.

128 Accounting for concessionary loans at the amount paid or received rather than fair value is not consistent with the accounting requirements set out in either Section 11 of FRS 102, EU-adopted IFRS or IPSAS 29 *Financial Instruments: Recognition and Measurement* (which require that such arrangements are measured and recognised in the financial statements at their fair value).

129 Nevertheless the Accounting Council advises that due to the difficulties that smaller PBEs may face with using fair value, PBEs that make or receive concessionary loans may have the option of measuring such loans at either the amount paid or received or at fair value. However, PBEs that make and receive concessionary loans must apply the same measurement method to both. Further the Accounting Council proposes that the same accounting may be applied by other wholly-owned entities in a public benefit entity group, to eliminate the need to restate concessionary loans made or received for the purposes of furthering the PBEs objectives on consolidation.

130 Presentation and disclosure of concessionary loan arrangements are an important part of the proposals for concessionary loans and the Accounting Council concluded that the disclosure requirements in FRS 102 will provide sufficient information to understand and interpret the impact of this type of transaction on the financial statements.

Property held for the provision of social benefits

131 Subsequent to FRED 45, the Accounting Council decided that the requirements for property held for the provision of social benefits should apply to all entities applying FRS 102 and should not be restricted to PBEs.

132 Consideration was given as to whether properties that are held for the provision of social benefits meet the definition of an investment property. The definition of investment property in paragraph 16.2 of FRS 102, excludes properties held for use in the production or supply of goods and services or for administrative purposes. A property held to earn rentals and/or for capital appreciation, but not used in the production or supply of goods or services, meets this definition. The Accounting Council noted that although many PBEs

that engage in the provision of social housing receive rental income, their primary purpose is to provide social benefits.

133 Provision of social housing is akin to supplying a service and therefore, property held for the primary purpose of providing social benefits should be excluded from the scope of investment property and be accounted for as property, plant and equipment.

134 The Accounting Council acknowledges that PBEs may hold 'investment properties' which are not held primarily to provide social benefits and will return market value rentals and/or are held for their capital appreciation. FRS 102 requires those properties to be accounted for as investment properties.

Public benefit entity combinations

135 In considering the issue of entity combinations involving two or more public benefit entities, the Accounting Council noted that there is some debate over whether the use of acquisition accounting for all combinations would be appropriate. In particular whether acquisition accounting reflects the substance of a transaction if there is a gift of one entity to another in a combination at nil or nominal consideration, or where two or more organisations genuinely merge to form a new entity.

136 Where there is a combination of entities at nil or nominal consideration which is in substance a gift, it is appropriate to follow the same accounting principles as donations of assets (as set out in Section 34 *Specialised Activities: Incoming Resources from Non-Exchange Transactions*) by recognising the fair value of the assets received and liabilities assumed as a gain or loss in income and expenditure.

137 Accounting for combinations that meet the definition of a merger requires a different methodology to acquisition accounting in order to reflect the true substance of the transaction. Whilst it is not anticipated that all combinations involving two or more public benefit entities are mergers or that merger accounting will generally be applicable to such combinations it is considered appropriate to retain merger accounting in certain circumstances. In considering this matter it was noted that the accounting requirements for PBEs in some jurisdictions, for example, the US and Australia have recently been reviewed and noted that merger accounting has been retained for the public and not-for-profit sectors.

138 In retaining merger accounting, the Accounting Council considered the criteria to be met for a merger. The criteria set out in FRS 6 *Acquisitions and Mergers* provided a starting point, but are framed in the context of the commercial sector and therefore the criteria have been adapted to make them more appropriate for public benefit entities. In particular, a criterion has been added to include consideration of the impact of the combination on beneficiaries and the benefits to which they are entitled.

139 One specific concern highlighted in relation to the requirements of FRS 6, is the need to restate comparatives by adding together the previous periods' reported figures of each of the combining entities. This does not reflect the substance of the transaction as the historical parties which formed the entity did not exist in the previous accounting period and therefore FRS 102 requires that comparatives are marked as 'combined' to make it clear that they are a combination of previously reported figures for the combining entities.

Impairment of assets

140 FRS 102 requires impaired assets to be measured at the lower of their fair value less costs to sell and their value in use. In a for-profit context, value in use is determined by measuring the present value of the cash flows derived from the asset. However, often PBE assets are held for their service potential rather than their ability to generate cash

flows. In such a case it is sometimes impossible to determine value in use by reference to cash flows and it is more appropriate to regard value in use as the present value of future service potential rather than cash flows.

141 International Public Sector Accounting Standard (IPSAS) 21 *Impairment of Non-Cash Generating Assets* permits value in use to be determined by any of three approaches:

(a) depreciated replacement cost (DRC);

(b) restoration cost; and

(c) the service units approach.

Restoration cost and the service units approach are applications of DRC as DRC is used as the starting point. DRC reflects the cash outflows that are saved through ownership of an asset and is likely to be widely applicable and appropriate for PBEs. Therefore FRS 102 permits a service potential driven valuation to be used for assets held for their service potential.

142 The use of DRC is not mandated; other methods that value service potential rather than cash flows may be used if those methods are more appropriate in those particular circumstances.

143 FRED 45 only allowed this alternative valuation method for PBEs, however subsequent to that consultation, the Accounting Council advises that any entity that holds an asset for service potential can use a service potential valuation method. It is not expected that, for example, headquarters buildings that do not generate cash flows independently of other assets or groups of assets but nevertheless contribute to the cash-generating activities of the entity, will usually be measured on the basis of their service potential.

144 The Accounting Council also discussed whether a restriction on the use of an asset would affect its fair value. As an asset's fair value is based on the amount that an entity could obtain, restrictions might impact on the fair value where they prevent a purchaser from using the asset for another purpose that would be more valuable than that required by the restriction. In addition, the costs to sell should include the costs of breaking the restriction.

145 Another issue for discussion was indicators of impairment. Although the indicators provided in FRS 102 are mainly linked to the expected cash flow of an asset and as such may not necessarily be relevant to some PBE assets, the Accounting Council considered that they must, as a minimum, be considered by PBEs as possible indicators of impairment.

146 In addition, the Accounting Council noted that other accounting literature (eg IPSAS 21 and SORPs) identified other indicators of impairment including:

(a) cessation, or near cessation of the demand or need for services provided by the asset;

(b) social, demographic or environmental changes resulting in a reduction of beneficiaries; and

(c) a major loss of key employees associated with particular activities.

147 The Accounting Council concluded that it would not be appropriate to include these indicators in FRS 102, as they are not exclusively relevant to PBEs and because the indicators given in FRS 102 will continue to apply to PBEs. Therefore, their inclusion would make such entities subject to a confusing list of overlapping indicators. The indicators given in FRS 102 are merely minimum requirements, and recognition of an impairment loss is required irrespective of whether any of the given indicators are met.

148 The Accounting Council also considered whether to specify that an indicator of impairment was present where an asset's service potential was not fully utilised and noted that an entity may require standby or surplus capacity to ensure that it has adequate capacity to provide services at all times. For example, a building that provides accommodation for the homeless may not be used to full capacity during the summer months but is utilised fully during winter. In this circumstance, the surplus capacity is part of the required service potential of the asset and the asset is not impaired. For this reason, it was concluded that it would be inappropriate to specify that the unutilised capacity should be treated as an indicator of impairment.

Funding commitments

149 The Accounting Council also discussed when to recognise a commitment to provide funding in a non-exchange transaction. The *Statement of Principles: Interpretation for Public Benefit Entities* previously addressed this issue, and it was considered necessary to incorporate these details into FRS 102 to be used in conjunction with Sections 2 *Concepts and Pervasive Principles* and 21 *Provisions and Contingencies*.

150 The issue was identified as being particularly important because many PBEs provide funding on an on-going basis and there is little guidance on how such multi-year commitments should be recognised.

151 The Accounting Council considered when a liability for such a commitment should be recognised and determined that an entity would only recognise a liability if the commitment to provide funding was made unconditionally, and the grantor could not realistically withdraw from the commitment. In this situation, an entity would recognise a liability for the present value of the total funding promised.

152 As this is an application of the principles in Sections 2 and 21, the Accounting Council advises that the requirements for funding commitments should apply to all entities and not just PBEs.

Incoming resources from non-exchange transactions

153 The receipt of resources from non-exchange transactions is an inflow of resources that is highly significant for many PBEs: the receipt of donations, grants and legacies from non-exchange transactions are a major source of their funding and this issue is not addressed in the IFRS for SMEs apart from in Section 24 *Government Grants*.

154 The Accounting Council considered that for PBE financial statements to be complete, they should reflect the benefit that the inflow of these resources had to the entity. FRS 102 requires, in principle, PBEs to value the resources they receive from non-exchange transactions at their fair value. The Accounting Council discussed whether using fair value would overstate the value of a donation where the entity is unable to exploit fully an asset, and the equivalent service potential could be derived from a lower value asset. Being able to achieve the same service potential from a lower value asset might suggest that the value of the donated asset should be at the lower value. However, FRS 102 requires donated assets to be valued at their fair value. This reflects that the circumstances described above would rarely occur. In many cases, an entity would be able to sell the donated asset and if appropriate, purchase a cheaper asset with the equivalent service potential.

155 Incorporating an exception for donated assets which may not be fully exploited would make the application of FRS 102 more onerous, as it would require all entities in receipt of donated assets (except those intended for resale) to consider whether they would be able to exploit the asset fully. This would be subjective and may incur the risk of understatement of the value of donated assets.

156 The Accounting Council noted that where goods are donated for subsequent sale (for example donations to charity shops), it could be argued that the donated goods should be valued only when they are sold. This is not consistent with the accruals concept which requires the financial statements to recognise goods when they are received. However, the Accounting Council advises, on pragmatic grounds, that donated goods should only be recognised as income on receipt when the item is material, can be measured reliably and if the benefits of recognising the item outweigh the costs. Further the Accounting Council proposes that the same accounting may be applied by other wholly-owned entities in a public benefit entity group, to eliminate the need to restate goods donated for subsequent sale on consolidation (for example where a charity operates it shops through a subsidiary that is a non-charitable company).

157 FRS 102 requires donated services that would otherwise have been purchased to be accounted for at their estimated value to the recipient. This is a pragmatic solution recognising that there are potential issues in determining a value for volunteer services and their contribution to the organisation and notes that quantifying this type of service may not be practicable. There is an argument to suggest that valuing volunteer services could be measured by reference to a metric such as the minimum wage, however this measure does not take into consideration an organisation's requirements for volunteers. In addition, this would be attributing an arbitrary value onto a volunteer's time which may not be reflective of their skills, experience or role and to determine a different method of valuation would be very subjective.

158 However, when a service is provided voluntarily for which the entity would otherwise have to pay (eg legal or financial advice) the value of that service should be recognised in the financial statements where, as will usually be the case, its value can be reasonably quantified.

Other PBE issues

159 The Accounting Council discussed the issue of reporting entity control and the indicators of control that may be specific to the PBE sectors. The indicators of control set out in Section 9 *Consolidated and Separate Financial Statements* of FRS 102 focus on benefits, and in the PBE sectors benefit can be in the form of indirect benefit through a PBE's beneficiaries or benefit which furthers a PBE's activities. Following discussion of these issues the Accounting Council advises that FRS 102 can be interpreted and applied to PBEs and therefore no separate guidance for PBEs is considered necessary.

160 A number of additional topics were identified through the development of FRS 102, which may be considered in the future and as possible updates to FRS 102. The following table summarises these subjects:

Narrative Reporting	To consider narrative reporting requirements for public benefit entities and any specific matters.
Fresh Start Accounting	To consider the concept of fresh start accounting as an alternative accounting treatment for entity combinations where the effect of a combination is to create a new entity that cannot be reasonably portrayed as the enlargement of a pre-existing party.
Social Benefit Obligations	To consider if and how social benefit obligations should be recognised and measured in the financial statements. The International Public Sector Accounting Standards Board currently have a project addressing this issue and it is likely to be most productive to await the outcome of that work.

Fund Accounting	To consider how fund accounting would be applied in accordance with the requirements of FRS 102 for segmental reporting.

Transition to FRS 102

161 The Accounting Council noted that FRS 102 does not permit goodwill to have an indefinite useful life, unlike current FRS. On transition to FRS 102 entities that previously determined that goodwill had an indefinite useful life will need to reassess goodwill to determine its remaining useful life, and subsequently amortise the goodwill over that period.

Effective date

162 FREDs 43 and 44 proposed an effective date for accounting periods beginning on or after 1 July 2013, with early application being permitted. Respondents' views regarding the proposals were very mixed with some calling for earlier adoption and others for deferral of the proposals.

163 The Accounting Council took into consideration its decision that FRS 102 would apply to a broader scope of entities and its revised guidelines for amending the IFRS for SMEs in relation to the effective date. The Accounting Council noted that:

(a) Although the revisions to its original proposals should ease the transition, an 18 month period between the publication of the final standard and effective date should be retained as there are significant changes to the accounting requirements for financial instruments.

(b) The IASB's decision to revise the effective date of IFRS 9 *Financial Instruments* to 2015. The ASB noted that entities that apply current FRS without FRS 26, who wished to move to the proposed reduced disclosure framework would not be able to apply IFRS 9 until it was adopted by the EU. Consequently such entities would need to apply IAS 39 *Financial Instruments: Recognition and Measurement* for an interim period. The costs associated with these changes were not justifiable.

(c) The effective date needed to take into consideration the updating of the SORPs that is required.

164 The Accounting Council advises that the effective date of FRS 102 should be accounting periods beginning on or after 1 January 2015.

165 The Accounting Council also considered whether to permit early application of FRS 102. It noted that as FRS 102 represents an improvement in financial reporting it would not be appropriate to prevent early application of its requirements. However, the Accounting Council advises that early application of FRS 102 should not be permitted for accounting periods before those ending on or after 31 December 2012, which is consistent with the first date at which it is likely to be practical for entities applying FRS 101 to apply that standard.

166 The Accounting Council also considered the early application of FRS 102 by entities that are within the scope of a SORP. It noted that most of the SORPs require updating for consistency with FRS 102, and for charities there are legal requirements relating to the application of the SORP. The Accounting Council therefore advises that early application should be permitted for entities applying a SORP provided that FRS 102 does not conflict with the requirements of a current SORP or legal requirements for the preparation of financial statements.

Approval of this advice

167 This advice to the FRC was approved by eight of the nine members of the Accounting Council on 17 January 2013. Mr Beale dissented from the approval of the advice and his dissenting view is set out in the Appendix to the Accounting Council's advice. The Accounting Council is comprised of the following members:

Roger Marshall   (Chair of the Accounting Council)

Nick Anderson

Dr Richard Barker

Edward Beale

Peter Elwin

Ken Lever

Robert Overend

Andy Simmonds

Pauline Wallace

Appendix to the Accounting Council's Advice to the FRC to issue FRS 102

Dissenting view of Mr Beale

1   Mr Beale agrees that it is fundamental that financial statements should provide useful information to users, who are defined as being: investors not involved in management, customers and suppliers, including suppliers of capital and of non-equity finance. He agrees with the Accounting Council that it is disappointing that despite extensive outreach activities, the Accounting Council has not received more feedback from users, both formal and informal, on whether or not financial statements prepared in accordance with FRS 102 will meet their information needs.

2   Mr Beale does not believe that the consultation responses from industry representative bodies[18], and from organisations which are both preparers and users, can be considered to be input from users since these responses are from a preparer perspective.

3   The informal input received by the FRC staff supports FRS 102 as drafted, and is generally consistent with the input from preparers and industry representative bodies. However, this informal input is inconsistent with the five[19] formal consultation responses received from users and the informal input received personally by Mr Beale. This inconsistency in the content of informal input may be due to the informal input received by FRC staff being from providers of non-equity finance whereas the informal input received by Mr Beale has been from directors (who are both users and preparers) and investors.

4   This informal input received by FRC staff in relation to FRS 102 differs from comments that FRC staff have recently received on other projects:

   (a)   from credit analysts and bond fund managers in relation to the financial statements of listed entities[20] (that there is not sufficient forward looking information on cash flows and challenging the usefulness of fair value); and

   (b)   as part of the Financial Reporting Laboratory's work on a single figure for remuneration[21] (regarding valuation of equity incentives and pension costs).

5   In Mr Beale's experience users are concerned with issues identified by the FRC in *Louder than Words*[22], which they believe have not been adequately addressed in FRS 102. In his analysis, the common thread behind these user concerns is a desire for clearer, more understandable, information, from which they can derive better predictions about future cash flows on a going concern basis, even at the expense of further divergence from IFRS. Understandability is crucial to confidence in the integrity of financial reporting, and thus maximising the benefits from accounts. Despite the importance of maintaining consistency with IFRS, Mr Beale believes that the FRC should not be issuing new accounting standards perpetuating problems identified in existing standards.

6   In particular Mr Beale believes that there are significant further opportunities to improve the balance between costs and benefits in the sections of FRS 102 dealing with: Financial Instruments, Deferred Tax, Defined Benefit Pension Schemes, and Equity Settled Share-based Payments. This is discussed further below. In his view FRS 102 could have achieved clearer reporting in the above areas by departing further from the IFRS for

---

[18]   Some of which have been classified in the Feedback Statements as 'user representative bodies'.

[19]   Four of these formal consultation responses are from users connected to Mr Beale and include three responses to FREDs 43 and 44, of which two were formally classified as being from preparers and one from an academic.

[20]   http://www.frc.org.uk/getattachment/b0eff085-b542-4eaf-bc36-d52e26eb3833/How-credit-analysts-view-and-use-the-financial-statements.aspx

[21]   http://frc.org.uk/getattachment/5310093d-c092-45e1-8106-278ae7ac1a4b/A-single-figure-for-remuneration.aspx

[22]   http://www.frc.org.uk/getattachment/7d952925-74ea-4deb-b659-e9242b09f2fa/Louder-than-words.aspx

SMEs, thus better meeting users' needs for high-quality financial information in line with the overriding objective.

7 The FRC needs to consider whether the extensive outreach activities undertaken constitute 'adequate consultation'. In Mr Beale's opinion the determination of 'adequate consultation' should be based on the outcome from the consultation process and, regrettably, there has been virtually no formal input from the people who will be using accounts prepared under FRS 102. Based on the consultation responses from users and the informal input from users that he has received, Mr Beale is advising that the FRC defer approval of FRS 102 until it has a better understanding of the degree of support from users, and in the meantime to work on improving the balance between costs and benefits in the areas outlined above.

8 In Mr Beale's experience, users do not consider UK GAAP to be in need of urgent replacement, and will not be concerned about any delays to FRS 102 necessary to determine the degree of user support and resolve any outstanding issues.

Further opportunities to improve the balance between costs and benefits

9 There are two issues of principle underpinning the areas of FRS 102 that, in Mr Beale's opinion, can be significantly improved:

(a) Since the purpose of accounts is to supply useful information to users, the most important concepts underpinning accounting standards should be 'relevance' (include information that is useful to users) and its converse, 'materiality' (exclude information that is not useful). All other accounting concepts should clearly be subsidiary to these. Such an emphasis on the priority attributable to 'relevance' and 'materiality' will promote measurement of assets and liabilities in a manner that conveys useful information to users, and will normally exclude mark to model valuations, and limit application of fair value elsewhere.

(b) At present some assets and liabilities are revalued, and some unrealised profits are taken to earnings. To ensure a principled base for accounting standards the FRC needs to determine general principles covering (i) when it is appropriate for assets and liabilities to be revalued, and (ii) whether unrealised profits arising from revaluations should be recognised in earnings or as a movement in reserves. A consistent approach to revaluation of items such as fixed assets and financial instruments, and a consistent approach to profit recognition, cannot be achieved without such principles. In his opinion, for the purposes of FRS 102: assets should be revalued when there is a sufficiently liquid market for their market value to be determined reliably, or when an impairment provision is necessary; liabilities should only be revalued when there are changes to the amount required to settle them when they fall due; and unrealised profits should not be included within earnings, except for profits on liquid investments.

In Mr Beale's opinion, opportunities to significantly improve the balance of costs and benefits within FRS 102 exist in four areas, two of general application: financial instruments, and deferred tax; and two of more limited application: equity settled share based payments and defined benefit pension schemes. These are summarised below.

Financial instruments

10 Current FRSs have been criticised in that they allow certain financial instruments not to be recorded. Such criticism is incorrect in that the existence of, and details about, these financial instruments should (where 'material') be recorded in the notes to the accounts. This criticism has been used by some to justify moving to an IFRS based approach to accounting for financial instruments, which has been widely criticised, and which is not the

most cost effective approach to providing users of accounts with the information that they desire.

11   Many different assets and liabilities fall within the definition of financial instruments and attempting to deal with all of these in the same manner introduces unnecessary complexity. The two sections on financial instruments include three to four pages of rules on which section should be applied, and are written in a language which is in places very difficult for people not accustomed to IFRS to understand. These sections have also been drafted to cater for financial institutions as well as ordinary businesses, and this exacerbates the difficulty that non-experts will have in applying them. Preparers of accounts will generally only refer to accounting standards once a year in the lead up to preparation of their annual accounts. FRS 102 needs to be readily understandable for such preparers, and there is a risk that if accounting standards are not sufficiently accessible they will be applied in a manner that generates unnecessary complexity and clutter.

12   The two sections on financial instruments should be redrafted in language that is understandable to the normal businessperson and is not the preserve of experts. Redrafting of these sections should focus on the information that users need relating to ordinary businesses, with additional requirements for financial institutions dealt with in the section for specialised activities, by expanding the part relating to financial institutions, and which can in turn refer to IAS 39 Financial Instruments: Recognition and Measurement, IFRS 7 Financial Instruments: Disclosure and IFRS 9 Financial Instruments where appropriate.

13   Users need different 'information sets' on financial instruments that are: fixed assets, current assets and liabilities; and FRS 102 should consider financial instruments in these three categories, rather than trying to cover all three categories with one set of rules. Prudence should be incorporated where necessary so that the treatment of assets is not necessarily the mirror of the treatment of liabilities.

Financial assets

14   For normal businesses, financial assets should be carried at fair value when the principles for revaluation set out above are met, and failing that at cost less any necessary impairment provision. Income should be recognised in a prudent manner: as it is earned (eg interest on a daily basis), or when it can be reliably measured (eg dividends).

15   Circumstances may arise which cause the valuation basis of financial assets to change, but such situations are unlikely to occur frequently outside financial institutions. Where they do occur, the consequences of reclassifications can be made obvious to users of accounts through note disclosures. Strict anti-abuse rules are not necessary. A clear analysis in the notes can highlight where reclassification is potentially being abused to manage earnings, so that users can discuss their concerns with management, auditors or regulators as appropriate. Any additional requirements considered necessary for financial institutions can be dealt with in the section for specialised activities.

Financial liabilities

16   When a financial liability is included in the balance sheet at a value which is different from the amount required to settle the liability when it falls due, disclosure of amount of principal repayable is necessary, so that users can understand the underlying cash flow. The notes then show two different values for the same liability. This duplication of valuation bases creates extra cost to both preparers and users of accounts and risks causing confusion. Confusion can be minimised by using the settlement value in the statement of financial position, rather than fair values or amortised cost, recognising deferred financing costs where necessary, and providing information in the notes about financing costs and settlement dates. Interested users will then have the information necessary to perform

their own comparisons with other businesses, as well as clearer information on the business's funding requirements.

17   The above approach to liabilities could lead to extensive disclosures for financial institutions and others where there are a large number of different types of financial liability. The section on specialised activities should set out an approach for the aggregation of necessary disclosures and allow an opt into IFRS 9/IAS 39.

Impairment of financial assets

18   Impairment provisions are only allowed in FRS 102 where there is 'objective evidence' of impairment. Businesses are not allowed to make provision for expected losses, even where there is past experience supporting the likelihood of such losses. Expected loss provisions should be allowed now, before IFRS 9 has been updated, to avoid assets being overvalued. A clear analysis in the notes will highlight where impairment provisions are potentially being abused to manage earnings, so that users can discuss their concerns with management, auditors or regulators as appropriate. Additional requirements may be imposed on financial institutions through the section on specialised activities.

Hedging

19   Hedge accounting is only permitted in FRS 102 if 'specified criteria' are met. In the past similar restrictions have led to businesses not hedge accounting for financial instruments acquired, or entered into, for hedging purposes. The purpose of accounting standards is not to promote good management but good reporting. Accounting standards are not the appropriate way to attempt to stop the miss-selling, or miss-buying, of derivatives. There needs to be transparency over hedges entered into so that the effect of hedges in managing risk can be understood by users of accounts. This can be achieved by linked accounting for hedges and items being hedged, so that accounting faithfully represents the underlying commercial activity.

20   Concerns over earnings management can be alleviated by disclosure of the impact on earnings of hedges closed out in a different period to the risk that they purported to hedge. Businesses other than financial institutions should be able to allay concerns over the effectiveness of hedges by explaining how their limited number of material risks are being hedged. Financial institutions may have too many hedges to be able to provide this information in a meaningful manner and an alternative approach for such businesses should be set out in the section on specialised activities.

Deferred tax

21   As the recent ASB/EFRAG discussion paper on tax identified, users want to know how future tax payments will differ from the amount calculated by applying the standard tax rate to future profits. This difference will be in part due to future actions and in part due to past actions.

22   The section of FRS 102 on deferred tax is not predicated on a going concern basis, and in effect identifies the impact on future tax payments if the business ceases trading. As such, except for the disclosure of amounts expected to reverse in the next period, the approach in FRS 102 is of little relevance to most users and will create disclosures which will generally be ignored by users.

23   The disclosure required by FRS 102 of the amount of the deferred tax provision which will be released in the next period is of limited usefulness. This is only part of the difference between expected tax cost and standard tax rate. Prediction of the element due to future actions is not currently required.

24   The information that users need can best be provided by way of disclosure of the expected future tax rate and any other material information that may influence future tax payments, eg losses carried forward. A deferred tax provision should not be made because this does not provide useful information in a cost effective manner. The exception to this is that the logic behind revaluing certain items dictates that, for consistency, the tax impact of such revaluations needs to be recognised too.

Equity settled share-based payments

25   As identified by the recent financial reporting laboratory work on valuation of remuneration, users do not understand the complex models used to value equity settled share based payments. The cost of creating these values is therefore wasted.

26   These valuation models also generate a substantial amount of clutter when trying to explain how the valuation is arrived at.

27   It should also be noted that the standard valuation models assume liquid markets and negligible spreads. These assumptions are not appropriate for the types of businesses that will be applying FRS 102. Given the lack of guidance in FRS 102, and the complexity of the valuation models, in Mr Beale's opinion it is highly likely that preparers will use inappropriate valuation models, or use valuation models in inappropriate ways, and that users will not have enough knowledge to identify this.

28   Unless there is a liquid market to provide a relevant value for equity settled share based payments, their existence should be disclosed in the notes to the accounts, and there should be no notional cost in the income statement.

Defined benefit pension schemes

29   The information relating to defined benefit pension schemes that users need is: the current cost of providing the benefit, the expected additional payments required to make good any funding deficit (or payment holiday because of funding surpluses) and an explanation of the contingent liability in respect of potential future funding shortfalls.

30   At present there is a requirement to prepare a fund valuation solely for accounting purposes and then to consolidate the net assets or, more usually, liabilities of the fund. Changes in the net assets/liabilities are then split into three parts and recognised in operating costs, financing costs and other comprehensive income. This is supplemented by extensive disclosures. However, the disclosures do not require information about the uncertainties or sensitivities attached to the valuation inputs eg the time periods over which payments out of the fund will be made, discount and inflation rates, and other risks inherent in the fund.

31   Most users do not understand pension scheme valuations. They see fund valuations which are massively volatile, and perceive most current requirements as adding to clutter and generating additional preparation costs for no benefit.

32   Clutter could be reduced by not consolidating the pension fund, but instead disclosing the level of normal contributions being made and providing for contributions required to make good any funding shortfall. Changes in this liability to make good any funding shortfall should be expensed and explained. In addition disclosures should be made describing the contingent liability to fund any future increases in fund deficits. Those users who do understand pension scheme valuations can obtain the more detailed information that they are likely to want about pension scheme funding from the fund valuation prepared for that purpose, which should be made available on demand or on a web site. Such an approach would save the costs associated with preparing a valuation solely for accounting purposes as well as reducing clutter in the accounts.

Training costs

33 Maintaining limited UK GAAP differences from IFRS will marginally increase the cost of training accountants, but should improve their employability, and will increase the challenge on the IASB to further improve IFRS, thereby improving the balance between benefits and costs overall.

The Accounting Council's Advice to the FRC to issue Amendments to FRS 102 – Basic financial instruments and Hedge accounting

Introduction

1   This report provides an overview of the main issues that have been considered by the Accounting Council in advising the Financial Reporting Council (FRC) to issue *Amendments to FRS 102 The Financial Reporting Standard applicable in the UK and Republic of Ireland – Basic financial instruments and Hedge accounting*.

2   The FRC, in accordance with the *Statutory Auditors (Amendment of Companies Act 2006 and Delegation of Functions etc) Order 2012* (SI 2012/1741), is a prescribed body for issuing accounting standards in the UK. The *Foreword to Accounting Standards* sets out the application of accounting standards in the Republic of Ireland.

3   In accordance with the *FRC Codes and Standards: procedures*, any proposal to issue, amend or withdraw a code or standard is put to the FRC Board with the full advice of the relevant Councils and/or the Codes & Standards Committee. Ordinarily, the FRC Board will only reject the advice put to it where:

(a)   it is apparent that a significant group of stakeholders has not been adequately consulted;

(b)   the necessary assessment of the impact of the proposal has not been completed, including an analysis of costs and benefits;

(c)   insufficient consideration has been given to the timing or cost of implementation; or

(d)   the cumulative impact of a number of proposals would make the adoption of an otherwise satisfactory proposal inappropriate.

4   The FRC has established the Accounting Council as the relevant Council to assist it in the setting of accounting standards.

Advice

5   The Accounting Council is advising the FRC to issue *Amendments to FRS 102 The Financial Reporting Standard applicable in the UK and Republic of Ireland – Basic financial instruments and Hedge accounting* to:

(a)   remove the unintended accounting consequences arising for the classification of certain financial instruments. It believes these changes will result in a reduction in the cost of compliance for entities within the scope of the standard; and

(b)   to make the application of the hedge accounting requirements easier and more cost effective to apply for entities that choose to take advantage of this option.

6   The Accounting Council's Advice to the FRC in FRS 102 *The Financial Reporting Standard applicable in the UK and Republic of Ireland* is supplemented by the inclusion of its advice on these amendments.

Background

7   The FRC issued FRS 102 in March 2013, which is effective for accounting periods beginning on or after 1 January 2015.

8   After the publication of FRS 102, feedback from constituents indicated that the implementation of the accounting requirements of FRS 102 for loans with common contractual features could have unintended consequences for many entities. The

amendments to Section 11 *Basic Financial Instruments* address the issues identified and take into account responses to FRED 54 *Draft Amendments to FRS 102 Financial Reporting Standard applicable in the UK and Ireland – Basic financial instruments.*

9   At the time of issue of FRS 102, the Accounting Council and the FRC were of the view that the standard should reflect up-to-date thinking on hedge accounting, but the IASB had not yet finalised the hedge accounting requirements in IFRS 9 *Financial Instruments*. The Accounting Council advised the FRC at that time that amending the hedge accounting requirements in FRS 102 prior to the IASB finalising the hedge accounting requirements in IFRS 9, would risk implementing hedge accounting requirements in FRS 102 that were inconsistent with IFRS.

10   The hedge accounting amendments to FRS 102 were developed based on the hedge accounting requirements in IFRS 9 and take into account the responses to FRED 51 *Draft Amendments to FRS 102 Financial Reporting Standard applicable in the UK and Ireland – Hedge Accounting.*

Objective

11   The FRC gives careful consideration to its objective and the intended effects when developing new accounting standards or requirements for the UK and Republic of Ireland. In developing accounting standards, including FRS 102, the overriding objective of the FRC is:

> To enable users of accounts to receive high-quality understandable financial reporting proportionate to the size and complexity of the entity and users' information needs.

12   In meeting this objective, the FRC aims to provide succinct financial reporting standards that:

(a)   have consistency with global accounting standards through the application of an IFRS-based solution unless an alternative clearly better meets the overriding objective;

(b)   reflect up-to-date thinking and developments in the way businesses operate and the transactions they undertake;

(c)   balance consistent principles for accounting by all UK and Republic of Ireland entities with practical solutions, based on size, complexity, public interest and users' information needs;

(d)   promote efficiency within groups; and

(e)   are cost-effective to apply.

Basic financial instruments

Rules vs principles-based solution

13   The classification of financial instruments as "basic" or "other" in FRS 102 is dependent on a list of prescriptive conditions. The Accounting Council considered whether a principles-based solution to relaxing the conditions, based on the principle articulated in IFRS 9 in respect of the classification of financial assets, would be more effective, but advises retaining the rules-based conditions of FRS 102 instead, for the following reasons:

(a)   the IFRS 9 principle is yet untested in practice and, at the time of giving the advice, the IASB is currently debating possible amendments to IFRS 9; and

(b) the IFRS 9 principle in relation to the classification of financial instruments only applies to financial assets. The classification conditions in FRS 102, however, apply equally to debt instruments that are assets or liabilities.

Interaction with Regulations or LLP Regulations on measurement of certain financial instruments

14 Subsequent to receiving the responses to FRED 54, the Accounting Council was made aware of an additional issue in relation to a conflict between the Regulations and LLP Regulations and the requirements in FRS 102, as originally issued, on measurement of some financial liabilities. The original text of FRS 102 could have resulted in the standard requiring certain financial liabilities to be measured at fair value where such measurement may be prohibited by the Regulations. The Regulations prohibit the measurement of financial liabilities at fair value, except for those held as part of a trading portfolio, that are derivatives or where permitted by EU-adopted IFRS.

15 For example, the original text of FRS 102 would have required certain financial liabilities, where the cash outflows are linked to non-financial variables specific to one party to the contract, to be classified as non-basic and measured at fair value. Fair value measurement is not permitted for such liabilities under EU-adopted IFRS and so would be prohibited by the Regulations.

16 Such liabilities commonly arise in insurance contracts where the amount an insurer is liable to pay depends on the occurrence of insured events specific to the insured party and its activities.

17 The Accounting Council is aware that there are divergent views on what constitutes a "non-financial variable" in other cases. For example, there is no clear consensus as to whether measures of performance such as turnover, profits or EBITDA are "non-financial variables...specific to a party to the contract". The Accounting Council is unable to resolve this divergence as to do so would involve interpreting EU-adopted IFRS on an issue that the IFRS Interpretations Committee has so far not reached a definitive conclusion.

18 Similarly, FRS 102 would have required that financial assets which are similarly linked to non-financial variables specific to one party to the contract, be classified as non-basic and measured at fair value through profit or loss. Although Regulations permit financial assets to be classified at fair value, this classification is only available as permitted by EU-adopted IFRS, which in some cases is restricted to fair value through other comprehensive income.

19 The Accounting Council also notes that there may be other non-basic financial assets and liabilities that EU-adopted IFRS, and hence the Regulations, would not permit to be measured at fair value through profit or loss although it expected that such instruments would be rare in practice.

20 As a result, the Accounting Council advises the inclusion of an exception in Section 12 in respect of non-basic financial instruments where the Regulations would not permit the use of fair value through profit or loss, instead requiring them to be measured at amortised cost. In advising this, the Accounting Council is conscious that this exception would be applicable to a small number of entities under a narrow set of circumstances.

Loans in the social housing sector

21 In response to FRED 54, a number of respondents from the social housing sector raised concerns about the classification of certain lending arrangements common within that sector. It was noted that a number of these arrangements were structured in different ways but often to achieve the same economic outcome. After detailed consideration the Accounting Council advises that a loan cannot be classified as basic if it includes

contractual terms giving the lender the unilateral option to change the terms of that loan, for example from a pre-determined fixed rate to a variable rate or to a different fixed rate chosen by the lender, even if the holder can avoid it by repaying the loan.

Structured financial instruments

22 In response to FRED 54, a number of respondents raised questions about the classification of certain financial instruments that were structured in a complex way and requested that the final amendment clarify their classification in accordance with FRS 102. The Accounting Council noted that such structured financial instruments are not based on contracts that are standardised across an industry. As a result, the repayment of principal and interest on such loans can be impacted in a complex way by a number of different variables defined in the contractual terms. The Accounting Council noted that it was not possible to conclude on the classification of such financial instruments without a close reading of the individual contracts and an understanding of the detailed clauses. Therefore, the Accounting Council advises that the reporting entity's directors should apply their judgement to determine whether the contractual terms enable a financial instrument to be classified as basic in accordance with the requirements in FRS 102.

Classification subsequent to initial recognition

23 The Accounting Council noted that the initial classification assessment of a financial instrument should take into account the relevant clauses dealing with the returns and any subsequent contractual variations relating to returns, prepayments and extensions of terms etc. Once the classification of a financial instrument is determined at initial recognition, no re-assessment is required at subsequent dates unless there is a modification of contractual terms.

Hedge accounting

24 The previous hedge accounting requirements in FRS 102 narrowly defined the types of permitted arrangements that may qualify for hedge accounting, which was not necessarily representative of an entity's risk management objectives and hedging practices.

25 The Accounting Council's aim was to develop new hedge accounting requirements that allow for a reflection of an entity's hedging activities in the financial statements that is consistent with the entity's risk management objectives and are, as far as appropriate for constituents of FRS 102, consistent with IFRS.

26 These amendments to FRS 102 have been developed on the basis of IFRS, and substantively adopt the terminology and hedge accounting requirements in IFRS 9, with notable exceptions described in more detail below. The Accounting Council has been mindful that the requirements in IFRS 9 deal with hedging transactions that can be far more complex than those typically entered into by entities applying FRS 102. The departures from the requirements in IFRS 9 are therefore intended to simplify the application of hedge accounting.

Eligible hedged items

27 The Accounting Council was requested to reconsider the exclusion of explicit macrohedging provisions in FRS 102, similar to those in IAS 39 *Financial Instruments: Recognition and Measurement*. After consideration of the specific concerns of entities that raised this as an issue, the Accounting Council concluded that in the interest of developing straight-forward hedge accounting requirements that are relevant for a majority of entities, it retains its previous advice stated in FRED 51. Entities wishing to apply the IFRS macrohedging provisions are able to apply the accounting policy choice in FRS 102 to apply IAS 39 and/or IFRS 9 instead.

Qualifying hedge accounting conditions

28   The qualifying hedge accounting conditions in FRS 102 have been simplified compared to the criteria set out in IFRS 9, with the aim of making hedge accounting easier to apply.

29   Under the amended hedge accounting requirements it is not necessary to achieve a prescribed level of effectiveness in a hedging relationship in order to qualify for hedge accounting, but an economic relationship between the hedged item and the hedging instrument has to exist. In response to feedback on FRED 51, an explanation has been added of when an economic relationship between a hedged item and a hedging instrument exists, which is in line with IFRS 9.

30   The Accounting Council notes that although a quantitative assessment of hedge effectiveness is not required, it is nevertheless important for entities to identify the different factors that affect the valuation of the hedging instrument and hedged item, including factors that may be a source of hedge ineffectiveness. Entities are therefore required to identify and document causes of hedge ineffectiveness before they commence hedge accounting, to ensure that ineffectiveness is properly captured in profit or loss.

31   Entities are required to document a hedging relationship, to avoid hedge accounting being misused. The hedge documentation requirements are, however, relatively informal and undemanding and should not be an administrative burden for entities in practice.

Discontinuing hedge accounting

32   These amendments permit entities to discontinue hedge accounting voluntarily. This is a departure from IFRS 9. The Accounting Council considered that the restrictions in IFRS 9 on discontinuance are unnecessarily onerous, and instead has retained the existing option of voluntary discontinuation. An entity must document the election to discontinue hedge accounting, which is consistent with the requirement for documentation at the start of hedge accounting.

Disclosure

33   These amendments retain substantially the disclosure requirements of FRS 102. The disclosure requirements in relation to the hedge accounting requirements in IFRS 9, contained in IFRS 7 *Financial Instruments: Disclosure* focus on risks and risk mitigation through hedging. The Accounting Council notes that risk disclosures are not generally required in FRS 102, except for financial institutions.

Transitional provisions for first-time adopters of FRS 102

34   The Accounting Council's aim was to develop transitional provisions that are consistent with the permissive hedge accounting regime of FRS 102 and give entities a choice over whether to commence, continue or end hedge accounting on transition to FRS 102. Some respondents to FRED 51 were concerned that this flexibility may be abused, as it allows entities to apply a degree of hindsight. The Accounting Council is mindful of this possible exploitation of the transitional provisions. Nevertheless, on balance it believes that in the interests of the majority of entities, especially entities that have not applied hedge accounting before, flexibility should take precedence over restrictions aimed at preventing abuse.

35   The Accounting Council is conscious that entities may have applied diverse hedge accounting practices before the adoption of FRS 102. Entities may have applied the hedge accounting requirements in accordance with FRS 26 (IAS 39) *Financial Instruments: Recognition and Measurement* or may have applied synthetic accounting practices permitted under SSAP 20 *Foreign currency translation*. Accommodating these

different accounting practices introduces complexity that the transitional provisions need to address. Under the transitional provisions, regardless of what accounting practices were applied previously, entities have the choice to continue hedge accounting in accordance with FRS 102, provided the conditions for hedge accounting are met. Entities that elect not to apply the FRS 102 hedge accounting requirements, have to comply with the applicable measurement requirements for assets and liabilities set out elsewhere in FRS 102 from the date of transition.

36 The amendments are issued after the date of transition to FRS 102 for many entities. The transitional provisions take this into account by providing an extended deadline for hedge documentation on first-time adoption.

Alternative reporting of economic hedges

37 The Accounting Council advises modifying the provision in Section 11 to allow the designation of loan commitments at fair value through profit or loss (in addition to the designation of debt instruments at fair value through profit or loss). This will have the effect of allowing economic hedge accounting where an entity balances the risks from a first instrument by taking out a second which is measured at fair value: it will be able to choose to measure the first at fair value too, thus matching the movements in profit and reflecting, in financial reporting, the combined economic effect of the instruments.

Impairment provisions

38 Originally it was planned to amend FRS 102 prior to its effective date in respect of the requirements relating to hedge accounting and the impairment of financial assets. The IASB's project on the new IFRS impairment model is delayed and the FRC's consultation on introducing equivalent requirements in FRS 102 has therefore been deferred. Respondents to FRED 51 requested the exemption of certain entities from the requirement to adopt the impairment accounting requirements in FRS 102 until the new impairment requirements in FRS 102 are finalised.

39 The Accounting Council deliberated on the likely impact of the adoption of the impairment accounting requirements in FRS 102. It concluded that the incurred loss impairment model in FRS 102 is consistent with UK GAAP, as applicable prior to the introduction of FRS 102. The Accounting Council considers that it is therefore unnecessary to provide a temporary relief from the impairment accounting requirements in FRS 102.

Effective date

40 The Accounting Council advises that the amendments should be effective from the effective date of FRS 102 (ie accounting periods beginning on or after 1 January 2015), and therefore no amendment to the effective date is required.

Approval of this advice

41 This advice to the FRC was approved by the Accounting Council on 19 June 2014.

The Accounting Council's Advice to the FRC to issue Amendments to FRS 102 – Pension obligations

Introduction

1   This report provides an overview of the main issues that have been considered by the Accounting Council in advising the Financial Reporting Council (FRC) to issue *Amendments to FRS 102 The Financial Reporting Standard applicable in the UK and Republic of Ireland – Pension obligations*.

2   The FRC, in accordance with the *Statutory Auditors (Amendment of Companies Act 2006 and Delegation of Functions etc) Order 2012* (SI 2012/1741), is a prescribed body for issuing accounting standards in the UK. The *Foreword to Accounting Standards* sets out the application of accounting standards in the Republic of Ireland.

3   In accordance with the *FRC Codes and Standards: procedures*, any proposal to issue, amend or withdraw a code or standard is put to the FRC Board with the full advice of the relevant Councils and/or the Codes & Standards Committee. Ordinarily, the FRC Board will only reject the advice put to it where:

    (a)   it is apparent that a significant group of stakeholders has not been adequately consulted;

    (b)   the necessary assessment of the impact of the proposal has not been completed, including an analysis of costs and benefits;

    (c)   insufficient consideration has been given to the timing or cost of implementation; or

    (d)   the cumulative impact of a number of proposals would make the adoption of an otherwise satisfactory proposal inappropriate.

4   The FRC has established the Accounting Council as the relevant Council to assist it in the setting of accounting standards.

Advice

5   The Accounting Council is advising the FRC to issue *Amendments to FRS 102 The Financial Reporting Standard applicable in the UK and Republic of Ireland – Pension obligations*.

6   The amendments will resolve an issue of uncertainty over the requirements of FRS 102 in relation to a commitment to make payments under a 'schedule of contributions' to a defined benefit pension plan which the entity accounts for on a defined benefit basis, and therefore reduce potential diversity in practice and the cost of compliance with FRS 102.

7   The Accounting Council's Advice to the FRC to issue FRS 102 *The Financial Reporting Standard applicable in the UK and Republic of Ireland* was set out in that standard. The Accounting Council's Advice to the FRC on these amendments will be included in the revised FRS 102.

Background

8   After the publication of FRS 102 in March 2013 the FRC issued, in October 2013, a Press Notice[23] addressing the accounting in accordance with EU-adopted IFRS for a 'schedule of contributions' payable by an entity to a defined benefit pension plan. Subsequently the

---

[23] FRC PN 089 *Findings of the FRC in respect of the accounts of WH Smith Plc for the year ended 31 August 2012.*

FRC received enquiries about the accounting for similar circumstances by entities applying FRS 102.

9   The issue concerns whether or not an entity applying FRS 102 should have regard to the principles of IFRIC 14 *IAS 19 – The Limit on a Defined Benefit Asset, Minimum Funding Requirements and their Interaction* where it might be relevant to its circumstances. There appeared to be a diversity of views on the matter, and because the potential implications for an entity's financial statements could be significant the FRC decided to address the matter outside the intended three-yearly review cycle for FRS 102.

10   The Accounting Council considered the responses to the consultation FRED 55 *Draft Amendments to FRS 102 – Pension obligations*, which was issued in August 2014, in developing its advice.

Objective

11   In developing its advice to the FRC, the Accounting Council was guided by the overriding objective to enable users of accounts to receive high-quality understandable financial reporting proportionate to the size and complexity of the entity and users' information needs.

12   In meeting this objective, the FRC aims to provide succinct financial reporting standards that:

(a)   have consistency with international accounting standards through the application of an IFRS-based solution unless an alternative clearly better meets the overriding objective;

(b)   reflect up-to-date thinking and developments in the way entities operate and the transactions they undertake;

(c)   balance consistent principles for accounting by all UK and Republic of Ireland entities with practical solutions, based on size, complexity, public interest and users' information needs;

(d)   promote efficiency within groups; and

(e)   are cost-effective to apply.

Proportionate measurement of the net defined benefit liability for a defined benefit plan

13   The Accounting Council considered whether FRS 102 required an entity with a defined benefit plan to consider the principles of IFRIC 14 in interpreting its requirements to measure the net defined benefit liability. The Accounting Council noted that there appeared to be uncertainty over this issue and that there was the possibility of significant diversity arising in accounting practice, particularly because the amounts that might be recognised (or not) could be very significant.

14   The Accounting Council considers that for entities applying FRS 102, the recognition of the net defined benefit liability or asset (which may be limited by paragraph 28.22) for a defined benefit pension plan as the net total of the present value of the obligations under the plan and the fair value of the plan assets is a proportionate way to measure the present obligation to employees as a result of service rendered. It noted that in some circumstances IFRIC 14 would result in an additional liability being recognised in relation to a schedule of contributions that had been agreed with the defined benefit plan in order to address a deficit that had arisen on the basis of the funding assumptions. It further noted that the measurement of the present value of the obligations under the plan for funding purposes differs from the measurement for accounting purposes, but they are different measurements of the same obligation, not separate obligations.

15 Therefore the Accounting Council advises that, as a practical and proportionate solution, in measuring its defined benefit obligation an entity need not include the present value of contributions payable that arise from an agreement with the defined benefit plan to fund a deficit. The Accounting Council also advises that Section 28 *Employee Benefits* explicitly states that, in applying FRS 102, no additional liabilities shall be recognised in respect of an agreement with the defined benefit plan to fund a deficit (such as a schedule of contributions). This should ensure there are no divergent interpretations of the scope of Section 21 *Provisions and Contingencies* in relation to a schedule of contributions, because they are clearly within the scope of Section 28, and therefore outside the scope of Section 21.

16 The Accounting Council considered another potential solution to determining whether or not an additional obligation should be recognised in certain circumstances. It noted the interaction with the recognition of a defined benefit plan asset, and considered whether removing the restriction on recognising a defined benefit plan asset in some circumstances might be an alternative solution. However, the Accounting Council rejected this because it could have the unintended consequence of permitting an asset to be recognised where other factors would indicate the reporting entity was not able to recover the surplus.

17 These amendments to FRS 102 do not affect the accounting for a schedule of contributions or other funding agreement between a reporting entity and a multi-employer plan, which is set out in paragraph 28.11A of FRS 102. Where an entity participates in a defined benefit plan that is a multi-employer plan accounted for as if it were a defined contribution plan, it shall recognise a liability for the contributions payable that arise from the agreement (to the extent that they relate to a deficit) because this is the most cost-effective way of recognising the entity's obligation to employees as a result of service rendered. This contrasts with the approach for defined benefit plans because the obligation has already been recognised as the net defined benefit liability.

18 The majority of respondents to FRED 55 supported the proposal.

Effect of a restriction on the recoverability of a plan surplus

19 The Accounting Council also noted that FRS 102 does not specify where an entity shall recognise the effects of a restriction on the recoverability of a plan surplus, and therefore FRS 102 would require it to be recognised in profit or loss. A plan surplus may be irrecoverable because the entity is not able to recover the surplus through reduced contributions in the future or through refunds from the plan (see paragraph 28.22 of FRS 102). The Accounting Council considers that, except for any amount included in net interest on the net defined benefit liability, the effect of any such restriction should be recognised in other comprehensive income and advises that paragraph 28.25 is amended so that any such amounts are part of remeasurements, and therefore recognised in other comprehensive income. This is consistent with IAS 19 *Employee Benefits*.

Disclosure

20 Four respondents to FRED 55 commented on the benefits of an entity disclosing the amounts it had committed to pay under a schedule of contributions, and some requested clarification that the requirement in paragraph 28.41(a) of FRS 102 to disclose the funding policy was intended to include such disclosure.

21 The Accounting Council agreed that the disclosure of information about the amount and timing of payments intended to fund a deficit in a defined benefit plan would be useful information for users of financial statements. Although this should already be covered by the requirement to describe the funding policy, the Accounting Council advises that paragraph 28.41(a) is amended to clarify this.

Effective date

22 The Accounting Council advises that these amendments should be effective from the effective date of FRS 102 (ie accounting periods beginning on or after 1 January 2015), and therefore no amendment to the effective date of FRS 102 is required.

Approval of this Advice

23 This advice to the FRC was approved by the Accounting Council on 15 January 2015.

The Accounting Council's Advice to the FRC to issue Amendments to FRS 102 – Small entities and other minor amendments

Introduction

1   This report provides an overview of the main issues that have been considered by the Accounting Council in advising the Financial Reporting Council (FRC) to issue *Amendments to FRS 102 The Financial Reporting Standard applicable in the UK and Republic of Ireland – Small entities and other minor amendments* incorporating the Council's advice following the Consultation Document *Accounting standards for small entities – Implementation of the EU Accounting Directive,* FRED 59 *Draft Amendments to FRS 102 The Financial Reporting Standard applicable in the UK and Republic of Ireland – Small entities and other minor amendments* and FRED 61 *Draft amendments to FRS 102 – Share-based payment arrangements with cash alternatives.*

2   The FRC, in accordance with the *Statutory Auditors (Amendment of Companies Act 2006 and Delegation of Functions etc) Order 2012* (SI 2012/1741), is a prescribed body for issuing accounting standards in the UK. The *Foreword to Accounting Standards* sets out the application of accounting standards in the Republic of Ireland.

3   In accordance with the *FRC Codes and Standards: procedures,* any proposal to issue, amend or withdraw a code or standard is put to the FRC Board with the full advice of the relevant Councils and/or the Codes & Standards Committee. Ordinarily, the FRC Board will only reject the advice put to it where:

   (a)   it is apparent that a significant group of stakeholders has not been adequately consulted;

   (b)   the necessary assessment of the impact of the proposal has not been completed, including an analysis of costs and benefits;

   (c)   insufficient consideration has been given to the timing or cost of implementation; or

   (d)   the cumulative impact of a number of proposals would make the adoption of an otherwise satisfactory proposal inappropriate.

4   The FRC has established the Accounting Council as the relevant Council to assist it in the setting of accounting standards.

Advice

5   The Accounting Council is advising the FRC to issue *Amendments to FRS 102 The Financial Reporting Standard applicable in the UK and Republic of Ireland – Small entities and other minor amendments.*

6   The Accounting Council advises that these proposals will maintain consistency of accounting standards with company law and will improve the financial reporting by small entities by, for example, requiring the recognition of various financial instruments that the *Financial Reporting Standard for Smaller Entities (effective January 2015)* (FRSSE) does not currently require.

7   The Accounting Council's Advice to the FRC to issue FRS 102 *The Financial Reporting Standard applicable in the UK and Republic of Ireland* was set out in the standard. The Accounting Council's Advice to the FRC in respect of these amendments will be included in the revised FRS 102.

Background

8   The new EU Accounting Directive (Directive 2013/34/EU of the European Parliament and of the Council of 26 June 2013) is being implemented in the UK and Republic of Ireland. In doing so there are changes to company law to reflect new requirements and, where considered appropriate, to take advantage of new options that are available. Accounting standards are developed within the context set by company law; when company law changes, amendments may also be required to accounting standards.

9   In September 2014, the FRC issued a Consultation Document *Accounting standards for small entities – Implementation of the EU Accounting Directive*[24] (the Consultation Document), outlining its proposal that small entities will apply FRS 102 *The Financial Reporting Standard applicable in the UK and Republic of Ireland*. It was proposed that a new section would be inserted into FRS 102 setting out the presentation and disclosure requirements applicable to small entities, which would be based on the new legal provisions, and as a consequence the FRSSE would be withdrawn. A small number of other amendments to FRS 102 would also be necessary to maintain consistency with company law. The Accounting Council considered the responses to the Consultation Document in developing FRED 59. It has also considered the responses to FRED 59, which was issued in February 2015, in developing its advice on these amendments.

10   In addition, in April 2015 the FRC issued FRED 61 to address an implementation issue in relation to FRS 102. The responses to FRED 61 have also been considered in developing this advice.

Objective

11   In developing its advice to the FRC, the Accounting Council was guided by the overriding objective to enable users of accounts to receive high-quality understandable financial reporting proportionate to the size and complexity of the entity and users' information needs.

12   In meeting this objective, the FRC aims to provide succinct financial reporting standards that:

(a)   have consistency with international accounting standards through the application of an IFRS-based solution unless an alternative clearly better meets the overriding objective;

(b)   reflect up-to-date thinking and developments in the way entities operate and the transactions they undertake;

(c)   balance consistent principles for accounting by all UK and Republic of Ireland entities with practical solutions, based on size, complexity, public interest and users' information needs;

(d)   promote efficiency within groups; and

(e)   are cost-effective to apply.

Small entities regime

13   In the Consultation Document, the FRC proposed that the FRSSE should be withdrawn and that, for small entities ineligible for the micro-entities regime, it should be replaced with a new Section 1A *Small Entities* within FRS 102. It was proposed that Section 1A would set out the presentation and disclosure requirements applicable to small entities, whilst the recognition and measurement requirements of the remainder of FRS 102 would apply.

---

[24] Available on the FRC website (www.frc.org.uk).

This proposal was supported by the majority of respondents. In particular, respondents supported the proposals that:

(a) the FRSSE should be withdrawn (see FRED 60 *Draft amendments to FRS 100 and FRS 101*);

(b) Section 1A should apply to all entities (that are required to prepare financial statements that present a true and fair view) meeting the relevant criteria and not just companies; and

(c) small entities should apply the same recognition and measurement criteria as other entities applying FRS 102.

14 FRED 59 set out these proposals in more detail.

15 The Accounting Council notes that, whilst the financial statements of a small company must give a true and fair view, the new legal framework for small companies restricts the specific disclosures that may be required of small companies. As these restrictions do not apply to entities that are not companies, the Accounting Council considered whether to have two small entities regimes, one applying to companies and one to other entities. As set out in the Consultation Document and FRED 59, the Accounting Council advises that it may be confusing to have two different sets of presentation and disclosure requirements for small entities, depending on legal form, particularly when the overall objective of the financial statements is the same (that they give a true and fair view), and therefore Section 1A should apply to all entities meeting the relevant criteria.

16 Eligibility for the small companies regime is set out in company law. The Accounting Council advises that Section 1A should apply to companies eligible for the small companies regime, LLPs eligible for the small LLPs regime and any other entity that would have met the criteria for the small companies regime had they been companies. This is broadly the same as the scope of the FRSSE. At the time of giving this advice the Accounting Council notes that different thresholds apply to the small companies regime and the small LLPs regime and entities will need to take care to ensure they are eligible to apply Section 1A.

Presentation and disclosure

17 A key feature of the new small companies regime set out in the new Accounting Directive is that it specifies the maximum mandatory disclosures to be included in a small company's financial statements, which may not be added to. However, the financial statements of a small company must still give a true and fair view of the financial performance and financial position of the entity; this has been emphasised in Section 1A. The directors of a company will need to consider whether additional disclosures are necessary to give a true and fair view and, if so, provide those additional disclosures.

18 The Accounting Council advises that, as the disclosures required by FRS 102 of larger entities are those that are usually considered necessary (but not necessarily sufficient) to give a true and fair view, a small entity should be encouraged to consider all of these disclosures in order to determine the additional disclosures necessary in its own circumstances.

19 In addition, the Accounting Council considers that it will be helpful to small entities applying FRS 102 for the disclosures required by law to be included and cross-referenced to the same or similar disclosures elsewhere in FRS 102. This has been set out in Appendix C to Section 1A, where the drafting of the disclosures is as close as possible to the company law requirements, with a note of the source of the legal requirement, and an indication of which paragraphs of FRS 102 address similar requirements.

20 There are a small number of specific disclosures that the Accounting Council considers will be particularly useful to users of the financial statements of a small entity, including a statement of compliance with FRS 102 and a note of dividends declared and paid or payable. The Accounting Council advises specifically encouraging small entities to provide these disclosures.

21 Another feature of the small companies regime is that additional 'statements' may not be required of small companies. This includes a statement of comprehensive income, a statement of changes in equity and the cash flow statement. Section 1A makes it clear that such statements are not required of small entities, but the Accounting Council considers that a statement of comprehensive income and a statement of changes in equity (or statement of income and retained earnings) will be useful to users of the financial statements of a small entity in explaining the financial performance for the reporting period and the effect that this has had on financial position. Therefore the Accounting Council advises that a small entity is encouraged to provide these statements.

22 The Accounting Council notes that, although the FRSSE encouraged the presentation of a cash flow statement by small entities, FRS 1 (Revised 1996) *Cash flow statements* simply exempted small entities from presenting a cash flow statement on the basis that it was not required by company law for a small company. The Accounting Council advises retaining the exemption from FRS 1. As a result, a small entity choosing to apply 'full' FRS 102 is not required to present a cash flow statement.

Recognition and measurement

23 The Accounting Council advises that small entities should follow the recognition and measurement requirements of FRS 102. This will improve financial reporting by small entities by, for example, requiring the recognition of various financial instruments that the FRSSE does not currently require, such as derivatives like interest rate swaps and forward foreign currency contracts. Almost all respondents to FRED 59 agreed with this; those that did not generally suggested that changes should be made to FRS 102 that would apply to all entities. These suggestions will be considered as part of the triennial review of FRS 102.

24 In FRS 105 *The Financial Reporting Standard applicable to the Micro-entities Regime* the Accounting Council has considered and applied a set of principles for simplifying the recognition and measurement requirements for micro-entities. For the larger small entities within the scope of FRS 102 the Accounting Council advises that the principle it has applied is that there should not be recognition and measurement differences from the requirements applicable to larger entities. This reinstates the principle of consistency in accounting policies between those entities that are smaller and those that are larger that applied when the FRSSE was originally developed.

25 A small number of additional transitional provisions have been provided for small entities applying FRS 102 for the first time for an accounting period that commences before 1 January 2017 (see paragraphs 42 to 44).

Other matters relating to the small entities regime

26 Some respondents to FRED 59 noted that Section 1A did not address situations where a small entity voluntarily chooses to prepare consolidated financial statements. The Accounting Council advises that this is addressed in Section 1A.

27 Company law and the new Accounting Directive restrict the disclosures that can be required of small companies in relation to related party transactions. In particular, disclosure can only be required of transactions not conducted under normal market conditions. Respondents noted that it could be burdensome for a small entity to identify

those related party transactions that were not conducted under normal market conditions, because a significant degree of judgement would be involved. Instead, disclosure of all transactions with the specified related parties would meet the legal disclosure requirement. The Accounting Council notes that the Accounting Regulatory Committee reached a conclusion in 2007 that disclosing all related party transactions would comply with the requirement to disclose those not conducted under normal market conditions (as previously set out in paragraph 36 of Appendix IV to FRS 8 *Related Party Disclosures*). Therefore it advises including guidance in Appendix C to Section 1A that notes that although disclosure is only required of material transactions with the specified related parties that have not been concluded under normal market conditions, small entities disclosing all transactions with such related parties would still be compliant with company law.

True and fair view

28   In Section 1A the drafting of various requirements is as close as possible to the company law requirements, reflecting the need for the financial statements of a small entity to give a true and fair view. The Accounting Council noted that Section 3 *Financial Statement Presentation* expressed some of the same requirements in a different way, and advises that Section 3 is amended to more closely reflect the requirements of company law. These changes are not considered to have any substantive effect as 'true and fair' and 'presents fairly' are synonymous, being different articulations of the same concept, as confirmed by legal opinion.

Other minor amendments

29   A small number of other amendments were also necessary to maintain consistency between FRS 102 and company law. This was not a comprehensive review of the requirements of FRS 102.

30   The amendments include:

(a)   Greater flexibility in relation to the format of the profit and loss account and balance sheet, which will allow entities choosing this option to adopt a presentation that is closer to that applied by entities preparing 'IAS accounts'. The Accounting Council advises that these new options available in company law should be available to entities applying FRS 102, but that a framework should be provided in FRS 102 to assist entities applying it.

(b)   Revisions to certain requirements relating to financial instruments that are, or may be, measured at fair value. The new Accounting Directive permits measurement of certain financial instruments at fair value where it is in accordance with EU-adopted IFRS; previously this was restricted to IFRS endorsed by 5 September 2006. The consequences of this change, as well as any interaction with IFRS 9 *Financial Instruments* that was issued in July 2014 and which an entity may make an accounting policy choice to apply under paragraphs 11.2(c) and 12.2(c), have been considered. As a result, the Accounting Council advises that some amendments are made for compliance with company law, although these are only likely to affect a minority of entities applying FRS 102. In addition, Appendix IV: *Note on legal requirements* advises that entities applying IFRS 9 will need to consider an override of the Regulations for the purposes of giving a true and fair view, in order to recognise certain fair value gains or losses in other comprehensive income.

(c)   Revising the 'seriously prejudicial' exemption that applies, in extremely rare circumstances, to disclosure of provisions and contingencies. The Accounting Council notes that company law requires certain disclosures in relation to provisions and contingencies, and that it advises consistency of disclosure by entities that are companies and those that are not. Therefore the 'seriously prejudicial' exemption has been redrafted to remind companies of the legal disclosure requirements and ensure that equivalent disclosures are provided by all entities.

(d) Revising the maximum period over which goodwill and other intangible assets may be amortised to 10 years, in those exceptional cases where an entity is unable to make a reliable estimate of the asset's useful economic life. The Accounting Council advises that, as this only applies in exceptional cases, the change in the maximum period so soon after it was introduced in the first edition of FRS 102 should have a limited impact in practice.

(e) Prohibiting the reversal of impairment losses for goodwill.

(f) Clarifying that a public benefit entity may apply merger accounting to an entity combination that is a merger provided that it is permitted by the statutory framework under which it reports. The new Accounting Directive only permits companies to apply merger accounting for group reconstructions and the Accounting Council advises that this amendment is made to ensure merger accounting is not applied by public benefit entities that are companies where not permitted in law. Some respondents to FRED 59 suggested that FRS 102 should continue to require the use of merger accounting by all public benefit entity combinations meeting the definition and criteria of a merger, through requiring the use of the true and fair override. The Accounting Council noted that 'true mergers' (other than those that might be considered group reconstructions) are not likely to be common. However, Appendix IV: *Note on legal requirements* notes that an individual public benefit entity may apply the true and fair override if it considers it appropriate to its circumstances, and provides the corresponding disclosures.

(g) Amending the definitions of a 'related party' and 'turnover' in accordance with changes in company law.

(h) Clarifying in paragraph 1.12(c) that, because company law requires certain disclosures relating to financial instruments, a qualifying entity choosing to provide reduced disclosures will not be exempt from all the disclosure requirements of Sections 11 and 12. This was previously addressed in paragraph A4.10, which notes that preparers need to have regard to the requirements of company law in addition to accounting standards.

31 The Accounting Council noted that in relation to small entities, Section 1A of FRS 102 will include all the disclosure requirements set out in company law, but that FRS 102 does not presently include all the equivalent disclosures for larger entities. The majority of respondents to the Consultation Document agreed that the current approach for larger entities should not be amended because this would increase the length of FRS 102 and make it potentially less user-friendly, especially as a significant number of larger entities applying FRS 102 are not companies and the additional disclosure requirements would not be applicable to them. Some respondents suggested including any additional disclosures as an appendix, but noted that this could be considered as part of the triennial review of FRS 102. The Accounting Council advises not amending FRS 102 for additional disclosures for larger entities at present, but notes that the suggestion of an appendix could be reconsidered at a later date.

32 The Accounting Council noted that in some areas the amendments made to the Regulations and the Small Companies Regulations make new accounting options available alongside existing requirements. In these areas it is not necessary to amend FRS 102, as it already complies with the existing requirements. The Accounting Council considered the following two areas:

(a) Equity method in individual accounts – paragraph 29A of the Regulations and the Small Companies Regulations permits participating interests to be accounted for in the financial statements of an investor using the equity method. FRS 102 already includes a number of options for accounting for such investments (see paragraph 9.26) and the Accounting Council does not advise introducing this option at present.

(b) Contingent consideration in a business combination – an amendment to paragraph 36 of the Regulations and the Small Companies Regulations would permit contingent consideration in a business combination to be measured and remeasured at fair value, which would be consistent with EU-adopted IFRS (IFRS 3 *Business Combinations* (revised 2008)). The Accounting Council notes that the requirements of FRS 102 are based on IFRS 3 (issued 2004) and does not advise amending the accounting for contingent consideration outside the context of a wider review of the accounting for business combinations. Therefore an amendment to accounting for contingent consideration in a business combination is not proposed at present.

33 In addition, the following amendments are advised:

(a) Two of the examples following paragraph 11.13 are being amended for clarity.

(b) The reduced disclosures for subsidiaries, set out in paragraphs 1.8 to 1.13, have been amended in relation to financial instruments measured at fair value through profit or loss to ensure they are consistent with company law disclosure requirements.

Residents' Management Companies

34 In considering the feedback received from the FRC's previous consultations, the Accounting Council noted that no clear consensus existed amongst respondents on the appropriate basis of accounting in the statutory financial statements of residents' management companies[25] where service charge monies are held on trust in accordance with section 42 of the Landlord and Tenant Act 1987. However, there was general agreement that no change should be made to FRS 102, or any other relevant financial reporting standard (including FRS 105), to address such a narrow and sector-specific issue.

35 The Accounting Council considered this issue carefully. It assessed the case for further intervention by reference to the FRC's published *Principles for the development of Codes, Standards and Guidance*[26] and, in particular, the extent to which the anticipated benefits from any changes to current practices would outweigh the costs incurred by the entities involved. It agreed with respondents that this matter does not merit a change in accounting standards, and therefore advises that no changes are made to FRS 102 (or FRS 105) that are specific to residents' management companies.

Share-based payment arrangements with cash alternatives

36 After the introduction of FRS 102, it was brought to the FRC's attention that the accounting it required for share-based payment transactions that give the reporting entity an option to settle in cash or equity could result in the recognition of a liability even though the conditions for the recognition of a liability under the standard were not clearly met. The Accounting Council notes that the requirement to account for such transactions as cash-settled is more onerous than the requirements under EU-adopted IFRS, under which they would generally be treated as equity-settled, since it requires the measurement of the obligation at fair value at each reporting date.

---

[25] An organisation which may be referred to in the lease, which is responsible for the provision of services, and manages and arranges maintenance of the property, but which does not necessarily have any legal interest in the property.

[26] This can be found on the FRC's website at www.frc.org.uk/FRC-Documents/FRC/About-the-FRC/Principles-for-the-development-of-Codes.pdf.

37   The Accounting Council therefore advises that FRS 102 should be amended with the result that such transactions are accounted for as equity-settled share-based payment arrangements unless the option to settle in equity has no commercial substance or the entity has created a valid expectation that it would settle in cash.

38   In some schemes the recipient may have an option to request settlement in cash or equity instruments. If an entity cannot avoid settling in cash should the recipient request it, FRS 102 requires the entity to account for the transaction as cash-settled by measuring the goods or services acquired at the fair value of the liability unless the cash settlement option has no commercial substance. The Accounting Council notes that this requirement is different to EU-adopted IFRS which requires the separate recognition of debt and equity components. The Accounting Council continues to believe that the simpler requirements of FRS 102 provide a practical and proportionate solution for those applying the standard and notes that this is generally consistent with the requirements in the IFRS for SMEs. In FRED 61 the exemption from cash-settlement accounting when the option to settle in cash has no commercial substance was omitted and the Accounting Council advises that this be retained in FRS 102.

39   The FRC had consulted on additional amendments that would have resulted in cash-settlement treatment for all share-based payment arrangements with terms that could result in the transfer of cash on the occurrence of an event outside the control of either party to the transaction. Some respondents commented that this could result in the recognition of a liability in situations when the probability of settlement in cash is remote. They also noted that the accounting for such transactions is under consideration by the IASB and its Interpretation Committee who have so far been unable to reach a conclusion. For the reasons noted by these respondents, the Accounting Council advises that FRS 102 should not be amended in this regard, but the need for further amendment be re-considered as part of the next review of the standard.

40   The FRC did not propose any additional transitional exemptions for entities that had chosen to early adopt FRS 102 and had granted awards under share-based payment arrangements that would be affected by the changes in FRED 61. The majority of respondents agreed that there was no need for additional transitional exemptions as such instances would be very rare and early adopters would have had the benefit of the transitional exemption for awards granted before the date of transition.

41   However, some respondents did identify an issue with the transitional exemption where greater clarity is needed. The transitional exemption in paragraph 35.10(b) of FRS 102 refers only to equity instruments granted before the date of transition. Some respondents noted that it was not clear if this reference also applies to the equity components of instruments that had been treated as compound instruments under FRS 20 or IFRS 2. The Accounting Council notes that the transitional exemption was intended to alleviate the costs of transition in respect of equity-settled share-based payment arrangements for companies that had previously applied the FRSSE, where such arrangements were not recognised, and for companies that had previously applied FRS 20 / IFRS 2 should FRS 102 require different accounting. As FRS 20 / IFRS 2 can result in compound instruments being partly accounted for as equity-settled and partly as cash-settled, the Accounting Council agrees it should be clarified that the reference to equity instruments includes the equity component of compound instruments accounted for in accordance with FRS 20 / IFRS 2. The Accounting Council also notes that there is no need for transitional exemptions to be added for liabilities not settled at the transition date, including those arising from arrangements previously treated as compound instruments, because the liability will not continue to be measured in the same way under FRS 102, being the fair value of the liability.

Transitional provisions for small entities

42   The Accounting Council considered whether transitional provisions should be provided for small entities applying FRS 102 for the first time. The Accounting Council noted that FRS 102 already includes Section 35 *Transition to this FRS*, which applies to any first-time adopter of FRS 102, which has a significant number of optional exemptions from full retrospective application of FRS 102 that are designed to reduce the burden of first-time adoption. This is particularly where it may be difficult to restate historical transactions on the basis otherwise required by FRS 102 because the relevant data would not have been obtained at the time the transaction occurred.

43   The Accounting Council advised in FRED 59 that no further transitional provisions were necessary for small entities that are not already provided for. Although the majority of respondents to FRED 59 agreed with this assessment, a small number of respondents suggested that additional transitional provisions should be made available. These suggestions related to areas where additional burdens may be incurred in applying FRS 102 for the first time because an entity's transition date to FRS 102 occurred before these amendments were finalised.

44   The Accounting Council considered these suggestions carefully and agreed to provide additional transitional exemptions for all small entities applying FRS 102 for the first time for an accounting period that commences before 1 January 2017. These relate to equity-settled share-based payment arrangements, financial instruments measured at fair value and financing transactions with related parties. On first-time application they provide relief from the full application of FRS 102 in the comparative period.

Effective date

45   The Accounting Council advises that, other than the replacement of paragraph 26.15 with new paragraphs 26.15 to 26.15B, these amendments should be effective for accounting periods beginning on or after 1 January 2016, with early application:

    (a)   permitted for accounting periods beginning on or after 1 January 2015 provided that *The Companies, Partnerships and Groups (Accounts and Reports) Regulations 2015* (SI 2015/980) are applied from the same date; and

    (b)   required if an entity applies *The Companies, Partnerships and Groups (Accounts and Reports) Regulations 2015* (SI 2015/980) to a reporting period beginning before 1 January 2016.

46   The Accounting Council advises that the replacement of paragraph 26.15 with new paragraphs 26.15 to 26.15B shall be effective for accounting periods beginning on or after 1 January 2015, with early application permitted in line with FRS 102 generally.

Approval of this Advice

47   This advice to the FRC was approved by the Accounting Council on 16 June 2015.

Appendix I: Glossary

This glossary is an integral part of the Standard.

accounting policies	The specific principles, bases, conventions, rules and practices applied by an entity in preparing and presenting **financial statements**.
accrual basis (of accounting)	The effects of transactions and other events are recognised when they occur (and not as **cash** or its equivalent is received or paid) and they are recorded in the accounting records and reported in the **financial statements** of the periods to which they relate.
accumulating compensated absences	Compensated absences that are carried forward and can be used in future periods if the current period's entitlement is not used in full.
acquisition date	The date on which the acquirer obtains **control** of the acquiree.
Act	The Companies Act 2006
active market	A market in which all the following conditions exist: (a) the items traded in the market are homogeneous; (b) willing buyers and sellers can normally be found at any time; and (c) prices are available to the public.
actuarial assumptions	An entity's unbiased and mutually compatible best estimates of the demographic and financial variables that will determine the ultimate cost of providing post-employment benefits.
actuarial gains and losses	Changes in the **present value** of the **defined benefit obligation** resulting from: (a) experience adjustments (the effects of differences between the previous **actuarial assumptions** and what has actually occurred); and (b) the effects of changes in actuarial assumptions.
agent	An entity is acting as an agent when it does not have exposure to the significant risks and rewards associated with the sale of goods or the rendering of services. One feature indicating that an entity is acting as an agent is that the amount the entity earns is predetermined, being either a fixed fee per transaction or a stated percentage of the amount billed to the customer.
agricultural activity	The management by an entity of the biological transformation of **biological assets** for sale, into agricultural produce or into additional biological assets.
agricultural produce	The harvested product of the entity's **biological assets**.
amortisation	The systematic allocation of the **depreciable amount** of an **asset** over its **useful life**.

amortised cost (of a financial asset or financial liability)	The amount at which the **financial asset** or **financial liability** is measured at initial **recognition** minus principal repayments, plus or minus the cumulative **amortisation** using the **effective interest method** of any difference between that initial amount and the maturity amount, and minus any reduction (directly or through the use of an allowance account) for impairment or uncollectability.
asset	A resource controlled by the entity as a result of past events and from which future economic benefits are expected to flow to the entity.

asset held by a long-term employee benefit fund	An **asset** (other than non-transferable financial instruments issued by the reporting entity) that:
	
	(a) is held by an entity (a fund) that is legally separate from the reporting entity and exists solely to pay or fund **employee benefits**; and
	
	(b) is available to be used only to pay or fund employee benefits, is not available to the reporting entity's own creditors (even in bankruptcy), and cannot be returned to the reporting entity, unless either:
	
	    (i) the remaining assets of the fund are sufficient to meet all the related employee benefit obligations of the plan or the reporting entity; or
	
	    (ii) the assets are returned to the reporting entity to reimburse it for employee benefits already paid.

associate	An entity, including an unincorporated entity such as a partnership, over which the investor has **significant influence** and that is neither a **subsidiary** nor an interest in a **joint venture**.
biological asset	A living animal or plant.
borrowing costs	Interest and other costs incurred by an entity in connection with the borrowing of funds.
business	An integrated set of activities and **assets** conducted and managed for the purpose of providing: (a) a return to investors; or (b) lower costs or other economic benefits directly and proportionately to policyholders or participants. A business generally consists of inputs, processes applied to those inputs, and resulting outputs that are, or will be, used to generate **revenues**. If **goodwill** is present in a transferred set of activities and assets, the transferred set shall be presumed to be a business.
business combination	The bringing together of separate entities or **businesses** into one reporting entity.
carrying amount	The amount at which an **asset** or **liability** is recognised in the **statement of financial position**.
cash	Cash on hand and demand deposits.
cash equivalents	Short-term, highly liquid investments that are readily convertible to known amounts of **cash** and that are subject to an insignificant risk of changes in value.

cash flows	Inflows and outflows of **cash** and **cash equivalents**.
cash-generating unit	The smallest identifiable group of **assets** that generates cash inflows that are largely independent of the cash inflows from other assets or groups of assets.
cash-settled share-based payment transaction	A **share-based payment transaction** in which the entity acquires goods or services by incurring a **liability** to transfer **cash** or other **assets** to the supplier of those goods or services for amounts that are based on the price (or value) of the entity's shares or other equity instruments of the entity or another group entity.
change in accounting estimate	An adjustment of the **carrying amount** of an **asset** or a **liability**, or the amount of the periodic consumption of an asset, that results from the assessment of the present status of, and expected future benefits and obligations associated with, assets and liabilities. Changes in accounting estimates result from new information or new developments and, accordingly, are not corrections of **errors**.
class of assets	A grouping of **assets** of a similar nature and use in an entity's operations.
close members of the family of a person	Those family members who may be expected to influence, or be influenced by, that person in their dealings with the entity including: (a) that person's children and spouse or domestic partner; (b) children of that person's spouse or domestic partner; and (c) dependants of that person or that person's spouse or domestic partner.
closing rate	The spot exchange rate at the end of the **reporting period**
combination that is in substance is a gift	A combination carried out at nil or nominal consideration that is not a fair value exchange but in substance the gift of one entity to another.
commencement of lease term	The date from which the lessee is entitled to exercise its right to use the leased asset. It is the date of initial **recognition** of the **lease** (ie the recognition of the **assets**, **liabilities**, **income** or **expenses** resulting from the lease, as appropriate).
component of an entity	Operations and **cash flows** that can be clearly distinguished, operationally and for financial reporting purposes, from the rest of the entity.
compound financial instrument	A financial instrument that, from the issuer's perspective, contains both a **liability** and an **equity** element.
consolidated financial statements	The financial statements of a **parent** and its **subsidiaries** presented as those of a single economic entity.
construction contract	A contract specifically negotiated for the construction of an **asset** or a combination of assets that are closely interrelated or interdependent in terms of their design, technology and function or their ultimate purpose or use.

constructive obligation	An obligation that derives from an entity's actions where: (a) by an established pattern of past practice, published policies or a sufficiently specific current statement, the entity has indicated to other parties that it will accept certain responsibilities; and (b) as a result, the entity has created a valid expectation on the part of those other parties that it will discharge those responsibilities.
contingent asset	A possible **asset** that arises from past events and whose existence will be confirmed only by the occurrence or non-occurrence of one or more uncertain future events not wholly within the control of the entity.

contingent liability	(a) a possible obligation that arises from past events and whose existence will be confirmed only by the occurrence or non-occurrence of one or more uncertain future events not wholly within the control of the entity; or
	
	(b) a present obligation that arises from past events but is not recognised because:
	
	    (i) it is not **probable** that an outflow of resources embodying economic benefits will be required to settle the obligation; or
	
	    (ii) the amount of the obligation cannot be measured with sufficient **reliability**.

contingent rent	That portion of the lease payments that is not fixed in amount but is based on the future amount of a factor that changes other than with the passage of time (eg percentage of future sales, amount of future use, future price indices, and future market rates of interest).
control (of an entity)	The power to govern the financial and operating policies of an entity so as to obtain benefits from its activities.
credit risk	The risk that one party to a financial instrument will cause a financial loss for the other party by failing to discharge an obligation.
current assets	**Assets** of an entity which: (a) for an entity choosing to apply paragraph 1A(1) of Schedule 1 to the Regulations, are not **non-current assets**; or (b) for all other entities, are not fixed assets.
current liabilities (for the purposes of an entity applying paragraph 1A(1) of Schedule 1 to the Regulations)	**Liabilities** of the entity which: (a) it expects to settle in its normal operating cycle; (b) it holds primarily for the purpose of trading; (c) are due to be settled within 12 months after the **reporting period**; or (d) it does not have an unconditional right to defer settlement for at least 12 months after the reporting period.
current tax	The amount of income tax payable (refundable) in respect of the taxable profit (tax loss) for the current period or past **reporting periods**.
date of transition	The beginning of the earliest period for which an entity presents full comparative information in a given standard in its first **financial statements** that comply with that standard.

deemed cost	An amount used as a surrogate for cost or depreciated cost at a given date. Subsequent **depreciation** or **amortisation** assumes that the entity had initially recognised the **asset** or **liability** at the given date and that its cost was equal to the deemed cost.
deferred acquisition costs	Costs arising from the conclusion of **insurance contracts** that are incurred during a **reporting period** but which relate to a subsequent reporting period.
deferred tax	Income tax payable (recoverable) in respect of the **taxable profit (tax loss)** for future **reporting periods** as a result of past transactions or events.
deferred tax assets	Income tax recoverable in future **reporting periods** in respect of: (a) future tax consequences of transactions and events recognised in the **financial statements** of the current and previous periods; (b) the carry forward of unused tax losses; and (c) the carry forward of unused tax credits.
deferred tax liabilities	Income tax payable in future **reporting periods** in respect of future tax consequences of transactions and events recognised in the **financial statements** of the current and previous periods.
defined benefit obligation (present value of)	The **present value**, without deducting any **plan assets**, of expected future payments required to settle the obligation resulting from employee service in the current and prior periods.
defined benefit plans	**Post-employment benefit plans** other than **defined contribution plans**.
defined contribution plans	**Post-employment benefit plans** under which an entity pays fixed contributions into a separate entity (a fund) and has no legal or **constructive obligation** to pay further contributions or to make direct benefit payments to employees if the fund does not hold sufficient **assets** to pay all **employee benefits** relating to employee service in the current and prior periods.
depreciable amount	The cost of an **asset**, or other amount substituted for cost (in the **financial statements**), less its residual value.
depreciated replacement cost	The most economic cost required for the entity to replace the **service potential** of an **asset** (including the amount that the entity will receive from its disposal at the end of its **useful life**) at the **reporting date**.
depreciation	The systematic allocation of the **depreciable amount** of an **asset** over its **useful life**.
derecognition	The removal of a previously recognised **asset** or **liability** from an entity's **statement of financial position**.

derivative	A financial instrument or other contract with all three of the following characteristics: (a) its value changes in response to the change in a specified interest rate, financial instrument price, commodity price, foreign exchange rate, index of prices or rates, credit rating or credit index, or other variable (sometimes called the 'underlying'), provided in the case of a non-financial variable that the variable is not specific to a party to the contract; (b) it requires no initial net investment or an initial net investment that is smaller than would be required for other types of contracts that would be expected to have a similar response to changes in market factors; and (c) it is settled at a future date.
development	The application of **research** findings or other knowledge to a plan or design for the production of new or substantially improved materials, devices, products, processes, systems or services before the start of commercial production or use.
discontinued operation	A **component of an entity** that has been disposed of and: (a) represented a separate major line of **business** or geographical area of operations; (b) was part of a single co-ordinated plan to dispose of a separate major line of business or geographical area of operations; or (c) was a **subsidiary** acquired exclusively with a view to resale.

discretionary participation feature	A contractual right to receive, as a supplement to guaranteed benefits, additional benefits:
	
	(a) that are likely to be a significant portion of the total contractual benefits;
	
	(b) whose amount or timing is contractually at the discretion of the issuer; and
	
	(c) that are contractually based on:
	
	    (i) the performance of a specified pool of contracts or a specified type of contract;
	
	    (ii) realised and/or unrealised investment returns on a specified pool of **assets** held by the issuer; or
	
	    (iii) the **profit or loss** of the company, fund or other entity that issues the contract.

disposal group	A group of **assets** to be disposed of, by sale or otherwise, together as a group in a single transaction, and **liabilities** directly associated with those assets that will be transferred in the transaction. The group includes **goodwill** acquired in a **business combination** if the group is a **cash-generating unit** to which goodwill has been allocated in accordance with the requirements of paragraphs 27.24 to 27.27 of this FRS.
effective interest method	A method of calculating the **amortised cost** of a **financial asset** or a **financial liability** (or a group of financial assets or financial liabilities) and of allocating the interest income or interest expense over the relevant period.

effective interest rate	The rate that exactly discounts estimated future cash payments or receipts through the expected life of the financial instrument or, when appropriate, a shorter period to the **carrying amount** of the **financial asset** or **financial liability**.
employee benefits	All forms of consideration given by an entity in exchange for service rendered by employees.
entity combination	See **business combination**.
equity	The residual interest in the **assets** of the entity after deducting all its **liabilities**.
equity-settled share-based payment transaction	A **share-based payment transaction** in which the entity: (a) receives goods or services as consideration for its own equity instruments (including shares or **share options**); or (b) receives goods or services but has no obligation to settle the transaction with the supplier.
errors	Omissions from, and misstatements in, the entity's **financial statements** for one or more prior periods arising from a failure to use, or misuse of, reliable information that: (a) was available when financial statements for those periods were authorised for issue; and (b) could reasonably be expected to have been obtained and taken into account in the preparation and presentation of those financial statements.
expenses	Decreases in economic benefits during the **reporting period** in the form of outflows or depletions of **assets** or incurrences of **liabilities** that result in decreases in **equity**, other than those relating to distributions to equity investors.
EU-adopted IFRS	IFRS that have been adopted in the European Union in accordance with EU Regulation 1606/2002.
fair value	The amount for which an **asset** could be exchanged, a **liability** settled, or an equity instrument granted could be exchanged, between knowledgeable, willing parties in an arm's length transaction. In the absence of any specific guidance provided in the relevant section of this FRS, the guidance in paragraphs 11.27 to 11.32 shall be used in determining fair value.
fair value less costs to sell	The amount obtainable from the sale of an **asset** or **cash-generating unit** in an arm's length transaction between knowledgeable, willing parties, less the costs of disposal.
finance lease	A **lease** that transfers substantially all the risks and rewards incidental to ownership of an **asset**. Title may or may not eventually be transferred. A lease that is not a finance lease is an operating lease.

financial asset	Any **asset** that is:
	
	(a) **cash**;
	
	(b) an equity instrument of another entity;
	
	(c) a contractual right:
	
	    (i) to receive cash or another financial asset from another entity, or
	
	    (ii) to exchange financial assets or **financial liabilities** with another entity under conditions that are potentially favourable to the entity; or
	
	(d) a contract that will or may be settled in the entity's own equity instruments and:
	
	    (i) under which the entity is or may be obliged to receive a variable number of the entity's own equity instruments; or
	
	    (ii) that will or may be settled other than by the exchange of a fixed amount of cash or another financial asset for a fixed number of the entity's own equity instruments. For this purpose the entity's own equity instruments do not include instruments that are themselves contracts for the future receipt or delivery of the entity's own equity instruments.

financial guarantee contract	A contract that requires the issuer to make specified payments to reimburse the holder for a loss it incurs because a specified debtor fails to make payments when due in accordance with the original or modified terms of a debt instrument.

financial institution	Any of the following:
	
	(a) a bank which is:
	
	    (i) a firm with a Part IV permission[27] which includes accepting deposits and:
	
	        (a) which is a credit institution; or
	
	        (b) whose Part IV permission includes a requirement that it complies with the rules in the General Prudential sourcebook and the Prudential sourcebook for Banks, Building Societies and Investment Firms relating to banks, but which is not a building society, a friendly society or a credit union;
	
	    (ii) an EEA bank which is a full credit institution;
	
	(b) a building society which is defined in section 119(1) of the Building Societies Act 1986 as a building society incorporated (or deemed to be incorporated) under that act;
	
	(c) a credit union, being a body corporate registered under the Industrial and Provident Societies Act 1965 as a credit union in accordance with the Credit Unions Act 1979, which is an authorised person;
	
	(d) custodian bank, broker-dealer or stockbroker;

---

[27] As defined in section 40(4) of the *Financial Services and Markets Act 2000* or references to equivalent provisions of any successor legislation.

	(e) an entity that undertakes the business of effecting or carrying out **insurance contracts**, including general and life assurance entities;
	(f) an incorporated friendly society incorporated under the Friendly Societies Act 1992 or a registered friendly society registered under section 7(1)(a) of the Friendly Societies Act 1974 or any enactment which it replaced, including any registered branches;
	(g) an investment trust, Irish investment company, venture capital trust, mutual fund, exchange traded fund, unit trust, open-ended investment company (OEIC);
	(h) a **retirement benefit plan**; or
	(i) any other entity whose principal activity is to generate wealth or manage risk through financial instruments. This is intended to cover entities that have business activities similar to those listed above but are not specifically included in the list above.
	A **parent** entity whose sole activity is to hold investments in other group entities is not a financial institution.
financial instrument	A contract that gives rise to a **financial asset** of one entity and a **financial liability** or equity instrument of another entity.
financial liability	Any **liability** that is: (a) a contractual obligation: 　(i) to deliver **cash** or another **financial asset** to another entity; or 　(ii) to exchange financial assets or financial liabilities with another entity under conditions that are potentially unfavourable to the entity, or (b) a contract that will or may be settled in the entity's own equity instruments and: 　(i) under which the entity is or may be obliged to deliver a variable number of the entity's own equity instruments; or 　(ii) will or may be settled other than by the exchange of a fixed amount of cash or another financial asset for a fixed number of the entity's own equity instruments. For this purpose the entity's own equity instruments do not include instruments that are themselves contracts for the future receipt or delivery of the entity's own equity instruments.
financial position	The relationship of the **assets**, **liabilities** and **equity** of an entity as reported in the **statement of financial position**.
financial statements	Structured representation of the **financial position**, financial **performance** and **cash flows** of an entity.

financial risk	The risk of a possible future change in one or more of a specified interest rate, financial instrument price, commodity price, foreign exchange rate, index of prices or rates, credit rating or credit index or other variable, provided in the case of a non-financial variable that the variable is not specific to a party to the contract.
financing activities	Activities that result in changes in the size and composition of the contributed **equity** and borrowings of the entity.
firm commitment	A binding agreement for the exchange of a specified quantity of resources at a specified price on a specified future date or dates.
first-time adopter of this FRS	An entity that presents its first annual **financial statements** that conform to this FRS, regardless of whether its previous accounting framework was **EU-adopted IFRS** or another set of accounting standards.
fixed assets	**Assets** of an entity which are intended for use on a continuing basis in the entity's activities.
forecast transaction	An uncommitted but anticipated future transaction.
foreign operation	An entity that is a **subsidiary**, **associate**, **joint venture** or branch of a reporting entity, the activities of which are based or conducted in a country or currency other than those of the reporting entity.
FRS 100	FRS 100 *Application of Financial Reporting Requirements*
FRS 101	FRS 101 *Reduced Disclosure Framework*
FRS 102	FRS 102 *The Financial Reporting Standard applicable in the UK and Republic of Ireland*
FRS 103	FRS 103 *Insurance Contracts*
FRS 104	FRS 104 *Interim Financial Reporting*
FRS 105	FRS 105 *The Financial Reporting Standard applicable to the Micro-entities Regime*
functional currency	The currency of the primary economic environment in which the entity operates.
funding (of post-employment benefits)	Contributions by an entity, and sometimes its employees, into an entity, or fund, that is legally separate from the reporting entity and from which the **employee benefits** are paid.
gains	Increases in economic benefits that meet the definition of **income** but are not **revenue**.
general purpose financial statements (generally referred to simply as financial statements)	**Financial statements** directed to the general financial information needs of a wide range of users who are not in a position to demand reports tailored to meet their particular information needs.

going concern	An entity is a going concern unless management either intends to liquidate the entity or to cease trading, or has no realistic alternative but to do so.
goodwill	Future economic benefits arising from **assets** that are not capable of being individually identified and separately recognised.
government grant	Assistance by government in the form of a transfer of resources to an entity in return for past or future compliance with specified conditions relating to the **operating activities** of the entity. Government refers to government, government agencies and similar bodies whether local, national or international.
grant date	The date at which the entity and another party (including an employee) agree to a share-based payment arrangement, being when the entity and the counterparty have a shared understanding of the terms and conditions of the arrangement. At grant date the entity confers on the counterparty the right to **cash**, other **assets**, or equity instruments of the entity, provided the specified vesting conditions, if any, are met. If that agreement is subject to an approval process (for example, by shareholders), grant date is the date when that approval is obtained.
gross investment in a lease	The aggregate of: (a) the **minimum lease payments** receivable by the lessor under a **finance lease**; and (b) any unguaranteed **residual value** accruing to the lessor.
group	A **parent** and all its **subsidiaries**.
group reconstruction	Any one of the following arrangements: (a) the transfer of an equity holding in a **subsidiary** from one group entity to another; (b) the addition of a new **parent** entity to a **group**; (c) the transfer of equity holdings in one or more subsidiaries of a group to a new entity that is not a group entity but whose equity holders are the same as those of the group's parent; or (d) the combination into a group of two or more entities that before the combination had the same equity holders.
hedging gain or loss	The change in fair value of a hedged item that is attributable to the hedged risk.
held exclusively with a view to subsequent resale	An interest: (a) for which a purchaser has been identified or is being sought, and which is reasonably expected to be disposed of within approximately one year of its date of acquisition; or (b) that was acquired as a result of the enforcement of a security, unless the interest has become part of the continuing activities of the **group** or the holder acts as if it intends the interest to become so; or (c) which is **held as part of an investment portfolio**.

held as part of an investment portfolio	An interest is held as part of an investment portfolio if its value to the investor is through **fair value** as part of a directly or indirectly held basket of investments rather than as media through which the investor carries out **business**. A basket of investments is indirectly held if an investment fund holds a single investment in a second investment fund which, in turn, holds a basket of investments.
heritage assets	Tangible and **intangible assets** with historic, artistic, scientific, technological, geophysical, or environmental qualities that are held and maintained principally for their contribution to knowledge and culture.
highly probable	Significantly more likely than **probable**.
IAS Regulation	EU Regulation 1606/2002
IFRS (International Financial Reporting Standards)	Standards and interpretations issued (or adopted) by the International Accounting Standards Board (IASB). They comprise: (a) International Financial Reporting Standards; (b) International Accounting Standards; and (c) Interpretations developed by the IFRS Interpretations Committee (IFRIC) or the former Standing Interpretations Committee (SIC).
impairment loss	The amount by which the **carrying amount** of an **asset** exceeds: (a) in the case of **inventories**, its selling price less costs to complete and sell; or (b) in the case of other assets, its **recoverable amount**.
impracticable	Applying a requirement is impracticable when the entity cannot apply it after making every reasonable effort to do so.
imputed rate of interest	The more clearly determinable of either: (a) the prevailing rate for a similar instrument of an issuer with a similar credit rating; or (b) a rate of interest that discounts the nominal amount of the instrument to the current cash sales price of the goods or services.
inception of the lease	The earlier of the date of the lease agreement and the date of commitment by the parties to the principal provisions of the **lease**.
income	Increases in economic benefits during the **reporting period** in the form of inflows or enhancements of **assets** or decreases of **liabilities** that result in increases in **equity**, other than those relating to contributions from equity investors.
income and expenditure	The total of **income** less **expenses**, excluding the components of **other comprehensive income**. In the for-profit sector this is known as **profit or loss**.
income statement	**Financial statement** that presents all items of **income** and **expense** recognised in a **reporting period**, excluding the items of **other comprehensive income** (referred to as the profit and loss account in the **Act**).

income tax	All domestic and foreign taxes that are based on **taxable profits**. Income tax also includes taxes, such as withholding taxes, that are payable by a **subsidiary**, **associate** or **joint venture** on distributions to the reporting entity.
individual financial statements	The accounts that are required to be prepared by an entity in accordance with the Act or relevant legislation, for example: (a) 'individual accounts', as set out in section 394 of the Act; (b) 'statement of accounts', as set out in section 132 of the Charities Act 2011; or (c) 'individual accounts', as set out in section 72A of the Building Societies Act 1986. **Separate financial statements** are included in the meaning of this term.
infrastructure assets	Infrastructure for public services, such as roads, bridges, tunnels, prisons, hospitals, airports, water distribution facilities, energy supply and telecommunications networks.
insurance contract	A contract under which one party (the insurer) accepts significant insurance risk from another party (the policyholder) by agreeing to compensate the policyholder if a specified uncertain future event (the insured event) adversely affects the policyholder.
intangible asset	An identifiable non-monetary asset without physical substance. Such an **asset** is identifiable when: (a) it is separable, ie capable of being separated or divided from the entity and sold, transferred, licensed, rented or exchanged, either individually or together with a related contract, asset or **liability**; or (b) it arises from contractual or other legal rights, regardless of whether those rights are transferable or separable from the entity or from other rights and obligations.

interest rate implicit in the lease	The discount rate that, at the **inception of the lease**, causes the aggregate **present value** of:
	
	(a) the **minimum lease payments**; and
	
	(b) the unguaranteed **residual value** to be equal to the sum of:
	
	   (i) the **fair value** of the leased asset; and
	
	   (ii) any initial direct costs of the lessor.

interim financial report	A financial report containing either a complete set of **financial statements** or a set of condensed financial statements for an **interim period**.
interim period	A financial **reporting period** shorter than a full financial year.
intrinsic value	The difference between the fair value of the shares to which the counterparty has the (conditional or unconditional) right to subscribe or which it has the right to receive, and the price (if any) the counterparty is (or will be) required to pay for those shares. For example, a share option with an exercise price of CU15, on a share with a fair value of CU20, has an intrinsic value of CU5.

inventories	**Assets**: (a) held for sale in the ordinary course of business; (b) in the process of production for such sale; or (c) in the form of materials or supplies to be consumed in the production process or in the rendering of services.
inventories held for distribution at no or nominal consideration	**Assets** that are: (a) held for distribution at no or nominal consideration in the ordinary course of operations; (b) in the process of production for distribution at no or nominal consideration in the ordinary course of operations; or (c) in the form of material or supplies to be consumed in the production process or in the rendering of services at no or nominal consideration.
investing activities	The acquisition and disposal of long-term assets and other investments not included in **cash equivalents**.
investment property	Property (land or a building, or part of a building, or both) held by the owner or by the lessee under a **finance lease** to earn rentals or for capital appreciation or both, rather than for: (a) use in the production or supply of goods or services or for administrative purposes, or (b) sale in the ordinary course of **business**.
joint control	The contractually agreed sharing of **control** over an economic activity. It exists only when the strategic financial and operating decisions relating to the activity require the unanimous consent of the parties sharing control (the **venturers**).
joint venture	A contractual arrangement whereby two or more parties undertake an economic activity that is subject to **joint control**. Joint ventures can take the form of jointly controlled operations, jointly controlled assets, or **jointly controlled entities**.
jointly controlled entity	A **joint venture** that involves the establishment of a corporation, partnership or other entity in which each **venturer** has an interest. The entity operates in the same way as other entities, except that a contractual arrangement between the venturers establishes **joint control** over the economic activity of the entity.
key management personnel	Those persons having authority and responsibility for planning, directing and controlling the activities of the entity, directly or indirectly, including any director (whether executive or otherwise) of that entity.
lease	An agreement whereby the lessor conveys to the lessee in return for a payment or series of payments the right to use an **asset** for an agreed period of time.

lease incentives	Incentives provided by the lessor to the lessee to enter into a new or renew an operating lease. Examples of such incentives include up-front cash payments to the lessee, the reimbursement or assumption by the lessor of costs of the lessee (such as relocation costs, leasehold improvements and costs associated with pre-existing lease commitments of the lessee), or initial periods of the **lease** provided by the lessor rent-free or at a reduced rent.
lease term	The non-cancellable period for which the lessee has contracted to **lease** the **asset** together with any further terms for which the lessee has the option to continue to lease the asset, with or without further payment, when at the **inception of the lease** it is reasonably certain that the lessee will exercise the option.
lessee's incremental borrowing rate (of interest)	The rate of interest the lessee would have to pay on a similar **lease** or, if that is not determinable, the rate that, at the **inception of the lease**, the lessee would incur to borrow over a similar term, and with a similar security, the funds necessary to purchase the **asset**.
liability	A present obligation of the entity arising from past events, the settlement of which is expected to result in an outflow from the entity of resources embodying economic benefits.
liquidity risk	The risk that an entity will encounter difficulty in meeting obligations associated with **financial liabilities** that are settled by delivering **cash** or another **financial asset**.
LLP Regulations	The Large and Medium-sized Limited Liability Partnerships (Accounts) Regulations 2008 (SI 2008/1913)
loans payable	**Financial liabilities** other than short-term trade payables on normal credit terms.
market condition	A condition upon which the exercise price, vesting or exercisability of an equity instrument depends that is related to the market price of the entity's equity instruments, such as attaining a specified share price or a specified amount of **intrinsic value** of a **share option**, or achieving a specified target that is based on the market price of the entity's equity instruments relative to an index of market prices of equity instruments of other entities.
market risk	The risk that the **fair value** or future **cash flows** of a financial instrument will fluctuate because of changes in market prices. Market risk comprises three types of risk: currency risk, interest rate risk and other price risk. Interest rate risk – the risk that the fair value or future cash flows of a financial instrument will fluctuate because of changes in market interest rates. Currency risk – the risk that the fair value or future cash flows of a financial instrument will fluctuate because of changes in foreign exchange rates. Other price risk – the risk that the fair value or future cash flows of a financial instrument will fluctuate because of changes in market prices (other than those arising from interest rate risk or currency risk), whether those changes are caused by factors specific to the financial instrument or its issuer, or factors affecting all similar financial instruments traded in the market.

material	Omissions or misstatements of items are material if they could, individually or collectively, influence the economic decisions of users taken on the basis of the **financial statements**. Materiality depends on the size and nature of the omission or misstatement judged in the surrounding circumstances. The size or nature of the item, or a combination of both, could be the determining factor.
measurement	The process of determining the monetary amounts at which the elements of the **financial statements** are to be recognised and carried in the **statement of financial position** and **statement of comprehensive income**.
merger	An **entity combination** that results in the creation of a new reporting entity formed from the combining parties, in which the controlling parties of the combining entities come together in a partnership for the mutual sharing of risks and benefits of the newly formed entity and in which no party to the combination in substance obtains **control** over any other, or is otherwise seen to be dominant. All of the following criteria must be met for an entity combination to meet the definition of a merger: (a) no party to the combination is portrayed as either acquirer or acquiree, either by its own board or management or by that of another party to the combination; (b) there is no significant change to the classes of beneficiaries of the combining entities or the purpose of the benefits provided as a result of the combination; and (c) all parties to the combination, as represented by the members of the board, participate in establishing the management structure of the combined entity and in selecting the management personnel, and such decisions are made on the basis of a consensus between the parties to the combination rather than purely by exercise of voting rights.

minimum lease payments	The payments over the **lease term** that the lessee is or can be required to make, excluding **contingent rent**, costs for services and taxes to be paid by and reimbursed to the lessor, together with:
	
	(a) for a lessee, any amounts guaranteed by the lessee or by a party related to the lessee; or
	
	(b) for a lessor, any **residual value** guaranteed to the lessor by:
	
	   (i) the lessee;
	
	   (ii) a party related to the lessee; or
	
	   (iii) a third party unrelated to the lessor that is financially capable of discharging the obligations under the guarantee.
	
	However, if the lessee has an option to purchase the **asset** at a price that is expected to be sufficiently lower than **fair value** at the date the option becomes exercisable for it to be reasonably certain, at the **inception of the lease**, that the option will be exercised, the minimum lease payments comprise the minimum payments payable over the lease term to the expected date of exercise of this purchase option and the payment required to exercise it.

monetary items	Units of currency held and **assets** and **liabilities** to be received or paid in a fixed or determinable number of units of currency.
multi-employer (benefit) plans	**Defined contribution plans** (other than **state plans**) or **defined benefit plans** (other than state plans) that: (a) pool the **assets** contributed by various entities that are not under common control, and (b) use those assets to provide benefits to employees of more than one entity, on the basis that contribution and benefit levels are determined without regard to the identity of the entity that employs the employees concerned.
net assets available for benefits	The **assets** of a plan less **liabilities** other than the actuarial **present value** of promised retirement benefits
net defined benefit liability	The **present value** of the **defined benefit obligation** at the **reporting date** minus the **fair value** at the reporting date of **plan assets** (if any) out of which the obligations are to be settled.
net investment in a foreign operation	The amount of the reporting entity's interest in the net assets of that operation.
net investment in a lease	The **gross investment in a lease** discounted at the **interest rate implicit in the lease**.
non-controlling interest	The **equity** in a **subsidiary** not attributable, directly or indirectly, to a **parent**.
non-current assets	**Assets** of the entity which: (a) it does not expect to realise, or intend to sell or consume, in its normal operating cycle; (b) it does not hold primarily for the purpose of trading; (c) it does not expect to realise within 12 months after the **reporting period**; or (d) are **cash** or **cash equivalents** restricted from being exchanged or used to settle a **liability** for at least 12 months after the reporting period.
non-current liabilities	**Liabilities** of the entity which are not **current liabilities.**
non-exchange transaction	A transaction whereby an entity receives value from another entity without directly giving approximately equal value in exchange, or gives value to another entity without directly receiving approximately equal value in exchange.
notes (to financial statements)	Notes contain information in addition to that presented in the **statement of financial position**, **statement of comprehensive income**, **income statement** (if presented), combined **statement of income and retained earnings** (if presented), **statement of changes in equity** and **statement of cash flows**. Notes provide narrative descriptions or disaggregations of items presented in those statements and information about items that do not qualify for **recognition** in those statements.

notional amount	The quantity of currency units, shares, bushels, pounds or other units specified in a financial instrument contract.
objective of financial statements	To provide information about the **financial position**, **performance** and, when required to be presented, **cash flows** of an entity that is useful for economic decision-making by a broad range of users who are not in a position to demand reports tailored to meet their particular information needs.
onerous contract	A contract in which the unavoidable costs of meeting the obligations under the contract exceed the economic benefits expected to be received under it.
operating activities	The principal revenue-producing activities of the entity and other activities that are not investing or **financing activities**.
operating lease	A **lease** that does not transfer substantially all the risks and rewards incidental to ownership. A lease that is not an operating lease is a **finance lease**.
operating segment	An operating segment is a **component of an entity**: (a) that engages in business activities from which it may earn **revenues** and incur **expenses** (including revenues and expenses relating to transactions with other components of the same entity); (b) whose operating results are regularly reviewed by the entity's chief operating decision maker to make decisions about resources to be allocated to the segment and assess its **performance**; and (c) for which discrete financial information is available.
ordinary share	An equity instrument that is subordinate to all other classes of equity instrument.
other comprehensive income	Items of **income** and **expense** (including reclassification adjustments) that are not recognised in **profit or loss** as required or permitted by this FRS.
owners	Holders of instruments classified as **equity**.
parent	An entity that has one or more **subsidiaries**.
performance	The relationship of the **income** and **expenses** of an entity, as reported in the **statement of comprehensive income**.
performance-related condition	A condition that requires the performance of a particular level of service or units of output to be delivered, with payment of, or entitlement to, the resources conditional on that performance.
permanent differences	Differences between an entity's **taxable profits** and its **total comprehensive income** as stated in the **financial statements**, other than **timing differences**.
plan assets (of an employee benefit plan)	(a) **assets held by a long-term employee benefit fund**; and (b) **qualifying insurance policies.**

post-employment benefits	**Employee benefits** (other than **termination benefits** and short-term employee benefits) that are payable after the completion of employment.
post-employment benefit plans	Formal or informal arrangements under which an entity provides **post-employment benefits** for one or more employees.
potential ordinary share	A financial instrument or other contract that may entitle its holder to **ordinary shares**.
present value	A current estimate of the present discounted value of the future net **cash flows** in the normal course of **business**.
presentation currency	The currency in which the **financial statements** are presented.
prevailing market rate	The rate of interest that would apply to the entity in an open market for a similar financial instrument.
principal	An entity is acting as a principal when it has exposure to the significant risks and rewards associated with the sale of goods or the rendering of services. Features that indicate that an entity is acting as a principal include: (a) the entity has the primary responsibility for providing the goods or services to the customer or for fulfilling the order, for example by being responsible for the acceptability of the products or services ordered or purchased by the customer; (b) the entity has inventory risk before or after the customer order, during shipping or on return; (c) the entity has latitude in establishing prices, either directly or indirectly, for example by providing additional goods or services; and (d) the entity bears the customer's credit risk for the amount receivable from the customer.
probable	More likely than not.
profit or loss	The total of **income** less **expenses**, excluding the components of **other comprehensive income**.
projected unit credit method	An actuarial valuation method that sees each period of service as giving rise to an additional unit of benefit entitlement and measures each unit separately to build up the final obligation (sometimes known as the accrued benefit method pro-rated on service or as the benefit/years of service method).
property, plant and equipment	Tangible assets that: (a) are held for use in the production or supply of goods or services, for rental to others, or for administrative purposes, and (b) are expected to be used during more than one period.

prospectively (applying a change in accounting policy)	Applying the new **accounting policy** to transactions, other events and conditions occurring after the date as at which the policy is changed.
provision	A **liability** of uncertain timing or amount.
prudence	The inclusion of a degree of caution in the exercise of the judgements needed in making the estimates required under conditions of uncertainty, such that **assets** or **income** are not overstated and **liabilities** or **expenses** are not understated.
public benefit entity	An entity whose primary objective is to provide goods or services for the general public, community or social benefit and where any **equity** is provided with a view to supporting the entity's primary objectives rather than with a view to providing a financial return to equity providers, shareholders or members.[28]
public benefit entity concessionary loan	A loan made or received between a **public benefit entity** or an entity within a **public benefit entity group** and another party: (a) at below the **prevailing market rate** of interest; (b) that is not repayable on demand; and (c) is for the purposes of furthering the objectives of the public benefit entity or public benefit entity **parent**.
public benefit entity group	A **public benefit entity parent** and all of its wholly-owned **subsidiaries**.
publicly traded (debt or equity instruments)	Traded, or in process of being issued for trading, in a public market (a domestic or foreign stock exchange or an over-the-counter market, including local and regional markets).

[28] The term 'public benefit entity' does not necessarily imply that the purpose of the entity is for the benefit of the public as a whole. For example, many PBEs exist for the direct benefit of a particular group of people, although it is possible that society as a whole also benefits indirectly. The important factor is what the primary purpose of such an entity is, and that it does not exist primarily to provide economic benefit to its investors. Organisations such as mutual insurance companies, other mutual co-operative entities and clubs that provide dividends or other economic benefits directly and proportionately to their owners, members or participants are not PBEs.

Some PBEs undertake certain activities that are intended to make a surplus in order to fund their primary activities. Consideration should be given to the primary purpose of an entity's (or group's) activities in assessing whether it meets the definition of a PBE.

PBEs may have received contributions in the form of equity, even though the entity does not have a primary profit motive. However, because of the fundamental nature of public benefit entities, any such contributions are made by the equity holders of the entity primarily to enable the provision of goods or services to beneficiaries rather than with a view to a financial return for themselves. This is different from the position of lenders; loans do not fall into the category of equity.

qualifying asset	An **asset** that necessarily takes a substantial period of time to get ready for its intended use or sale. Depending on the circumstances any of the following may be qualifying assets: (a) **inventories**; (b) manufacturing plants; (c) power generation facilities; (d) **intangible assets**; and (e) **investment properties**. **Financial assets**, and inventories that are produced over a short period of time, are not qualifying assets. Assets that are ready for their intended use or sale when acquired are not qualifying assets.
qualifying entity (for the purposes of this FRS)	A member of a **group** where the **parent** of that group prepares publicly available **consolidated financial statements** which are intended to give a true and fair view (of the **assets**, **liabilities**, **financial position** and **profit or loss**) and that member is included in the consolidation[29].

qualifying insurance policies	An insurance policy[30] issued by an insurer that is not a **related party** of the reporting entity, if the proceeds of the policy:
	
	(a) can be used only to pay or fund **employee benefits** under a **defined benefit plan**; and
	
	(b) are not available to the reporting entity's own creditors (even in bankruptcy) and cannot be paid to the reporting entity, unless either:
	
	    (i) the proceeds represent surplus **assets** that are not needed for the policy to meet all the related employee benefit obligations; or
	
	    (ii) the proceeds are returned to the reporting entity to reimburse it for employee benefits already paid.

recognition	The process of incorporating in the **statement of financial position** or **statement of comprehensive income** an item that meets the definition of an asset, liability, equity, income or expense and satisfies the following criteria: (a) it is **probable** that any future economic benefit associated with the item will flow to or from the entity; and (b) the item has a cost or value that can be measured with **reliability**.
recoverable amount	The higher of an **asset's** (or **cash-generating unit's**) **fair value less costs to sell** and its value in use.
Regulations	The Large and Medium-sized Companies and Groups (Accounts and Reports) Regulations 2008 (SI 2008/410)

---

[29] As set out in section 474(1) of the Act.

[30] A qualifying insurance policy is not necessarily an insurance contract.

reinsurance contract	An **insurance contract** issued by one insurer (the reinsurer) to compensate another insurer (the cedant) for losses on one or more contracts issued by the cedant.

related party	A related party is a person or entity that is related to the entity that is preparing its **financial statements** (the reporting entity).
	
	(a) A person or a close member of that person's family is related to a reporting entity if that person:
	
	   (i) has **control** or **joint control** over the reporting entity;
	
	   (ii) has **significant influence** over the reporting entity; or
	
	   (iii) is a member of the **key management personnel** of the reporting entity or of a **parent** of the reporting entity.
	
	(b) An entity is related to a reporting entity if any of the following conditions apply:
	
	   (i) the entity and the reporting entity are members of the same **group** (which means that each parent, **subsidiary** and fellow subsidiary is related to the others).
	
	   (ii) one entity is an **associate** or **joint venture** of the other entity (or of a member of a group of which the other entity is a member).
	
	   (iii) both entities are joint ventures of the same third entity.
	
	   (iv) one entity is a joint venture of a third entity and the other entity is an associate of the third entity.
	
	   (v) the entity is a **post-employment benefit plan** for the benefit of employees of either the reporting entity or an entity related to the reporting entity. If the reporting entity is itself such a plan, the sponsoring employers are also related to the reporting entity.
	
	   (vi) the entity is controlled or jointly controlled by a person identified in (a).
	
	   (vii) a person identified in (a)(i) has significant influence over the entity or is a member of the key management personnel of the entity (or of a parent of the entity).
	
	   (viii) the entity, or any member of a group of which it is a part, provides key management personnel services to the reporting entity or to the parent of the reporting entity.

related party transaction	A transfer of resources, services or obligations between a reporting entity and a **related party**, regardless of whether a price is charged.
relevance	The quality of information that allows it to influence the economic decisions of users by helping them evaluate past, present or future events or confirming, or correcting, their past evaluations.
reliability	The quality of information that makes it free from **material error** and bias and represents faithfully that which it either purports to represent or could reasonably be expected to represent.
reporting date	The end of the latest period covered by **financial statements** or by an **interim financial report**.

reporting period	The period covered by **financial statements** or by an **interim financial report**.
research	Original and planned investigation undertaken with the prospect of gaining new scientific or technical knowledge and understanding.
residual value (of an asset)	The estimated amount that an entity would currently obtain from disposal of an **asset**, after deducting the estimated costs of disposal, if the asset were already of the age and in the condition expected at the end of its **useful life**.
restriction	A requirement that limits or directs the purposes for which a resource may be used that does not meet the definition of a **performance-related condition**.
restructuring	A restructuring is a programme that is planned and controlled by management and materially changes either: (a) the scope of a business undertaken by an entity; or (b) the manner in which that business is conducted.
retirement benefit plan	Arrangements whereby an entity provides benefits for employees on or after termination of service (either in the form of an annual **income** or as a lump sum) when such benefits, or the contributions towards them, can be determined or estimated in advance of retirement from the provisions of a document or from the entity's practice.
retrospective application (of an accounting policy)	Applying a new **accounting policy** to transactions, other events and conditions as if that policy had always been applied.
revenue	The gross inflow of economic benefits during the period arising in the course of the ordinary activities of an entity when those inflows result in increases in **equity**, other than increases relating to contributions from equity participants.
separate financial statements	Those presented by a **parent** in which the investments in **subsidiaries**, **associates** or **jointly controlled entities** are accounted for either at cost or **fair value** rather than on the basis of the reported results and net assets of the investees. Separate financial statements are included within the meaning of **individual financial statements**.
service concession arrangement	An arrangement whereby a public sector body or a **public benefit entity** (the grantor) contracts with a private sector entity (the operator) to construct (or upgrade), operate and maintain **infrastructure assets** for a specified period of time (the concession period).
service potential	The economic utility of an **asset**, based on the total benefit expected to be derived by the entity from use (and/or through sale) of the asset.

share-based payment transaction	A transaction in which the entity: (a) receives goods or services (including employee services) as consideration for its own equity instruments (including shares or **share options**); or (b) receives goods or services but has no obligation to settle the transaction with supplier; or (c) acquires goods or services by incurring **liabilities** to the supplier of those goods or services for amounts that are based on the price (or value) of the entity's shares or other equity instruments of the entity or another group entity.
share option	A contract that gives the holder the right, but not the obligation, to subscribe to the entity's shares at a fixed or determinable price for a specific period of time.
significant influence	Significant influence is the power to participate in the financial and operating policy decisions of the **associate** but is not **control** or **joint control** over those policies.
Small Companies Regulations	The Small Companies and Groups (Accounts and Directors' Report) Regulations 2008 (SI 2008/409)
small entity	(a) A company meeting the definition of a small company as set out in section 382 or 383 of the **Act** and not excluded from the small companies regime by section 384; (b) an LLP qualifying as small and not excluded from the small LLPs regime, as set out in LLP Regulations; or (c) any other entity that would have met the criteria in (a) had it been a company incorporated under company law.
Small LLP Regulations	The Small Limited Liability Partnership (Accounts) Regulations 2008 (SI 2008/1912)
Statement of Recommended Practice (SORP)	An extant Statement of Recommended Practice developed in accordance with *SORPs: Policy and Code of Practice*. SORPs recommend accounting practices for specialised industries or sectors. They supplement accounting standards and other legal and regulatory requirements in the light of the special factors prevailing or transactions undertaken in a particular industry or sector.
state	A national, regional, or local government.
state (employee benefit) plan	Employee benefit plans established by legislation to cover all entities (or all entities in a particular category, for example a specific industry) and operated by national or local government or by another body (for example an autonomous agency created specifically for this purpose) which is not subject to control or influence by the reporting entity.
statement of cash flows	**Financial statement** that provides information about the changes in **cash** and **cash equivalents** of an entity for a period, showing separately changes during the period from operating, investing and **financing activities**.

statement of comprehensive income	**Financial statement** that presents all items of **income** and **expense** recognised in a period, including those items recognised in determining **profit or loss** (which is a subtotal in the statement of comprehensive income) and items of **other comprehensive income**. If an entity chooses to present both an **income statement** and a statement of comprehensive income, the statement of comprehensive income begins with profit or loss and then displays the items of other comprehensive income.
statement of financial position	**Financial statement** that presents the relationship of an entity's **assets**, **liabilities** and **equity** as of a specific date (referred to as the balance sheet in the **Act**).
statement of income and retained earnings	**Financial statement** that presents the **profit or loss** and changes in retained earnings for a **reporting period**.
subsidiary	An entity, including an unincorporated entity such as a partnership, that is **controlled** by another entity (known as the **parent**).
substantively enacted	Tax rates shall be regarded as substantively enacted when the remaining stages of the enactment process historically have not affected the outcome and are unlikely to do so. A UK tax rate shall be regarded as having been substantively enacted if it is included in either: (a) a Bill that has been passed by the House of Commons and is awaiting only passage through the House of Lords and Royal Assent; or (b) a resolution having statutory effect that has been passed under the Provisional Collection of Taxes Act 1968. (Such a resolution could be used to collect taxes at a new rate before that rate has been enacted. In practice, corporation tax rates are now set a year ahead to avoid having to invoke the Provisional Collection of Taxes Act for the quarterly payment system.) A Republic of Ireland tax rate can be regarded as having been substantively enacted if it is included in a Bill that has been passed by the Dail.
tax expense	The aggregate amount included in **total comprehensive income** or **equity** for the **reporting period** in respect of **current tax** and **deferred tax**.
taxable profit (tax loss)	The profit (loss) for a **reporting period** upon which income taxes are payable or recoverable, determined in accordance with the rules established by the taxation authorities. Taxable profit equals taxable income less amounts deductible from taxable income.
termination benefits	**Employee benefits** provided in exchange for the termination of an employee's employment as a result of either: (a) an entity's decision to terminate an employee's employment before the normal retirement date; or (b) an employee's decision to accept voluntary redundancy in exchange for those benefits.

timing differences	Differences between **taxable profits** and **total comprehensive income** as stated in the **financial statements** that arise from the inclusion of **income** and **expenses** in tax assessments in periods different from those in which they are recognised in financial statements.
timeliness	Providing the information in **financial statements** within the decision time frame.
total comprehensive income	The change in **equity** during a period resulting from transactions and other events, other than those changes resulting from transactions from equity participants (equal to the sum of **profit or loss** and **other comprehensive income**).
transaction costs (financial instruments)	Incremental costs that are directly attributable to the acquisition, issue or disposal of a **financial asset** or **financial liability**, or the issue or reacquisition of an entity's **own equity instrument**. An incremental cost is one that would not have been incurred if the entity had not acquired, issued or disposed of the financial asset or financial liability, or had not issued or reacquired its own equity instrument.
treasury shares	An entity's own equity instruments, held by that entity or other members of the consolidated group.
turnover	The amounts derived from the provision of goods and services after deduction of: (a) trade discounts; (b) value added tax; and (c) any other taxes based on the amounts so derived.
understandability	The presentation of information in a way that makes it comprehensible by users who have a reasonable knowledge of **business** and economic activities and accounting and a willingness to study the information with reasonable diligence.
useful life	The period over which an **asset** is expected to be available for use by an entity or the number of production or similar units expected to be obtained from the asset by an entity.
value in use	The **present value** of the future **cash flows** expected to be derived from an **asset** or **cash-generating unit**.
value in use (in respect of assets held for their service potential)	When the future economic benefits of an **asset** are not primarily dependent on the asset's ability to generate net cash inflows, **value in use** (in respect of assets held for their **service potential**) is the **present value** to the entity of the asset's remaining service potential if it continues to be used, plus the net amount that the entity will receive from its disposal at the end of its **useful life**.
venturer	A party to a **joint venture** that has **joint control** over that joint venture.
vest	Become an entitlement. Under a share-based payment arrangement, a counterparty's right to receive **cash**, other **assets** or equity instruments of the entity vests when the counterparty's entitlement is no longer conditional on the satisfaction of any vesting conditions.
vested benefits	Benefits, the rights to which, under the conditions of a **retirement benefit plan**, are not conditional on continued employment.

Appendix II: Significant differences between FRS 102 and the IFRS for SMEs

Section		Changes to the IFRS for SMEs (July 2009)
1	Scope of this FRS	This section of the IFRS for SMEs has been replaced. The IFRS for SMEs applies to small and medium sized entities that do not have public accountability and publish general purpose financial statements. FRS 100 *Application of Financial Reporting Requirements* sets out the scope of entities applying this FRS. Paragraphs 1.14A and 1.14B are added to provide transitional provisions in respect of the designation of financial instruments at fair value and hedge accounting which are available to entities that have authorised for issue financial statements compliant with this FRS prior to 1 August 2014.
1A	Small Entities	This section has been inserted to set out the information that is to be presented and disclosed in the financial statements of a small entity, based on the legal framework for small companies.
2	Concepts and Pervasive Principles	No significant changes.
3	Financial Statement Presentation	The drafting of the requirements has been more closely aligned with the drafting of company law. The requirements in paragraph 3.7 are deleted. Paragraph 3.16 is amended to clarify the role of materiality in the preparation of financial statements. Paragraph 3.16A is inserted to specify that disclosures are not required if the information is not material.
4	Statement of Financial Position	The requirements of this section have predominantly been removed and replaced by the requirements set out in the Act. Entities that do not report under the Act comply with the requirements of this section, and of the Regulations, except to the extent that these requirements are not permitted by any statutory framework under which such entities report.
5	Statement of Comprehensive Income and Income Statement	The requirements of this section have predominantly been removed and replaced by the requirements set out in the Act. Entities that do not report under the Act comply with the requirements of this section and of the Regulations except to the extent that these requirements are not permitted by any statutory framework under which such entities report. Paragraph 5.10 has been amended and paragraphs 5.10A and 5.10B are inserted to comply with the Regulations and include the definition of an extraordinary item.

Section		Changes to the IFRS for SMEs (July 2009)
6	Statement of Changes in Equity and Statement of Income and Retained Earnings	Paragraph 6.3A is inserted to require presentation for each component of equity an analysis of other comprehensive income by item, either in the notes, or in the statement of changes in equity.
7	Statement of Cash Flows	The scope of this section is amended to exclude mutual life assurance companies, pension funds and certain investment funds. Paragraphs 7.10A to 7.10E are inserted to require the reporting of cash flows on a net basis in some circumstances. Paragraphs 7.11 and 7.12 are amended to provide some relaxation of the exchange rates permitted to be used.
8	Notes to the Financial Statements	No significant changes.
9	Consolidated and Separate Financial Statements	The scope of this section is amended to clarify that it applies to all parent entities that present consolidated financial statements intended to give a true and fair view. The requirements to present consolidated financial statements are amended to comply with the Act. Paragraph 9.9 requires a subsidiary that is held exclusively with a view to subsequent resale because it is held as part of an investment portfolio, to be excluded from consolidation. Such subsidiaries are required to be measured at fair value with changes recognised in profit or loss. This exemption is required irrespective of whether the subsidiary was previously consolidated under previous GAAP, prior to transition to FRS 102. In addition paragraphs 14.4B and 15.9B are inserted to require an investor that has investments in associates or jointly controlled entities that are held as part of an investment portfolio to measure those investments at fair value with the changes recognised in profit or loss in their consolidated financial statements. Clarification is added to paragraph 9.10 that Employee Share Ownership Plans and similar arrangements are Special Purpose Entities. Paragraph 9.16 is amended to comply with paragraph 2(2) of Schedule 6 to the Regulations in order to require a subsidiary's financial statements, which are included in the consolidated financial statements, to be for the same reporting period (financial year) and as at the same reporting date (year-end). Where it is not practicable to align the subsidiary's reporting date (year-end) with the parent's, paragraph 9.16 has been amended to specify which financial statements of the subsidiary are permitted to be used in the consolidation.

Section	Changes to the IFRS for SMEs (July 2009)
	Paragraphs 9.18A and 9.18B are inserted to clarify the treatment of a disposal where control is lost.
	Paragraph 9.19A is inserted to clarify the treatment of the disposal where control is retained.
	Paragraph 9.19B is inserted to clarify the treatment of an acquisition made in stages.
	Paragraphs 9.19C and 9.19D are inserted to clarify the treatment of non-controlling interest when a parent changes its holding in a subsidiary but control is retained.
	Paragraphs 9.23A to 9.25 are amended to clarify the distinction between the individual financial statements and separate financial statements and that the Act specifies when individual financial statements are required to be prepared.
	Paragraphs 9.28 to 9.30 relating to combined financial statements are deleted.
	Paragraphs 9.31 and 9.32 provide guidance on exchanges of businesses or other non-monetary assets for an interest in a subsidiary, joint venture or associate. This guidance was previously contained in UITF Abstract 31 *Exchanges of businesses or other non-monetary assets for an interest in a subsidiary, joint venture or associate*.
	Paragraphs 9.33 to 9.38 are inserted to provide guidance on the accounting treatment for intermediate payment arrangements. These were previously contained in UITF Abstract 32 *Employee benefit trusts and other intermediate payment arrangements*.
10	Accounting Policies, Estimates and Errors	Paragraph 10.5 clarifies when an entity is required to refer to SORPs in developing an accounting policy.
		Paragraph 10.10A is inserted to bring the accounting treatment for changes in accounting policy relating to property, plant and equipment (Section 17) and intangible assets (Section 18) in line with IAS 10 *Accounting Policies, Estimate and Errors*.
11	Basic Financial Instruments	The scope of Section 11 is amended to clarify that certain financial instruments are not within its scope.
		Paragraph 11.2A is inserted to ensure that an entity choosing to apply the recognition and measurement requirements of IFRS 9 complies with the Regulations.
		Paragraph 11.8(b) is amended to clarify that instruments as described in paragraph 11.6(b) are not debt instruments accounted for under Section 11.

Section		Changes to the IFRS for SMEs (July 2009)
		Paragraph 11.9(a) is amended to clarify the permissible contractual returns to the lender.
		Paragraph 11.9(aA) is added to include some contractual provisions that provide for a linkage of repayments and/or returns to the lender based on inflation.
		Paragraph 11.9(aB) is added to permit certain variations of the return to the holder during the life of the instrument.
		Paragraph 11.9(c) is amended to clarify that contractual prepayment provisions which are contingent future events exclude those which protect the holder from credit deterioration, changes in central bank levies or tax changes and to clarify when compensation payments do not breach the condition.
		The text of paragraph 11.9(d) is deleted as it is no longer needed.
		Paragraph 11.9(e) is added to permit certain contractual extension options.
		Examples are inserted after paragraph 11.9 to illustrate the application of paragraph 11.9.
		Paragraphs 11.11(b) and (c) are deleted as the instruments shown as examples are excluded from debt instruments within the scope of Section 11 under paragraph 11.8(b).
		Paragraph 11.14(b) is inserted to clarify that entities may choose to designate debt instruments and loan commitments as fair value through profit or loss under certain circumstances.
		Paragraph 11.38A is inserted to allow offsetting of certain financial assets and financial liabilities in the statement of financial position.
		Paragraph 11.48A is inserted to provide disclosures required in accordance with the Regulations for certain financial instruments held at fair value.
		Paragraphs 11.48B and 11.48C require additional disclosures for financial institutions.
12	Other Financial Instruments Issues	The scope of Section 12 is amended to exclude financial instruments issued by an entity with a discretionary participation feature, reimbursement assets and financial guarantee contracts.
		Paragraph 12.2A is inserted to ensure that an entity choosing to apply the recognition and measurement requirements of IFRS 9 complies with the Regulations.

Section		Changes to the IFRS for SMEs (July 2009)
		Paragraph 12.8(c) is added to clarify when financial instruments within the scope of Section 12 should be measured at amortised cost.

Paragraphs 12.15 to 12.29 are deleted and replaced with paragraphs 12.15 to 12.29A to include revised hedge accounting requirements which have the following effect:

(a) the scope of permissible hedged items and hedging instruments is expanded;

(b) the hedge accounting conditions are revised and simplified;

(c) it determines three hedge accounting models, ie cash flow, fair value and net investment hedges;

(d) it clarifies that the cumulative amount of foreign exchange differences relating to a hedge of a net investment in a foreign operation is not reclassified to profit or loss on disposal or partial disposal; and

(e) it introduces a documentation requirement in cases of voluntary hedge accounting discontinuation.

Paragraph 12.25B is inserted to allow offsetting of certain financial assets and financial liabilities in the statement of financial position.

Paragraph 12.26 is amended to comply with requirements set out in the Act.

The Appendix to Section 12 is inserted to illustrate by way of example the application of the hedge accounting requirements. |
| 13 | Inventories | Paragraph 13.3 is amended to permit inventory to be measured at fair value less costs to sell through profit or loss in certain circumstances.

Paragraphs 13.4A and 13.20A are inserted to provide guidance on inventories held for distribution at no or nominal consideration.

Paragraph 13.5A is inserted to provide guidance on inventory acquired through non-exchange transactions.

Paragraph 13.8A is inserted to clarify the treatment for provisions made against dismantling and restoration costs (of PPE) in the cost of inventory.

Paragraph 13.12 is deleted because of the revisions to the hedge accounting requirements.

Paragraph 13.15 is amended to allow for the inclusion of a cost model for agricultural produce in Section 34 *Specialised Activities*. |

Section		Changes to the IFRS for SMEs (July 2009)
14	Investments in Associates	The scope of this section is amended to clarify its application to consolidated financial statements and to the financial statements of an entity that is not a parent but which holds investments in associates.
		Paragraph 14.4(b) of the IFRS for SMEs is deleted as the equity method of accounting for investments in associates in individual financial statements is not compliant with company law. Paragraph 14.4(d) is inserted to allow non-parent investors to account for investments in associates at fair value with changes recognised in profit or loss.
		Paragraphs 14.4B is inserted to require an investor that is a parent which has investments in associates that are held as part of an investment portfolio to measure those investments at fair value with the changes recognised in profit or loss in their consolidated financial statements.
		Paragraph 14.9 is amended to require transaction costs to be included as part of the transaction price on initial recognition.
		Paragraph 14.10 is amended to require changes in fair value to be recognised through other comprehensive income, in accordance with paragraphs 17.15E and 17.15F, when the fair value model is applied, rather than through profit or loss.
		Paragraph 14.15A is inserted to provide information about associates held by entities that are not parents.
15	Investments in Joint Ventures	The scope of this section is amended to clarify its application to consolidated financial statements and to the financial statements of a venture that is not a parent.
		Paragraph 15.9(b) of the IFRS for SMEs is deleted as the equity method of accounting for interests in jointly controlled entities in individual financial statements is not compliant with company law. Paragraph 15.9(d) is inserted to allow non-parent investors to account for investments in jointly controlled entities at fair value with the changes recognised in profit or loss.
		Paragraph 15.9B is inserted to require an investor that is a parent which has investments in jointly controlled entities that are held as part of an investment portfolio to measure those investments at fair value with the changes recognised in profit or loss in their consolidated financial statements.
		Paragraph 15.14 is amended to require transaction costs to be included as part of the transaction price on initial recognition.

Section		Changes to the IFRS for SMEs (July 2009)
		Paragraph 15.15 is amended to require changes in fair value to be recognised through other comprehensive income, in accordance with paragraphs 17.15E and 17.15F, when the fair value model is applied, rather than through profit or loss. Paragraph 15.21A is inserted to provide information about associates held by entities that are not parents.
16	Investment Property	No significant changes.
17	Property, Plant and Equipment	Section 17 is amended to provide, after initial recognition, that an entity may use the cost model or revaluation model.
18	Intangible Assets other than Goodwill	Section 18 is amended to permit entities to recognise intangible assets that result from expenditure incurred on the internal development of an intangible item (subject to certain criteria). The section provides guidance on what comprises the cost of an internally generated intangible asset and the criteria for initial recognition. The section is also amended to provide, after initial recognition, that an entity may use the cost model or revaluation model.
19	Business Combinations and Goodwill	Section 19 is amended to permit the use of the merger accounting method for group reconstructions. The merger method is set out in paragraphs 19.29 to 19.33. Paragraphs 19.15A to 19.15C are inserted to provide guidance on the treatment of deferred tax assets or liabilities, employee benefit arrangements and share-based payments of a subsidiary on acquisition. Paragraph 19.24 is amended and paragraph 19.26A is inserted to comply with the requirements of the Act for bargain purchases (negative goodwill).
20	Leases	The scope of Section 20 is amended to include operating leases that are onerous within its scope. Paragraphs 20.15A and 20.25A are inserted to clarify the treatment of operating lease incentives for lessees and lessors respectively. Paragraph 20.15B is inserted to provide guidance on the treatment of onerous operating lease contracts.
21	Provisions and Contingencies	The scope of Section 21 is amended to include financial guarantee contracts. Paragraph 21.17A is inserted to provide guidance on the accounting treatment of financial guarantee contracts. Paragraph 21.17 is amended to comply with disclosure requirements set out in the Regulations.

Section		Changes to the IFRS for SMEs (July 2009)
22	Liabilities and Equity	Paragraph 22.3A is inserted to clarify that a financial instrument where the issuer does not have the unconditional right to avoid settling in cash or by delivery of another financial asset (or otherwise to settle it in such a way that it would be a financial liability); and where settlement is dependent on the occurrence or non-occurrence of uncertain future events beyond the control of the issuer and the holder, is a financial liability of the issuer unless specific circumstances apply. The requirement for an entity to recognise a liability at fair value when non-cash assets are distributed to owners is removed and only disclosure is required in paragraph 22.18.
23	Revenue	No significant changes.
24	Government Grants	Paragraphs 24.5C to 24.5G are inserted to allow an additional model of accounting for grants (the accrual model). The model permits entities to recognise grant income on a systematic basis over the period in which the entity recognises the related costs for which the grant is intended to compensate.
25	Borrowing Costs	Section 25 is amended to allow an option that permits entities to capitalise borrowing costs that are directly attributable to the acquisition, construction or production of a qualifying asset.
26	Share-based Payment	The definition of equity-settled share based payments has been amended to align with the revised IFRS 2 definition. It is clarified that option pricing models do not have to be applied in all circumstances. Paragraph 26.15 has been replaced with new paragraphs 26.15 to 26.15B to bring the accounting for share-based payment arrangements with cash alternatives closer to that required by IFRS 2 when the entity has the settlement choice.
27	Impairment of Assets	Paragraph 27.20A is inserted to provide guidance on the treatment of impairments on assets held for their service potential. Paragraph 27.33A is inserted to include a descriptive disclosure requirement of the events and circumstances that led to the recognition or reversal of the impairment loss.
28	Employee Benefits	The presentation of the cost of a defined benefit plan and the accounting for group plans have been amended to be consistent with the requirements of IAS *19 Employee Benefits* as amended in 2011. Paragraph 28.11A is inserted to require the recognition of a liability on a defined benefit multi-employer plan, which is accounted as defined

Section		Changes to the IFRS for SMEs (July 2009)
		contribution scheme, where funding of a deficit has been agreed.

Paragraph 28.19 is deleted to remove the option to use a simplified valuation method in measuring the liability. |
29	Income Tax	Section 29 of the IFRS for SMEs has been entirely replaced with revised requirements.
30	Foreign Currency Translation	No significant changes.
31	Hyperinflation	No significant changes.
32	Events after the End of the Reporting Period	Paragraphs 32.7A and 32.7B are inserted to provide guidance on the impact of changes in an entity's going concern status.
33	Related Party Disclosures	Paragraph 33.1A is inserted to include the exemption from disclosure of related party transactions for wholly-owned entities available in the Act.

The definition of a related party in paragraph 33.2 is amended for consistency with company law. |
| 34 | Specialised Activities | Agriculture – this sub-section is amended to allow the option to hold biological assets and agricultural produce at cost.

Extractives – this sub-section has been amended to require application of IFRS 6.

Service concession arrangements – this sub-section is amended to clarify the accounting by operators and provide guidance to grantors.

The following additional sub-sections are inserted:
<ul><li>Financial Institutions;</li><li>Retirement Benefit Plans: Financial Statements;</li><li>Heritage Assets;</li><li>Funding Commitments;</li><li>Incoming Resources from Non-Exchange Transactions;</li><li>Public Benefit Entity Combinations; and</li><li>Public Benefit Entity Concessionary Loans.</li></ul> |
| 35 | Transition to this FRS | Amendments to this section reflect the changes in preceding sections and the different effective date for small entities. |

Appendix III: Table of equivalence for UK Companies Act terminology

The following table compares company law terminology with broadly equivalent terminology used in FRS 102. In some cases there are minor differences between the broadly equivalent definitions, which are also summarised below.

Company law terminology	FRS 102 terminology
Accounting reference date	Reporting date
Accounts	Financial statements
Associated undertaking	Associate
Balance sheet	Statement of financial position
Capital and reserves	Equity
Cash at bank and in hand	Cash[31]
Debtors	Trade receivables
Diminution in value [of assets]	Impairment
Financial year	Reporting period
Group [accounts]	Consolidated [financial statements]
IAS	EU-adopted IFRS
Individual [accounts]	Individual [financial statements]
Interest payable and similar charges	Finance costs
Interest receivable and similar income	Finance income/Investment income
Minority interests	Non-controlling interest
Net realisable value [of any current asset]	Estimated selling price less costs to complete and sell
Parent undertaking	Parent
Profit and loss account	Income statement (under the two-statement approach) Part of the statement of comprehensive income (under the single- statement approach)
Related undertakings[32]	Subsidiaries, associates and joint ventures
Stocks	Inventories
Subsidiary undertaking	Subsidiary
Tangible assets	Includes: Property, plant equipment; Investment property
Trade creditors	Trade payables

---

[31] FRS 102 requires the cash flow statement to reconcile the movement in 'cash and cash equivalents'. Disclosure is required of reconciliation between amounts presented in the statement of financial position (ie cash) and 'cash and cash equivalents'.

[32] This would also include entities in which a company has at least a 20 per cent holding, but which are not a subsidiary, joint venture or an associate. A shareholding of 20 per cent is presumed to give significant influence to the holder, such that the investment would be classified as an associate, therefore in practice there are unlikely to be many related undertakings that are not subsidiaries, joint ventures or associates.

Appendix IV: Note on legal requirements

Introduction

A4.1   This appendix provides an overview of how the requirements in FRS 102 address United Kingdom company law requirements. It is therefore written from the perspective of a company to which the Companies Act 2006 applies[33]. Appendix VI discusses the Republic of Ireland legal references.

A4.2   Many entities that are not constituted as companies apply accounting standards promulgated by the FRC for the purposes of preparing financial statements that present a true and fair view[34]. A brief consideration of the legal framework for some other entities can be found at A4.41 and A4.42. For those entities that are within the scope of a Statement of Recommended Practice (SORP), the relevant SORP will provide more details on the legal framework.

A4.3   References to the Act in this appendix are to the *Companies Act 2006*. References to the Regulations are to *The Large and Medium-sized Companies and Groups (Accounts and Reports) Regulations 2008* (SI 2008/410) as amended by *The Companies, Partnerships and Groups (Accounts and Reports) Regulations 2015* (SI 2015/980) following the implementation of the EU Accounting Directive. References to specific provisions are to Schedule 1 to the Regulations; entities applying Schedules 2, 3 or 6 should read them as referring to the equivalent paragraph in those schedules; and small entities applying the Small Companies Regulations should read them as referring to the equivalent paragraph in Schedule 1 to the Small Companies Regulations. Similar provisions generally also apply to limited liability partnerships applying the Small LLP Regulations or the LLP Regulations although some differences do exist (see paragraphs A4.43 to A4.47).

Applicable accounting framework

A4.4   Group accounts of certain parent entities (those with securities admitted to trading on a regulated market in an EU Member State) are required by Article 4 of EU Regulation 1606/2002 (IAS Regulation) to be prepared in accordance with EU-adopted IFRS.

A4.5   All other entities, except those that are eligible to apply FRS 105 *The Financial Reporting Standard applicable to the Micro-entities Regime*, must apply[35] either FRS 102 *The Financial Reporting Standard applicable in the UK and Republic of Ireland*, EU-adopted IFRS or FRS 101 *Reduced Disclosure Framework* (if the financial statements are the individual financial statements of a qualifying entity eligible to apply FRS 101).

A4.6   Section 395(1) of the Act states:

'A company's individual accounts may be prepared—

(a)   in accordance with section 396 ("Companies Act individual accounts"), or

(b)   in accordance with international accounting standards ("IAS individual accounts").'

---

[33] Some charities are also companies, and are therefore required to apply the requirements of both the *Companies Act 2006* and the *Charities Act 2011*.

[34] More information about the 'true and fair' concept can be found on the FRC's website at http://www.frc.org.uk/Our-Work/Codes-Standards/Accounting-and-Reporting-Policy/True-and-Fair.aspx.

[35] Under company law in the Republic of Ireland, certain entities are permitted to prepare Companies Act accounts using accounting standards other than those issued by the FRC.

Section 403(2) of the Act states:

'The group accounts of other companies may be prepared—

(a) in accordance with section 404 ("Companies Act group accounts"), or

(b) in accordance with international accounting standards ("IAS group accounts").'

A4.7   Accounts prepared in accordance with FRS 102 are classified as either 'Companies Act individual accounts', including those of qualifying entities applying FRS 102, or 'Companies Act group accounts' and are therefore required to comply with the applicable provisions of Parts 15 and 16 of the Act and with the Regulations.

Consistency of financial reporting within groups

A4.8   Section 407 of the Act requires that the directors of the parent company secure that individual accounts of a parent company and each of its subsidiaries are prepared using the same financial reporting framework, except to the extent that in the directors' opinion there are good reasons for not doing so.

In addition, consistency is not required in the following situations:

(a) when the parent company does not prepare consolidated financial statements; or

(b) when some subsidiaries are charities (consistency is not needed between the framework used for these and for other subsidiaries).

Where the directors of a parent company prepare IAS group accounts and IAS individual accounts, there only has to be consistency across the individual financial statements of the subsidiaries.

A4.9   All companies, other than those which elect or are required to prepare IAS individual accounts in accordance with the Act, prepare Companies Act individual accounts.

Application of FRS 102

Compliance with company law

A4.10   The FRS has been developed for application in the UK and Republic of Ireland, using the IFRS for SMEs as a basis. Part of that development process included making amendments to the IFRS for SMEs to ensure compliance with the Act and the Regulations. For example, changes were made to eliminate options that are not permitted by company law. However, FRS 102 is not intended to be a one-stop-shop for all accounting and legal requirements, and although the FRC believes FRS 102 is not inconsistent with company law, compliance with FRS 102 alone will often be insufficient to ensure compliance with all the disclosure requirements set out in the Act and the Regulations. As a result preparers will continue to be required to have regard to the requirements of company law in addition to accounting standards.

A4.11   This appendix does not list every legal requirement, but instead focuses on those areas where greater judgement might be required in determining compliance with the law.

Small companies

A4.11A The definition of a small company is contained in sections 382 and 383 of the Act; certain companies are excluded from the small companies regime by section 384. Subject to certain conditions and exclusions, the qualifying conditions are met by a company in a year in which it does not exceed two or more of the following criteria:

(a) Turnover £10.2 million

(b) Balance sheet total £5.1 million

(c) Average number of employees 50

A4.11B A parent company qualifies as a small company in relation to a financial year only if the group that it heads qualifies as small (as set out in section 383 of the Act).

A4.11C The Small Companies Regulations set out the small companies regime. Although FRS 102 was developed on the basis of the Regulations (which apply to large and medium-sized companies) the recognition and measurement requirements of FRS 102 should also be consistent with the Small Companies Regulations.

A4.11D In accordance with section 393 of the Act the directors of any company, including a small company, must not approve accounts unless they are satisfied that they give a true and fair view of the assets, liabilities, financial position and profit or loss of the company. In order to achieve this, a company, including a small company, may need to provide disclosures additional to those required by company law. In relation to small companies, paragraph 1A.16 of FRS 102 reflects this requirement and paragraph 1A.17 encourages a small company to consider all other disclosures in FRS 102 to determine any additional disclosures to provide.

A4.11E The Small Companies Regulations include options for small companies to prepare an abridged balance sheet and an abridged profit and loss account. In order to take this option small companies must comply with the additional legal requirement that all members of the company have consented to the drawing up of abridged financial statements (which may only be given in respect of the preceding financial year). In accordance with paragraph 1A(4) of Schedule 1 to the Small Companies Regulations this option is not available to small entities that are charities. When a small entity that is not a company chooses to prepare abridged financial statements it should ensure that:

(a) similar consent is obtained from the members of its governing body, taking into account its legal form; and

(b) abridged financial statements would not be prohibited by relevant laws or regulation.

Financial instruments measured at fair value

A4.12 All preparers of Companies Act accounts must comply with the requirements of paragraph 36 of Schedule 1 to the Regulations, which provides that:

'(1) Subject to sub-paragraphs (2) to (5), financial instruments (including derivatives) may be included at fair value.

(2) Sub-paragraph (1) does not apply to financial instruments that constitute liabilities unless—

a. they are held as part of a trading portfolio,

b. they are derivatives, or

c. they are financial instruments falling within sub-paragraph (4).

(3) Unless they are financial instruments falling within sub-paragraph (4), sub-paragraph (1) does not apply to –

    a.   financial instruments (other than derivatives) held to maturity,

    b.   loans and receivables originated by the company and not held for trading purposes,

    c.   interests in subsidiary undertakings, associated undertakings and joint ventures,

    d.   equity instruments issued by the company,

    e.   contracts for contingent consideration in a business combination, or

    f.   other financial instruments with such special characteristics that the instruments, according to generally accepted accounting principles or practice, should be accounted for differently from other financial instruments.

(4) Financial instruments which under international accounting standards may be included in accounts at fair value, may be so included, provided that the disclosures required by such accounting standards are made.

(5) [...]'

A4.12A   In limited circumstances, an entity applying this FRS to its financial instruments that are classified as non-basic in accordance with Section 11 *Basic Financial Instruments* may be prohibited, by paragraph 36 of Schedule 1 to the Regulations, to measure those financial instruments at fair value through profit or loss in accordance with the requirements of this FRS. The Regulations prohibit the measurement of certain financial instruments at fair value through profit or loss, unless the instruments could be designated for such measurement under EU-adopted IFRS. EU-adopted IFRS permits designation at fair value through profit or loss upon initial recognition for financial instruments where: doing so eliminates or reduces a measurement or recognition inconsistency; or a group of financial instruments is managed and their performance evaluated on a fair value basis; or for a hybrid financial instruments which contains a component that, if recognised separately, would meet the definition of a derivative. Paragraph 12.8(c) of this FRS is applicable to the measurement of financial instruments prohibited under the Regulations to be measured at fair value through profit or loss and requires them to be measured at amortised cost.

A4.12B   Further, an entity that has made the accounting policy choice in paragraph 11.2(c) or paragraph 12.2(c) to apply the recognition and measurement provisions of IFRS 9 *Financial Instruments* shall depart from those provisions of IFRS 9 where the measurement of financial assets at fair value through profit or loss is not permitted by paragraph 36 of Schedule 1 to the Regulations. This can occur in relation to financial assets because the classification and measurement requirements of IFRS 9 are not identical to the equivalent requirements of IAS 39 *Financial Instruments: Recognition and Measurement*, which is the standard presently adopted by the EU and is therefore the reference point for paragraph 36(4) of Schedule 1 to the Regulations.

A4.12C   Paragraph 40 of Schedule 1 to the Regulations requires companies to include fair value gains and losses on financial instruments measured at fair value in the profit and loss account, except when the financial instrument is a hedging instrument or an available for sale security. Therefore, for those companies making the accounting policy choice, in accordance with paragraph 11.2(c) and 12.2(c) of FRS 102, to apply the recognition and measurement requirements of IFRS 9 *Financial Instruments*, recording fair value gains and losses attributable to changes in credit risk in other comprehensive income in accordance with IFRS 9 will usually be a departure from the requirement of paragraph 40 of Schedule 1 to the Regulations, for the overriding purpose of giving a true and fair view.

A4.12D Entities that are preparing Companies Act accounts must provide the disclosures required by paragraph 55 of Schedule 1 to the Regulations, which sets out requirements relating to financial instruments measured at fair value through profit or loss. Most of these disclosures will be satisfied by equivalent requirements of FRS 102, but entities will need to take care to ensure appropriate disclosure of derivatives is provided.

A4.13 An entity applying this FRS and holding financial instruments measured at fair value may be required to provide the disclosures required by paragraph 36(4) of Schedule 1 to the Regulations. The disclosures required by paragraph 36(4) have been incorporated into Section 11. Some of the Section 11 disclosure requirements apply to all financial instruments measured at fair value, whilst others (see paragraph 11.48A of FRS 102) apply only to certain financial instruments (this does not include financial liabilities held as part of a trading portfolio nor derivatives). The disclosure requirements of paragraph 11.48A will predominantly apply to certain financial liabilities, however, there may be instances where paragraph 36(3) of Schedule 1 to the Regulations requires that the disclosures must also be provided in relation to financial assets, for example investments in subsidiaries, associates or jointly controlled entities measured at fair value (see paragraph 9.27B of FRS 102).

Requirement to present financial statements

A4.14 FRS 102 does not prescribe which entities prepare financial statements and preparers should apply the requirements of the Act in determining whether financial statements (either individual or consolidated) are required. FRS 102 sets out the requirements for a complete set of financial statements that give a true and fair view of the financial position, financial performance and, where required to be presented, cash flows of an entity, where these are required by law, or other regulation or requirement.

A4.15 A parent company preparing consolidated financial statements under section 434(2) of the Act must publish its company financial statements together with the consolidated financial statements, although section 408 of the Act provides an exemption from including the company's individual profit and loss account.

Subsidiaries excluded from consolidation

A4.16 Paragraph 9.9(b) of Section 9 *Consolidated and Separate Financial Statements* requires a group to exclude subsidiaries from consolidation on the grounds that they are held exclusively with a view to subsequent resale. By defining 'held exclusively with a view to subsequent resale' in FRS 102 to include those interests that are held as part of an investment portfolio, subsidiaries held as part of such an investment portfolio are excluded from consolidation in accordance with section 405(3) of the Act and an entity will not need to apply the true and fair override in this circumstance.

A4.17 Paragraph 9.9B(a) requires a group to measure subsidiaries excluded from consolidation by virtue of paragraph 9.9(b) and held as part of an investment portfolio, at fair value through profit or loss. The measurement at fair value through profit and loss, in circumstances where it would not be required by IFRS 10 *Consolidated Financial Statements*, is a departure from the requirements of paragraph 36 of Schedule 1 to the Regulations, for the overriding purpose of giving a true and fair view in the consolidated financial statements. In this circumstance entities must provide, in the notes to the financial statements, the 'particulars of the departure, the reasons for it and its effect' (paragraph 10(2) of Schedule 1 to the Regulations).

Calculation of goodwill where a business combination is achieved in stages

A4.18 Paragraph 9 of Schedule 6 to the Regulations sets out the requirements for the acquisition method of accounting, which results in goodwill (or negative goodwill) being calculated as the difference between:

(a) the fair value of the group's share of identifiable assets and liabilities of the subsidiary at the date control is achieved; and

(b) the total acquisition cost of the interests held by the group in that subsidiary.

This applies even where part of the acquisition cost arises from purchases at earlier dates.

A4.19 In most cases, this method provides a practical means of applying acquisition accounting because it does not require retrospective assessments of the fair value of the identifiable assets and liabilities of the subsidiary. In certain circumstances, however, not using fair values at the dates of earlier purchases while using acquisition costs which in part relate to earlier purchases may result in accounting that is inconsistent with the way the investment has been treated previously and, for that reason, may fail to give a true and fair view.

A4.20 For example, an undertaking that has been treated as an associate may then be acquired by that group as a subsidiary. Using the method required by the Regulations and paragraph 9.19B of FRS 102 to calculate goodwill on such an acquisition has the effect that the group's share of profits or losses and reserve movements of its associate becomes reclassified as goodwill (usually negative goodwill). A similar problem may arise where the group has substantially restated its investment in an undertaking that subsequently becomes its subsidiary. For example, where such an investment has been written down because it is impaired, the effect of applying the Regulations' method of acquisition accounting would be to increase reserves and create an asset (goodwill).

A4.21 In the rare cases where the method for calculating goodwill set out in the Regulations and in paragraph 9.19B of FRS 102 would be misleading, the goodwill should be calculated as the sum of goodwill arising from each purchase of an interest in the relevant undertaking adjusted as necessary for any subsequent impairment. Goodwill arising on each purchase should be calculated as the difference between the cost of that purchase and the fair value at the date of that purchase of the identifiable assets and liabilities attributable to the interest purchased. The difference between the goodwill calculated using this method and that calculated using the method provided by the Regulations and FRS 102 is shown in reserves. Section 404(5) of the Act sets out the disclosures required in cases where the statutory requirement is not applied. Paragraph 3.5 of FRS 102 sets out the disclosures when an entity departs from a requirement of FRS 102 or from a requirement of applicable legislation.

Netting

A4.22 FRS 102 permits an expense relating to a provision to be presented net of the amount recognised for a reimbursement (which may only be recognised if it is virtually certain it will be received) (see paragraph 21.9 of FRS 102). Paragraph 8 of Schedule 1 to the Regulations requires that 'Amounts in respect of items representing assets or income may not be set off against amounts in respect of items representing liabilities or expenditure (as the case may be), or vice versa.' The reimbursement asset is recognised separately from the underlying obligation to reflect the fact that the entity often will continue to be liable if the third party from which the reimbursement is due fails to pay. On the other hand, the net presentation in the income statement reflects the cost to the entity and net presentation therefore does not conflict with the Regulations.

A4.23　FRS 102 requires that a financial asset and financial liability are offset and the net amount presented in the statement of financial position, if certain criteria are met (see paragraph 11.38A of FRS 102). The net presentation does not conflict with paragraph 8 of Schedule 1 to the Regulations, because provided the criteria for the net presentation are met, the presentation reflects the expected net cash flows from settling two or more separate financial instruments.

Recording investments at cost

A4.24　Paragraph 9.26 of FRS 102 requires that in an investor's separate financial statements its investments in subsidiaries are accounted for at cost less impairment, or at fair value. Where the cost model is applied, sections 611 to 615 of the Act set out the treatment where 'merger relief' or 'group reconstruction relief' are available. These reliefs reduce the amount required to be included in share premium; they also (in section 615) allow the initial carrying amount to be adjusted downwards so it is equal to either the previous carrying amount of the investment in the transferor's books or the nominal value of the shares issued, depending on which relief applies. If the fair value model in paragraph 9.26 is used, then the relief in section 615 is not available, so the investment's carrying value may not be reduced, although the provisions in sections 611 and 612 remain relevant in respect of amounts required to be recorded in share premium.

Realised profits

A4.25　Paragraph 13(a) of Schedule 1 to the Regulations requires that only profits realised at the reporting date are included in profit or loss, a requirement modified from that in Article 31.1(c)(aa) of the Fourth Directive which refers to profits 'made' at the balance sheet date.

A4.26　Paragraph 36 and paragraph 39 of Schedule 1 to the Regulations allow financial instruments, stocks, investment property, and living animals and plants to be held at fair value in Companies Act accounts.

A4.27　Paragraph 40(2) of Schedule 1 to the Regulations then requires that movements in the value of financial instruments, investment properties and living animals and plants are recognised in the profit and loss account, notwithstanding the usual restrictions allowing only realised profits and losses to be included in the profit and loss account. Paragraph 40 of Schedule 1 to the Regulations thereby overrides the requirements of paragraph 13(a) of Schedule 1.

A4.28　Entities measuring financial instruments, investment properties, and living animals and plants at fair value should note that they may transfer such amounts to a separate non-distributable reserve, instead of a transfer to retained earnings, but are not required to do so. Presenting fair value movements, that are not distributable profits, in the separate reserve may assist with the identification of profits available for that purpose.

A4.29　The determination of profits available for distribution is a complex area where accounting and company law interface. In determining profits available for distribution an entity may refer to Technical Release 02/10 *Guidance on realised and distributable profits under the Companies Act 2006* issued by the Institute of Chartered Accountants in England and Wales and the Institute of Chartered Accountants of Scotland, or any successor document, to determine profits available for distribution.

Merger accounting

A4.30   Paragraph 10 of Schedule 6 to the Regulations states:

'The conditions for accounting for an acquisition as a merger are—

(a)   that the undertaking whose shares are acquired is ultimately controlled by the same party both before and after the acquisition,

(b)   that the control referred to in paragraph (a) is not transitory, and

(c)   that adoption of the merger method accords with generally accepted accounting principles or practice.'

Therefore, paragraph 10 of Schedule 6 to the Regulations permits the use of merger accounting in certain limited circumstances, which is generally consistent with paragraph 19.27 of FRS 102 (group reconstructions). If an entity considers that, for the overriding purpose of giving a true and fair view, merger accounting should be applied in circumstances other than those set out in paragraph 10 of Schedule 6 to the Regulations, it may do so providing the relevant disclosures are made in the notes to the financial statements.

A4.30A   Section 34 *Specialised Activities* requires that combinations by public benefit entities meeting certain criteria are accounted for as a merger, unless this is not permitted by the relevant statutory framework. FRS 102 therefore does not extend the use of merger accounting beyond its applicability in company law, or other relevant statutory framework. If a public benefit entity that is a company considers that, for the overriding purpose of giving a true and fair view, merger accounting should be applied in circumstances other than those set out in paragraph 10 of Schedule 6 to the Regulations, it may do so providing the relevant disclosures are made in the notes to the financial statements.

Treasury shares

A4.31   Paragraph 22.16 of FRS 102 sets out the accounting requirements when an entity purchases its own equity instruments (ie treasury shares).

A4.32   Companies subject to the Act, need to comply with the accounting requirements of paragraph 22.16 as well as with the requirements of the Act when they purchase their own equity and hold it in treasury (Sections 690 to 708 and 724 to 732, respectively).

Measurement of investments in associates and jointly controlled entities for an investor, which is not a parent

A4.33   Paragraph 36 of Schedule 1 to the Regulations sets out the fair value accounting rules and permits investments in associates and joint ventures to be measured at fair value through profit or loss only where they are permitted to be treated as financial instruments in accordance with IAS Regulation. EU-adopted IFRS does allow investments in subsidiaries, associates and jointly controlled entities to be measured in accordance with IAS 39 *Financial Instruments Recognition and Measurement* within separate financial statements (as set out in IAS 27 *Consolidated and Separate Financial Statements*).

A4.34   Therefore, where the fair value model is applied by an investor, changes in fair value may be recognised through profit or loss, or other comprehensive income. Under the alternative accounting rules set out in Section C of Schedule 1 to the Regulations, the initial recognition of the investment must include any expenses that are incidental to the acquisition of the investment.

Measurement of inventories held for distribution at no or nominal value

A4.35   Paragraph 24(1) of Schedule 1 to the Regulations requires that if the net realisable value of any current asset is lower than its purchase price or production cost, the amount to be included in respect of that asset must be the net realisable value. However, paragraph 39 permits stocks to be included at their fair value, when applying fair value accounting.

A4.36   Inventories held for distribution at no or nominal value include items that might be distributed to beneficiaries by public benefit entities and items such as advertising and promotional material. As the items will be distributed at no or nominal cost, the net realisable value will usually be lower than the purchase price.

A4.37   Paragraph 13.4A of FRS 102 requires inventories held for distribution at no or nominal cost to be measured at the lower of cost (adjusted for any loss in service potential) and replacement cost. This is an application of fair value accounting. For inventories, including those held for distribution at no or nominal value (particularly items distributed to beneficiaries by public benefit entities), there is unlikely to be a significant difference between replacement cost and fair value.

Amortisation of intangible assets

A4.37A   Paragraph 22 of Schedule 1 to the Regulations requires intangible assets to be written off over their useful economic lives. This is broadly consistent with paragraph 18.21 of FRS 102, except that FRS 102 allows for the possibility that an intangible asset will have a residual value, in which case it is the depreciable amount that shall be amortised, not the cost (or revalued amount) of the intangible asset. In practice it will be uncommon for an intangible asset to have a residual value (paragraph 18.23 requires an entity to assume that the residual value is zero other than in specific circumstances). In those cases where an intangible asset has a residual value that is not zero, the amortisation of the depreciable amount of an intangible asset over its useful economic life is a departure from the requirements of paragraph 22 of Schedule 1 to the Regulations for the overriding purpose of giving a true and fair view. In these circumstances entities must provide, in the notes to the financial statements, the 'particulars of the departure, the reasons for it and its effect' (paragraph 10(2) of Schedule 1 to the Regulations).

Accounts formats

A4.38   Sections 1A, 4 and 5 of FRS 102 require entities to apply one of the profit and loss account and balance sheet formats set out in the Small Companies Regulations, the Regulations, the Small LLP Regulations and the LLP Regulations, when preparing their statement of comprehensive income (single-statement approach) or income statement (two-statement approach) and statement of financial position, respectively. The *General Rules* preceding *The Required Formats for Accounts* include certain flexibilities for companies (but not LLPs at present), this includes permitting adaptation of the formats, providing the adapted presentation is equivalent to that set out in the formats and that it is consistent with generally accepted accounting practice. For entities within its scope FRS 102 sets out a framework for the information to be presented by those entities choosing to adapt the formats.

Discontinued operations

A4.39   FRS 102 requires an entity with discontinued operations, to provide an analysis between continuing operations and discontinued operations of each of the line items on the face of the statement of comprehensive income, or income statement, up to and including post-tax profit or loss for the period and illustrates this presentation in a columnar format. This is in order to present the post-tax results of those operations, combined with the profit or loss on their disposal, as a single line item while still complying with the requirement of company law to show totals for ordinary activities of items such as turnover, profit or loss before taxation and tax.

Long-term debtors

A4.40   UITF Abstract 4 *Presentation of long-term debtors in current assets* addressed the inclusion of debtors due after more than one year within 'current assets'; that UITF consensus has been withdrawn, but its conclusions remain valid and have been included in paragraph 4.4A of FRS 102.

Entities not subject to company law

A4.41   Many entities that apply FRS 102 are not companies, but are nevertheless required by their governing legislation, or other regulation or requirement to prepare financial statements that present a true and fair view of the financial performance and financial position of the reporting entity. However, the FRC sets accounting standards within the framework of the Act and therefore it is the company law requirements that the FRC primarily considered when developing FRS 102. Entities preparing financial statements within other legal frameworks will need to satisfy themselves that FRS 102 does not conflict with any relevant legal obligations.

A4.42   However, the FRC notes the following:

Legislation	Overview of requirements
Building Societies Act 1986	The annual accounts of a building society shall give a true and fair view of the income and expenditure for the year and the balance sheet shall give a true and fair view of the state of affairs of the society at the end of the financial year. Regulations make further requirements about the form and content of building society accounts, which do not appear inconsistent with the requirement of FRS 102.
Charity law in England and Wales: Charities Act 2011 and regulations made thereunder	All charities are required to prepare accounts. The regulations require financial statements (other than cash-based receipts and payments accounts prepared by smaller charities) to present a true and fair view of the incoming resources, application of resources and the balance sheet, and to be prepared in accordance with the SORP. However company charities prepare their accounts in accordance with UK company law to give a 'true and fair view'. The Charities SORP (FRS 102) is compatible with the legal requirements, clarifying how they apply to accounting by charities applying FRS 102. UK company law prohibits charities from preparing IAS accounts.

Legislation	Overview of requirements
Charity law in Scotland: Charities and Trustee Investments Act (Scotland) 2005 and regulations made thereunder	All charities are required to prepare accounts. The regulations require financial statements (other than cash-based receipts and payments accounts prepared by smaller charities) to present a true and fair view of the incoming resources, application of resources and the balance sheet, and to be prepared in accordance with the SORP. These regulations apply equally to company charities.
Charity law in Northern Ireland: Charities Act (Northern Ireland) 2008	The Charities Act 2008 has yet to come fully into effect. The Act provides for all charities to prepare accounts. The Act provides for regulations concerning the financial statements. The financial statements other than cash-based receipts and payments accounts prepared by smaller charities are to present a true and fair view of the incoming resources, application of resources and the balance sheet.

However company charities prepare their accounts in accordance with UK company law to give a 'true and fair view'. |
| Friendly and Industrial and Provident Societies Act 1968 | Every Society shall prepare a revenue account and a balance sheet giving a true and fair view of the income and expenditure and state of affairs of the Society.

FRS 102 does not appear to give rise to any legal conflicts for Societies. However, Societies often carry out activities that are regulated and may be required to comply with additional regulations on top of the legal requirements and accounting standards. Some Societies fall within the scope of SORPs, which reflect the requirements of FRS 102. |
| Friendly Societies Act 1992 | Every society shall prepare a balance sheet and an income and expenditure account for each financial year giving a true and fair view of the affairs of the society and its income and expenditure for the year.

The Regulations[36] make further requirements about the form and content of friendly society accounts, which do not appear inconsistent with the requirements of FRS 102. |
| The Occupational Pension Schemes (Requirement to obtain Audited Accounts and a Statement from the Auditor) Regulations 1996 | The accounts of pension funds within the scope of the regulations should show a true and fair view of the transactions during the year, assets held at the end of the year and liabilities of the scheme, other than those to pay pensions and benefits.

FRS 102 includes retirement benefit plans as a specialised activity. |

---

[36] *The Friendly Societies (Accounts and Related Provisions) Regulations 1994* (as amended).

A4.43   Limited liability partnerships (LLPs) will be applying FRS 102 in conjunction with the LLP Regulations or the Small LLP Regulations. In many cases these regulations are similar to the Regulations or the Small Companies Regulations, which reduces the situations in which legal matters relevant to the financial statements of LLPs are not addressed in this Appendix. However, the amendments made to the Regulations and the Small Companies Regulations by *The Companies, Partnerships and Groups (Accounts and Reports) Regulations 2015* (SI 2015/980) have not been reflected in the LLP Regulations or the Small LLP Regulations. This gives rise to some differences for LLPs.

Small LLPs

A4.44   The thresholds that are part of the qualifying conditions of a small company and a small LLP have diverged, with the thresholds for a small LLP being lower than those for a small company. Of LLPs, only those qualifying as small (and not otherwise excluded) in accordance with the LLP Regulations, will be able to apply Section 1A *Small Entities*.

A4.45   A small LLP choosing to apply Section 1A shall provide the following disclosures:

(a)   those set out in Appendix C to Section 1A;

(b)   those required by the Small LLP Regulations that are additional to those set out in Appendix C to Section 1A; and

(c)   any additional disclosures necessary to meet the requirement to give a true and fair view, as set out in paragraph 1A.17.

In accordance with paragraph 1A.20 a small LLP is also encouraged to provide the disclosures set out in Appendix D to Section 1A.

All LLPs

A4.46   In a relatively small number of areas *The Companies, Partnerships and Groups (Accounts and Reports) Regulations 2015* (SI 2015/980) made changes to the recognition and measurement requirements applicable to companies. These changes have not been made to the LLP Regulations or the Small LLP Regulations and therefore, in a small number of cases, the requirements of FRS 102 will be inconsistent with the LLP Regulations and the Small LLP Regulations. Areas where this may have an impact include:

(a)   the flexibility available in relation to the format of the balance sheet and of the profit and loss account;

(b)   the scope of financial instruments that can be measured at fair value through profit or loss;

(c)   the reversal of impairment losses in relation to goodwill; and

(d)   the application of merger accounting.

If following the requirements of FRS 102 would lead to a conflict with applicable legislation, an LLP shall instead apply its own legal requirements and consider whether disclosure of a departure from FRS 102 is required.

LLP consolidated financial statements

A4.47   When LLPs prepare consolidated financial statements, whether mandatorily or voluntarily, there will also be differences between company law and the similar requirements applicable to LLPs. If following the requirements of FRS 102 would lead to a conflict with applicable legislation, an LLP shall instead apply its own legal requirements and consider whether disclosure of a departure from FRS 102 is required.

Appendix V: Previous consultations

A5.1   The requirements in FRSs 100 to 102 are the outcome of a lengthy and extensive consultation. The FRC (and formerly the ASB) together with the Department for Business, Innovation and Skills have consulted on the future of accounting standards in the UK and Republic of Ireland (RoI) over a ten-year period.

Table 1 – Consultations conducted

Year	Consultation
2002	DTI[37] consults on adoption of IAS Regulation
2004	Discussion Paper – Strategy for Convergence with IFRS
2005	Exposure Draft – Policy Statement: The Role of the ASB
2006	Public Meeting and Proposals for Comment
2006	Press Notice seeking views
2007	Consultation Paper – Proposed IFRS for SMEs
2009	Consultation Paper – Policy Proposal: The future of UK GAAP
2010	Request for Responses – Development of the Impact Assessment
2010	Financial Reporting Exposure Drafts 43 and 44
2011	Financial Reporting Exposure Draft 45
2012	Financial Reporting Exposure Drafts 46, 47 and 48
2012	Financial Reporting Exposure Draft: Amendment to FRED 48

2004

A5.2   In 2004 the Discussion Paper contained two key elements underpinning the proposals: firstly that UK and Republic of Ireland (RoI) accounting standards should be based on IFRS and secondly that a phased approach to the introduction of the standards should be adopted.

A5.3   The ASB embarked on the phased approach and issued a number of standards based on IFRS. The majority of respondents agreed with a framework based on IFRS, and although supportive overall, the response to the phased approach was mixed.

2005

A5.4   In its 2005 Exposure Draft (2005 ED) of a Policy Statement *Accounting standard-setting in a changing environment: The role of the Accounting Standards Board*, amongst other aspects of its role, the ASB identified its intention to converge with IFRS by implementing new IFRS in the UK as soon as possible. It also proposed to continue the phased approach to adopting UK accounting standards based on older IFRSs, but recognised there was little case for being more prescriptive than IFRS.

---

[37] The Department of Trade and Industry (DTI) was a United Kingdom government department which was replaced with the announcement of the creation of the Department for Business, Enterprise and Regulatory Reform and the Department for Innovation, Universities and Skills on 28 June 2007, which were themselves merged into the Department for Business, Innovation and Skills (BIS) on 6 June 2009.

A5.5   Although the ASB had, in the 2005 ED, wanted to move the debate on to how it would seek to influence the IASB's agenda, respondents' main concern remained about convergence. In 2005, the ASB issued an exposure draft proposing the IASB's standard on Business Combinations be adopted in the UK and RoI. This exposure draft highlighted the complexity of a mixed set of UK accounting standards, with some based on IFRSs and others developed independently by the ASB. The majority of respondents continued to agree with the aim of basing UK accounting standards on IFRS, but a broader set of views on how to achieve this was emerging.

A5.6   As time progressed the ASB formed the view that convergence by adopting certain IFRSs was not meeting the needs of its constituents, which no longer included quoted groups. The ASB was concerned about the complexity of certain IFRSs, and it noted that introducing them piecemeal created complications and anomalies within the body of current FRSs. This arose because IFRS-based standards were not an exact replacement for current FRSs and many consequential amendments were required to 'fit' each replacement IFRS-based standard into the existing body of UK FRS. The ASB agreed to continue with its convergence programme, but decided to re-examine how to achieve this.

2006

A5.7   The ASB published revised proposals to be discussed at the 2006 public meeting. By this time the IASB had started its IFRS for SMEs project, and the ASB decided this might have a role as one of the tiers in the UK financial reporting framework. The ASB proposed a 'big bang' with new IFRS-based UK accounting standards mandatory from a single date, 1 January 2009. The ASB's proposal was for a three-tier system, with Tier 1 being EU-adopted IFRS, and the other two tiers being developed as the IASB progressed with its project on the IFRS for SMEs.

A5.8   Those attending the public meeting supported the aim of basing UK and RoI accounting standards on IFRS and adapting them to ensure they were appropriate for the entities applying them.

A5.9   Taking this feedback into account, later in 2006 the ASB issued a Press Notice (PN 289) seeking views on its current thinking:

(a)   All quoted and publicly accountable companies should apply EU-adopted IFRS.

(b)   The FRSSE should be retained and extended to include medium-sized entities.

(c)   UK subsidiaries of groups applying full IFRS should apply EU-adopted IFRS, but with reduced disclosure requirements.

(d)   No firm decision on the remainder (Tier 2), but options included extending the FRSSE, extending full IFRS, maintaining separate UK accounting standards or some combination of these.

A5.10   The responses were mixed, but there was agreement that whatever the solution, it should be based on IFRS and there should be different reporting tiers to ensure proportionality.

2007

A5.11   The IASB published an exposure draft of its IFRS for SMEs in early 2007; shortly afterwards the ASB published its own consultation paper. This sought views on how the IFRS for SMEs might fit into the future UK financial reporting framework, for example whether it might be appropriate for Tier 2, with the FRSSE continuing for those eligible for the small companies' regime.

A5.12 Feedback on the IFRS for SMEs was largely positive: it would be suitable for Tier 2, it was international, it was compatible with IFRS, and it represented a significant simplification. Overall, it was seen as a workable alternative to IFRS. In addition, respondents wanted to retain the FRSSE (because it reduces the regulatory burden on smaller entities) and to give subsidiaries the option of applying the IFRS for SMEs as well as a reduced disclosure regime if applying full IFRS.

2009

A5.13 The IFRS for SMEs was published in 2009, allowing the ASB to further develop its proposals in the Consultation Paper *Policy Proposal: The future of UK GAAP*. The proposals were largely consistent with the cumulative results of the preceding consultations and included:

(a) a move to an IFRS-based framework;

(b) a three-tier approach;

(c) publicly accountable entities would be Tier 1 and would apply EU-adopted IFRS;

(d) small companies would be Tier 3 and continue to apply the FRSSE; and

(e) other entities would be Tier 2 and should apply a UK and RoI accounting standard based on the IFRS for SMEs.

A5.14 The only significant proposal that was inconsistent with respondents' previous comments was that subsidiaries should simply apply the requirement of the tier they individually met – respondents had wanted subsidiaries to be able to take advantage of disclosure exemptions, and at that time the ASB had yet to be convinced that significant cost savings were available from a reduced disclosure framework. Taking into account the feedback received, this proposal was subsequently reversed and the reduced disclosure framework was incorporated into FREDs 43 and then 46, and it is now set out in FRS 101.

A5.15 In addition to the many useful and detailed points made, some common themes included general agreement that change was needed to UK accounting standards and that there was support for many of the changes proposed in the consultation paper.

2010 onwards

A5.16 The request for responses to aid development of the Impact Assessment focused on obtaining feedback on the expected costs, benefits and impact of the proposals subsequently set out in FREDs 43 and 44, rather than on the accounting principles. As the focus was on costs and benefits no specific question was asked about the principle of the proposed introduction of an IFRS-based framework, but nevertheless respondents commented on this: of the 32 responses received only 12.5 per cent did not agree with the introduction of an IFRS-based framework.

A5.17 FRED 43 and 44 issued in October 2010 set out the draft suggested text for two new accounting standards that would replace the majority of extant Financial Reporting Standards (current FRS) in the UK and RoI. The ASB issued a supplementary FRED addressing specific needs of public benefit entities (FRED 45) in March 2011. The ASB then updated FREDs 43, 44 and 45, replacing them with the revised FREDs 46, 47 and 48 in January 2012, by eliminating the concept of public accountability and by introducing a number of accounting treatment options that are available in EU-adopted IFRS. The Accounting Council's advice to the FRC to issue FRSs 100 to 102 includes more discussion of the feedback received on FREDs 43 to 48 and how the proposals have been refined and developed into the standards.

How have the proposals been developed?

A5.18   As set out above, the FRC, the Accounting Council (and previously the ASB) have consulted regularly on the future of financial reporting in the UK and RoI. Over the consultations the ASB's (and the Accounting Council's) thinking has evolved based on careful consideration of the feedback at each stage. Whilst responses were sometimes mixed, there has been agreement that:

(a)   current FRS, which are a mixture of Statements of Standard Accounting Practice (SSAPs) issued by the Consultative Committee of Accounting Bodies, FRSs developed and issued by the ASB and IFRS-based standards issued by the ASB to converge with international standards, are an uncomfortable mismatch that lack strong underlying principles or cohesion; and

(b)   whatever the solution, it should be based on IFRS and there should be different reporting tiers to ensure proportionality.

A5.19   During the consultation process to date, the Accounting Council and formerly the ASB have been guided by the following principles:

(a)   The framework must be fit for purpose, so that each entity required to produce true and fair financial statements under UK and RoI law will deliver financial statements that are suited to the needs of its primary users. The Accounting Council has kept in close contact with constituent users on this point, including investors, creditor institutions and the tax authorities.

(b)   The framework must be proportionate, so that preparing entities are not unduly burdened by costs that outweigh the benefit to them and to the primary users of information in their financial statements. The FRC believes that the proposals will produce a lower cost regime, while enhancing user benefits. It has carried out a consultation stage impact assessment with input from interested parties, and will continue to assess cost-benefit issues.

(c)   The framework must be in line with UK company law. This determines which entities must produce true and fair financial statements. Exemptions within the law have generally been retained. The detailed requirements of the Companies Act 2006 are driven to a great extent by the European Accounting Directives, which are being revised[38].

(d)   The framework must be future-proofed, where possible. The FRC will continue to monitor the situation and has sovereignty over UK accounting standards (subject to the law). Changes to the Accounting Directives may lead to further developments, for example the European Council and European Parliament decision to permit Member States an option to treat micro-entities as a separate category of Company and exempt them from certain accounting requirements.

Summary of outreach

A5.20   During the development and throughout the consultation period of FREDs 43 to 48, the ASB undertook an extensive programme of outreach aimed at raising awareness of the proposals and to address the view (held by some) that previous consultations had not gathered sufficient evidence to support and test the assumptions made.

A5.21   As part of the outreach programme to obtain both formal and informal feedback, a series of meetings and events took place with users, including with lenders to small and medium-sized entities. Lenders noted that financial statements are an important part of their decision-making process when considering whether to provide finance

---

[38] The EU's consultation process on review of the Accounting Directives is summarised at http://ec.europa.eu/internal_market/accounting/sme_accounting/review_directives_en.htm

and, whilst a decision to provide finance is not based on financial statements alone, they provide useful information and verification to the lender.

A5.22 Although the ASB and the Accounting Council employed their best efforts to obtain feedback from users (a constituent group historically difficult to engage with formally) it is disappointing that limited formal responses were received and the Accounting Council has not been more successful in obtaining input from users.

A5.23 In addition, a review was made of academic research that addressed the users of the financial statements of small and medium-sized entities. The conclusion drawn from the research was that many entities requested financial statements from Companies House when considering whether to trade with another entity. The European Federation of Accountants and Auditors (EFAA) issued, in May 2011, a statement that identified the users of financial statements, noting who the users of SMEs' financial statements are and that information on the public record assists all users of financial statements of SMEs by providing, in an efficient manner, basic information that protects their rights.

A5.24 The ASB considered that the outreach programme had gleaned information from people who would not normally submit formal responses to a consultation and provided very useful information that could be used in developing the next stage of the project. The ASB noted that whilst this information was not part of the public record, as are formal consultation responses, it could use the information to assist in developing the revised FREDs 46 to 48, supplementing information contained in responses, and would seek further comment in the next stage of its deliberations.

A5.25 The Accounting Council continued the work of the ASB in finalising FRSs 100 to 102. The responses to FREDs 46 to 48 were analysed and discussed, and engagements were conducted to take into account the views and suggestions of all relevant associations and contacts. Respondents and outreach contacts were satisfied with FREDs 46 to 48, and many of the response letters were forthcoming in their overall praise for the proposals. A significant number of constituents anticipated cost savings arising from the application of FRS 101. Many respondents considered that FRS 102 would improve UK accounting standards, in particular by introducing requirements for accounting for financial instruments. Further they considered that the improvements will be achieved in a way that will be proportionate to the needs of users, and that once the transition phase has been overcome, it will have the effect of reducing the reporting burden on those UK companies that adopt it.

Appendix VI: Republic of Ireland (RoI) legal references

A6.1   Appendix VI: *Republic of Ireland (RoI) legal references* will be updated as appropriate for both the Companies Act 2014 and the Irish legislation implementing the EU Accounting Directive once the latter has been made. This will be made available on the FRC website and included in the next edition of FRS 102.

COPYRIGHT NOTICE

International Financial Reporting Standards (IFRSs) together with their accompanying documents are issued by the International Accounting Standards Board (IASB):

30 Cannon Street, London, EC4M 6XH, United Kingdom.
Tel: +44 (0)20 7246 6410 Fax: +44 (0)20 7246 6411
Email: info@ifrs.org Web: www.ifrs.org

Copyright © 2015 IFRS Foundation

The IASB, the IFRS Foundation, the authors and the publishers do not accept responsibility for loss caused to any person who acts or refrains from acting in reliance on the material in this publication, whether such loss is caused by negligence or otherwise.

IFRSs (which include International Accounting Standards and Interpretations) are copyright of the International Financial Reporting Standards (IFRS) Foundation. The authoritative text of IFRSs is that issued by the IASB in the English language. Copies may be obtained from the IFRS Foundation Publications Department. Please address publication and copyright matters to:

IFRS Foundation Publications Department
30 Cannon Street, London, EC4M 6XH, United Kingdom.
Tel: +44 (0)20 7332 2730 Fax: +44 (0)20 7332 2749
Email: publications@ifrs.org Web: www.ifrs.org

All rights reserved. No part of this publication may be translated, reprinted or reproduced or utilised in any form either in whole or in part or by any electronic, mechanical or other means, now known or hereafter invented, including photocopying and recording, or in any information storage and retrieval system, without prior permission in writing from the IFRS Foundation.

The IFRS Foundation logo, the IASB logo, the IFRS for SMEs logo, the "Hexagon Device", "IFRS Foundation", "eIFRS", "IAS", "IASB", "IASC Foundation", "IASCF", "IFRS for SMEs", "IASs", "IFRS", "IFRSs", "International Accounting Standards" and "International Financial Reporting Standards" are Trade Marks of the IFRS Foundation.